W9-AUX-476

Better Homes and Gardens®

the *ultimate* low-calorie book

More than **400** light and
healthy meals for every day

WILEY

John Wiley & Sons, Inc.

This book is printed on acid-free paper. ♾

Copyright © 2012 by Meredith Corporation, Des Moines, IA. All rights reserved

Published by John Wiley & Sons, Inc., Hoboken, New Jersey

Published simultaneously in Canada

No part of this publication may be reproduced, stored in a retrieval system, or transmitted in any form or by any means, electronic, mechanical, photocopying, recording, scanning, or otherwise, except as permitted under Section 107 or 108 of the 1976 United States Copyright Act, without either the prior written permission of the Publisher, or authorization through payment of the appropriate per-copy fee to the Copyright Clearance Center, Inc., 222 Rosewood Drive, Danvers, MA 01923, (978) 750–8400, fax (978) 750–4470, or on the web at www.copyright.com. Requests to the Publisher for permission should be addressed to the Permissions Department, John Wiley & Sons, Inc., 111 River Street, Hoboken, NJ 07030, (201) 748–6011, fax (201) 748–6008, or online at http://www.wiley.com/go/permissions.

Limit of Liability/Disclaimer of Warranty: While the publisher and author have used their best efforts in preparing this book, they make no representations or warranties with respect to the accuracy or completeness of the contents of this book and specifically disclaim any implied warranties of merchantability or fitness for a particular purpose. No warranty may be created or extended by sales representatives or written sales materials. The advice and strategies contained herein may not be suitable for your situation. You should consult with a professional where appropriate. Neither the publisher nor author shall be liable for any loss of profit or any other commercial damages, including but not limited to special, incidental, consequential, or other damages.

For general information on our other products and services or for technical support, please contact our Customer Care Department within the United States at (877) 762–2974, outside the United States at (317) 572–3993 or fax (317) 572–4002.

Wiley also publishes its books in a variety of electronic formats. Some content that appears in print may not be available in electronic books. For more information about Wiley products, visit our web site at www.wiley.com.

Library of Congress Cataloging-in-Publication Data:
The ultimate low-calorie book : more than 400 light and healthy recipes for every day / [editor, Jan Miller].
        p. cm.
    At head of title: Better Homes and Gardens
ISBN 978-1-118-03814-7 (pbk.), 978-1-118-11980-8 (ebk.),
978-1-118-11981-5 (ebk.), 978-1-118-11982-2 (ebk.)
  1. Entrées (Cooking) 2. Low-fat diet--Recipes.
I. Miller, Jan. II. Title: Better Homes and Gardens.
  TX740.U48 2011
  641.5'6384--dc23
                                        2011030366

Printed in the United States of America
10 9 8 7 6 5 4 3 2 1

Meredith Corporation

Editorial Manager: Jan Miller

Editor: Sheena Chihak, R.D.

Recipe Development and Testing: Better Homes and Gardens® Test Kitchen

John Wiley & Sons, Inc.

Publisher: Natalie Chapman

Associate Publisher: Jessica Goodman

Executive Editor: Anne Ficklen

Senior Editor: Linda Ingroia

Production Editor: Abby Saul

Production Director: Diana Cisek

Interior Design: Jill Budden

Layout: Holly Wittenberg

Manufacturing Manager: Tom Hyland

Our seal assures you that every recipe in *The Ultimate Low-Calorie Book* has been tested in the Better Homes and Gardens® Test Kitchen. This means that each recipe is practical and reliable and meets our high standards of taste appeal. We guarantee your satisfaction with this book for as long as you own it.

table of
contents

3

357

61

◄ *Recipes ready to eat in 30 minutes or less*

◄ *Recipes with 5 grams of fiber or more*

◄ *Recipes with 400 mg of sodium or less per entrée and 200 mg or less for sides and snacks*

Look for these tabs throughout to guide your recipe choices

start eating better today

As someone with an eye on health you want foods that are good for you and taste great but also help shed excess pounds. Armed with this book, you can eat foods you love while watching your waistline, and you can do it without giving in to the latest fads or suffering the food blahs of diet deprivation.

You will quickly discover this cookbook is perfect for everyday family meals. The recipes are lower in calories, fat, and sodium but there are no "diet foods" here. Enjoy your fill of pizzas, burgers, soups, casseroles, and desserts all specially developed to fit a healthy eating plan. And because each recipe has been rigorously tested in the Better Homes & Gardens® Test Kitchen, you can rest assured that they'll taste great too.

Kick off your efforts to eat better and lose weight with our opening chapter of healthy eating basics. Learn to determine your specific calorie needs, choose proper portions, and make healthier swaps and substitutions at each meal.

One healthy choice leads to another. You chose this book now choose a recipe and get cooking!

Cherry-Kissed Tacos
with Feta Cheese,
page 77

healthy eating

ba

1

When traveling to the New You, plan your journey and plot your path. This guide provides everything you need to know— before you pass go.

sics

tricks for trimming

With a few smart ingredient swaps you can save hundreds of calories. Use these ideas to start trimming calories (and your waistline).

breakfast A smart breakfast helps keep your appetite in check all day. Protein is the nutrient that works hardest at helping you feel full and satisfied. Pork loin cutlets, leftover chicken breast, and lean roast beef are just as tasty with eggs or in breakfast sandwiches as processed breakfast meats yet save on fat and sodium. Skim milk, nonfat Greek yogurt, and low-fat cheese also provide protein (and calcium) in breakfast recipes. Boost satisfaction by bulking up breakfast fare with fiber-rich whole grains and low-calorie vegetables and fruits. Try spinach in egg dishes or berries in whole grain muffins.

omelet fillers

choose this ↓

Raw tomato
diced (1/4 cup)

8 cal., 0 g fat, 2 mg sodium

Leftover cooked pork loin chop
cubed (1 ounce)

60 cal., 3 g fat, 18 mg sodium

Yellow summer squash and zucchini
thinly sliced (1/2 cup)

12 cal., 0 g fat, 1 mg sodium

Vegetarian sausage-style crumbles
cooked (1 ounce)

46 cal., 1 g fat, 216 mg sodium

not this ↓

Sundried tomatoes
packed in oil, drained (1/4 cup)

59 cal., 4 g fat, 73 mg sodium

Crumbled bacon
(1 ounce)

153 cal., 12 g fat, 655 mg sodium

Corn
(1/2 cup)

62 cal., 1 g fat, 11 mg sodium

Pork sausage crumbles
cooked (1 ounce)

100 cal., 10 g fat, 190 mg sodium

sandwiches It's easy for excess calories and sodium to sneak into sandwiches. Starting with a slim yet hearty whole grain wrap, pita, or thin bun can help control calories, or try an open-faced hot sandwich with half the bread. Opt for low-fat meats, cheeses, and spreads and choose lower-sodium options, when possible. Leftover chicken breast and roast beef slices are also good alternatives to salty processed meats. Your sandwich will be more filling and flavorful if you load it with lots of fresh vegetables such as broccoli sprouts, cucumber slices, and bell pepper strips. Thin slices of apple or pear add a sweet crunch in sandwiches, too.

smart sandwich staples

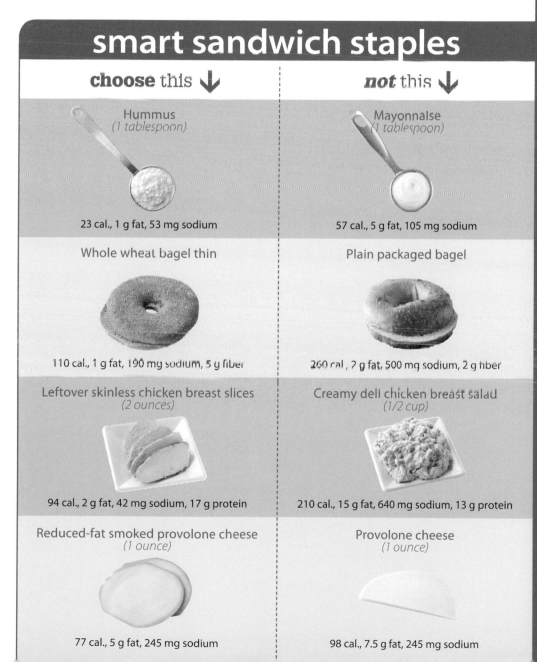

choose this ⬇	**not** this ⬇
Hummus *(1 tablespoon)*	Mayonnaise *(1 tablespoon)*
23 cal., 1 g fat, 53 mg sodium	57 cal., 5 g fat, 105 mg sodium
Whole wheat bagel thin	Plain packaged bagel
110 cal., 1 g fat, 190 mg sodium, 5 g fiber	260 cal., 2 g fat, 500 mg sodium, 2 g fiber
Leftover skinless chicken breast slices *(2 ounces)*	Creamy deli chicken breast salad *(1/2 cup)*
94 cal., 2 g fat, 42 mg sodium, 17 g protein	210 cal., 15 g fat, 640 mg sodium, 13 g protein
Reduced-fat smoked provolone cheese *(1 ounce)*	Provolone cheese *(1 ounce)*
77 cal., 5 g fat, 245 mg sodium	98 cal., 7.5 g fat, 245 mg sodium

salads With just 5 calories per cup of shredded lettuce, it's easy to see why green salads are a dieter's friend. What you add to the lettuce, however, can make or break the calorie count. Although it's smart to top salad with lots of colorful vegetables, don't forget to add protein. Protein-rich lean meats, low-fat cheeses, beans, nuts, and seeds lend more staying power to salads. And although you should avoid high-fat salad dressings, you don't have to choose fat-free. In fact, it's important to get at least 3 to 5 grams of fat in your salad (whether from the dressing or other ingredients) to best absorb certain vitamins in the vegetables. Avoid drenching your greens in salad dressing—about 1 tablespoon dressing per 2 cups lettuce should be enough.

salad bar toppers

choose this ↓   ***not*** this ↓

choose this ↓	***not*** this ↓
Part-skim mozzarella cheese *(1 ounce)*	Cheddar cheese *(1 ounce)*
72 cal., 5 g fat, 132 mg sodium	114 cal., 9 g fat, 176 mg sodium
Fresh fruit, chopped *(1/4 cup)*	Dried fruit bits *(1/4 cup)*
16 cal., 0 g fat, 0 mg sodium	120 cal., 0 g fat, 20 mg sodium
Roasted chicken breast without skin *(3 ounces)*	Fried chicken breast *(3 ounces)*
142 cal., 3 g fat, 64 mg sodium	187 cal., 8 g fat, 64 mg sodium
Hard cooked egg *(1 large egg)*	Egg salad *(1/3 cup)*
78 cal., 5 g fat, 62 mg sodium	131 cal., 10 g fat, 195 mg sodium

soups and stews Low-fat soups and stews typically contain more water and vegetables than other one-dish entrées, resulting in a satisfying portion with fewer calories per bite. Start with low-sodium broth, low-fat milk, or evaporated skim milk, then pump up the protein with lean meats or fiber-rich beans. Nonstarchy vegetables are easy add-ins when you keep frozen ones on hand. Fiber-rich grains—such as barley, quinoa, or whole grain pasta—can either be cooked in soups and stews or added precooked closer to serving time.

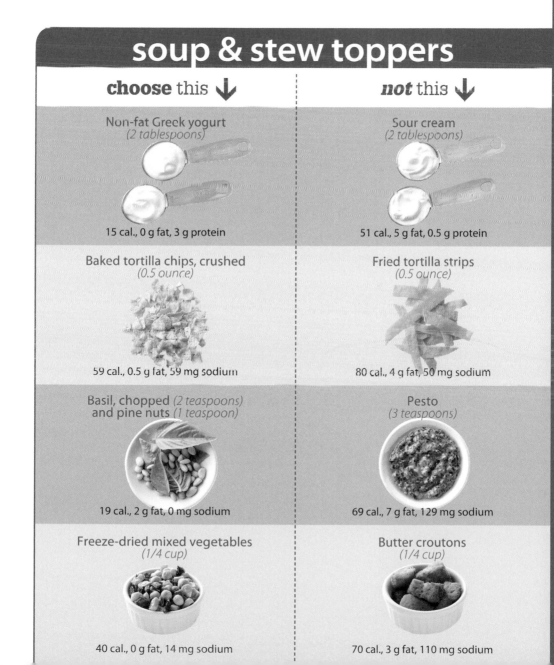

soup & stew toppers

choose this ↓	**not** this ↓
Non-fat Greek yogurt *(2 tablespoons)*	Sour cream *(2 tablespoons)*
15 cal., 0 g fat, 3 g protein	51 cal., 5 g fat, 0.5 g protein
Baked tortilla chips, crushed *(0.5 ounce)*	Fried tortilla strips *(0.5 ounce)*
59 cal., 0.5 g fat, 59 mg sodium	80 cal., 4 g fat, 50 mg sodium
Basil, chopped *(2 teaspoons)* and pine nuts *(1 teaspoon)*	Pesto *(3 teaspoons)*
19 cal., 2 g fat, 0 mg sodium	69 cal., 7 g fat, 129 mg sodium
Freeze-dried mixed vegetables *(1/4 cup)*	Butter croutons *(1/4 cup)*
40 cal., 0 g fat, 14 mg sodium	70 cal., 3 g fat, 110 mg sodium

meat, poultry, and seafood Meat is rich in hunger-satisfying protein, so don't skip it just because you're counting calories. You can find lean cuts of beef, pork, and lamb by looking for the words "loin" or "round" in the name. Skinless white-meat chicken and turkey are smart choices, too, but carefully read the label of ground poultry—it may include higher-fat dark meat and skin. Decrease the amount of ground meat used in recipes by adding vegetables with a meaty texture, such as eggplant, mushrooms, or beans. At least twice a week, eat fish, especially ones rich in heart-healthy omega-3 fats, such as salmon. Plain seafood is often sold frozen, so it's easy to move it from freezer to refrigerator first thing in the morning to let it thaw for the evening meal.

lean & meaty

choose this ↓	**not** this ↓
Beef sirloin steak *(4 ounces grilled)*	**Beef rib-eye steak** *(4 ounces grilled)*
149 cal., 4.5 g fat (1.5 g sat. fat), 25 g protein	300 cal., 23 g fat (9 g sat. fat), 20 g protein
Skinless chicken breast *(4 ounces grilled)*	**Skinless chicken thigh** *(4 ounces grilled)*
124 cal., 1.5 g fat (0.5 g sat. fat), 26 g protein	143 cal., 5 g fat (1 g sat. fat), 24 g protein
Extra-lean ground turkey breast *(4 ounces raw)*	**Ground turkey** *(4 ounces raw)*
120 cal., 1 g fat (0 g sat. fat), 28 g protein	240 cal., 17 g fat (4.5 g sat. fat), 20 g protein
Portabella mushroom *(4 ounces cooked)*	**Hamburger patty, 85 percent lean** *(4 ounces cooked)*
25 cal., 0 g fat (0 g sat. fat), 2 g protein	243 cal., 17 g fat (6.5 g sat. fat), 21 g protein

grilling Grilling is a low-fat way to add lots of flavor to lean meat, chicken, fish, vegetables, and even fruit. In general, marinate meats before cooking, even if just for an hour. (Marinate fish just 30 minutes.) Opt for low-fat, low-sodium bottled marinades or make your own. A marinade that contains vinegar, citrus juice, or other acidic ingredients does a great job tenderizing meat. Most vegetables absorb little marinade, so just toss them quickly with a marinade before grilling to help prevent sticking. Although you can grill vegetables and fruit on skewers or in foil, you can cook almost anything outdoors with an inexpensive grilling tray that has small holes to prevent food from falling into the fire.

build a better burger

choose this ⬇   ### *not* this ⬇

choose this	not this
Tomato slice *(1 thick slice)*	Ketchup *(1 tablespoon)*
5 cal., 0 g fat, 1 mg sodium	15 cal., 0 g fat, 167 mg sodium
Roasted red sweet peppers *(1 tablespoon)*	Pickle relish *(1 tablespoon)*
5 cal., 0 g fat, 30 mg sodium	19 cal., 1 g fat, 164 mg sodium
Reduced-fat cheddar cheese *(1 ounce)*	American cheese *(1 ounce)*
49 cal., 3 g fat, 174 mg sodium	106 cal., 8 g fat, 356 mg sodium
Whole wheat bun *(1.5 ounces)*	White hamburger bun *(1.5 ounces)*
112 cal., 2 g fat, 195 mg sodium, 2 g fiber	123 cal., 2 g fat, 204 mg sodium, 1 g fiber

casseroles A bubbling, hot casserole is the ultimate comfort food, but high-fat sauces, meats, and dairy products can really pile on the calories. Luckily, it's not difficult to find slimmer casserole ingredients, such as low-fat condensed soup, lean meat, and reduced-fat cheese. It's also easy to swap regular pastas for higher-fiber whole grain versions. And don't forget the vegetables. You'll be able to enjoy a larger casserole serving with fewer calories if you mix in lots of nutrient-rich, nonstarchy veggies, such as broccoli, tomatoes, zucchini, carrots, celery, and sweet peppers.

casserole staples

choose this ↓ | **not** this ↓

Whole wheat panko bread crumbs
(1/4 cup)

70 cal., 0.5 g fat, 23 mg sodium

French fried onions
(1/4 cup)

90 cal., 7 g fat, 120 mg sodium

Long grain brown rice, cooked
(1/2 cup)

108 cal., 1 g fat, 3 g protein, 2 g fiber

White rice, cooked
(1/2 cup)

121 cal., 0 g fat, 2 g protein, 0 g fiber

Spaghetti squash, cooked
(1/2 cup)

21 cal., 0 g fat, 1 g fiber

Spaghetti, cooked
(1/2 cup)

111 cal., 1 g fat, 1 g fiber

Frozen hashbrowns
(3 ounces)

70 cal., 0 g fat, 0 mg sodium

Frozen tater tots
(3 ounces)

150 cal., 7 g fat, 420 mg sodium

baked goods There are many ways to trim fat and calories from baked goods and desserts. But too many changes to a baked good can have flat, gummy, or tasteless results so start small. When modifying your favorite recipes, start with one change and when you've fine-tuned that, try making additional tweaks. For example, use low-fat dairy ingredients instead of their full-fat cousins. If that works fine, go ahead and swap whole wheat flour for up to half of the all-purpose flour. If a recipe calls for nuts, cut the amount in half yet heighten their flavor by roasting them in oven, and you'll find a smaller serving of your treat is more satisfying.

better baking staples

choose this ↓	**not** this ↓
Pureed (baby food) pears *(1/2 cup)*	Vegetable oil *(1/2 cup)*
54 cal., 0 g fat, 4.5 g fiber, 31 mg vitamin C	964 cal., 109 g fat, 0 g fiber, 0 mg vitamin C
Toasted chopped walnuts *(1/4 cup)*	Chopped walnuts *(1/2 cup)*
191 cal., 19 g fat (1.5 g sat fat), 2 g fiber	383 cal., 38 g fat (3.5 g sat. fat), 4 g fiber
Semi-sweet mini chocolate chips *(1/4 cup)*	Semi-sweet chocolate chips *(1/2 cup)*
280 cal., 16 g fat (10 g sat. fat), 32 g sugars	560 cal., 32 g fat (20 g sat. fat), 64 g sugars
Whole wheat pastry flour *(1 cup)*	All-purpose flour *(1 cup)*
440 cal., 2 g fat (0 g sat. fat), 16 g fiber	455 cal., 1 g fat (0 g sat. fat), 3 g fiber

portion distortion

When is the last time you measured your plates? If your plates are 10 years old, they are probably about 10 inches in diameter. If they are older than that, they might be 9 inches. If they are new, chances are your plates are 12 or more inches in diameter. It's no coincidence that plate size has increased along with our waistlines.

Nobody wants to eat from a half-empty plate of food. You want a nicely filled plate, especially if you paid for that food at a restaurant. If you think your plates at home are big, restaurant plates are even bigger—more like platters than plates.

It's human nature to eat everything on your plate, even if you are full after eating just half. That's why we recommend to fill just the inner rim of your plate or to downsize to a plate that's a few inches smaller than the typical dinner plate.

Those are good ideas if you're eating at home, but if you eat out, you have to make a point of not eating the whole platterlike plate, which can be tough. Splitting a meal with a fellow diner is always an option. Or you could divide your plate in half as soon as you get it and eat only from one side. The trick is to make sure to stop as soon as you feel even a little bit full. Eating slower also helps you eat less since it takes about 20 minutes for your brain to get the "I'm full" message from your belly. Otherwise your natural habit to eat everything on your plate will take over.

plate check

Still not convinced that the plate size is a big deal? Check out this visual. Each plate has a normal serving of spaghetti—1 cup cooked pasta with $^1/_2$ cup pasta sauce. Which serving looks most appealing?

8 ½-inch plate

9 ¾ inch plate

11 ¼-inch plate

check your cups too

Plates aren't the only serving pieces that have grown in size. Cups and glasses have too! Just look at the coffee cups above. The one on the left is a coffee cup today, which holds about 16 ounces. The one on the right is what was typical about 20 years ago. It holds 6 ounces. It's easy to see how calories add up fast with today's big cups and glasses. We may be drinking the same beverages as we did years ago, but now we're drinking twice the amount or more (and that means more calories!).

For more information:

Learn more about nutrition, portion sizes, and calorie control at these websites:

eatright.org
Find current nutrition news, advice on weight control, and other helpful tips at this website of the American Dietetic Association.

calorieking.com
Quickly look up calorie levels for thousands of foods at this site.

what's the right amount?

You could be eating three or four times what you really need. Check the difference in sizes of the following common foods. The first food in each photo shows a typical portion today. The second food shows what an actual serving should be. It's easy to see how your version of one serving actually could contain multiple portions. And with multiple portions, the calories add up quickly.

cereal

2¼ cups (3 grain servings) = **330 calories**
1 oz or ¾ cup (1 grain serving) = **110 calories**

orange juice

12 oz (2 fruit servings) = **165 calories**
6 oz (1 fruit serving) = **83 calories**

bagel

3.5 oz (3½ grain servings) = **250 calories**
2 oz (2 grain servings) = **140 calories**

apple

7 oz (2 fruit servings) = **186 calories**
3 oz (1 fruit serving) = **80 calories**

potato

9 oz (2 vegetable servings) = **350 calories**
4½ oz (1 vegetable serving) = **175 calories**

steak

12 oz (3 meat servings) = **1,080 calories**
5 ounces (1⅓ meat serving) = **450 calories**

ice cream

3 scoops (1 milk servings) = **450 calories**
One ½-cup scoop (⅓ milk serving) = **150 calories**

determine your
healthy weight

A healthy body weight is one that is right for you. It is a weight that reduces your risk of disease and allows you to look and feel good. There are several ways to determine your healthy weight; one of them is Body Mass Index.

Body Mass Index (BMI)

	Normal						Overweight					Obese										Extremely Obese		
BMI	19	20	21	22	23	24	25	26	27	28	29	30	31	32	33	34	35	36	37	38	39	40	41	42
height												weight in pounds												
4'10"	91	96	100	105	110	115	119	124	129	134	138	143	148	153	158	162	167	172	177	181	186	191	196	201
4'11"	94	99	104	109	114	119	124	128	133	138	143	148	153	158	163	168	173	178	183	188	193	198	203	208
5'0"	97	102	107	112	118	123	128	133	138	143	148	153	158	163	168	174	179	184	189	194	199	204	209	215
5'1"	100	106	111	116	122	127	132	137	143	148	153	158	164	169	174	180	185	190	195	201	206	211	217	222
5'2"	104	109	115	120	126	131	136	142	147	153	158	164	169	175	180	186	191	196	202	207	213	218	224	229
5'3"	107	113	118	124	130	135	141	146	152	158	163	169	175	180	186	191	197	203	208	214	220	225	231	237
5'4"	110	116	122	128	134	140	145	151	157	163	169	174	180	186	192	197	204	209	215	221	227	232	238	244
5'5"	114	120	126	132	138	144	150	156	162	168	174	180	186	192	198	204	210	216	222	228	234	240	246	252
5'6"	118	124	130	136	142	148	155	161	167	173	179	186	192	198	204	210	216	223	229	235	241	247	253	260
5'7"	121	127	134	140	146	153	159	166	172	178	185	191	198	204	211	217	223	230	236	242	249	255	261	268
5'8"	125	131	138	144	151	158	164	171	177	184	190	197	203	210	216	223	230	236	243	249	256	262	269	276
5'9"	128	135	142	149	155	162	169	176	182	189	196	203	209	216	223	230	236	243	250	257	263	270	277	284
5'10"	132	139	146	153	160	167	174	181	188	195	202	209	216	222	229	236	243	250	257	264	271	278	285	292
5'11"	136	143	150	157	165	172	179	186	193	200	208	215	222	229	236	243	250	257	265	272	279	286	293	301
6'0"	140	147	154	162	169	177	184	191	199	206	213	221	228	235	242	250	258	265	272	279	287	294	302	309
6'1"	144	151	159	166	174	182	189	197	204	212	219	227	235	242	250	257	265	272	280	288	295	302	310	318
6'2"	148	155	163	171	179	186	194	202	210	218	225	233	241	249	256	264	272	280	287	295	303	311	319	326
6'3"	152	160	168	176	184	192	200	208	216	224	232	240	248	256	264	272	279	287	295	303	311	319	327	335

For most people, the BMI provides a fairly accurate estimation of body fat based on height and weight. It's used most commonly to define "overweight" and "obese." To calculate your BMI and the calories you need each day, follow the steps below.

1 Find your height in the left-hand column and your weight in the corresponding row.

2 The number in the top row is the BMI for your height and weight rounded to the nearest pound.

3 If your BMI is 25 or above, you may need to lose weight. See "How Many Calories Do I Need?," to the right.

The Ultimate Weight Loss Tool:

The ultimate weight loss tool may already be right at your fingertips— pen and paper. Studies show the simple act of keeping a food journal increases your chances of weight loss success by increasing awareness of your eating habits and holding you personally accountable.

how many calories do I need?

Here is a quick and easy way to determine approximately how many calories you need each day.

To Maintain Your Weight: Multiply your weight in pounds by 15 if you're moderately active (you do housework, gardening, and brisk walking for 30 to 60 minutes most days) or by 13 if you're sedentary (you sit all day with no planned exercise).

For example: If you're moderately active and weigh 150 pounds, your average intake should be 2,250 calories per day (150 × 15).

To Lose Weight: To drop 1 pound per week, you need to reduce your calories by 500 per day. That's because 3,500 calories (500 calories × 7 days) equals 1 pound of body fat. Losing 1 to 2 pounds a week is considered a healthy rate of weight loss.

If that's too much calculating for you, just consume fewer calories than you do now. Most women lose weight if they eat 1,200 to 1,500 calories per day, while most men lose weight if they eat between 1,600 and 1,800 calories per day.

guide to produce

	seasonality	selection	storage
1. asparagus	The peak season for asparagus lasts from February until June.	Look for firm, bright green stalks with fresh, tightly closed tips.	Store asparagus wrapped in a wet paper towel in the refrigerator for up to 7 days.
2. broccoli	The peak season for broccoli lasts from October through April.	Look for richly colored broccoli with tightly closed buds and crisp leaves.	Store unwashed broccoli in a perforated plastic bag in the crisper drawer for up to 4 days.
3. cabbage	Cabbage is readily available year-round, but reaches its peak in the fall.	Opt for heavy cabbage heads with crisp leaves that are firmly packed.	Store in a plastic bag in the crisper drawer of the refrigerator for up to 2 weeks.
4. carrots	Carrots are available year-round but are at their peak from October through April.	Look for firm, smooth carrots with fresh, brightly colored greenery.	Remove greenery and store in a plastic bag in the refrigerator for up to 2 weeks.
5. cauliflower	Cauliflower is available year-round but it's at its best in the fall months.	Look for firm cauliflower with compact florets and no signs of browning.	Wrap tightly in plastic and store in the refrigerator for 3 to 5 days.
6. corn	The peak season for fresh corn lasts from May through September.	Choose ears that are bright green, with tight-fitting husks and golden brown silk.	Corn is best cooked the day it is purchased, but it can be refrigerated with husks on in a plastic bag in the crisper drawer for up to 7 days.
7. cucumbers	Cucumbers reach their peak season from May to August.	Look for small to medium cucumbers that are firm and brightly colored.	Store unwashed cucumbers in the crisper drawer of the refrigerator for up to 7 days.

The best recipe results come when you cook with fruits and vegetables that are ripe and in season. Use this chart as a handy reference for spotting, buying, and storing the best produce to ensure delicious healthful dishes all year round.

	seasonality	selection	storage
 **8.** eggplant	Eggplant is available year-round but reaches its peak in August and September.	Eggplants should be heavy for their size and have firm, glossy skin free from bruising.	Store whole, unwashed eggplant in a plastic bag in the crisper drawer of the refrigerator for up to 5 days.
9. green beans	The peak season for green beans lasts from May to October.	Opt for slender beans that are crisp, brightly colored, and free from blemishes.	Store green beans in a plastic bag in the refrigerator for up 7 days.
10. lettuce	Different lettuce varieties reach their peaks throughout the year.	Choose crisp, dry salad greens that are free from blemishes.	Store washed lettuce wrapped in paper towels, in a plastic bag in the refrigerator for up to 3 days.
11. onions	Onions are available year-round, but most sweet onions are best during the summer.	Choose onions that are heavy for their size with dry, papery skins and free from soft spots.	Store fresh onions in a cool, dry, dark place with good air circulation for 2 months.
 **12.** peas	Look for the tastiest peas from mid spring through early summer.	Choose plump, crisp pea pods that possess a bright green color.	Store snap peas in a plastic bag in the refrigerator for up to 3 days.
 **13.** sweet peppers	The peak season for sweet peppers lasts from July through September.	Look for peppers with shiny skin that are firm, richly colored, and heavy for their size.	Store peppers in the refrigerator for up to 1 week.
 **14.** potatoes	Many varieties are available year-round. Look for new potatoes from spring to summer.	Look for firm potatoes with no green spots, soft spots, wrinkling, or sprouting.	Store in a cool, dry, dark place for up to 2 weeks. Use new potatoes within 3 days.

better brea

2

Wake up and smell the coffee—along with a nutritious breakfast. These luscious breakfasts give you 29 reasons to get up in the morning.

kfast

breakfast pizza

prep: 20 minutes bake: 20 minutes oven: 375°F makes: 10 slices

1	16-ounce loaf frozen whole wheat bread dough, thawed
1	cup sliced zucchini, halved, and/or green or red sweet pepper pieces
1	cup sliced fresh mushrooms
¼	teaspoon crushed red pepper (optional)
1	tablespoon cooking oil
8	eggs
½	cup milk
1	tablespoon butter or margarine
1½	cups shredded cheddar and/or mozzarella cheese (6 ounces)
2	slices bacon, crisp-cooked, drained, and crumbled Chunky salsa (optional)

1 Preheat oven to 375°F. Grease a 13-inch pizza pan; set aside. On a lightly floured surface, roll bread dough into a 14-inch circle. (If dough is difficult to roll out, stop and let it rest a few minutes.) Transfer dough to prepared pan. Build up edges slightly. Prick dough generously with a fork. Bake for 15 to 20 minutes or until light brown.

2 Meanwhile, in a large skillet cook zucchini, mushrooms, and crushed red pepper (if using) in hot oil about 5 minutes or until vegetables are almost tender. Remove zucchini mixture; drain well.

3 In a medium bowl beat together eggs and milk. In same skillet melt butter over medium heat. Pour in egg mixture. Cook, without stirring, until mixture begins to set on the bottom and around edges.

4 Using a large spatula, lift and fold partially cooked eggs so that the uncooked portion flows underneath. Continue cooking over medium heat for 2 to 3 minutes or until egg mixture is cooked through but is still glossy and moist. Immediately remove from heat.

5 Sprinkle half of the shredded cheese over the hot crust. Top with scrambled eggs, zucchini mixture, bacon, and the remaining cheese. Bake for 5 to 8 minutes more or until cheese melts. If desired, serve with salsa.

nutrition facts per slice: 283 cal., 15 g total fat (6 g sat. fat), 193 mg chol., 465 mg sodium, 23 g carb., 2 g dietary fiber, 16 g protein.

easy breakfast pizza: Omit the bread dough in Step 1 and substitute one 12-inch Italian bread shell (Boboli), baking according to the bread shell package. Or, substitute one 13.8-ounce package refrigerated pizza dough, baking as directed on the pizza dough package. Continue as directed in Steps 2 through 5. Makes 10 slices.

per slice easy breakfast pizza: 287 cal., 16 g total fat (6 g sat. fat), 196 mg chol., 462 mg sodium, 22 g carb., 0 g dietary fiber, 16 g protein.

Yes, this is great for breakfast and brunch, but don't let the name stop you. It is good for a light supper as well.

breakfast burritos

start to finish: 25 minutes makes: 6 servings

2 cups refrigerated or frozen egg product, thawed, or 8 eggs, lightly beaten

⅓ cup fat-free milk

6 ounces uncooked bulk turkey sausage

½ cup chopped green sweet pepper (1 small)

½ cup chopped fresh mushrooms

¼ cup chopped onion

2 cloves garlic, minced

½ cup chunky salsa

½ cup chopped romaine lettuce

2 tablespoons finely chopped fresh jalapeño chile pepper* (optional)

6 8- to 10-inch whole wheat flour tortillas, warmed

⅓ cup shredded reduced-fat cheddar cheese

Chunky salsa (optional)

1 In a medium bowl combine egg product and milk; set aside.

2 In a large skillet cook sausage, sweet pepper, mushrooms, onion, and garlic over medium heat until meat is brown and vegetables are tender. Drain off fat. Add egg mixture to skillet. Cook, without stirring, until mixture starts to set on the bottom and around the edges.

3 Using a large spatula, lift and fold partially cooked eggs so that the uncooked portion flows underneath. Continue cooking over medium heat for 2 to 3 minutes or until egg mixture is cooked through but is still glossy and moist. Immediately remove from heat. Stir in ½ cup salsa, romaine lettuce, and jalapeño chile pepper (if using).

4 Divide egg mixture among tortillas; sprinkle with cheese. Roll up tortillas. If desired, serve with additional salsa.

nutrition facts per serving: 291 cal., 9 g total fat (2 g sat. fat), 26 mg chol., 877 mg sodium, 31 g carb., 3 g dietary fiber, 22 g protein.

*tip: Because hot chile peppers contain volatile oils that can burn your skin and eyes, avoid direct contact with chiles as much as possible. When working with chile peppers, wear plastic or rubber gloves. If your bare hands do touch the chile peppers, wash your hands and fingernails well with soap and water when you are done.

bacon and egg
breakfast wraps

start to finish: 25 minutes makes: 4 wraps

4   slices bacon, chopped
1   cup chopped fresh
     mushrooms
½   cup chopped green
     sweet pepper
¼   teaspoon chili
     powder
¼   teaspoon ground
     black pepper
⅛   teaspoon salt
1   cup refrigerated egg
     product
¼   cup chopped seeded
     tomato
     Few drops bottled
     hot pepper sauce
4   8-inch flour tortillas,
     warmed

1 In a large nonstick skillet cook bacon over medium heat until crisp. Using a slotted spoon, remove bacon and drain on paper towels. Reserve 1 tablespoon of drippings in skillet; discard the remaining drippings.

2 Add mushrooms, sweet pepper, chili powder, black pepper, and salt to drippings in skillet; cook and stir about 3 minutes or until vegetables are tender.

3 Add egg product. Cook, without stirring, until mixture begins to set on the bottom and around edges. Using a spatula, lift and fold partially cooked eggs so that the uncooked portion flows underneath. Continue cooking over medium heat about 2 minutes or until egg mixture is cooked through but is still glossy and moist. Stir in bacon, tomato, and hot pepper sauce. Divide egg mixture among tortillas; roll up tortillas.

nutrition facts per wrap: 195 cal., 9 g total fat (3 g sat. fat), 11 mg chol., 462 mg sodium, 18 g carb., 1 g dietary fiber, 11 g protein.

tip: To warm tortillas, preheat oven to 350°F. Wrap tortillas tightly in foil. Bake about 10 minutes or until heated through.

cheesy grits and sausage

start to finish: 25 minutes makes: 4 (1-cup) servings

4   cups water
1   cup quick-cooking grits
¼   teaspoon salt
⅛   teaspoon ground black pepper
6   ounces uncooked bulk turkey sausage
½   cup chopped red sweet pepper
½   cup chopped onion
4   teaspoons finely chopped fresh jalapeño chile pepper*
2   cloves garlic, minced
½   cup shredded reduced-fat cheddar cheese (2 ounce)
2   tablespoons sliced green onion (1)

1 In a medium saucepan bring the water to boiling. Slowly add grits, salt, and black pepper, stirring constantly. Return to boiling; reduce heat. Cook and stir for 5 to 7 minutes or until the water is absorbed and mixture is thickened. Remove from heat. Cover; set aside.

2 In a large skillet cook the turkey sausage, sweet pepper, onion, jalapeño chile pepper, and garlic over medium-high heat until sausage is brown and vegetables are tender. Drain well.

3 Stir cooked turkey sausage mixture into grits. Divide grits among four bowls. Sprinkle each serving with cheese and green onion.

nutrition facts per 1 cup: 244 cal., 7 g total fat (2 g sat. fat), 40 mg chol., 510 mg sodium, 33 g carb., 3 g dietary fiber, 15 g protein.

*tip: Because hot chile peppers contain volatile oils that can burn your skin and eyes, avoid direct contact with them as much as possible. When working with chile peppers, wear plastic or rubber gloves. If your bare hands do touch the peppers, wash your hands and fingernails well with soap and water when you are done.

mushroom, artichoke, and basil egg white omelet

start to finish: 15 minutes makes: 1 serving

½   cup sliced fresh
     cremini mushrooms
⅛   teaspoon garlic salt
     or sea salt
1   teaspoon olive oil
¼   cup coarsely chopped,
     drained, canned
     artichoke hearts
3   egg whites, or
     1 whole egg and
     2 egg whites
     Nonstick cooking
     spray or olive oil
2   tablespoons snipped
     fresh basil
3   tablespoons
     shredded Italian
     blend cheeses
¼   cup chopped red
     sweet pepper or
     tomato
     Cracked black pepper
     Mixed baby greens
     with fat-free
     balsamic vinaigrette
     dressing (optional)

1 In an 8-inch nonstick skillet cook mushrooms and garlic salt in the 1 teaspoon hot olive oil about 5 minutes or until mushrooms are tender, stirring occasionally. Stir in artichoke hearts. Transfer mushroom mixture to a small bowl; set aside. Cool skillet slightly.

2 In a small bowl whisk together egg whites with a fork or whisk just until frothy. Wipe out skillet with a clean paper towel. Coat skillet with cooking spray.

3 Sprinkle basil in the center of the skillet to within 1 inch of edge of skillet. Slowly pour egg white mixture around the edge of the basil and then over the top of the basil. Place skillet over medium heat. Cook, without stirring, over medium heat until mixture begins to set on the bottom and around edges. Using a large spatula, lift and fold partially cooked eggs so that the uncooked portion flows underneath. Continue cooking and lifting over medium heat for 2 to 3 minutes or until egg mixture is almost cooked but surface is still glossy and moist.

4 Sprinkle 2 tablespoons of the cheese across the center; top with mushroom mixture. Using a spatula lift and fold one side of the omelet up over the filling. Repeat with the remaining side of omelet. Remove from heat. Carefully transfer omelet to a serving plate. Top with sweet pepper, the remaining 1 tablespoon cheese, and cracked black pepper. If desired, serve with a salad and vinaigrette.

nutrition facts per serving: 196 cal., 10 g total fat (4 g sat. fat), 15 mg chol., 692 mg sodium, 8 g carb., 3 g dietary fiber, 19 g protein.

nutrition note

Put leftover artichoke hearts to good use—while snagging their potassium, magnesium, and folate benefits—by starring them on top of pizza or nachos.

Kale makes this dish a vitamin A powerhouse.

kale-goat cheese frittata

start to finish: 25 minutes makes: 6 servings

2 cups coarsely torn fresh kale

1 medium onion, halved and thinly sliced

2 teaspoons olive oil

6 eggs

4 egg whites

¼ teaspoon salt

⅛ teaspoon ground black pepper

¼ cup goat cheese, crumbled (1 ounce)

¼ cup oil-packed dried tomatoes, drained and thinly sliced

1 Preheat broiler. In a 10-inch ovenproof nonstick skillet cook kale and onion in hot oil over medium heat about 10 minutes or until onion is tender, stirring occasionally.

2 Meanwhile, in medium bowl whisk together eggs, egg whites, salt, and pepper. Cook, without stirring, over medium heat until mixture begins to set on the bottom and around edges. Using a large spatula, lift and fold partially cooked eggs so that the uncooked portion flows underneath. Continue cooking and lifting over medium heat for 2 to 3 minutes or until egg mixture is almost cooked but surface is still glossy and moist. Immediately remove from heat. Sprinkle with goat cheese and dried tomatoes.

3 Place skillet under the broiler 4 to 5 inches from the heat. Broil for 1 to 2 minutes or until top is just set and cheese melts.

nutrition facts per serving: 145 cal., 9 g total fat (3 g sat. fat), 216 mg chol., 242 mg sodium, 6 g carb., 1 g dietary fiber, 11 g protein.

ham and vegetable frittata

start to finish: 25 minutes makes: 4 servings

4   eggs, lightly beaten
1   cup refrigerated egg
    product
1   tablespoon snipped
    fresh basil or
    1 teaspoon dried
    basil, crushed
¼   teaspoon salt
¼   teaspoon ground
    black pepper
2   tablespoons olive oil
2   cups chopped fresh
    vegetables, such
    as summer squash,
    broccoli, roma
    tomatoes, and/or
    sweet peppers
⅓   cup thinly sliced
    green onions (3)
½   cup cubed cooked
    meat, such as ham,
    kielbasa, chicken,
    turkey, and/or
    crumbled pork
    sausage
½   cup shredded
    reduced-fat
    cheddar, Monterey
    Jack, or Swiss
    cheese (2 ounces)

1 Preheat broiler. In a medium bowl combine eggs, egg product, basil, salt, and black pepper; set aside. In a large ovenproof skillet heat oil over medium heat. Add desired fresh vegetables and green onions. Cook about 5 minutes or until vegetables are crisp-tender, stirring occasionally. Stir in desired cooked meat.

2 Pour egg mixture over vegetable mixture in skillet. Cook, without stirring, until mixture begins to set on the bottom and around edges. Using a large spatula, lift and fold partially cooked eggs so that the uncooked portion flows underneath. Continue cooking and lifting over medium heat for 2 to 3 minutes or until egg mixture is almost cooked but surface is still glossy and moist. Immediately remove from heat. Sprinkle with cheese.

3 Place skillet under the broiler 4 to 5 inches from heat. Broil for 1 to 2 minutes or until top is just set and cheese melts. (Or, preheat oven to 400°F; bake about 5 minutes or until top is set.)

nutrition facts per serving: 241 cal., 16 g total fat (5 g sat. fat), 229 mg chol., 656 mg sodium, 5 g carb., 1 g dietary fiber, 20 g protein.

eggs benedict strata

prep: 30 minutes stand: 8 to 12 hours chill: 2 to 24 hours bake: 55 minutes
oven: 325°F makes: 6 servings

8   slices whole wheat
    or whole grain
    white bread
6   cups baby spinach
    leaves or torn fresh
    kale
2   teaspoons canola oil
4   ounces Canadian-
    style bacon (about
    7 slices), torn into
    bite-size pieces
4   eggs, beaten
2   egg whites, beaten
¼   cup light sour cream
2   tablespoons all-
    purpose flour
1   teaspoon dry mustard
1   teaspoon finely
    shredded lemon
    peel
¼   teaspoon ground
    black pepper
1⅔ cups fat-free milk
⅓   cup light sour cream
2   teaspoons Dijon-style
    mustard
1   to 2 tablespoons
    fat-free milk
    Fresh thyme sprigs
    (optional)

1 Place bread slices in a single layer on a wire rack; cover loosely with a clean kitchen or paper towel and let stand 8 to 12 hours or until bread is dried out. (Or, preheat oven to 300°F. Place bread slices in a 15×10×1 inch baking pan. Bake for 10 to 15 minutes or until bread is dried out, turning once halfway through baking.) Tear bread slices into large pieces.

2 In a very large nonstick skillet cook spinach in hot oil over medium heat for 1 to 2 minutes or just until spinach wilts, turning frequently with tongs. (If using kale, cook for 6 to 8 minutes or just until tender.) Coarsely chop spinach or kale.

3 In a lightly greased 2-quart rectangular baking dish arrange half of the bread pieces. Top with the spinach and the Canadian-style bacon. Top with remaining bread pieces.

4 In a medium bowl whisk together the eggs, egg whites, ¼ cup sour cream, flour, dry mustard, lemon peel, and pepper. Stir in 1⅔ cups milk until well combined. Evenly pour egg mixture over the layers in dish. Cover and chill for 2 to 24 hours.

5 Preheat oven to 325°F. Bake strata, uncovered, for 55 to 60 minutes or until a knife inserted near center comes out clean. Let stand for 10 minutes before serving.

6 Meanwhile, for sauce, in a small bowl stir together ⅓ cup sour cream, Dijon-style mustard, and 1 to 2 tablespoons milk to make a sauce of drizzling consistency. Drizzle sauce over strata to serve. If desired, garnish with fresh thyme sprigs.

nutrition facts per serving: 241 cal., 9 g total fat (3 g sat. fat), 158 mg chol., 521 mg sodium, 23 g carb., 3 g dietary fiber, 17 g protein.

egg and potato casserole

prep: 20 minutes bake: 50 minutes stand: 5 minutes oven: 350°F
makes: 6 servings

Nonstick cooking
spray
2 cups frozen diced
hash brown
potatoes with onion
and peppers
1 cup loose-pack frozen
cut broccoli or
asparagus
⅓ cup finely chopped
Canadian-style
bacon or lean
cooked ham
(2 ounces)
⅓ cup evaporated fat-
free milk
2 tablespoons all-
purpose flour
8 eggs
½ cup shredded
reduced-fat cheddar
cheese (2 ounces)
1 tablespoon snipped
fresh basil or
1 teaspoon dried
basil, crushed
¼ teaspoon salt
¼ teaspoon ground
black pepper

1 Preheat oven to 350°F. Lightly coat a
2-quart square baking dish with cooking
spray. Arrange hash brown potatoes and
frozen broccoli in bottom of baking dish; top
with Canadian-style bacon. Set aside.

2 In a medium bowl whisk together evaporated
milk and flour. In another medium bowl
beat eggs with a rotary beater or wire whisk until
combined. Stir milk mixture, ¼ cup of the cheese,
the basil, salt, and pepper into the egg mixture.
Pour mixture over vegetables in baking dish.

3 Bake about 50 minutes or until a knife
inserted near center comes out clean.
Sprinkle with the remaining ¼ cup cheese. Let
stand for 5 minutes before serving.

nutrition facts per serving: 216 cal., 10 g total fat
(4 g sat. fat), 296 mg chol., 529 mg sodium, 16 g carb.,
1 g dietary fiber, 16 g protein.

make-ahead directions: Prepare as
directed through Step 2. Cover and chill for
at least 4 hours or up to 24 hours. Uncover
and bake as directed in Step 3.

Lox is a luscious form of brined, cold-smoked salmon especially popular in Jewish-American cuisine.

bagel, lox, and egg strata

prep: 30 minutes   chill: 4 to 24 hours   bake: 45 minutes   stand: 10 minutes
oven: 350°F   makes: 12 servings

Nonstick cooking
   spray
8 cups plain bagels cut
   into bite-size pieces
   (3 to 4 bagels)
2 cups shredded Swiss
   cheese or Monterey
   Jack cheese
   (8 ounces)
1 3-ounce package
   thinly sliced
   smoked salmon
   (lox-style), cut into
   small pieces
¼ cup snipped fresh
   chives
8 eggs, beaten
2 cups fat-free milk
1 cup low-fat cottage
   cheese
¼ teaspoon ground
   black pepper

1 Lightly coat a 3-quart rectangular baking dish with cooking spray. Spread half of the bagel pieces evenly in prepared baking dish. Sprinkle cheese, lox, and chives evenly over bagel pieces. Top with the remaining bagel pieces. In a large bowl combine eggs, milk, cottage cheese, and pepper. Evenly pour over layers in baking dish.

2 Press all of the ingredients gently with the back of a spoon to moisten. Cover and chill for at least 4 or up to 24 hours.

3 Preheat oven to 350°F. Bake, uncovered, about 45 minutes or until set and edges are puffed and golden brown. Let stand for 10 minutes before serving.

nutrition facts per serving: 204 cal., 10 g total fat (5 g sat. fat), 163 mg chol., 384 mg sodium, 13 g carb., 0 g dietary fiber, 16 g protein

spiced pumpkin-apple oatmeal

start to finish: 15 minutes   makes: 4 (¾-cup) servings

1⅓   cups water
⅔   cup apple juice
½   cup canned pumpkin
⅓   cup snipped dried apples
1¼   cups quick-cooking rolled oats
1   tablespoon packed brown sugar
1   teaspoon ground cinnamon
¼   teaspoon ground nutmeg
Ground cinnamon (optional)
½   cup vanilla fat-free yogurt

1 In a medium saucepan combine the water, apple juice, pumpkin, and dried apples. Bring to boiling. In a small bowl combine oats, brown sugar, 1 teaspoon cinnamon, and nutmeg. Add oat mixture all at once to boiling mixture; cook and stir, uncovered, for 1 minute.

2 Divide oatmeal among four bowls. If desired, sprinkle with additional cinnamon. Serve with yogurt.

nutrition facts per ¾ cup: 168 cal., 2 g total fat (0 g sat. fat), 1 mg chol., 30 mg sodium, 35 g carb., 4 g dietary fiber, 5 g protein.

nutrition note
Behold the mighty power of pumpkin! Its vitamin A promotes vision, helps your immune system, and works as an antioxidant.

overnight **apple-cinnamon** oatmeal

prep: 15 minutes   slow cook: 6 to 7 hours (low)   makes: 8 servings

4   cups water
1½   cups apple juice
1   cup steel-cut oats
½   cup regular barley
     (not quick-cooking)
½   teaspoon ground
     cinnamon
½   teaspoon grated
     fresh ginger or
     ¼ teaspoon ground
     ginger
¼   teaspoon salt
¼   cup packed brown
     sugar or pure maple
     syrup
2   medium apples,
     coarsely chopped
⅓   cup coarsely chopped
     pecans, toasted
     Ground cinnamon
     (optional)
     Honey and/or fat-free
     milk (optional)

1 Line a 3½- or 4-quart slow cooker with a plastic slow cooker liner. In prepared slow cooker combine the water, apple juice, oats, barley, ½ teaspoon cinnamon, ginger, and salt.

2 Cover and cook on low-heat setting for 6 to 7 hours. Stir in brown sugar.

3 Top each serving with apples and pecans. If desired, sprinkle with additional ground cinnamon and serve with honey and/or milk.

nutrition facts per serving: 218 cal., 5 g total fat (0 g sat. fat), 0 mg chol., 81 mg sodium, 40 g carb., 5 g dietary fiber, 5 g protein.

This oatmeal uses steel-cut oats, which retain a lot of nutrients since they are minimally processed. Preparing the oatmeal ahead like this allows you virtually no prep time in the morning when you are ready for breakfast.

spiced oatmeal

prep: 15 minutes chill: 12 hours to 3 days cool: 5 minutes
cook: 8 minutes makes: 5 (⅔-cup) servings

1½ cups water
¾ cup steel-cut oats
¾ cup fat-free milk
1 6-ounce carton plain low-fat yogurt
½ cup dried fruit, such as cranberries, blueberries, snipped apples, snipped apricots, snipped plums (prunes), and/or dried fruit bits
2 tablespoons honey
¼ teaspoon apple pie spice or pumpkin pie spice
⅛ teaspoon salt
1 tablespoon honey (optional)
⅓ cup coarsely chopped almonds, toasted
Banana, sliced (optional)

1 In a 2-quart saucepan combine the water and steel-cut oats. Bring to boiling; reduce heat. Simmer, uncovered, for 8 minutes. (Oats will not be tender at this point.) Remove from heat; transfer to a medium bowl. Cool for 5 minutes. Stir in milk, yogurt, dried fruit, 2 tablespoons honey, apple pie spice, and salt. Cover and chill for at least 12 hours or up to 3 days.

2 To serve, heat oatmeal mixture through in a saucepan over low heat. Stir in 1 tablespoon honey (if using). Divide oatmeal among five serving bowls. Top each serving with almonds and, if desired, banana slices.

nutrition facts per ⅔ cup: 228 cal., 5 g total fat (1 g sat. fat), 3 mg chol., 102 mg sodium, 38 g carb., 4 g dietary fiber, 8 g protein.

tip: Oatmeal may also be served without heating, just let stand at room temperature for 15 minutes before serving.

cranberry-almond
cereal mix

prep: 10 minutes   cook: 12 minutes   makes: 14 (⅓-cup) servings

1   cup rolled oats
1   cup quick-cooking
    barley
1   cup bulgur or cracked
    wheat
1   cup dried cranberries,
    raisins, and/or
    snipped dried
    apricots
¾   cup sliced almonds,
    toasted
⅓   cup sugar
1   tablespoon ground
    cinnamon
¼   teaspoon salt
    Fat-free milk
    (optional)

1 For cereal mix, in an airtight container stir together oats, barley, bulgur, cranberries, almonds, sugar, cinnamon, and salt. Cover; seal. Store at room temperature for up to 2 months or freeze for up to 6 months.

2 For two breakfast servings, in a small saucepan bring 1⅓ cups water to boiling. Stir cereal mix before measuring; add ⅔ cup of the cereal mix to the boiling water. Reduce heat. Simmer, covered, for 12 to 15 minutes or until cereal reaches desired consistency. If desired, serve with milk.

nutrition facts per ⅓ cup: 177 cal., 3 g total fat (0 g sat. fat), 0 mg chol., 44 mg sodium, 35 g carb., 5 g dietary fiber, 4 g protein.

microwave directions: For one breakfast serving, in a microwave-safe 1-quart bowl combine ¾ cup water and ⅓ cup cereal mix. Microwave, uncovered, on 50 percent power (medium) for 8 to 11 minutes or until cereal reaches desired consistency, stirring once. Stir before serving. If desired, serve with milk.

Fruit is a powerful ally against heart disease; aim for 4 to 5 servings per day, this can be your first.

morning parfait

start to finish: 20 minutes makes: 4 servings

¼ cup raisins
2 tablespoons orange juice
1 teaspoon vanilla
½ of an 8-ounce package reduced-fat cream cheese (Neufchâtel), softened
1 tablespoon sugar
1 teaspoon finely shredded orange peel
2 cups fresh fruit, such as raspberries, blueberries, sliced strawberries, and/ or cut-up peaches
½ cup low-fat granola
Honey (optional)
Shredded orange peel (optional)

1 To plump raisins, in a small microwave-safe bowl combine raisins and orange juice. Microwave, covered, on 100 percent power (high) for 30 to 45 seconds; let stand for 1 minute. Stir in vanilla; set aside.

2 In a medium bowl combine cream cheese and sugar. Beat with an electric mixer on low to medium speed until smooth. Stir in raisin mixture and 1 teaspoon orange peel.

3 Layer half the cream cheese mixture, half of the fresh fruit, and half the granola equally among four tall glasses. Repeat layers. If desired, drizzle with honey and top with additional orange peel.

nutrition facts per serving: 209 cal., 8 g total fat (4 g sat. fat), 22 mg chol., 149 mg sodium, 32 g carb., 4 g dietary fiber, 5 g protein.

This works for breakfast or for a fall dessert too.

apples and granola
breakfast crisp

prep: 15 minutes   cook: 10 minutes   stand: 10 minutes
makes: 4 (½-cup) servings

1   tablespoon butter
2   medium apples, such
      as Rome or Pink
      Lady, peeled if
      desired, cored, and
      quartered
1   tablespoon packed
      brown sugar
½   teaspoon grated
      fresh ginger or
      ¼ teaspoon ground
      ginger
      Dash ground
      cardamom or
      ground cinnamon
1   6-ounce container
      fat-free plain Greek
      yogurt, such as
      Fage, or fat-free
      plain yogurt
1   teaspoon finely
      shredded lemon
      peel
4   teaspoons honey
¼   cup low-fat granola

1 In a medium skillet heat butter over medium heat. Add apples; cook about 5 minutes or until apples are golden brown, turning occasionally. Reduce heat to medium low. Stir in brown sugar, ginger, and cardamom; cook and stir about 5 minutes more or until apples are nearly tender. Remove skillet from heat. Cover and let stand about 10 minutes or until apples are tender.

2 Meanwhile, combine yogurt with lemon peel. Divide cooked apples among four individual plates or bowls. Top with yogurt mixture. Drizzle with honey and sprinkle with granola.

nutrition facts per ½ cup: 145 cal., 3 g total fat (2 g sat. fat), 8 mg chol., 56 mg sodium, 26 g carb., 2 g dietary fiber, 5 g protein.

whole grain brown sugar pancakes

start to finish: 25 minutes makes: 16 pancakes

1½ cups whole wheat flour
1 cup bran cereal flakes with or without raisins
2 tablespoons packed brown sugar
1 tablespoon baking powder
½ teaspoon salt
2 eggs, lightly beaten
1¾ cups buttermilk
2 tablespoons cooking oil
Light maple-flavored syrup (optional)
Fresh fruit (optional)

1 In a large bowl combine whole wheat flour, bran flakes, brown sugar, baking powder, and salt. In a medium bowl use a fork to combine eggs, buttermilk, and oil. Add egg mixture all at once to flour mixture. Stir just until moistened (batter should be slightly lumpy).

2 Heat a lightly greased griddle or heavy skillet over medium heat until a few drops of water dance across the surface. For each standard-size pancake, pour about ¼ cup batter onto the hot griddle. Spread batter, if necessary.

3 Cook for 1 to 2 minutes on each side or until pancakes are golden brown. Turn over when surfaces are bubbly and edges are slightly dry. Serve warm. If desired, top with syrup and fruit. Or keep warm in a loosely covered ovenproof dish in a 200°F oven for up to 30 minutes.

nutrition facts per pancake: 91 cal., 3 g total fat (1 g sat. fat), 28 mg chol., 196 mg sodium, 14 g carb., 2 g dietary fiber, 4 g protein.

tip: For even more raisin-packed pancakes, add ¼ cup raisins to the batter.

nutrition note

Whole wheat flour is made from the entire grain; all-purpose flour is not. The choice is easy: Go for whole wheat whenever you can for added nutrients and fiber.

chocolate-hazelnut
pancakes with raspberry sauce

prep: 25 minutes cook: 3 minutes per batch makes: about 10 pancakes

1¼ cups all purpose flour
2 teaspoons baking
    powder
¼ teaspoon salt
¼ cup chocolate-
    hazelnut spread
    (Nutella)
1 egg
1 tablespoon sugar
1¼ cups milk
1 recipe Raspberry
    Sauce

1 In a medium bowl whisk together the flour, baking powder, and salt; set aside. In another medium bowl whisk together the chocolate-hazelnut spread, egg, and sugar until combined. Whisk in milk until combined. Add milk mixture all at once to flour mixture and whisk until nearly smooth.

2 Heat a lightly greased large skillet or griddle over medium heat until a few drops of water dance across the surface. For each standard-size pancake, pour about ¼ cup batter into the skillet. Spread batter, if necessary.

3 Cook for 2 to 3 minutes. Turn when edges look dry and bubbles appear across the surface. Cook for 1 to 2 minutes more or until light brown on the bottom.

4 Serve pancakes with warm Raspberry Sauce.

nutrition facts per pancake: 151 cal., 4 g total fat (1 g sat. fat), 24 mg chol., 157 mg sodium, 20 g carb., 3 g dietary fiber, 4 g protein.

raspberry sauce: In a medium saucepan combine one 12-ounce package frozen raspberries and 2 tablespoons sugar, breaking up berries with a wooden spoon. Cook over medium heat until bubbly. In a small bowl stir together ¼ cup cold water and 1 tablespoon cornstarch until combined. Add to berry mixture; cook and stir until thickened and bubbly. Cook and stir for 2 minutes more. Serve warm. Makes 1¾ cups.

streusel-crunch
french toast

prep: 20 minutes chill: 2 to 24 hours bake: 30 minutes stand: 5 minutes
oven: 375°F makes: 6 servings

Nonstick cooking
  spray
3 eggs
1 cup evaporated fat-
  free milk
3 tablespoons sugar
2 teaspoons vanilla
½ teaspoon ground
  cinnamon
¼ teaspoon ground
  nutmeg
6 1-inch slices crusty
  whole wheat
  country-style bread
  or French bread
2 tablespoons sugar
½ teaspoon ground
  cinnamon
⅔ cup crushed
  shredded wheat
  biscuits
1 tablespoon butter,
  melted
2 cups sliced fresh
  strawberries

1 Lightly coat a 3-quart rectangular baking dish with cooking spray; set aside. In a medium bowl lightly beat eggs with a rotary beater or wire whisk. Beat in evaporated milk, 3 tablespoons sugar, vanilla, ½ teaspoon cinnamon, and nutmeg. Arrange bread slices in a single layer in prepared baking dish. Evenly pour egg mixture over bread. Cover and chill for 2 to 24 hours, turning bread slices once with a wide spatula.

2 Preheat oven to 375°F. In a small bowl combine 2 tablespoons sugar and ½ teaspoon cinnamon; set aside. In another small bowl combine crushed biscuits, melted butter, and 2 teaspoons of the cinnamon-sugar mixture. Sprinkle evenly over bread slices in dish.

3 Bake, uncovered, about 30 minutes or until light brown. Let stand for 5 minutes before serving. Meanwhile, in a small bowl combine strawberries and the remaining cinnamon-sugar mixture. Serve strawberries with French toast.

nutrition facts per serving: 248 cal., 6 g total fat (2 g sat. fat), 113 mg chol., 273 mg sodium, 40 g carb., 4 g dietary fiber, 10 g protein.

As you finish baking each waffle, keep them warm in a 300°F oven. Just be sure to put them in a single layer on a large baking sheet or tray, rather than stacking them on a plate. Stacking creates steam, which can make the waffles soggy.

banana-pecan waffles

prep: 20 minutes   cook: 3 minutes per waffle   makes: about 9 waffles

1¾ cups all-purpose flour
2 tablespoons sugar
1 tablespoon baking powder
½ teaspoon ground cinnamon
¼ teaspoon salt
¾ cup mashed bananas (2 small)
2 eggs, lightly beaten
1 cup milk
¼ cup vegetable oil or melted butter
1 teaspoon vanilla
½ cup finely chopped pecans, toasted
Light maple-flavored syrup, berries, sliced bananas, and/or desired chopped fruit (optional)

1 In large bowl stir together flour, sugar, baking powder, cinnamon, and salt. Make a well in the center of flour mixture; set aside.

2 In medium bowl beat together banana and eggs. Stir in milk, oil, and vanilla. Add banana mixture all at once to the flour mixture. Stir just until moistened (batter should be slightly lumpy). Stir in pecans.

3 Lightly grease waffle iron. Add batter to waffle iron according to manufacturer's directions. Bake according to manufacturer's directions for 3 to 4 minutes or until golden brown. Using a fork, lift waffle off grid. Repeat with the remaining batter. Serve warm with desired toppings.

nutrition facts per waffle: 241 cal., 12 g total fat (2 g sat. fat), 49 mg chol., 172 mg sodium, 28 g carb., 2 g dietary fiber, 5 g protein.

peachy corn bread muffins

prep: 15 minutes bake: 14 minutes cool: 5 minutes
oven: 400°F makes: 12 muffins

1	cup yellow cornmeal
¾	cup all-purpose flour
¼	cup sugar
2½	teaspoons baking powder
½	teaspoon salt
½	teaspoon apple pie spice
¾	cup milk
2	eggs
¼	cup butter, melted
¾	cup chopped fresh or frozen unsweetened peaches
	Light vegetable oil spread (optional)

1 Preheat oven to 400°F. Grease twelve 2½-inch muffin cups; set aside. In a medium bowl stir together cornmeal, flour, sugar, baking powder, salt, and apple pie spice. Make a well in the center of flour mixture; set aside.

2 In a small bowl whisk together milk, eggs, and melted butter. Stir in peaches. Add peach mixture all at once to flour mixture. Stir just until moistened. Spoon batter into prepared muffin cups, filling cups two-thirds full.

3 Bake for 14 to 15 minutes or until edges are firm and golden brown. Cool in muffin cups on a wire rack for 5 minutes. Remove from muffin cups; serve warm. If desired, serve with vegetable oil spread.

nutrition facts per muffin: 145 cal., 5 g total fat (3 g sat. fat), 47 mg chol., 219 mg sodium, 21 g carb., 1 g dietary fiber, 3 g protein.

ham-and-cheddar scones

prep: 25 minutes bake: 18 minutes oven: 375°F makes: 10 to 12 scones

1¾ cups all-purpose flour
¼ cup whole wheat flour
2 teaspoons baking powder
1 teaspoon sugar
½ teaspoon baking soda
⅛ teaspoon salt
½ cup butter
½ cup reduced-fat shredded sharp cheddar cheese (2 ounces)
¼ cup diced cooked ham
1 tablespoon snipped fresh dill or 1 teaspoon dried dill
1 egg, lightly beaten
¾ cup light sour cream
1 tablespoon Dijon-style mustard
Snipped fresh dill (optional)

1 Preheat oven to 375°F. Line a baking sheet with parchment; set aside. In a large bowl combine all-purpose flour, whole wheat flour, baking powder, sugar, baking soda, and salt. Using a pastry blender or two knives, cut in butter until mixture resembles coarse crumbs. Stir in cheese, ham, and 1 tablespoon dill. Make a well in center of flour mixture.

2 In a small bowl combine egg, sour cream, and mustard. Add egg mixture all at once to flour mixture. Using a fork, stir just until moistened (do not overmix).

3 Turn dough out onto a lightly floured surface. Knead dough by folding and gently pressing it for four to six strokes or just until dough holds together and is nearly smooth. Pat or lightly roll dough until ¾ inch thick. Cut dough with a floured 2½- to 3-inch biscuit cutter. Reroll scraps as necessary, dipping cutter into flour between cuts. Place dough circles 1 inch apart on prepared baking sheet.

4 Bake for 18 to 20 minutes or until golden. Remove scones from baking sheet; serve warm. If desired, sprinkle with additional fresh dill.

nutrition facts per scone: 223 cal., 13 g total fat (8 g sat. fat), 56 mg chol., 369 mg sodium, 21 g carb., 1 g dietary fiber, 6 g protein.

cornmeal-blueberry
scones

prep: 25 minutes bake: 12 minutes oven: 450°F makes: 12 scones

Nonstick cooking
   spray
1⅓ cups all-purpose flour
  ⅔ cup yellow cornmeal
  2 tablespoons
    granulated sugar
  2 tablespoons packed
    brown sugar
1½ teaspoons baking
    powder
  ½ teaspoon salt
  ¼ teaspoon baking soda
  ⅓ cup cold butter, cut up
  ½ cup buttermilk
  1 egg
1½ teaspoons finely
    shredded lime peel
  1 cup blueberries
  1 teaspoon cornstarch
  1 cup powdered sugar
  3 to 4 teaspoons lime
    juice
  3 tablespoons chopped
    almonds, toasted

1 Preheat oven to 450°F. Coat large baking sheet with cooking spray; set aside.

2 In large bowl combine flour, cornmeal, granulated sugar, brown sugar, baking powder, salt, and baking soda. Using a pastry blender or two knives, cut in butter until flour mixture resembles coarse crumbs. Make a well in the center of flour mixture. In a small bowl combine buttermilk, egg, and lime peel. Add buttermilk mixture all at once to flour mixture. Using a fork, stir just until moistened.

3 Toss blueberries with cornstarch; add to flour mixture. Stir gently for 3 to 5 turns just until berries are combined (do not overmix). Using a large spoon, drop dough into 12 mounds on prepared baking sheet, leaving 1 inch between mounds.

4 Bake for 12 to 15 minutes or until tops are golden. For icing, in a small bowl stir together powdered sugar and enough lime juice to make an icing of drizzling consistency. Drizzle over warm scones. Sprinkle with nuts. Serve warm.

nutrition facts per scone: 203 cal., 7 g total fat (4 g sat. fat), 32 mg chol., 225 mg sodium, 33 g carb., 1 g dietary fiber, 2 g protein.

Substitute these for a sugary pastry in the morning and you'll feel better. Instead of butter and eggs, these cinnamon-laced cookies contain peanut butter and a potassium-rich banana.

banana oat breakfast cookie

prep: 20 minutes bake: 14 minutes per batch oven: 350°F
makes: 12 breakfast cookies

Nonstick cooking
  spray
½ cup mashed banana
  (1 large)
½ cup chunky natural
  peanut butter
  (unsalted and
  unsweetened) or
  regular chunky
  peanut butter
½ cup honey
1 teaspoon vanilla
1 cup rolled oats
½ cup whole wheat
  flour
¼ cup nonfat dry milk
  powder
2 teaspoons ground
  cinnamon
¼ teaspoon baking soda
1 cup dried cranberries
  or raisins

1 Preheat oven to 350°F. Lightly coat two cookie sheets with cooking spray; set aside. In a large bowl stir together banana, peanut butter, honey, and vanilla. In a small bowl combine oats, flour, milk powder, cinnamon, and baking soda. Stir oat mixture into banana mixture until combined. Stir in dried cranberries.

2 Use a ¼-cup measure or scoop to drop mounds of dough about 3 inches apart onto prepared baking sheets. Dip a thin metal or small plastic spatula into water; flatten and spread each mound of dough into a 2¾-inch round, about ½ inch thick.

3 Bake, one cookie sheet at a time, for 14 to 16 minutes or until light brown. Transfer to wire racks; cool completely.

4 Layer cookies between sheets of waxed paper in an airtight container; cover. Store at room temperature for up to 3 days or freeze for up to 2 months.

nutrition facts per cookie. 227 cal., 6 g total fat (1 g sat. fat), 0 mg chol., 77 mg sodium, 37 g carb., 4 g dietary fiber, 6 g protein.

nutrition note

No need to choose between a healthy breakfast and a morning workout— with these grab-and-go breakfast cookies, you'll have time for both.

apricot maple logs

prep: 25 minutes bake: 15 minutes cool: 5 minutes oven: 350°F
makes: 9 cookie logs

1	cup rolled oats
¾	cup whole wheat pastry flour
¼	cup nonfat dry milk powder
½	teaspoon baking soda
½	teaspoon ground cinnamon
⅛	teaspoon salt
3	tablespoons corn oil or canal oil
½	cup maple-flavored syrup
1	teaspoon vanilla
¾	cup dried apricot halves, chopped
¼	cup raw sunflower seeds

1 Preheat oven to 350°F. Grease a cookie sheet or line with parchment paper; set aside.

2 In a large bowl stir together oats, flour, dry milk, baking soda, cinnamon, and salt. In a medium bowl combine oil, maple syrup, and vanilla. Add oil mixture all at once to flour mixture. Stir just until combined. Stir in apricots and sunflower seeds.

3 For each cookie, use damp hands to shape ¼ cup of dough into a 4-inch log. Place logs on prepared baking sheet.

4 Bake about 15 minutes or until light brown and edges are set (cookies will still be soft). Cool on cookie sheet for 5 minutes. Transfer to a wire rack; cool completely.

5 Store cookies in a resealable plastic bag or wrap individually in plastic wrap at room temperature for up to 3 days or freeze for up to 1 month. To serve, thaw frozen cookies at room temperature about 30 minutes or until completely thawed.

nutrition facts per log: 249 cal., 8 g total fat
(1 g sat. fat), 0 mg chol., 125 mg sodium, 40 g carb.,
4 g dietary fiber, 6 g protein.

Sweet, spicy pumpkin and crunchy pumpkin seeds make these tasty bars high in beta carotene, fiber, and minerals. Heart-healthy oats and whole wheat flour round out a chewy breakfast bar.

double pumpkin bars

prep: 15 minutes bake: 20 minutes oven: 350°F makes: 8 bars

1 cup rolled oats
½ cup whole wheat pastry flour or white whole wheat flour
½ teaspoon baking soda
½ teaspoon ground cinnamon
½ teaspoon ground allspice
¼ teaspoon salt
1 egg
½ cup canned pumpkin
¼ cup sugar
¼ cup canola oil
1 teaspoon vanilla
½ cup chopped pitted dates
¼ cup pumpkin seeds (pepitas) or chopped walnuts

1 Preheat oven to 350°F. Lightly grease an 8×8×2-inch baking pan or 2-quart square baking dish; set aside.

2 In a medium bowl stir together oats, flour, baking soda, cinnamon, allspice, and salt. In a small bowl whisk together egg, pumpkin, sugar, oil, and vanilla. Add pumpkin mixture to flour mixture. Stir just until combined. Stir in dates and pumpkin seeds. Spread mixture evenly into the prepared baking pan.

3 Bake about 20 minutes or until top is firm and a toothpick inserted near center comes out clean. Cool in pan on a wire rack. Cut into bars. If desired, cut each bar diagonally.

nutrition facts per bar: 264 cal., 12 g total fat (2 g sat. fat), 27 mg chol., 163 mg sodium, 34 g carb., 4 g dietary fiber, 8 g protein

make-ahead directions: Prepare and cool as directed. Wrap bars individually in plastic wrap and store in the refrigerator for up to 1 week.

A sparkly dusting of cinnamon sugar makes these apple-studded cookies seem like a cheat, but they are made with whole wheat, fat-free yogurt, and applesauce. The whole grain flour provides heart-healthy antioxidants and fiber, so enjoy them instead of doughnuts.

breakfast apple
snickerdoodles

prep: 25 minutes   bake: 10 minutes   oven: 375°F   makes: about 14 cookies

1   cup whole wheat
    pastry flour
½   cup nonfat dry milk
    powder
¼   teaspoon baking soda
¼   teaspoon ground
    cinnamon
    Dash salt
½   cup fat-free vanilla
    yogurt
¼   cup honey
2   tablespoons
    unsweetened
    applesauce
1   tablespoon canola oil
½   cup snipped or diced
    dried apples
1   tablespoon sugar
½   teaspoon ground
    cinnamon
    Honey (optional)

1 Preheat oven to 375°F. In a large bowl combine flour, milk powder, baking soda, ¼ teaspoon cinnamon, and salt; set aside. In a medium bowl whisk together yogurt, honey, applesauce, and oil. Stir applesauce mixture into flour mixture all at once. Stir just until combined. Stir in dried apples just until combined.

2 Drop dough by rounded tablespoons 2 inches apart onto an ungreased cookie sheet. In a small bowl combine sugar and ½ teaspoon cinnamon. Sprinkle lightly over dough.

3 Bake for 10 to 12 minutes or until edges are light brown. Transfer to a wire rack; cool completely. If desired, drizzle with honey just before serving.

nutrition facts per cookie: 73 cal., 1 g total fat (0 g sat. fat), 0 mg chol., 54 mg sodium, 15 g carb., 1 g dietary fiber, 2 g protein.

blueberry-pineapple
smoothie

start to finish: 10 minutes makes: 2 (1-cup) servings

1 In a blender combine spinach, 1 cup blueberries, banana, yogurt, ¼ cup pineapple, cherries, and orange juice. Cover and blend until nearly smooth, stopping to scrape down sides of container as necessary. Divide between two glasses. If desired, top with additional pineapple and/or blueberries.

2   cups fresh baby spinach
1   cup frozen blueberries
1   banana
½   cup fat-free vanilla yogurt
¼   cup chopped fresh pineapple
¼   cup frozen dark sweet cherries
¼   cup orange juice
    Chopped fresh pineapple and/or fresh blueberries (optional)

nutrition facts per 1 cup: 195 cal., 1 g total fat (1 g sat. fat), 3 mg chol., 86 mg sodium, 43 g carb., 5 g dietary fiber, 6 g protein.

protein-packed smoothie

start to finish: 10 minutes makes: 4 (1-cup) servings

1 In a blender combine yogurt, bananas, sliced strawberries, honey, and peanut butter. Cover and blend until nearly smooth, stopping to scrape down sides of container as necessary. Divide among four glasses. If desired, garnish with whole strawberries.

2   cups plain fat-free yogurt
2   ripe medium bananas
2   cups sliced fresh strawberries or frozen unsweetened strawberries
2   tablespoons honey
2   tablespoons peanut butter
    Whole fresh strawberries (optional)

nutrition facts per 1 cup: 223 cal., 5 g total fat (1 g sat. fat), 2 mg chol., 133 mg sodium, 39 g carb., 3 g dietary fiber, 10 g protein.

sandwiches and pi

3

Hold out your hand and be ready—a lean and lovely, simple and satisfying meal is within your grasp.

zza

bagel beef sandwiches

prep: 15 minutes   stand: 15 minutes   broil: 12 minutes   makes: 4 sandwiches

¼   cup sliced dried tomatoes (not oil-packed)
2   teaspoons olive oil
1   small red onion, sliced
12   ounces boneless beef top sirloin steak, cut about ¾ inch thick
¼   teaspoon garlic salt
¼   teaspoon ground black pepper
½   cup chopped onion (1 medium)
2   tablespoons light mayonnaise
1   tablespoon yellow mustard
4   small whole wheat bagels, split and toasted (8 ounces total)
2   cups mixed spring salad greens or finely shredded romaine lettuce

1 Preheat broiler. Place dried tomatoes in a 2-cup microwave-safe glass measuring cup or small bowl; add enough water to cover. Microwave, uncovered, on 100 percent (high) for 1 minute. Let stand for 15 minutes.

2 Meanwhile, brush oil on red onion slices. Trim fat from meat. Sprinkle meat with garlic salt and pepper. Arrange meat and onion slices on the unheated rack of a broiler pan. Broil 3 to 4 inches from the heat for 12 to 16 minutes for medium rare (145°F) or desired doneness, turning once halfway through broiling. Transfer meat to a cutting board. Thinly slice meat across the grain into bite-size strips.

3 For sauce, drain and finely chop tomatoes. In a small bowl combine tomatoes, ½ cup chopped onion, mayonnaise, and mustard.

4 To serve, top bagel bottoms with salad greens. Top with meat, onion slices, sauce, and bagel tops.

nutrition facts per sandwich: 323 cal., 10 g total fat (2 g sat. fat), 38 mg chol., 524 mg sodium, 36 g carb., 6 g dietary fiber, 27 g protein.

chipotle–bbq
steak sandwiches

prep: 25 minutes marinate: 4 to 6 hours grill: 17 minutes stand: 5 minutes
makes: 4 sandwiches

1 8-ounce can no-salt-added tomato sauce plus 1 clove garlic, minced
3 tablespoons no-salt-added tomato paste
2 tablespoons water
1 tablespoon Dijon-style mustard
1 tablespoon Worcestershire sauce
2 teaspoons honey
1 teaspoon finely chopped canned chipotle chile peppers in adobo sauce*
1 12-ounce beef flank steak
1 medium green sweet pepper, seeded and quartered
4 ½-inch slices sweet onion, such as Vidalia, Walla Walla, or Maui
   Nonstick cooking spray
4 ciabatta rolls or hamburger buns, split and toasted (10 ounces)

1 For marinade, in a small bowl stir together tomato sauce, tomato paste, the water, mustard, Worcestershire sauce, honey, and chipotle chile peppers; set aside.

2 Trim fat from meat. Score both sides of meat in a diamond pattern by making shallow diagonal cuts at 1-inch intervals. Place meat in a large resealable plastic bag set in a shallow dish. Pour marinade over meat. Seal bag; turn to coat meat. Marinate meat in the refrigerator for 4 to 6 hours, turning bag occasionally.

3 Drain steak, reserving marinade. Lightly coat sweet pepper and onion with cooking spray.

4 For a charcoal grill, place meat, sweet pepper, and onion on the rack of an uncovered grill directly over medium coals. Grill until meat is medium doneness (160°F) and vegetables are tender, turning once halfway through grilling. Allow 17 to 21 minutes for the meat and 8 to 12 minutes for the vegetables. (For a gas grill, preheat grill. Reduce heat to medium. Place meat, sweet pepper, and onion on grill rack over heat. Cover and grill as directed.)

5 Meanwhile, for sauce, pour reserved marinade into a small saucepan. Bring to boiling; reduce heat. Simmer, uncovered, about 5 minutes or until desired consistency.

6 Let meat stand for 5 minutes. Thinly slice meat across the grain. Thinly slice sweet pepper lengthwise. To serve, top ciabatta roll bottoms with steak slices, sweet pepper strips, onion slices, sauce, and ciabatta roll tops.

nutrition facts per sandwich: 417 cal., 9 g total fat (3 g sat. fat), 35 mg chol., 667 mg sodium, 56 g carb., 4 g dietary fiber, 28 g protein.

*tip: Because hot chile peppers contain volatile oils that can burn your skin and eyes, avoid direct contact with them as much as possible. When working with chile peppers, wear plastic or rubber gloves. If your bare hands do touch the peppers, wash your hands and fingernails well with soap and water when you are done.

open-face beef, lettuce, and peach sandwiches

prep: 25 minutes marinate: 4 to 24 hours grill: 17 minutes
makes: 4 servings

1 pound beef flank steak
¼ cup balsamic vinegar
2 tablespoons olive oil
1 tablespoon snipped fresh rosemary
2 cloves garlic, minced
¼ teaspoon salt
⅛ teaspoon ground black pepper
4 ½-inch-thick slices multigrain or whole grain crusty country bread
2 medium peaches and/or plums, halved and pitted
¼ cup slivered red onion
2 tablespoons balsamic vinegar
1 cup coarsely shredded lettuce

1 Score both sides of meat in a diamond pattern by making shallow diagonal cuts at 1-inch intervals. Place meat in a large resealable plastic bag set in a shallow dish. For marinade, in a small bowl whisk together ¼ cup vinegar, 1 tablespoon of the oil, the rosemary, and garlic. Pour marinade over the meat. Seal bag; turn to coat meat. Marinate in the refrigerator for 4 to 24 hours, turning bag occasionally.

2 Drain meat, discarding marinade. Sprinkle meat with salt and pepper. For a charcoal grill, grill meat on the rack of an uncovered grill directly over medium coals for 17 to 21 minutes for medium (160°F), turning once halfway through grilling. Meanwhile, brush bread slices with the remaining 1 tablespoon oil. While meat is grilling, add bread slices and peach and/or plum halves, cut sides down, to grill. Grill for 1 to 2 minutes or until bread is lightly toasted on both sides and peaches and/or plums are charred and softened slightly. (For a gas grill, preheat grill. Reduce heat to medium. Place meat, then bread and peaches and/or plums on grill rack over heat. Cover and grill as above.)

3 Coarsely chop grilled peaches and/or plums. In a small bowl combine peaches and/or plums, red onion, and the 2 tablespoons vinegar; toss to coat. Thinly slice meat across the grain.

4 To serve, top bread slices with lettuce, meat slices, and peach and/or plum mixture.

nutrition facts per serving: 325 cal., 11 g total fat (3 g sat. fat), 37 mg chol., 347 mg sodium, 26 g carb., 6 g dietary fiber, 29 g protein.

62

open-face
italian beef
sandwiches

start to finish: 20 minutes makes: 4 sandwiches

¼ cup white wine
   vinegar or cider
   vinegar
1 teaspoon sugar
½ teaspoon salt
½ teaspoon ground
   black pepper
1 17-ounce package
   refrigerated cooked
   Italian-style beef
   roast au jus,
   undrained
1 cup thinly sliced baby
   or regular red and/
   or yellow sweet
   pepper
2 square whole grain
   ciabatta buns, split
4 slices provolone
   cheese (4 ounces)
2 tablespoons snipped
   fresh Italian (flat-
   leaf) parsley
   Snipped fresh Italian
   (flat-leaf) parsley
   (optional)

1 Preheat broiler. In a large microwave-safe bowl combine vinegar, sugar, salt, and black pepper. Stir in meat with juices and sweet pepper. Microwave, covered, on 100 percent power (high) for 4 minutes.

2 Meanwhile, place buns, cut sides up, on a baking sheet. Broil 3 to 4 inches from the heat about 1 minute or until lightly toasted. Top with cheese. Broil for 1 to 2 minutes more or until cheese melts.

3 Using a fork, coarsely shred meat. Stir in the 2 tablespoons parsley. Using a slotted spoon, mound meat mixture onto toasted bun halves. If desired, sprinkle with additional parsley. Serve with any remaining meat juices.

nutrition facts per sandwich: 341 cal., 15 g total fat (8 g sat. fat), 78 mg chol., 774 mg sodium, 22 g carb., 2 g dietary fiber, 31 g protein.

nutrition note
Sandwiches can go from being a "no-no" to a "yes, please"—even if you're watching your carbohydrate intake—when you opt for an open-face sandwich like this. Or, use a sandwich thin in place of traditional bread.

poached salmon on ciabatta

start to finish: 30 minutes makes: 4 sandwiches

½ cup dry white wine
or water

½ cup water

12 ounces skinless
salmon fillet, about
1 inch thick

¼ cup tub-style
whipped cream
cheese with garlic
and herbs

2 tablespoons fat-free
milk

1 tablespoon snipped
fresh dill

1 teaspoon finely
shredded lemon
peel

⅛ teaspoon coarsely
cracked black
pepper

4 2-ounce ciabatta rolls,
split and toasted, if
desired

1 cup fresh baby
spinach

1 In a large nonstick skillet combine wine and the water. Bring to boiling; add fish. Reduce heat. Simmer, covered, for 8 to 12 minutes or until fish begins to flake when tested with fork. Remove fish from cooking liquid; discard liquid. Let fish cool to room temperature; break into large chunks.

2 Meanwhile, in a small bowl combine cream cheese, milk, dill, lemon peel, and pepper. Spread cream cheese mixture on cut sides of the ciabatta rolls. Top with spinach, fish chunks, and roll tops, spread sides down.

nutrition facts per sandwich: 345 cal, 16 g total fat (5 g sat. fat), 57 mg chol., 458 mg sodium, 30 g carb., 2 g dietary fiber, 23 g protein.

nutrition note

While most vitamin-D rich foods on grocery store shelves need to be fortified with the nutrient, salmon provides it naturally. So dig in, knowing that you're giving your bones a boost.

chicken salad sandwiches

start to finish: 20 minutes makes: 4 sandwiches

¼ cup light sour cream
2 tablespoons snipped fresh Italian (flat-leaf) parsley or basil
1 tablespoon white balsamic vinegar or cider vinegar
¼ teaspoon freshly ground black pepper
1½ cups chopped cooked chicken*
⅓ cup chopped seeded cucumber
¼ cup chopped roasted red sweet pepper
8 slices whole wheat bread, toasted
4 small tomato slices
4 lettuce leaves

1 In a medium bowl stir together sour cream, parsley, vinegar, and black pepper. Add chicken, cucumber, and roasted sweet pepper; toss to coat. Cover and chill for up to 4 hours if not serving immediately.

2 To serve, spread chicken mixture on half of the bread slices. Top with tomato slices, lettuce, and the remaining bread slices. Cut sandwiches in half.

nutrition facts per sandwich: 235 cal., 5 g total fat (2 g sat. fat), 49 mg chol., 286 mg sodium, 23 g carb., 4 g dietary fiber, 23 g protein.

*tip: For quick, cooked chicken, use a purchased deli-roasted chicken. Use the breast meat for the fewest calories and remove the skin. If you choose to cook your own chicken breast meat, sprinkle it lightly with salt.

zucchini and mozzarella panini

start to finish: 30 minutes makes: 4 sandwiches

8 slices sourdough bread
1½ tablespoons olive oil
¼ cup light mayonnaise
2 medium tomatoes, thinly sliced
1 medium zucchini, thinly sliced diagonally
1 small red onion, thinly sliced
¼ cup oil-packed dried tomatoes, drained and snipped
½ to ¾ cup fresh basil leaves
½ to ¾ cup shredded mozzarella cheese (2 to 3 ounces)

1 Brush one side of bread slices with oil. Spread the other side of four of the bread slices with mayonnaise. Layer the mayonnaise-topped bread with tomato slices, zucchini, red onion, and dried tomato. Sprinkle with basil and cheese. Top with the remaining four bread slices, oil sides up.

2 Heat a 12-inch skillet over medium-low heat. Place sandwiches in skillet. Weight sandwiches down with a heavy skillet. Cook until bread is lightly toasted. Turn sandwiches over, weight down, and cook until bread is lightly toasted and cheese melts.

nutrition facts per sandwich: 322 cal., 15 g total fat (4 g sat. fat), 13 mg chol., 567 mg sodium, 38 g carb., 3 g dietary fiber, 11 g protein.

chicken and hummus wraps

start to finish: 15 minutes   makes: 4 wraps

1   7-ounce carton
    desired-flavor
    hummus or one
    8-ounce tub cream
    cheese spread with
    garden vegetables
4   10-inch flour tortillas
⅓   cup plain low-fat
    yogurt or sour
    cream
1   6-ounce package
    refrigerated cooked
    chicken breast
    strips
¾   cup coarsely chopped
    roma tomatoes
    (2 large)
⅓   of a medium
    cucumber, cut into
    2-inch matchsticks

1 Spread hummus evenly on tortillas. Spread yogurt over hummus. Top with chicken, tomatoes, and cucumber. Roll up tortillas.

nutrition facts per wrap: 288 cal., 9 g total fat (2 g sat. fat), 31 mg chol., 713 mg sodium, 36 g carb., 3 g dietary fiber, 16 g protein.

nutrition note
All tortillas are not created equal! Read their nutrition labels and reach for those high in fiber and protein and lower in calories and fat.

avocado-lime tuna wraps

start to finish: 10 minutes makes: 4 wraps

1 ripe avocado, halved,
   seeded, peeled, and
   coarsely mashed
¼ cup salsa
¼ cup chopped green
   onions (2)
1 tablespoon lime juice
1 6-ounce can chunk
   white tuna
   (waterpack),
   drained and broken
   into chunks
4 8- to 10-inch flour
   tortillas
1¼ cups shredded
   lettuce
½ cup shredded
   cheddar or Colby
   and Monterey Jack
   cheese (2 ounces)

1 In a medium bowl combine avocado, salsa,
green onions, and lime juice. Add the tuna;
mix gently to combine.

2 Spread tuna mixture evenly over tortillas.
Top with lettuce and cheese. Fold edge
over filling; fold in the sides and roll up.
Serve immediately.

nutrition facts per wrap: 270 cal., 13 g total fat
(4 g sat. fat), 38 mg chol., 534 mg sodium, 20 g carb.,
3 g dietary fiber, 18 g protein.

tuna–red pepper
salad wraps

start to finish: 15 minutes makes: 2 servings

1 5-ounce pouch chunk
   light tuna
¼ cup light mayonnaise
   or salad dressing
¼ cup chopped roasted
   sweet red pepper
1 tablespoon chopped
   sweet gherkin
6 Bibb lettuce leaves
1 slice whole wheat
   bread, toasted and
   cut into 6 strips

1 In a small bowl combine tuna, mayonnaise,
roasted sweet pepper, and gherkin. Spoon
tuna mixture onto each lettuce leaf near one
edge. Top each with a strip of toast. Roll up
lettuce, starting from the edge with the
tuna mixture.

nutrition facts per 3 wraps: 216 cal., 11 g total fat
(2 g sat. fat), 48 mg chol., 599 mg sodium, 10 g carb.,
2 g dietary fiber, 19 g protein.

grilled jamaican jerk
fish wraps

prep: 30 minutes   grill: 4 minutes to 6 minutes per ½-inch thickness
makes: 4 servings

1   pound fresh or frozen
     skinless flounder,
     cod, or sole fillets
1½   teaspoons Jamaican
     jerk seasoning
4   7- to 8-inch whole
     grain flour tortillas
2   cups packaged fresh
     baby spinach
¾   cup chopped, seeded
     tomato
¾   cup chopped fresh
     mango or pineapple
2   tablespoons snipped
     fresh cilantro
1   tablespoon finely
     chopped, seeded
     fresh jalapeno chile
     pepper*
1   tablespoon lime juice

1 Thaw fish, if frozen. Rinse fish; pat dry with paper towels. Sprinkle both sides of fish fillets with Jamaican jerk seasoning; rub in with your fingers. Measure thickness of fish.

2 For a charcoal grill, grill tortillas on the greased rack of an uncovered grill directly over medium coals about 1 minute or until bottoms of tortillas have grill marks. Remove from grill; set aside.

3 Add fish to the grill. Grill for 4 to 6 minutes per ½-inch thickness or until fish begins to flake when tested with fork, carefully turning once halfway through grilling. (For a gas grill, preheat grill. Reduce heat to medium. Place tortillas, then fish on greased grill rack over heat. Cover and grill as above.) Coarsely flake the fish.

4 Meanwhile, in a medium bowl combine spinach, tomato, mango, cilantro, jalapeño chile pepper, and lime juice; toss gently to coat.

5 To serve, place tortillas, grill mark sides down, on a flat work surface. Divide spinach mixture and fish among tortillas. Fold tortillas over to enclose filling.

nutrition facts per serving: 254 cal., 4 g total fat (1 g sat. fat), 48 mg chol., 509 mg sodium, 23 g carb., 11 g dietary fiber, 29 g protein.

*tip: Because chiles contain volatile oils that can burn your skin and eyes, avoid direct contract with them as much as possible. When working with chiles, wear plastic or rubber gloves. If your bare hands do touch the peppers, wash your hands and nails well with soap and warm water.

ginger beef
lettuce wraps

prep: 20 minutes freeze: 30 minutes marinate: 4 to 6 hours
cook: 8 minutes makes: 4 servings

1	pound beef flank steak or boneless beef top round steak
1	medium yellow or green sweet pepper, seeded and cut into bite-size strips
1	small zucchini, trimmed and cut into thin bite-size strips
½	medium red onion, cut into thin wedges
⅓	cup ginger beer or ginger ale
3	tablespoons reduced-sodium soy sauce
2	cloves garlic, minced
½	teaspoon cornstarch
2	teaspoons canola oil
2	tablespoons finely chopped fresh ginger
12	Bibb or leaf lettuce leaves (about 2 heads)
¼	cup fresh cilantro leaves

1 Trim fat from meat. For easier slicing, if desired, wrap meat in plastic wrap and partially freeze for 30 to 45 minutes or until firm. Thinly slice across the grain into bite-size strips. Place meat in a resealable plastic bag set in a shallow dish. In a second resealable plastic bag combine sweet pepper, zucchini, and red onion.

2 For marinade, in a small bowl combine ginger beer, soy sauce, and garlic. Pour marinade over meat and vegetables, evenly dividing between the two bags. Seal bags; turn each to coat. Marinate in the refrigerator for 4 to 6 hours, turning bags occasionally. Drain both of the marinades into a small bowl. Stir in cornstarch; set aside.

3 Pour oil into a large nonstick wok or extra-large nonstick skillet; heat wok over medium-high heat. Add ginger; cook and stir for 15 seconds. Add marinated vegetables; cook and stir for 3 to 5 minutes or until crisp-tender. Remove from wok. Add half of the meat to wok; cook and stir for 2 to 3 minutes or until meat is slightly pink in center. Remove from wok. Repeat with remaining meat. Return meat to wok. Push from center of wok. Stir marinade mixture; add to center of wok. Cook and stir until thickened and bubbly. Return vegetables to wok; stir all ingredients together to coat with sauce. Cook and stir for 30 seconds.

4 To serve, divide meat mixture among lettuce leaves. Top with cilantro and roll up.

nutrition facts per 3 wraps: 258 cal., 11 g total fat (4 g sat. fat), 46 mg chol., 517 mg sodium, 12 g carb., 2 g dietary fiber, 27 g protein.

Served on hearty bread and dripping with Swiss cheese, this unusual onion burger is sure to hit your taste-bud target with each and every bite. With the addition of kale, the sandwich also hits a nutritional mark with a bit of vitamin K.

bull's-eye onion burgers

prep: 20 minutes   grill: 10 minutes   makes: 4 servings

1	large sweet onion, such as Vidalia or Walla Walla
1	pound lean ground beef
1½	teaspoons garlic powder
¼	teaspoon salt
¼	teaspoon ground black pepper
4	slices reduced-fat Swiss cheese (3 ounces)
8	red and/or green kale leaves, stems removed
2	teaspoons olive oil
4	¾-inch slices crusty country bread or Texas toast, toasted

1 Peel and cut onion into four ¼ inch-thick slices. (Reserve the remaining onion for another use.) Shape ground meat into four ½-inch-thick patties. Sprinkle with garlic powder, salt, and pepper. Press 1 of onion slices into the center of each patty; press edges of meat against onion, keeping top of onion flush with the surface of the meat patty.

2 For a charcoal grill, grill meat patties, onion sides up, on the rack of an uncovered grill directly over medium coals for 10 to 13 minutes or until meat is done (160°F), turning once halfway through grilling. Top meat patty with cheese during the last 1 minute of grilling. (For a gas grill, preheat grill. Reduce heat to medium. Place meat patties on grill rack over heat. Cover and grill as above.) Brush kale leaves lightly with oil; add to grill the last 1 to 1½ minutes of grilling.

3 To serve, place 2 of the kale leaves on each bread slice. Top with a burger, onion side up.

nutrition facts per burger: 321 cal., 10 g total fat (4 g sat. fat), 78 mg chol., 387 mg sodium, 22 g carb., 2 g dietary fiber, 34 g protein.

If you enjoy new flavor combinations, try this zesty burger. It showcases ground venison dressed up with coffee, cocoa powder, chili powder, and whiskey.

spiced whiskey burgers

prep: 15 minutes   grill: 25 minutes for garlic   grill: 10 minutes for burgers
makes: 4 burgers

2   bulbs garlic
2   teaspoons olive oil
1   teaspoon instant coffee crystals
1   teaspoon unsweetened cocoa powder
¾   teaspoon chili powder
¼   teaspoon salt
1   tablespoon whiskey or water
1   pound ground venison or lean ground beef
4   small whole wheat hamburger buns, split and toasted
    Lettuce leaves (optional)
    Thin fresh jalapeño chile peppers slices (optional)
    Tomato slices (optional)
    Thin red onion slices (optional)
    Dill pickle slices (optional)

1   For garlic, cut off the top ¼ to ½ inch of each garlic bulb to expose the cloves. Remove the papery outer skins, leaving the cloves intact. Place each garlic bulb on a 6-inch square of heavy foil; drizzle bulbs with oil. Wrap foil up around bulbs; seal.

2   For a charcoal grill, grill garlic on the rack of an uncovered grill directly over medium coals about 25 minutes or until garlic is soft. (For a gas grill, preheat grill. Reduce heat to medium. Place foil-wrapped garlic bulbs on grill rack over heat. Cover and grill as above.) Remove garlic from grill and cool slightly.

3   For burgers, in a medium bowl combine coffee crystals, cocoa powder, chili powder, and salt. Stir in whiskey. Add venison; mix well. Shape meat mixture into four ½-inch-thick patties.

4   For a charcoal grill, grill patties on the greased rack of an uncovered grill directly over medium coals for 10 to 13 minutes or until meat is done (160°F), turning once halfway through grilling. (For a gas grill, preheat grill. Reduce heat to medium. Place patties on grill rack over heat. Cover and grill as above.)

5   Meanwhile, squeeze garlic cloves from the skins into a small bowl. Mash garlic with a fork. Spread garlic on bun bottoms; add lettuce (if using) and grilled patties. If desired, top with chile peppers, tomato, red onion, and/or pickles. Add bun tops.

nutrition facts per burger: 315 cal., 6 g total fat (1 g sat. fat), 96 mg chol., 422 mg sodium, 30 g carb., 3 g dietary fiber, 32 g protein.

turkey tomatillo
burgers

prep: 20 minutes   grill: 14 minutes   makes: 2 burgers

1   egg white, lightly beaten
2   tablespoons fine dry bread crumbs
1   tablespoon snipped fresh cilantro
1   teaspoon chopped canned chipotle chile pepper in adobo sauce*
1   clove garlic, minced
¼   teaspoon chili powder
⅛   teaspoon freshly ground black pepper
8   ounces uncooked ground turkey breast
4   slices tomatillo and/ or tomato
2   ¾-ounce slices Muenster cheese
2   whole wheat hamburger buns, split and toasted

1 In a medium bowl combine egg white, bread crumbs, cilantro, chipotle pepper in adobo sauce, garlic, chili powder, and black pepper. Add ground turkey; mix well. Shape turkey mixture into two ¾-inch-thick patties. (If mixture is sticky, moisten hands with water.)

2 For a charcoal grill, grill burgers on the lightly greased rack of an uncovered grill directly over medium coals for 14 to 18 minutes or until no longer pink (165°F),** turning once halfway through grilling. Add tomatillo and/or tomato slices to the grill. Top each burger with a slice of cheese for the last 2 minutes of grilling. (For a gas grill, preheat grill. Reduce heat to medium. Place burgers, and later tomatillos and/or tomato slices, on grill rack over heat. Cover and grill as above.)

3 To serve, top bun bottoms with grilled burgers, tomatillo and/or tomato slices in buns, and bun tops.

nutrition facts per burger: 360 cal., 9 g total fat (4 g sat. fat), 91 mg chol., 492 mg sodium, 28 g carb., 3 g dietary fiber, 40 g protein.

*tip: Because chile peppers contain volatile oils that can burn your skin and eyes, avoid direct contact with them as much as possible. When working with chile peppers, wear plastic or rubber gloves. If your bare hands do touch the peppers, wash your hands and nails well with soap and warm water.

**tip: The internal color of a burger is not a reliable doneness indicator. A turkey patty cooked to 165°F is safe, regardless of color. To measure the doneness of a patty, insert an instant-read thermometer through the side of the patty to a depth of 2 to 3 inches.

greek fusion burgers

prep: 25 minutes grill: 10 minutes makes: 4 burgers

1   pound uncooked
    ground turkey
    breast
2   teaspoons finely
    chopped canned
    chipotle chile
    peppers in adobo
    sauce*
1   teaspoon dried
    oregano, crushed
¼   cup light tub-style
    cream cheese,
    softened
¼   cup shredded
    reduced-fat cheddar
    cheese
1   tablespoon finely
    chopped green
    onion
⅛   teaspoon salt
2   large whole wheat
    pita bread rounds,
    halved crosswise
½   of a medium
    cucumber, cut into
    thin bite-size strips
8   small slices tomato

1 In a medium bowl combine ground turkey, 1 teaspoon of the chipotle chile peppers, and the oregano. Shape meat mixture into four ½-inch-thick oval patties.

2 For a charcoal grill, grill patties on the rack of an uncovered grill directly over medium heat for 10 to 13 minutes or until meat is done (165°F), turning once halfway through grilling. (For a gas grill, preheat grill. Reduce heat to medium. Place patties on grill rack over heat. Cover and grill as above.)

3 Meanwhile, in a small bowl combine the remaining 1 teaspoon chipotle chile pepper, the cream cheese, cheddar cheese, green onion, and salt.

4 Open cut sides of halved pita bread rounds to make pockets. Spread cream cheese mixture into pockets. Add cucumber, grilled patties, and tomato slices.

nutrition facts per burger: 272 cal., 6 g total fat (3 g sat. fat), 58 mg chol., 473 mg sodium, 22 g carb., 3 g dietary fiber, 33 g protein.

*tip: Because hot chile peppers contain volatile oils that can burn your skin and eyes, avoid direct contact with chiles as much as possible. When working with chile peppers, wear plastic or rubber gloves. If your bare hands do touch the chile peppers, wash your hands and fingernails well with soap and water when you are done.

cannellini bean burgers

prep: 25 minutes   cook: 10 minutes   makes: 4 servings

1   15- to 16-ounce can
cannellini beans
(white kidney
beans), rinsed and
drained
¾   cup soft whole wheat
bread crumbs
(1 slice)
½   cup chopped onion
(1 medium)
¼   cup broken walnuts,
toasted if desired
2   tablespoons coarsely
snipped fresh basil
or 1 teaspoon dried
basil, crushed
2   cloves garlic,
quartered
1   tablespoon olive oil
4   whole grain
hamburger buns,
split and toasted
2   tablespoons bottled
light ranch salad
dressing
2   cups fresh spinach
leaves
½   of a medium tomato,
sliced

1 In a food processor combine cannellini beans, ¼ cup of the bread crumbs, the onion, walnuts, basil, and garlic. Cover and process until mixture is coarsely chopped and holds together.

2 Shape the bean mixture into four ½-inch-thick patties. Place the remaining ½ cup bread crumbs in a shallow dish. Carefully brush both sides of each patty with oil. Dip patties into bread crumbs, turning to coat.

3 Preheat a grill pan or large skillet over medium heat. Add patties; cook for 10 to 12 minutes or until heated through, turning once halfway through cooking. (Reduce heat to medium low if patties brown too quickly.)

4 Spread cut sides of bun bottoms with ranch salad dressing. Top with patties, spinach, tomato slices, and bun tops.

nutrition facts per burger: 299 cal., 11 g total fat (1 g sat. fat), 2 mg chol., 497 mg sodium, 44 g carb., 9 g dietary fiber, 13 g protein.

The tomato that tops off this satisfying meatless sandwich is a great source of lycopene, a phytonutrient that scientists believe helps combat a number of cancers including colorectal, breast, lung, and prostate cancer.

falafel pitas

prep: 25 minutes   cook: 8 minutes   makes: 4 servings

¼ cup fine dry bread crumbs

1 15-ounce can no-salt-added garbanzo beans, rinsed and drained

½ cup chopped onion

2 cloves garlic, minced

1 teaspoon ground cumin

¼ teaspoon salt

¼ cup snipped fresh Italian (flat-leaf) parsley

2 tablespoons all-purpose flour
   Skim milk

1 tablespoon olive oil

2 large whole wheat pita bread rounds, halved crosswise
   Shredded romaine lettuce leaves

1 small tomato, thinly sliced

½ of a small cucumber, thinly sliced

¼ cup plain fat-free yogurt

2 teaspoons lemon juice

1 teaspoon cracked black pepper

1 clove garlic, minced

1 Place the bread crumbs in a shallow dish; set aside. In a food processor combine garbanzo beans, onion, garlic, cumin, and salt. Cover and process until mixture is coarsely ground. Stir in parsley and flour.

2 Shape the bean mixture into four 3-inch-thick round or oval patties. Carefully brush patties with milk, coat both sides with bread crumbs.

3 In a large nonstick skillet heat oil over medium heat. Add patties; cook for 8 to 10 minutes or until patties are light brown, turning once halfway through cooking. (Add more oil as necessary during cooking.)

4 To serve, fill pita halves with patties, lettuce, tomato slices, and cucumber slices. In a small bowl combine yogurt, lemon juice, pepper, and garlic. Drizzle falafel with yogurt mixture.

nutrition facts per serving: 314 cal., 6 g total fat (1 g sat. fat), 0 mg chol., 454 mg sodium, 53 g carb., 9 g dietary fiber, 13 g protein.

cherry-kissed tacos with feta cheese salsa

start to finish: 25 minutes makes: 12 tacos

1 pound lean ground lamb or pork
1 cup finely chopped onion (1 large)
1 teaspoon curry powder
½ cup mango chutney
½ cup dried tart cherries, snipped
1 tablespoon lemon juice
¼ teaspoon salt
¼ teaspoon ground black pepper
12 taco shells, warmed
1 recipe Feta Cheese Salsa

1 In a large skillet cook ground meat and onion on medium-high heat until meat is brown and onion is tender, using a wooden spoon to break up meat as it cooks. Drain off fat. Add curry powder; cook and stir for 1 minute.

2 Snip any large pieces of chutney. Stir chutney, cherries, lemon juice, salt, and pepper into meat mixture. Bring to boiling; reduce heat. Simmer, covered, for 5 minutes.

3 To serve, spoon meat mixture into taco shells. Using a slotted spoon, top with Feta Cheese Salsa.

nutrition facts per taco: 207 cal., 9 g total fat (3 g sat. fat), 26 mg chol., 274 mg sodium, 21 g carb., 1 g dietary fiber, 8 g protein.

feta cheese salsa: In a medium bowl combine ½ cup seeded and finely chopped tomato (1 medium), ⅓ cup finely chopped cucumber, ¼ cup crumbled reduced-fat feta cheese (1 ounce), ¼ cup finely chopped red onion, ¼ cup finely chopped green sweet pepper, 1 tablespoon olive oil, 1 tablespoon lemon juice, ⅛ teaspoon salt, and ⅛ teaspoon ground black pepper. Makes 2½ cups.

shrimp tacos

prep: 20 minutes   marinate: 30 minutes   broil: 4 minutes   makes: 8 servings

1   pound fresh or frozen medium shrimp in shells
2   tablespoons canola oil
1   teaspoon finely shredded lime peel
2   tablespoons fresh lime juice
¼   teaspoon salt
¼   teaspoon cayenne pepper
¼   teaspoon ground cumin
¼   teaspoon freshly ground black pepper
1   clove garlic, minced
⅓   cup mayonnaise or light salad dressing
⅓   cup light sour cream
2   tablespoons snipped fresh Italian (flat-leaf) parsley
½   of a fresh medium jalapeño chile pepper, seeded and finely chopped*
⅛   teaspoon cayenne pepper
⅛   teaspoon ground cumin
1½   cups shredded cabbage
½   cup chopped tomato (1 medium)
8   white corn taco shells, warmed according to package directions
¼   cup sliced green onions (2)
Fresh lime wedges

1 Thaw shrimp, if frozen. Peel and devein shrimp, removing tails. Rinse shrimp; pat dry with paper towels. Place shrimp in large resealable plastic bag set in a shallow bowl.

2 For marinade, in a small bowl combine oil, lime peel, lime juice, salt, ¼ teaspoon cayenne pepper, ¼ teaspoon cumin, black pepper, and garlic. Pour marinade over shrimp. Seal bag; turn bag to coat shrimp. Marinate in the refrigerator for 30 minutes.

3 Meanwhile, in a small bowl combine mayonnaise, sour cream, parsley, jalapeño chile pepper, ⅛ teaspoon cayenne pepper, and ⅛ teaspoon cumin. Add cabbage and tomato, stirring to coat. Cover; chill until serving.

4 Preheat broiler. Drain shrimp, discard marinade. Arrange shrimp on unheated rack of a broiler pan. Broil 4 to 5 inches from heat for 2 minutes. Turn shrimp over; broil for 2 to 4 minutes more or until shrimp are opaque.

5 To serve, divide cabbage mixture among taco shells; top with shrimp. Sprinkle with green onions. Serve with lime wedges.

nutrition facts per serving: 185 cal., 9 g total fat (2 g sat. fat), 92 mg chol., 244 mg sodium, 13 g carb., 2 g dietary fiber, 13 g protein.

*tip: Because hot chile peppers contain volatile oils that can burn your skin and eyes, avoid direct contact with chiles as much as possible. When working with chile peppers, wear plastic or rubber gloves. If your bare hands do touch the chile peppers, wash your hands and fingernails well with soap and water when you are done.

grilled **beef** and **avocado** pitas

prep: 20 minutes marinate: 24 hours grill: 17 minutes makes: 6 servings

12 ounces beef flank steak
½ cup bottled reduced-calorie clear Italian salad dressing
½ teaspoon finely shredded lime peel
¼ cup lime juice
2 tablespoons snipped fresh cilantro
¼ cup finely chopped onion
¼ teaspoon salt
¼ teaspoon ground black pepper
4 cups mixed spring salad greens
1 cup red sweet pepper cut into thin bite-size strips (1 medium)
1 medium avocado, seeded, peeled, and thinly sliced
3 large whole wheat pita bread rounds, halved crosswise

1 Trim fat from meat. Score both sides of meat in a diamond pattern by making shallow diagonal cuts at 1-inch intervals. Place meat in a resealable plastic bag set in a shallow dish.

2 In a screw-top jar combine Italian dressing, lime peel, lime juice, and cilantro. Cover and shake well. Pour half of the dressing mixture into a small bowl; add onion. Cover; chill until serving. Pour the remaining dressing mixture over meat. Seal bag; turn to coat meat. Marinate in the refrigerator for 24 hours, turning bag occasionally. Drain meat, discarding marinade. Sprinkle meat with salt and black pepper.

3 For a charcoal grill, grill meat on the rack of an uncovered grill directly over medium coals for 17 to 21 minutes for medium doneness (160°F), turning once halfway through grilling. (For a gas grill, preheat grill. Reduce heat to medium. Place steak on grill rack over heat. Cover and grill as above.)

4 To serve, thinly slice meat diagonally across the grain into thin bite-size strips. In a large bowl combine meat, salad greens, sweet pepper, avocado, and the reserved dressing mixture; toss to coat. Fill pita halves with meat mixture.

nutrition facts per serving: 254 cal., 11 g total fat (3 g sat. fat), 23 mg chol., 425 mg sodium, 24 g carb., 5 g dietary fiber, 17 g protein.

broiling directions: Preheat broiler. Place meat on the unheated rack of a broiler pan. Broil 3 to 4 inches from the heat for 17 to 21 minutes for medium doneness (160°F), turning once halfway through broiling.

whole wheat pizza with the works

prep: 20 minutes bake: 20 minutes oven: 425°F makes: 8 servings

Nonstick cooking
　　spray
1　16-ounce loaf frozen
　　whole wheat bread
　　dough, thawed
½　cup reduced-sodium
　　pizza sauce
½　of a 6-ounce package
　　thinly sliced cooked
　　turkey pepperoni
　　or pizza-style
　　Canadian-style
　　bacon
1½　cups thinly sliced
　　fresh mushrooms
½　of a small green
　　sweet pepper,
　　sliced into strips
¼　cup chopped onion
1　cup shredded
　　reduced-fat four-
　　cheese Italian blend
　　cheese or part-skim
　　mozzarella cheese
　　(4 ounces)
2　tablespoons snipped
　　fresh flat-leaf
　　(Italian) parsley

1 Preheat oven to 425°F. Lightly coat a 12- to 14-inch pizza pan with cooking spray. Pat dough evenly into prepared pan, building up edges slightly. (If dough is hard to pat out, allow to rest for 10 minutes.) Prick dough all over with a fork.

2 Bake about 10 minutes or until light brown.

3 Spread pizza sauce onto partially baked crust. Top with pepperoni, mushrooms, sweet pepper strips, and onion. Sprinkle with cheese.

4 Bake for 10 to 15 minutes more or until cheese melts and edge of crust is light brown. Sprinkle with parsley.

nutrition facts per serving: 232 cal., 7 g total fat (2 g sat. fat), 21 mg chol., 660 mg sodium, 31 g carb., 3 g dietary fiber, 15 g protein.

taco pizza

prep: 20 minutes   bake: 19 minutes   oven: 425°F   makes: 8 servings

Nonstick cooking
    spray
1   16-ounce loaf frozen
    whole wheat bread
    dough, thawed
12 ounces lean ground
    beef
½   cup chopped onion
    (1 medium)
½   cup salsa
1½ cups chopped
    tomatoes
    (3 medium)
½   cup shredded
    cheddar cheese
    (2 ounces)
½   to 1 cup shredded
    lettuce and/or fresh
    spinach leaves
1   cup baked tortilla
    chips, coarsely
    crushed

1 Preheat oven to 425°F. Lightly coat a 12- to 13-inch pizza pan with cooking spray. Pat dough evenly into prepared pan, building up edges slightly. (If dough is hard to pat out, allow to rest for 10 minutes.) Prick dough all over with a fork. Bake for 12 minutes.

2 Meanwhile, in a large skillet cook ground beef and onion over medium-high heat until meat is brown and onion is tender, using a wooden spoon to break up meat as it cooks. Drain off fat. Stir in the salsa.

3 Spread meat mixture evenly over hot crust. Bake for 5 minutes. Sprinkle with tomatoes and cheese. Bake for 2 to 3 minutes more or until cheese melts.

4 To serve, top pizza with lettuce. Sprinkle with crushed tortilla chips.

nutrition facts per serving: 279 cal., 9 g total fat (3 g sat. fat), 35 mg chol., 500 mg sodium, 33 g carb., 3 g dietary fiber, 18 g protein.

jambalaya pizza

prep: 30 minutes   bake: 30 minutes   oven: 450°F/425°F   makes: 6 to 8 servings

Nonstick cooking
spray
3   cups cooked long
grain rice, cooled
1   cup finely shredded
Monterey Jack
cheese with
jalapeño peppers
2   eggs, lightly beaten
¼   cup chopped celery
¼   cup chopped onion
¼   cup chopped green
sweet pepper
1   tablespoon butter
⅓   cup thinly sliced
smoked cooked
sausage
⅓   cup diced cooked
ham
⅓   cup coarsely chopped
cooked shrimp
1   clove garlic, minced
1   cup chunky salsa,
drained
¾   cup shredded part-
skim mozzarella
cheese (3 ounces)

1 Preheat oven to 450°F. Lightly coat a
12-inch pizza pan with cooking spray. In
a large bowl combine rice, Monterey Jack
cheese, and eggs. Spread rice mixture evenly
in pan. Bake 20 minutes. Remove from oven;
reduce oven temperature to 425°F.

2 Meanwhile, for topping, in large skillet cook
celery, onion, and sweet pepper in hot
butter over medium heat for 8 to 10 minutes or
until tender, stirring occasionally. Stir in sausage,
ham, shrimp, and garlic; heat through.

3 Spread salsa over rice crust, leaving a ½-inch
border. Spread vegetable-meat mixture over
salsa. Sprinkle with mozzarella cheese.

4 Bake for 10 to 15 minutes or until heated
through and cheese melts. Cut into
wedges to serve.

nutrition facts per serving: 316 cal., 15 g total fat
(8 g sat. fat), 129 mg chol., 707 mg sodium, 26 g carb.,
2 g dietary fiber, 17 g protein.

original pizza margherita

prep: 15 minutes   bake: 15 minutes   oven: 400°F   makes: 6 servings

Nonstick cooking
   spray
1 11-ounce package
   refrigerated thin
   crust pizza dough
1 tablespoon olive oil
2 cups grape tomatoes,
   halved
8 ounces small fresh
   mozzarella cheese
   balls, sliced
2 cloves garlic, minced
½ cup fresh basil leaves
   Coarse ground black
   pepper (optional)

1 Preheat oven to 400°F. Coat a 15×10×1-inch baking pan with cooking spray. Unroll pizza dough into prepared pan. Press dough evenly, building up edges up slightly. Brush with oil. Bake for 7 minutes. Top partially baked crust with tomatoes, cheese, and garlic.

2 Bake for 8 to 10 minutes more or until crust is golden brown. Tear or snip basil. Sprinkle pizza with basil and pepper (if using).

nutrition facts per serving: 291 cal., 15 g total fat (7 g sat. fat), 27 mg chol., 418 mg sodium, 27 g carb., 2 g dietary fiber, 12 g protein.

garden fresh pizza

prep: 30 minutes stand: 12 hours rise: 1 hour bake: 20 minutes
oven: 400°F makes: 6 servings

2 cups all-purpose flour
½ cup white whole wheat flour or whole-wheat flour
½ cup cornmeal
1 teaspoon salt
¼ teaspoon active dry yeast
1¼ cups warm water (120°F to 130°F)
Olive oil
½ cup no-salt-added tomato sauce
½ teaspoon dried Italian seasoning
3 to 4 cups fresh vegetables, such as halved yellow cherry tomatoes, sliced roma tomatoes, red onion slices, and/or broccoli florets
1 cup mushrooms, halved or sliced
2 ounces chorizo sausage or ground beef, cooked and drained
½ cup crumbled feta cheese or 1 cup shredded mozzarella cheese
Shredded radicchio (optional)

1 In a large bowl combine all-purpose flour, whole wheat flour, cornmeal, salt, and yeast; gradually add the warm water, stirring until mixture is moistened (will be a soft, sticky dough). Cover; let stand at room temperature for 12 to 24 hours.

2 Line a 15×10×1-inch baking pan with parchment paper. Brush parchment with oil. Turn dough out onto prepared pan. Using well-oiled hands or a rubber spatula, gently push dough to edges and corners of pan (dough will be sticky), building up edges slightly. Cover; let rise for 1 to 1½ hours or until puffy and dough pulls away slightly from edges of baking pan.

3 Preheat oven to 400°F. Bake crust for 10 minutes. In a small bowl combine tomato sauce and Italian seasoning; spread over hot crust. Top with desired vegetables, mushrooms, chorizo, and cheese.

4 Bake for 10 to 15 minutes more or until bubbly. Remove from oven. If desired, top pizza with radicchio. Serve immediately.

nutrition facts per serving: 336 cal., 8 g total fat (3 g sat. fat), 19 mg chol., 659 mg sodium, 54 g carb., 4 g dietary fiber, 12 g protein.

A container of barbecue sauce with shredded chicken makes a tasty pizza topping. If you like a spicy barbecue, stir in a dash of bottled hot pepper sauce.

barbecued chicken
pizza

prep: 20 minutes   bake: 19 minutes   oven: 425°F   makes: 6 servings

Nonstick cooking
  spray
1 13.8-ounce package
  refrigerated pizza
  dough
1 18-ounce tub
  refrigerated
  barbecue sauce
  with shredded
  chicken
2 cups shredded pizza
  cheese (8 ounces)
¼ cup snipped fresh
  cilantro

1 Preheat oven to 425°F. Coat a 15×10×1-inch baking pan with cooking spray. Unroll pizza dough in the prepared pan. Press dough into a 12×10-inch rectangle, building up edges slightly. Bake for 7 minutes.

2 Spread chicken in sauce evenly over hot crust. Sprinkle with cheese and cilantro. Bake for 12 to 15 minutes more or until light brown.

nutrition facts per serving: 324 cal., 13 g total fat (6 g sat. fat), 39 mg chol., 683 mg sodium, 33 g carb., 1 g dietary fiber, 20 g protein.

thai chicken pizza

prep: 20 minutes   bake: 11 minutes   oven: 475°F   makes: 8 servings

⅓   cup natural creamy
     peanut butter
¼   cup warm water
2   teaspoons sugar
2   teaspoons rice
     vinegar
¼   to ½ teaspoon
     crushed red pepper
12 ounces skinless
     boneless chicken
     breast, cut into
     bite-size pieces
2   teaspoons canola oil
½   cup thinly sliced
     green onions (4)
2   cloves garlic, minced
     Nonstick cooking
     spray
1   16-ounce loaf frozen
     whole wheat bread
     dough, thawed
1   cup thin red sweet
     pepper strips
½   cup shredded part-
     skim mozzarella
     cheese (2 ounces)
½   cup snipped fresh
     cilantro
     Green onion curls
     (optional)

1 Preheat oven to 475°F. In a small bowl combine peanut butter, the warm water, sugar, vinegar, and crushed red pepper; set aside.

2 In a medium skillet cook and stir chicken in hot oil over medium heat until no longer pink. Add green onions and garlic; cook and stir for 1 minute more. Add 2 tablespoons of the peanut butter mixture; cook and stir over low heat until chicken is coated. Remove from heat.

3 Lightly coat a 12- to 14-inch pizza pan, large baking sheet, or pizza screen with cooking spray. Pat dough evenly into prepared pan, building up edges slightly. (If dough is hard to pat out, allow to rest for 10 minutes.)

4 Spread dough with the remaining peanut butter mixture, adding water if needed to make it spreading consistency. Top with chicken mixture, sweet pepper, and cheese.

5 Bake for 11 to 14 minutes or until cheese melts and crust is light brown. Sprinkle with cilantro. If desired, garnish with green onion curls.

nutrition facts per serving: 306 cal., 10 g total fat (2 g sat. fat), 29 mg chol., 430 mg sodium, 32 g carb., 4 g dietary fiber, 21 g protein.

nutrition note
Consider pizza a catchall way to use up leftover veggies you have around, and you'll be doing your budget and your body a favor. That handful of spinach, those bright red sweet peppers, and that half an onion can nutritionally add up in your favor.

main-dish

sal

4

Rabbit food? Think again! When lean proteins mingle with crisp and crunchy vegetables, salads become oh-so-substantial.

salads

This recipe provides nearly 25% of daily iron needs. Vitamin C in the dressing helps your body absorb iron.

pasta salad with
orange dressing

prep: 30 minutes **chill:** 2 to 24 hours **makes:** 4 servings

6	ounces dried multigrain or regular farfalle (bow-tie) or penne pasta
1	15-ounce can black beans, rinsed and drained
1½	cups green sweet pepper cut into thin bite-size strips
1	cup chopped cooked chicken (5 ounces)
½	cup thin red onion wedges (optional)
1	8-ounce carton light sour cream
1½	teaspoons finely shredded orange peel
3	tablespoons orange juice
¼	teaspoon salt
¼	teaspoon ground black pepper
1	to 2 tablespoons milk
1½	cups lightly packed arugula leaves
3	tablespoons snipped fresh cilantro

1 Cook pasta according to package directions; drain. Rinse with cold water; drain again. Transfer to a large bowl. Add beans, sweet pepper, chicken, and red onion (if using); set aside.

2 For dressing, in a small bowl combine sour cream, orange peel, orange juice, salt, and black pepper.

3 Pour dressing over pasta mixture; toss gently to coat. Cover and chill for 2 to 24 hours.

4 Before serving, stir enough of the milk into pasta mixture to reach desired consistency. Stir in arugula and cilantro.

nutrition facts per serving: 390 cal., 10 g total fat (5 g sat. fat), 51 mg chol., 624 mg sodium, 57 g carb., 9 g dietary fiber, 23 g protein.

Toasted walnuts add a rich favor and pleasant crunch to this wilted spinach salad.

warm chicken spinach salad

start to finish: 20 minutes **makes:** 4 servings

4 skinless, boneless
   chicken breast halves
   (about 1¼ pounds total)
¼ teaspoon salt
¼ teaspoon ground
   black pepper
1 tablespoon
   vegetable oil
1½ cups sliced fresh mushrooms
1 10-ounce package fresh
   baby spinach
⅓ cup chopped
   walnuts, toasted
2 tablespoons
   finely shredded
   Parmesan cheese

1 Sprinkle chicken with salt and pepper. In a 12-inch skillet heat oil over medium heat. Add chicken; cook for 8 to 12 minutes or until chicken is no longer pink (170°F), turning once. Remove chicken from skillet; cover and keep warm.

2 Add mushrooms to skillet; cook for 2 minutes, stirring occasionally. Add spinach; cook, covered, for 1 to 2 minutes or just until spinach is wilted, gently stirring once. Stir in walnuts. Season to taste with additional salt and pepper.

3 Transfer spinach mixture to a serving bowl; sprinkle with cheese. Serve chicken with spinach mixture.

nutrition facts per serving: 285 cal., 12 g total fat (2 g sat. fat), 84 mg chol., 336 mg sodium, 5 g carb., 3 g dietary fiber, 38 g protein.

asian chicken salad

start to finish: 20 minutes **makes:** 6 servings

1 16-ounce package
   shredded cabbage with
   carrot (coleslaw mix)
3 cups shredded
   cooked chicken
1 cup fresh snow pea pods,
   trimmed and
   halved crosswise
1 cup red or yellow sweet
   pepper cut into thin strips
   (1 medium)
⅓ cup diagonally sliced
   green onions
⅔ cup bottled reduced-calorie
   Asian salad dressing
½ cup packaged garlic-ginger
   or wasabi ranch crisp
   wonton strips or toasted
   sliced almonds

1 In an extra-large bowl combine coleslaw mix, chicken, pea pods, sweet pepper, and green onions. Pour dressing over chicken mixture; toss gently to coat. Top with wonton strips.

nutrition facts per serving: 170 cal., 4 g total fat (1 g sat. fat), 43 mg chol., 443 mg sodium, 15 g carb., 3 g dietary fiber, 18 g protein.

nutrition note
Cast a keen eye on the nutrition labels of bottled salad dressings. Those low in calories and fat may soar when it comes to sodium or sugar.

healthful caesar salad with grilled portobello mushrooms

prep: 25 minutes grill: 12 minutes oven: 350°F makes: 4 servings

2	fresh portobello mushrooms (about 4 ounces each)
1	pound skinless, boneless chicken breast halves
	Nonstick cooking spray
¼	teaspoon salt
¼	teaspoon ground black pepper
1	tablespoon lemon juice
1	tablespoon red wine vinegar
2	teaspoons Dijon-style mustard
1	teaspoon Worcestershire sauce
1	clove garlic, minced
⅛	teaspoon ground black pepper
½	cup light mayonnaise or salad dressing
8	cups torn romaine lettuce
1	recipe Whole Wheat Croutons or ½ cup packaged whole wheat croutons
2	tablespoons finely shredded Parmesan cheese

1 Remove stems and gills from mushrooms. Lightly coat both sides of mushrooms and chicken with cooking spray. Sprinkle chicken with salt and ¼ teaspoon pepper.

2 For a charcoal grill, grill mushrooms and chicken on the rack of an uncovered grill directly over medium coals until mushrooms are tender and chicken is no longer pink (170°F), turning once halfway through grilling. Allow 10 to 12 minutes for mushrooms and 12 to 15 minutes for chicken. (For a gas grill, preheat grill. Reduce heat to medium. Place mushrooms and chicken on grill rack over heat. Cover and grill as above.)

3 Meanwhile, for dressing, in a small bowl combine lemon juice, vinegar, mustard, Worcestershire sauce, garlic, and ⅛ teaspoon pepper. Whisk in mayonnaise.

4 Divide lettuce among dinner plates. Slice mushrooms and chicken; arrange on top of lettuce. Spoon dressing over salads. Sprinkle with Whole Wheat Croutons and cheese.

nutrition facts per serving: 304 cal, 13 g total fat (3 g sat. fat), 79 mg chol., 612 mg sodium, 16 g carb., 4 g dietary fiber, 32 g protein.

whole wheat croutons: Preheat oven to 350°F. Cut 2 slices whole wheat bread into ½- to 1-inch pieces; place in a shallow baking pan. Lightly coat bread pieces with nonstick cooking spray; turn pieces over. Lightly coat again with nonstick cooking spray. Bake about 10 minutes or until bread is light brown and crisp. Cool completely.

The deep color of their outer layer is what sets black beans apart from other beans. It contains at least eight different flaveonoids, making these beans extra rich in antioxidants.

citrus chicken and black bean salad

start to finish: 25 minutes **makes:** 4 servings

¼ cup snipped
   fresh cilantro
2 tablespoons
   lime juice
2 tablespoons
   orange juice
2 tablespoons olive oil
1 clove garlic, minced
⅛ teaspoon salt
1 tablespoon olive oil
½ teaspoon chili
   powder
½ teaspoon ground
   cumin
¼ teaspoon salt
⅛ teaspoon cayenne
   pepper
12 ounces skinless,
   boneless chicken
   thighs or breast
   halves, cut into thin
   bite-size strips
1 15-ounce can no-salt-
   added black beans
   or pinto beans,
   rinsed and drained
2 large oranges, peeled
   and sectioned
2 slices red onion,
   halved and
   separated into rings
4 cups torn romaine
   lettuce or mixed
   salad greens
   Avocado slices
   (optional)

1 For dressing, in a screw-top jar combine cilantro, lime juice, orange juice, 2 tablespoons oil, garlic, and ⅛ teaspoon salt. Cover and shake well. Chill until ready to serve.

2 In a large skillet heat 1 tablespoon oil over medium-high heat. Add chili powder, cumin, ¼ teaspoon salt, and cayenne pepper; cook and stir for 30 seconds. Add chicken; cook and stir for 2 to 3 minutes or until chicken is no longer pink.

3 In a medium bowl combine chicken, beans, oranges, and red onion. Shake dressing. Pour dressing over chicken mixture; toss gently to coat. If desired, cover and chill for up to 2 hours.

4 Divide lettuce among dinner plates; top with chicken mixture. If desired, garnish with avocado.

nutrition facts per serving: 335 cal., 14 g total fat (2 g sat. fat), 71 mg chol., 314 mg sodium, 29 g carb., 9 g dietary fiber, 24 g protein.

almond chicken salad

start to finish: 15 minutes **makes:** 4 servings

- 2 6-ounce packages refrigerated grilled chicken breast strips, cut up
- 1 6-ounce package fresh baby spinach
- 1 cup seedless red grapes, halved
- 1 11-ounce can mandarin orange sections, drained
- ¼ cup sliced almonds
- ½ cup orange juice
- 2 tablespoons balsamic vinegar
- 1 tablespoon toasted sesame oil
- ¼ teaspoon ground black pepper

1 In an extra-large bowl combine chicken, spinach, grapes, orange sections, and almonds.

2 For dressing, in a screw-top jar combine orange juice, vinegar, oil, and pepper. Cover and shake well. Pour dressing over spinach mixture, toss gently to coat.

nutrition facts per serving: 249 cal., 8 g total fat (1 g sat. fat), 55 mg chol., 431 mg sodium, 25 g carb., 3 g dietary fiber, 22 g protein.

grilled chicken
wilted salad

start to finish: 30 minutes **makes:** 6 servings

1 pound chicken breast
tenderloins
1 medium onion, cut
into thin wedges
3 tablespoons olive oil
1 tablespoon snipped
fresh rosemary or
½ teaspoon dried
rosemary, crushed
¾ teaspoon coarse
ground black
pepper
½ teaspoon salt
¼ cup cranberry juice or
pomegranate juice
2 tablespoons red
wine vinegar
2 6-ounce packages
fresh baby spinach
¼ cup sliced pitted
kalamata olives*
¼ cup pine nuts or
slivered almonds,
toasted**

1 In a medium bowl combine chicken and
onion. Add 2 tablespoons of the oil, the
rosemary, ¼ teaspoon of the pepper, and
¼ teaspoon of the salt; toss gently to coat.

2 Preheat an indoor electric grill according
to the manufacturer's directions, or a grill
pan over medium heat. Place chicken and onion
on grill rack or in grill pan. If using a covered
indoor grill, close lid. Grill until chicken is no
longer pink (170°F) and onion is tender. (For a
covered grill, allow 4 to 5 minutes. For an uncovered
grill or grill pan, allow about 10 minutes,
turning once halfway through grilling.)

3 Meanwhile, for dressing, in a small saucepan
combine cranberry juice, vinegar, the
remaining 1 tablespoon oil, the remaining
½ teaspoon pepper, and the remaining
¼ teaspoon salt. Bring just to boiling; remove
from heat.

4 In an extra-large bowl combine chicken,
onion, spinach, olives, and pine nuts.
Pour warm dressing over spinach mixture;
toss gently to coat. Cover bowl with a large
plate for 1 to 2 minutes or just until spinach is
wilted; remove plate. Serve immediately.

nutrition facts per serving: 211 cal., 12 g total fat
(2 g sat. fat), 44 mg chol., 342 mg sodium, 7 g carb.,
2 g dietary fiber, 21 g protein.

*tip: kalamata olives are a variety of Greek olives
with a rich fruity flavor. They are a dark purple
color, almond shaped, and about ¹/₂- to 1-inch
long. They are available in the grocery store
packed in jars of oil or brine, or sometimes can be
found at the deli counter.

**tip: To toast pine nuts or almonds, preheat oven
to 350°F. Spread the nuts in a single layer in a shallow
baking pan. Bake for 5 to 10 minutes or until light
golden brown, watching carefully and stirring
once or twice so the nuts don't burn. If you like,
you can toast the nuts up to one day ahead.

turkey salad
with oranges
start to finish: 30 minutes **makes:** 4 servings

1   5-ounce package
    arugula or fresh
    baby spinach
2½ cups chopped roasted
    turkey (about
    12 ounces)
1   cup red sweet pepper
    strips (1 medium)
¼   cup snipped fresh
    cilantro
2   tablespoons peanut
    oil or canola oil
¼   cup orange juice
¼   cup honey
3   tablespoons
    lemon juice
1   tablespoon Dijon-
    style mustard
1   teaspoon ground
    cumin
¼   teaspoon ground
    black pepper
4   oranges, peeled and
    sectioned

1 In a large bowl combine arugula, turkey, sweet pepper, and cilantro.

2 For vinaigrette, in a screw-top jar combine oil, orange juice, honey, lemon juice, mustard, cumin, and black pepper. Cover and shake well.

3 Before serving, add orange sections to arugula mixture. Shake vinaigrette. Drizzle desired amount of vinaigrette over arugula mixture; toss gently to coat. Cover and chill any remaining vinaigrette for another use.

nutrition facts per serving: 338 cal., 8 g total fat (1 g sat. fat), 71 mg chol., 150 mg sodium, 39 g carb., 5 g dietary fiber, 29 g protein

nutrition note
Our bodies can't make vitamin C on their own. Fortunately, citrus fruits make it easy (and enjoyable) to get the recommended daily amounts of this powerful antioxidant. Men should aim for 90 mg per day, while women need 75 mg.

In addition to the pomegranate juice, this dish has two other good sources of antioxidants: spinach and almonds.

wilted chicken salad with
pomegranate dressing

start to finish: 30 minutes **makes:** 4 servings

¾	cup pomegranate juice
2	tablespoons olive oil
1	14- to 16-ounce package chicken breast tenderloins
½	of a medium red onion, cut into thin wedges
1	tablespoon snipped fresh oregano or ½ teaspoon dried oregano, crushed
¾	teaspoon coarse ground black pepper
½	teaspoon salt
2	tablespoons red wine vinegar
2	6-ounce packages fresh spinach leaves
½	cup pomegranate seeds
¼	cup slivered almonds, toasted*

1 In a small saucepan bring pomegranate juice to boiling; reduce heat. Boil gently, uncovered, for 5 to 8 minutes or until reduced to ¼ cup. Remove from heat; set aside.

2 Meanwhile, in a 12-inch skillet heat 1 tablespoon of the oil over medium-high heat. Add chicken; cook for 6 to 8 minutes or until chicken is no longer pink (170°F), turning occasionally. Remove chicken from skillet; cover and keep warm.

3 In same skillet combine the remaining 1 tablespoon oil, red onion, dried oregano (if using), pepper, and salt. Cook over medium heat for 3 to 5 minutes or just until onion is tender, stirring occasionally. Stir in reduced pomegranate juice and vinegar; bring to boiling. Boil, uncovered, for 1 minute. Remove from heat; stir in fresh oregano (if using). Gradually add spinach, tossing just until spinach is wilted.

4 Transfer spinach mixture to a large serving bowl. Top with chicken, pomegranate seeds, and almonds. Serve immediately.

nutrition facts per serving: 292 cal., 11 g total fat (2 g sat. fat), 58 mg chol., 425 mg sodium, 21 g carb., 4 g dietary fiber, 27 g protein.

*tip: To toast almonds, preheat oven to 350°F. Spread the nuts in a single layer in a shallow baking pan. Bake for 5 to 10 minutes or until light brown, watching carefully and stirring once or twice so the nuts don't burn. If you like, you can toast the nuts up to one day ahead.

Spreadable fruit helps keep the dressing for this chicken-studded coleslaw low in calories.

sweet-and-sour
chicken bowl

start to finish: 20 minutes **makes:** 4 servings

1 In a large bowl combine chicken, coleslaw mix, and pea pods; set aside.

2 For dressing, in a small bowl stir together spreadable fruit, oil, and vinegar. Stir in apple. Pour dressing over cabbage mixture; toss gently to coat. If desired, cover and chill for up to 1 hour before serving.

nutrition facts per serving: 285 cal., 10 g total fat (1 g sat. fat), 72 mg chol., 81 mg sodium, 21 g carb., 3 g dietary fiber, 28 g protein.

- 12 ounces shredded or chopped cooked chicken breast
- 4 cups packaged shredded cabbage with carrot (coleslaw mix)
- 1 cup fresh snow pea pods, trimmed and halved crosswise
- ¼ cup raspberry or strawberry spreadable fruit
- 2 tablespoons canola oil
- 4 teaspoons cider vinegar
- ⅔ cup chopped red apple (1 medium)

thai chicken and peach salad

start to finish: 35 minutes **makes:** 4 servings

4 ounces dried angel hair pasta

¼ cup reduced-sodium chicken broth

3 tablespoons reduced-sodium soy sauce

2 tablespoons hoisin sauce

1 tablespoon sugar

1 tablespoon vegetable oil or olive oil

2 teaspoons toasted sesame oil

3 cloves garlic, minced

1½ teaspoons grated fresh ginger

1 teaspoon crushed red pepper

3 cups sliced peeled peaches or unpeeled nectarines (3 medium)

2 cups cooked chicken cut into bite-size strips

2 cups torn mixed salad greens

¼ cup thinly sliced green onions (2)

1 Cook pasta according to package directions; drain. Return pasta to hot pan.

2 Meanwhile, for dressing, in a screw-top-jar combine broth, soy sauce, hoisin sauce, sugar, vegetable oil, sesame oil, garlic, ginger, and crushed red pepper. Cover and shake well.

3 Add 3 tablespoons of the dressing to cooked pasta; toss gently to coat. Divide pasta among shallow bowls or dinner plates. Top with peaches, chicken, salad greens, and green onions. Shake the remaining dressing; drizzle over salads.

nutrition facts per serving: 382 cal., 12 g total fat (2 g sat. fat), 63 mg chol., 662 mg sodium, 42 g carb., 4 g dietary fiber, 27 g protein.

strawberry-spinach salad with citrus dressing

start to finish: 30 minutes **makes:** 4 servings

4 skinless, boneless chicken breast halves (about 1¼ pounds total)

¼ teaspoon ground black pepper

⅛ teaspoon salt

1 cup reduced-sodium chicken broth

1 recipe Warm Citrus Dressing

6 cups fresh baby spinach and/ or watercress

2 cups halved fresh strawberries

¼ cup chopped pecans, toasted

1 Sprinkle chicken with pepper and salt. Pour broth into a large skillet. Bring to boiling. Add chicken; reduce heat. Simmer, covered, for 12 to 14 minutes or until chicken is no longer pink (170°F), turning once. Using a slotted spoon, remove chicken from broth; discard broth. Meanwhile, prepare the Warm Citrus Dressing

2 Thinly slice chicken. In a large salad bowl combine chicken, spinach and/or watercress, and strawberries.

3 Drizzle warm dressing over spinach mixture; sprinkle with nuts. Serve immediately.

nutrition facts per serving. 301 cal., 12 g total fat (1 g sat. fat), 82 mg chol., 417 mg sodium, 14 g carb., 4 g dietary fiber, 36 g protein.

warm citrus dressing: In a blender or food processor combine ½ cup cut-up fresh strawberries, ⅓ cup orange juice, 4 teaspoons canola oil, 2 teaspoons finely shredded lemon peel, 1 tablespoon lemon juice, 1 teaspoon sugar, ½ teaspoon chili powder (optional), ¼ teaspoon freshly ground black pepper, and ⅛ teaspoon salt. Cover and blend or process until smooth. Transfer to a small saucepan. Bring just to boiling; reduce heat. Simmer, uncovered, for 5 minutes, stirring occasionally. Keep warm over very low heat. Makes ¾ cup.

flank steak
vinaigrette salad

prep: 20 minutes grill: 15 minutes makes: 4 servings

1 recipe Cilantro-Pepper
Vinaigrette
8 ounces beef
flank steak
12 ounces tiny new
potatoes, quartered
8 ounces fresh sugar
snap pea pods,
trimmed (if desired)
6 cups mixed
salad greens

1 Prepare Cilantro-Pepper Vinaigrette. Cover and chill until needed.

2 Trim fat from meat. For a charcoal grill, grill meat on the rack of an uncovered grill directly over medium coals for 15 to 17 minutes for medium (160°F), turning once halfway through grilling. (For a gas grill, preheat grill. Reduce heat to medium. Place meat on grill rack over heat. Cover and grill as above.) Thinly slice meat. Transfer meat to a medium bowl; cover and chill until needed.

3 Meanwhile, in a covered large saucepan cook potatoes in enough boiling, lightly salted water to cover for 10 minutes. Add pea pods. Cook for 1 minute more; drain. Rinse with cold water; drain again.

4 In an extra-large bowl combine salad greens and potato mixture. Pour ½ cup of the vinaigrette over meat; toss gently to coat. Pour the remaining vinaigrette over greens mixture; toss gently to coat.

cilantro-pepper vinaigrette: In a medium bowl whisk together ⅓ cup cider vinegar, 3 tablespoons olive oil, 2 tablespoons snipped fresh cilantro, 1 to 2 teaspoons sugar, 1½ teaspoons red wine vinegar, 1 teaspoon coarse ground mustard, ¼ teaspoon salt, and ⅛ teaspoon ground black pepper. Stir in ¾ cup finely chopped green sweet pepper (1 medium), ¼ cup peeled and finely chopped jicama, 2 tablespoons finely chopped red onion, and half of a fresh serrano chile pepper, seeded and chopped.*

5 To serve, transfer greens mixture to a serving platter; top with meat.

nutrition facts per serving: 210 cal., 15 g total fat (3 g sat. fat), 26 mg chol., 225 mg sodium, 27 g carb., 5 g dietary fiber, 17 g protein.

*tip: Because chile peppers contain volatile oils that can burn your skin and eyes, avoid direct contact with them as much as possible. When working with chile peppers, wear plastic or rubber gloves. If your bare hands do touch the peppers, wash your hands and nails well with soap and warm water.

grilled steak, cucumber, and radish salad

prep: 20 minutes chill: 30 minutes grill: 10 minutes makes: 4 servings

1 pound boneless beef sirloin steak, cut 1 inch thick
1 tablespoon packed brown sugar
1 teaspoon five-spice powder
½ teaspoon salt
½ teaspoon ground black pepper
2 tablespoons seasoned rice vinegar
2 tablespoons orange juice
1 tablespoon toasted sesame oil
1 tablespoon honey
Dash salt
Dash ground black pepper
3 cups thinly sliced cucumbers
½ of a small sweet onion, halved and thinly sliced
¼ cup snipped fresh cilantro
2 large radishes, sliced
1 tablespoon black sesame seeds or toasted sesame seeds

1 Trim fat from meat. In a small bowl combine brown sugar, five-spice powder, ½ teaspoon salt, and ½ teaspoon pepper. Sprinkle mixture evenly over both sides of meat; rub in with your fingers. Cover and chill for 30 minutes.

2 For a charcoal grill, grill meat on the rack of an uncovered grill directly over medium coals for 10 to 12 minutes for medium-rare (145°F) or 12 to 15 minutes for medium (160°F), turning once halfway through grilling. (For a gas grill, preheat grill. Reduce heat to medium. Place meat on grill rack over heat. Cover and grill as above.) Remove meat from grill; cool slightly.

3 Meanwhile, for vinaigrette, in a large bowl whisk together vinegar, orange juice, oil, honey, dash salt, and dash pepper. Reserve about half of the vinaigrette. Add cucumbers, onion, cilantro, and radishes to the remaining vinaigrette; toss gently to coat.

4 Arrange cucumber mixture on a serving platter. Thinly slice meat across the grain; arrange on top of cucumber mixture. Drizzle with the reserved vinaigrette and sprinkle with sesame seeds.

nutrition facts per serving: 294 cal., 14 g total fat (5 g sat. fat), 63 mg chol., 476 mg sodium, 15 g carb., 1 g dietary fiber, 26 g protein.

Meal appeal comes from taste, aroma, presentation, and texture, an under-appreciated element that adds snap to a dish. This crunchy example includes crisp raw apples, jicama, and carrots, along with slices of beef.

beef and apple salad

start to finish: 30 minutes **makes:** 4 servings

1 For dressing, in a screw-top jar combine apple juice, oil, vinegar, and salt. Cover and shake well.

⅓ cup apple juice
2 tablespoons vegetable oil
2 tablespoons white wine vinegar
⅛ teaspoon salt
6 cups lettuce leaves or mixed baby salad greens
2 cups thinly sliced apples (2 medium)
8 ounces lean cooked beef, cut into thin bite-size strips (1½ cups)
1 cup peeled jicama cut into thin bite-size strips
1 cup carrots cut into thin bite-size strips (2 medium)
1 cup fresh pitted sweet cherries, halved
Coarse ground black pepper (optional)

2 Line dinner plates with lettuce. Arrange apples, meat, jicama, carrots, and cherries on top of lettuce. Shake dressing. Drizzle dressing over salads. If desired, sprinkle each serving with pepper.

nutrition facts per serving: 271 cal., 10 g total fat (2 g sat. fat), 39 mg chol., 147 mg sodium, 28 g carb., 6 g dietary fiber, 18 g protein.

nutrition note

Keep afternoon snacks from calling your name! Enjoy apples at lunch— they contain pectin, a soluble fiber that slows the digestion of food and helps you feel full longer.

roasted pork with
crunchy mango salad

prep: 25 minutes   roast: 25 minutes   stand: 10 minutes   oven: 425°F
makes: 4 servings

1	1-pound pork tenderloin
2	cloves garlic, minced
¼	teaspoon salt
¼	teaspoon ground black pepper
1	medium mango, seeded, peeled, and chopped
½	of a medium avocado, seeded, peeled, and chopped
½	cup red sweet pepper cut into thin bite-size strips
½	cup peeled and chopped jicama
¼	cup snipped fresh cilantro
1½	teaspoons finely shredded lime peel
⅛	teaspoon salt. Lime wedges (optional)

1 Preheat oven to 425°F. Trim fat from meat. Rub garlic over meat; sprinkle with ¼ teaspoon salt and black pepper. Place meat on a rack in a shallow roasting pan. Roast for 25 to 35 minutes or until done (155°F).

2 Remove meat from oven. Cover with foil; let stand for 10 minutes before slicing. (Temperature of the meat after standing should be 160°F.)

3 Meanwhile, in a medium bowl gently stir together mango, avocado, sweet pepper, jicama, cilantro, lime peel, and ⅛ teaspoon salt. Slice meat; serve meat with mango mixture and, if desired, lime wedges.

nutrition facts per serving: 211 cal., 7 g total fat (2 g sat. fat), 74 mg chol., 281 mg sodium, 13 g carb., 3 g dietary fiber, 25 g protein.

nutrition note
Don't pass the salt shaker—pass it up instead! Squeeze a fresh lemon or lime wedge over your dish for that extra punch of flavor you crave.

lemon-sage pork
taco salad

start to finish: 40 minutes **oven:** 425°F **makes:** 6 servings

1 Trim fat from meat. Cut meat into ¼-inch slices. Place meat in a large bowl. Add lemon peel, sage, cumin, pepper, and salt; toss gently to coat. Let stand at room temperature for 10 minutes.

1	pound pork tenderloin
1	tablespoon finely shredded lemon peel
6	fresh sage leaves, finely shredded
½	teaspoon ground cumin
¼	teaspoon ground black pepper
⅛	teaspoon salt
1	tablespoon olive oil
1	head leaf lettuce, torn
1½	cups chopped tomatoes (3 medium)
1	avocado, seeded, peeled, and chopped
1	cup canned black beans, rinsed and drained
½	cup sliced green onions (4)
1	recipe Hot Red Pepper Vinaigrette

2 In an extra-large skillet cook meat, half at a time, in hot oil over medium-high heat for 2 to 3 minutes or until meat is slightly pink in center, turning once. Remove from skillet.

3 Place lettuce on a serving platter. Top with tomatoes, avocado, beans, and green onions. Arrange meat slices on top of lettuce mixture. Drizzle with some of the Hot Red Pepper Vinaigrette; pass the remaining vinaigrette.

nutrition facts per serving: 266 cal., 14 g total fat (2 g sat. fat), 49 mg chol., 269 mg sodium, 17 g carb., 7 g dietary fiber, 21 g protein.

*tip: Because chiles contain volatile oils that can burn your skin and eyes, avoid direct contact with them as much as possible. When working with chiles, wear plastic or rubber gloves. If your bare hands do touch the peppers, wash your hands and nails well with soap and warm water.

hot red pepper vinaigrette: Preheat oven to 425°F. Cut 1 red sweet pepper and 1 fresh jalapeño chile pepper* in half lengthwise; remove stems, seeds, and membranes. Place pepper halves, cut sides down, on a baking sheet lined with foil. Roast for 20 to 25 minutes or until peppers are charred and very tender. Bring foil up around peppers and fold edges together to enclose. Let stand about 15 minutes or until cool enough to handle. Using a sharp knife, loosen edges of skins; gently pull off skins in strips and discard. Place peppers in a blender or food processor. Add 2 tablespoons lime juice, 2 tablespoons balsamic vinegar, 2 tablespoons olive oil, and ⅛ teaspoon salt. Cover and blend or process until smooth.

pasta primavera salad

start to finish: 30 minutes **makes:** 4 servings

1 tablespoon olive oil
1 tablespoon balsamic
   vinegar
1 teaspoon Dijon-style
   mustard
¼ teaspoon salt
¼ teaspoon ground
   black pepper
6 ounces dried
   vermicelli pasta
4 cups arugula leaves
1 cup yellow or orange
   sweet pepper cut
   into thin strips
   (1 medium)
½ cup carrot cut into
   thin strips
   (1 medium)
½ cup fresh sugar snap
   pea pods
4 red boiling onions,
   cut into thin
   wedges
4 ounces thinly sliced
   cooked ham or
   prosciutto, cut into
   1-inch strips
2 tablespoons finely
   shredded Parmesan
   cheese (optional)

1 For dressing, in a screw-top jar combine oil, vinegar, mustard, salt, and black pepper. Cover and shake well; set aside.

2 Cook pasta according to package directions; drain. Rinse with cold water; drain again. Divide cooked pasta among dinner plates; form each portion into a nest.

3 In a large bowl combine arugula, sweet pepper, carrot, pea pods, and onions. Mound arugula mixture in centers of pasta nests; top with ham. Shake dressing. Drizzle over salads. If desired, sprinkle with cheese.

nutrition facts per serving: 347 cal., 11 g total fat (3 g sat. fat), 22 mg chol., 579 mg sodium, 49 g carb., 4 g dietary fiber, 13 g protein.

nutrition note
To cook with cheese without piling on the fat, reach for reduced-fat products. Or, choose hard, boldly flavored cheeses, such as Parmesan and Asiago. A little of these goes a long way to add loads of flavor.

grilled tuna and cannellini bean salad

prep: 25 minutes grill: 8 minutes makes: 4 servings

2 5- to 6-ounce fresh or frozen tuna steaks, cut 1 inch thick

2 tablespoons lemon juice

2 tablespoons olive oil

1 tablespoon balsamic vinegar

1 tablespoon Dijon-style mustard

4 cups fresh baby spinach

2 15-ounce cans cannellini beans (white kidney beans), rinsed and drained

1 cup thinly sliced red onion

1 cup sliced celery (2 stalks)

¼ cup oil-packed dried tomatoes, drained and chopped

2 tablespoons snipped fresh Italian (flat-leaf) parsley

1 Thaw fish, if frozen. Rinse fish; pat dry with paper towels.

2 For a charcoal grill, grill fish on the greased rack of an uncovered grill directly over medium coals for 8 to 12 minutes or until fish flakes easily when tested with a fork, carefully turning once halfway through grilling. (For a gas grill, preheat grill. Reduce heat to medium. Place fish on greased grill rack over heat. Cover and grill as above.)

3 Meanwhile, for dressing, in a screw-top jar combine lemon juice, oil, vinegar, and mustard. Cover and shake well. Reserve 1 tablespoon of the dressing.

4 In a large bowl combine spinach, beans, red onion, celery, dried tomatoes, and parsley. Drizzle with the remaining dressing; toss gently to coat.

5 Arrange spinach mixture on a serving platter. Slice fish; place on top of spinach mixture. Drizzle fish with the reserved 1 tablespoon dressing.

nutrition facts per serving: 306 cal., 9 g total fat (1 g sat. fat), 32 mg chol., 515 mg sodium, 38 g carb., 12 g dietary fiber, 31 g protein.

grilled tuna salad niçoise

prep: 30 minutes **grill:** 8 minutes **makes:** 4 servings

1 pound fresh or frozen
   tuna steaks, cut
   1 inch thick
1 recipe Dijon Sherry
   Vinaigrette
8 ounces tiny new
   potatoes, quartered
6 ounces fresh
   green beans
6 cups butterhead
   (Boston or Bibb)
   lettuce leaves
¾ cup thinly sliced
   radishes
½ cup niçoise olives or
   ripe olives, pitted
   Finely chopped red
   onion (optional)
   Cracked black
   pepper (optional)

1 Thaw fish, if frozen. Rinse fish; pat dry with paper towels. Brush fish with 1 tablespoon of the Dijon Sherry Vinaigrette. Cover and chill the remaining vinaigrette until ready to serve.

2 For a charcoal grill, grill fish on the greased rack of an uncovered grill directly over medium coals for 8 to 12 minutes or until fish flakes easily when tested with a fork, carefully turning once halfway through grilling. (For a gas grill, preheat grill. Reduce heat to medium. Place fish on greased grill rack over heat. Cover and grill as above.)

3 Meanwhile, in a covered medium saucepan cook potatoes in a large amount of boiling water about 9 minutes or until potatoes are tender, adding green beans for the last 2 minutes of cooking; drain. Cool slightly.

4 Slice fish. On a serving platter arrange fish, potatoes, beans, lettuce, radishes, and olives. If desired, top with red onion and pepper. Stir the remaining vinaigrette. Pass with salad.

nutrition facts per serving: 282 cal., 10 g total fat (1 g sat. fat), 51 mg chol., 408 mg sodium, 17 g carb., 4 g dietary fiber, 31 g protein.

broiling directions: Thaw fish, if frozen. Preheat broiler. Prepare fish as directed in Step 1. Place on the greased unheated rack of a broiler pan. Broil about 4 inches from the heat for 8 to 12 minutes or until fish flakes easily when tested with a fork, carefully turning once halfway through broiling. Continue as directed.

dijon sherry vinaigrette: In a small bowl combine 3 tablespoons sherry vinegar and 2 tablespoons finely chopped shallot (1 medium). Whisk in 1 tablespoon Dijon-style mustard. Whisking constantly, drizzle in 2 tablespoons olive oil in a thin, steady stream. Stir in 1 anchovy fillet, rinsed and mashed; ⅛ teaspoon salt; and ⅛ teaspoon ground white pepper. Makes about ½ cup.

This quick from-the-pantry salad has a good supply of protein, fiber, and vitamin C, and requires no cooking.

creamy lemon-dill tuna salad

start to finish: 20 minutes **makes:** 6 servings

1   15- to 19-ounce can no-salt-added cannellini beans (white kidney beans), rinsed and drained

1   12-ounce can solid white tuna (water pack), drained and broken into chunks

½   cup halved red onion slices

½   cup roasted yellow or red sweet pepper, drained and chopped

½   cup sliced celery (1 stalk)

2   to 3 tablespoons drained capers or ½ cup stuffed green olives,* sliced (optional)

1   recipe Creamy Lemon-Dill Dressing

3   cups arugula or fresh baby spinach

2   large tomatoes, sliced

1 In a medium bowl combine beans, tuna, red onion, roasted sweet pepper, celery, and capers (if using). Gently stir in half of the Creamy Lemon-Dill Dressing.

2 Divide arugula and tomatoes among dinner plates; top with tuna mixture. Serve with the remaining dressing.

nutrition facts per serving: 260 cal., 12 g total fat (2 g sat. fat), 36 mg chol., 681 mg sodium, 20 g carb., 4 g dietary fiber, 19 g protein.

*tip: Look beyond pimiento-stuffed olives for olives stuffed with almonds, jalapeño pepper, onions, garlic, or other fun treats!

creamy lemon-dill dressing: In a small bowl combine ¾ cup light mayonnaise or salad dressing, 1 tablespoon snipped fresh dill, 1 tablespoon Dijon-style mustard, 1 tablespoon lemon juice, 1 tablespoon honey, ¼ teaspoon salt, and ⅛ teaspoon ground black pepper. Makes about 1 cup.

This tossed salad owes its Louisiana-style flavor to Cajun seasoning and shrimp.

lemon shrimp salad

start to finish: 20 minutes **makes:** 4 servings

12 ounces fresh or frozen peeled, cooked shrimp with tails

1 5-ounce package mixed baby salad greens

½ of a small red onion, thinly sliced

¼ cup light mayonnaise or salad dressing

2 tablespoons lemon juice

1 tablespoon water

¼ to ½ teaspoon Cajun seasoning
  Lemon slices (optional)

1 Thaw shrimp, if frozen. Rinse shrimp; pat dry with paper towels. In a large bowl combine shrimp, salad greens, and red onion.

2 For dressing, in a small bowl stir together mayonnaise, lemon juice, the water, and Cajun seasoning. Pour dressing over shrimp mixture; toss gently to coat. If desired, garnish with lemon slices.

nutrition facts per serving: 148 cal., 6 g total fat (1 g sat. fat), 171 mg chol., 310 mg sodium, 5 g carb., 0 g dietary fiber, 19 g protein.

Chicory, a curly salad green, is high in lutein and zeaxanthin-which keep eyes healthy.

shrimp on greens with garlic vinaigrette

start to finish: 35 minutes makes: 4 servings

1½ pounds fresh or
       frozen large shrimp
       in shells
       Sea salt
       Freshly ground
       black pepper
  2 tablespoons olive oil
  2 cloves garlic, minced
  2 tablespoons dry
       white wine or
       reduced-sodium
       chicken broth
  2 tablespoons white
       wine vinegar
  2 teaspoons snipped
       fresh thyme or
       ½ teaspoon dried
       thyme, crushed
1½ cups fresh chicory
       leaves, trimmed and
       coarsely torn
1½ cups packed fresh
       baby spinach
  1 head Belgian endive,
       trimmed and thinly
       sliced crosswise
  ¼ cup shaved Parmesan
       cheese (1 ounce)

1 Thaw shrimp, if frozen. Peel and devein shrimp, leaving tails intact, if desired. Rinse shrimp; pat dry with paper towels. Sprinkle lightly with salt and pepper.

2 For vinaigrette, in a small saucepan combine oil and garlic. Heat over low heat for 5 minutes to infuse the oil with garlic flavor. Whisk in wine, vinegar, and thyme. Keep warm over very low heat.

3 Meanwhile, heat a grill pan over medium-high heat. Add shrimp; cook for 3 to 5 minutes or until shrimp are opaque, turning once.

4 In a large bowl combine chicory, spinach, and endive. Pour warm vinaigrette over greens mixture; toss gently to coat. Divide greens mixture among dinner plates; top with shrimp and cheese.

nutrition facts per serving: 288 cal., 12 g total fat (3 g sat. fat), 264 mg chol., 588 mg sodium, 4 g carb., 1 g dietary fiber, 38 g protein.

spice-rubbed grouper with berry salad

start to finish: 30 minutes **makes:** 4 servings

1¼ pounds fresh or
     frozen skinless
     grouper or halibut
     fillets, ¾ to
     1 inch thick
2   cups water
½   cup bulgur
¼   teaspoon salt
1   tablespoon snipped
     fresh thyme or
     1 teaspoon dried
     thyme, crushed
2   teaspoons finely
     shredded
     orange peel
1   teaspoon ground
     coriander
¼   teaspoon salt
2   tablespoons olive oil
1   cup yellow and/or red
     sweet pepper cut
     into thin bite-size
     strips (1 medium)
1   cup fresh blueberries

1 Thaw fish, if frozen. Rinse fish; pat dry with paper towels. If necessary, cut fish into four serving-size portions; set aside. In a medium saucepan combine the water, bulgur, and ¼ teaspoon salt. Bring to boiling; reduce heat. Simmer, covered, about 15 minutes or until bulgur is tender; drain.

2 Meanwhile, in a small bowl combine thyme, orange peel, coriander, and ¼ teaspoon salt. Brush both sides of fish with 1 tablespoon of the oil. Sprinkle evenly with half of the spice mixture; rub in with your fingers. Set aside the remaining spice mixture. Measure thickness of fish.

3 For a charcoal grill, grill fish on the greased rack of an uncovered grill directly over medium coals for 4 to 6 minutes per ½-inch thickness or until fish flakes easily when tested with a fork, carefully turning once halfway through grilling. (For a gas grill, preheat grill; reduce heat to medium. Place fish on greased grill rack over heat. Cover and grill as above.)

4 Add the remaining spice mixture and the remaining 1 tablespoon oil to bulgur. Gently stir in sweet pepper and blueberries. Serve fish with bulgur mixture.

nutrition facts per serving: 285 cal., 9 g total fat (1 g sat. fat), 52 mg chol., 225 mg sodium, 22 g carb., 5 g dietary fiber, 30 g protein.

spaghetti-corn relish salad

start to finish: 30 minutes **makes:** 8 servings

1   **14- to 16-ounce package dried multigrain, whole wheat, or regular spaghetti**

4   **ears of corn, husks and silks removed, or 2 cups frozen whole kernel corn**

1¼   **cups seeded and chopped cucumber (1 small)**

1¼   **cups chopped red and/or yellow sweet pepper (1 large)**

1   **cup chopped zucchini or yellow summer squash (1 small)**

½   **cup thinly sliced celery (1 stalk)**

⅓   **cup finely chopped red onion (1 small)**

½   **cup cider vinegar**

¼   **cup olive oil**

1   **tablespoon sugar**

½   **teaspoon salt**

½   **teaspoon dry mustard**

½   **teaspoon celery seeds**

1 Cook spaghetti according to package directions, adding fresh or frozen corn to the water for the last 3 minutes of cooking. If using fresh corn, use tongs to transfer ears of corn to a cutting board. Drain spaghetti. Rinse with cold water; drain again.

2 Cool ears of corn until easy to handle. Holding each ear at an angle, use a sharp knife to cut down the length of the corn cob, cutting off corn in planks.

3 In a large bowl combine spaghetti, cucumber, sweet pepper, zucchini, celery, and red onion.

4 For dressing, in a screw-top jar combine vinegar, oil, sugar, salt, dry mustard, and celery seeds. Cover and shake well. Pour dressing over spaghetti mixture; toss gently to coat. Gently fold in corn planks. If desired, cover and chill for up to 24 hours.

nutrition facts per serving: 299 cal., 8 g total fat (1 g sat. fat), 0 mg chol., 183 mg sodium, 47 g carb., 6 g dietary fiber, 11 g protein.

orange, mint, and
asparagus pasta salad

prep: 25 minutes chill: 1 to 24 hours makes: 5 or 6 servings

8 ounces dried
campanelle or
farfalle (bow-tie)
pasta

1 pound fresh
asparagus spears,
trimmed and cut
diagonally into
1-inch pieces

½ cup thinly sliced
green onions (4)

⅓ cup snipped
fresh mint

⅓ cup crumbled
reduced-fat
feta cheese

3 large navel, Cara
Cara, and/or
blood oranges

2 tablespoons olive oil

1 tablespoon white
wine vinegar or
cider vinegar

½ teaspoon salt

¼ teaspoon ground
black pepper

1 Cook pasta according to package directions, adding asparagus to the water for the last 2 minutes of cooking; drain. Rinse with cold water; drain again. Transfer pasta mixture to a large serving bowl.

2 Add green onions, mint, and cheese to pasta mixture. Using a serrated knife, remove peel and white pith from two of the oranges. Halve oranges lengthwise, then slice crosswise. Add orange pieces to pasta mixture.

3 For dressing, finely shred enough peel from the remaining orange to measure 2 teaspoons. Squeeze enough juice from the remaining orange to measure 2 tablespoons. In a screw-top jar combine orange peel, orange juice, oil, vinegar, salt, and pepper. Cover and shake well.

4 Drizzle dressing over pasta mixture; toss gently to coat. Cover and chill for 1 to 24 hours. Toss again before serving.

nutrition facts per serving: 290 cal., 8 g total fat (2 g sat. fat), 8 mg chol., 350 mg sodium, 44 g carb., 4 g dietary fiber, 10 g protein.

sesame-ginger wheat berry salad

prep: 15 minutes   cook: 45 minutes   makes: 4 servings

1¼   cups water
½   cup wheat berries
1   15-ounce can black
     beans, rinsed
     and drained
1   medium mango,
     seeded, peeled,
     and chopped
¾   cup carrots cut into
     thin bite-size strips
¼   cup mango chutney
2   tablespoons
     rice vinegar
2   teaspoons toasted
     sesame oil
¼   teaspoon ground
     ginger
     Salt
1   small head napa
     cabbage, coarsely
     shredded

1 In a small saucepan combine the water and wheat berries. Bring to boiling; reduce heat. Simmer, covered, for 45 to 60 minutes or until tender. Drain off any liquid.

2 Stir beans, mango, carrots, chutney, vinegar, oil, and ginger into cooked wheat berries. Season to taste with salt. Serve with napa cabbage.

nutrition facts per serving: 265 cal., 3 g total fat (.4 g sat. fat), 0 mg chol., 419 mg sodium, 54 g carb., 10 g dietary fiber, 11 g protein.

taco salad cups

prep: 25 minutes bake: 30 minutes oven: 350°F makes: 4 servings

8   6-inch corn tortillas
     Nonstick cooking
       spray
½   cup chopped onion
       (1 medium)
1   clove garlic, minced
1   tablespoon canola oil
1   12-ounce package
       refrigerated or
       frozen cooked and
       crumbled ground
       meat substitute
       (soy protein)
1   8-ounce can no-salt-
       added tomato sauce
1   tablespoon
       cider vinegar
1   teaspoon ground
       cumin
¼   teaspoon crushed
       red pepper
4   cups shredded
       lettuce
12   cherry tomatoes,
       quartered, or 1 cup
       chopped tomatoes
       (2 medium)
¼   cup shredded
       reduced-fat cheddar
       cheese (1 ounce)
     Salsa (optional)

1 Preheat oven to 350°F. For tortilla bowls, stack tortillas and wrap in foil. Bake about 10 minutes or until warm and softened. Coat eight 10-ounce custard cups with cooking spray. Lightly coat both sides of each warm tortilla with cooking spray. Carefully press a tortilla into each cup. Bake about 20 minutes more or until golden brown and crisp. Remove from custard cups and cool on wire racks.

2 Meanwhile, in a large skillet cook onion and garlic in hot oil over medium heat until tender, stirring occasionally. Stir in crumbled meat substitute, tomato sauce, vinegar, cumin, and crushed red pepper. Bring to boiling; reduce heat. Simmer, uncovered, about 5 minutes or until mixture reaches desired consistency.

3 Divide tortilla bowls among dinner plates. Fill with lettuce and meat substitute mixture. Top with tomatoes, cheese, and, if desired, salsa.

nutrition facts per serving: 383 cal., 14 g total fat (2 g sat. fat), 4 mg chol., 560 mg sodium, 41 g carb., 10 g dietary fiber, 25 g protein.

make-ahead directions: Prepare tortilla bowls as directed in Step 1. Layer between paper towels and place in a large freezer container with paper towels crumpled around sides to protect the bowls. Seal, label, and freeze for up to 1 month.

120

tofu and mushrooms
over greens

start to finish: 30 minutes makes: 4 servings

8   ounces fresh button
and/or cremini
mushrooms,
quartered
3   cloves garlic, minced
2   tablespoons olive oil
1   tablespoon butter
1   tablespoon snipped
fresh thyme or
1 teaspoon dried
thyme, crushed
¼   teaspoon salt
⅛   teaspoon ground
black pepper
1   12-ounce package
firm, tub-style tofu
(fresh bean curd),
drained and cut into
½-inch slices
Salt
Ground black pepper
¼   cup balsamic vinegar
6   cups torn mixed
salad greens
¼   cup crumbled feta
cheese with garlic
and herb (1 ounce)
Baguette-style
French bread
slices, toasted

1 In a large skillet cook mushrooms and
garlic in hot oil and butter over medium
heat until mushrooms are tender and liquid is
evaporated, stirring occasionally. Stir in thyme,
¼ teaspoon salt, and ⅛ teaspoon pepper.
Remove from skillet; cover and keep warm.

2 Lightly sprinkle tofu with additional salt
and pepper. In the same skillet cook tofu,
half at a time if necessary, over medium-high
heat for 3 to 4 minutes or until light brown
and heated through, turning once. Remove
from skillet. Add vinegar to skillet. Bring to
boiling; reduce heat. Boil gently, uncovered,
for 1 minute.

3 Divide salad greens among dinner plates.
Top with tofu; drizzle with vinegar. Top
with mushroom mixture and cheese. Serve
with toasted bread slices.

nutrition facts per serving: 271 cal., 13 g total fat
(4 g sat. fat), 9 mg chol., 415 mg sodium, 28 g carb.,
3 g dietary fiber, 11 g protein.

ravioli and
greens salad

start to finish: 25 minutes makes: 4 servings

1 Cook ravioli according to package directions; drain. Rinse with cold water; drain again.

2 Divide salad greens among dinner plates. Top with cooked ravioli, sweet pepper, tomato, carrot, and herbs.

3 For dressing, in a screw-top jar combine vinegar, the water, oil, sugar, garlic, and black pepper. Cover and shake well. Drizzle dressing over salads.

1   9-ounce package
    refrigerated
    whole wheat
    4-cheese ravioli
1   5-ounce package
    mixed baby
    salad greens
1   cup red sweet pepper
    strips (1 medium)
1   cup tomato wedges
¼   cup coarsely
    shredded carrot
¼   cup snipped fresh
    basil, oregano,
    and/or dill
¼   cup white wine
    vinegar or
    white vinegar
2   tablespoons water
2   tablespoons olive oil
2   teaspoons sugar
2   cloves garlic, minced
¼   teaspoon ground
    black pepper

nutrition facts per serving: 302 cal., 14 g total fat (5 g sat. fat), 43 mg chol., 456 mg sodium, 33 g carb., 5 g dietary fiber, 11 g protein.

soups

and

ste

5

Simmer up some serenity.
These savory, soothing meals
in a bowl are the ultimate in
low cal comfort food.

WS

wild rice chicken soup

prep: 20 minutes cook: 40 minutes makes: 6 servings

2 cups water
½ cup uncooked wild rice, rinsed and drained
½ cup uncooked long grain brown rice
2 14-ounce cans reduced-sodium chicken broth
4 cloves garlic, minced
4 cups chopped tomatoes (8 small) or two 14.5-ounce cans diced tomatoes, undrained
2 cups chopped cooked chicken breast (10 ounces)
1 cup finely chopped zucchini (1 small)
¼ teaspoon freshly ground black pepper
1 tablespoon snipped fresh thyme or 1 teaspoon dried thyme, crushed
1 tablespoon Madeira or dry sherry (optional)

1 In a large saucepan bring the water to boiling. Stir in wild rice and brown rice. Return to boiling; reduce heat. Simmer, covered, for 40 to 45 minutes or until rice is tender and most of the liquid is absorbed. Remove from heat.

2 Meanwhile, in a 4-quart Dutch oven combine broth and garlic; bring to boiling. Stir in tomatoes, chicken, zucchini, and pepper. Return to boiling; reduce heat. Simmer, covered, for 5 minutes. Stir in cooked rice, thyme, and, if desired, Madeira; heat through.

nutrition facts per serving: 218 cal., 3 g total fat (1 g sat. fat), 40 mg chol., 361 mg sodium, 29 g carb., 3 g dietary fiber, 21 g protein.

mexican corn soup

prep: 25 minutes   cook: 10 minutes   makes: 6 servings

1   16-ounce package
    frozen whole kernel
    corn, thawed
1   cup chicken broth
1   4-ounce can diced
    green chile peppers,
    undrained
2   tablespoons butter or
    margarine
1   tablespoon snipped
    fresh oregano or
    1 teaspoon dried
    oregano, crushed
1   clove garlic, minced
¼   teaspoon salt
¼   teaspoon ground
    black pepper
2   cups milk
1   cup chopped cooked
    chicken (5 ounces)
1   cup chopped
    tomatoes
    (2 medium)
1   cup shredded
    Monterey Jack
    cheese (4 ounces)
    Snipped fresh parsley
    (optional)
    Fresh oregano sprigs
    (optional)

1 In a blender combine half of the corn
and the broth. Cover and blend until
nearly smooth.

2 In a large saucepan combine pureed corn,
the remaining corn kernels, the green chile
peppers, butter, dried oregano (if using), garlic,
salt, and black pepper. Bring to boiling; reduce
heat. Simmer, uncovered, for 10 minutes. Stir
in milk, chicken, tomatoes, and snipped fresh
oregano (if using); heat through. Remove
from heat.

3 Stir in cheese until melted. If desired,
sprinkle each serving with parsley and
garnish with oregano sprigs.

nutrition facts per serving: 279 cal., 14 g total fat
(8 g sat. fat), 56 mg chol., 479 mg sodium, 23 g carb.,
0 g dietary fiber, 18 g protein.

sage chicken
dumpling
soup

prep: 35 minutes   cook: 10 minutes   makes: 8 servings

2	cups sliced fresh mushrooms
1	cup chopped onion (1 large)
1	tablespoon olive oil
¼	cup all-purpose flour
6	cups reduced-sodium chicken broth
1	2- to 2½ -pound purchased roasted chicken, skinned, boned, and cut into bite-size pieces
2	cups fresh or frozen peas
½	cup pitted kalamata olives, halved
1	tablespoon lemon juice
1	teaspoon ground sage
1	recipe Buttermilk Dumplings
	Thinly sliced green onions (optional)
1	recipe Fried Sage Sprigs (optional)

1 In a 4-quart Dutch oven cook mushrooms and onion in hot oil over medium heat for 6 to 8 minutes or until mushrooms are tender and liquid is evaporated, stirring occasionally.

2 Stir in flour until combined. Slowly stir in broth. Cook and stir until thickened and bubbly. Stir in chicken, peas, olives, lemon juice, and ground sage. Return to boiling.

3 Drop the Buttermilk Dumpling batter from a tablespoon into eight mounds on top of chicken mixture. Simmer, covered, about 10 minutes or until a toothpick inserted near the center of a dumpling comes out clean.

4 If desired, sprinkle with green onions and top with Fried Sage Sprigs.

nutrition facts per serving: 367 cal., 12 g total fat (2 g sat. fat), 56 mg chol., 776 mg sodium, 37 g carb., 4 g dietary fiber, 25 g protein.

*tip: To make 1 cup sour milk, place 1 tablespoon lemon juice or vinegar in a glass measuring cup. Add enough milk to make 1 cup total liquid; stir. Let stand for 5 minutes before using.

buttermilk dumplings: In a medium bowl stir together 2 cups all-purpose flour, ½ teaspoon baking powder, ¼ teaspoon baking soda, and ¼ teaspoon salt. Stir in ¼ cup sliced green onions (2) and 1 tablespoon snipped fresh Italian (flat-leaf) parsley. Add 1 cup buttermilk or sour milk* and 2 tablespoons olive oil, stirring with a fork just until moistened.

fried sage sprigs: In a medium saucepan heat ¼ cup olive oil over medium heat until hot but not smoky. Add 8 small fresh sage sprigs, two at a time, and cook for 30 to 60 seconds or until crisp. Remove with a slotted spoon and drain sage sprigs on paper towels.

squash and quinoa soup

prep: 25 minutes   cook: 15 minutes   makes: 6 servings

12 ounces skinless, boneless
      chicken breast halves, cut
      into 1-inch pieces
⅓   cup finely chopped shallots
      or onion (1 small)
2   teaspoons olive oil
2   14-ounce cans reduced-
      sodium chicken broth
1   pound butternut squash,
      peeled, seeded, and cut
      into 1-inch pieces
¾   cup quinoa, rinsed and
      drained
1   5.5-ounce can apricot nectar
1   teaspoon ground cumin
2   small zucchini, halved
      lengthwise and cut into
      1-inch pieces

1 In a large saucepan cook chicken and
shallots in hot oil over medium heat for
2 to 3 minutes or until shallots are tender,
stirring occasionally. Stir in broth, butternut
squash, quinoa, apricot nectar, and cumin.

2 Bring to boiling; reduce heat. Simmer,
covered, for 5 minutes. Stir in zucchini.
Simmer, covered, about 10 minutes more or
until butternut squash and quinoa are tender.
Season to taste with salt and pepper.

nutrition facts per serving: 226 cal., 4 g total fat
(1 g sat. fat), 33 mg chol., 454 mg sodium, 31 g carb.,
3 g dietary fiber, 19 g protein.

quick chicken noodle soup

start to finish: 20 minutes   makes: 4 servings

12 ounces skinless boneless
      chicken breast halves, cut
      into bite-size pieces
1   tablespoon olive oil
1   14-ounce can reduced-
      sodium chicken broth
1½ cups water
3   cups coarsely chopped fresh
      kale or baby spinach
2   cups dried whole wheat
      noodles
1   cup fat-free garlic and herb
      pasta sauce*

1 In a large nonstick skillet cook chicken
in hot oil over medium-high heat for
3 minutes. Add broth and the water. Bring
to boiling; stir in kale and noodles. Return to
boiling; reduce heat. Simmer, covered, for 5 to
7 minutes or until chicken is no longer pink
and noodles are tender, stirring occasionally.

2 Stir in pasta sauce; heat through. Stir in
spinach (if using).

nutrition facts per serving: 257 cal., 5 g total fat
(1 g sat. fat), 49 mg chol., 479 mg sodium, 28 g carb.,
5 g dietary fiber, 26 g protein.

*tip: Check the nutrition label of the pasta sauce
to see if it is fat-free.

nutrition note

*When selecting leafy greens, steer towards dark side of the color
spectrum. In general, deeply colored greens have more vitamins and
fiber than lighter greens, such as iceberg lettuce.*

quick fiber high

tomatillo chicken soup

prep: 30 minutes slow cook: 6 to 7 hours (low) or 3 to 3½ hours (high)
makes: 4 to 6 servings

6 medium tomatillos, husks removed
1½ pounds skinless, boneless chicken breast halves
1 32-ounce carton reduced-sodium chicken broth
¾ cup chopped green sweet pepper (1 medium)
½ cup chopped red onion (1 medium)
½ cup chopped celery (1 stalk)
1 4-ounce can diced green chile peppers, undrained
2 tablespoons snipped fresh cilantro
1 fresh jalapeño chile pepper, seeded and finely chopped*
1 tablespoon ground cumin
1 tablespoon lime juice
2 teaspoons chili powder
2 cloves garlic, minced
1 teaspoon ground black pepper
Desired toppings, such as light sour cream, chopped red sweet pepper, sliced fresh jalapeño chile peppers,* snipped fresh cilantro, thinly sliced green onions, and/or tortilla chips (optional)

1 Chop three of the tomatillos; set aside. Place the remaining three tomatillos in a blender. Cover and blend until smooth.

2 In a 3½- or 4-quart slow cooker combine chopped and pureed tomatillos, chicken, broth, ¾ cup chopped sweet pepper, red onion, celery, green chile peppers, 2 tablespoons cilantro, finely chopped jalapeño chile pepper, cumin, lime juice, chili powder, garlic, and black pepper.

3 Cover and cook on low-heat setting for 6 to 7 hours or on high-heat setting for 3 to 3½ hours.

4 Using a slotted spoon, remove chicken from cooker. Using two forks, pull chicken apart into shreds. Return shredded chicken to cooker. If desired, top each serving with desired toppings.

nutrition facts per serving: 255 cal., 3 g total fat (1 g sat. fat), 99 mg chol., 760 mg sodium, 11 g carb., 4 g dietary fiber, 44 g protein.

*tip: Because chile peppers contain volatile oils that can burn your skin and eyes, avoid direct contact with them as much as possible. When working with chile peppers, wear plastic or rubber gloves. If your bare hands do touch the peppers, wash your hands and nails well with soap and warm water.

skillet beef stew

prep: 25 minutes cook: 55 minutes makes: 8 servings

2   pounds beef stew
    meat
2   tablespoons
    canola oil
6   medium carrots
    (1 pound),
    quartered
4   stalks celery, cut into
    2-inch pieces
2   medium onions, cut
    into ½-inch slices
2   teaspoons dried
    thyme or oregano,
    crushed
¼   teaspoon ground
    black pepper
6   cups lower-sodium
    beef broth
⅓   cup all-purpose flour
8   medium Yukon gold
    potatoes (about
    2¾ pounds)
1   cup fat-free milk or
    buttermilk
½   teaspoon ground
    black pepper
¼   teaspoon salt
    Cracked black pepper

1 Trim fat from meat. Cut meat into 1-inch pieces. In a 12-inch skillet cook meat, half at a time, in hot oil over medium-high heat until brown. Using a slotted spoon, remove meat from skillet. Add carrots, celery, and onions to skillet; cook and stir over medium heat for 5 minutes. Return meat to skillet; sprinkle with thyme and ¼ teaspoon pepper.

2 In a medium bowl stir together broth and flour; stir into meat mixture. Bring to boiling; reduce heat. Simmer, covered, for 45 minutes. Simmer, uncovered, for 10 to 15 minutes more or until meat and vegetables are tender.

3 Meanwhile, place four of the potatoes in a large microwave-safe bowl; cover with vented lid or plastic wrap.* Microwave on 100 percent power (high) for 8 minutes. Remove cooked potatoes from bowl; set aside. Repeat with the remaining four potatoes. Return all of the potatoes to the bowl. Using the back of a wooden spoon, break up any larger potatoes. Add milk, ½ teaspoon pepper, and salt. Using a potato masher, mash until nearly smooth or desired consistency.

4 To serve, spread potatoes to cover bottom of each of eight soup bowls. Spoon stew on top of potatoes. Sprinkle each serving with cracked black pepper.

nutrition facts per serving: 375 cal., 10 g total fat (2 g sat. fat), 62 mg chol., 557 mg sodium, 40 g carb., 6 g dietary fiber, 32 g protein.

*tip: To vent plastic wrap, pull back one corner of the wrap.

southwestern
noodle bowl

start to finish: 30 minutes makes: 8 servings

1½ pounds beef flank
       steak or beef top
       round steak
  1 teaspoon ground
       cumin
  ¼ teaspoon salt
  ⅛ teaspoon ground
       black pepper
  2 tablespoons
       canola oil
  2 cloves garlic, minced
  2 14-ounce cans lower-
       sodium beef broth
  1 14-ounce can
       reduced-sodium
       chicken broth
  6 ounces dried angel
       hair pasta
1½ cups chopped red
       or yellow sweet
       peppers (2 medium)
  6 green onions, cut
       diagonally into
       1-inch pieces
  ½ cup hot-style salsa
  ¼ cup snipped fresh
       oregano
       Salsa
       Garlic pepper
       seasoning (optional)

1 Trim fat from meat. Cut meat into thin bite-size strips. Season meat with cumin, salt, and black pepper; set aside.

2 Pour 1 tablespoon of the oil into a wok or extra-large skillet; heat wok over medium-high heat. Add garlic; cook and stir for 15 seconds. Add half of the meat; cook and stir for 2 to 3 minutes or until slightly pink in center. Remove from wok. Repeat with the remaining oil and meat. Return all of the meat to wok. Add broths; bring to boiling.

3 Stir in pasta, sweet peppers, and green onions; return to boiling. Cook about 3 minutes or until pasta is tender, stirring occasionally. Stir in ½ cup salsa and oregano; heat through.

4 Ladle mixture into shallow soup bowls. If desired, swirl pasta into nests in bowls. Top with additional salsa and, if desired, sprinkle with garlic pepper seasoning.

nutrition facts per serving: 260 cal., 9 g total fat (2 g sat. fat), 28 mg chol., 616 mg sodium, 21 g carb., 2 g dietary fiber, 24 g protein.

nutrition note
If canola oil isn't already in your pantry, consider it time for an oil change. This choice has less saturated fat and more omega-3 fatty acids than any other oil. Plus, its mild taste lets the flavors of other ingredients really take off.

This power-packed stew is brimming with colorful, nutritious vegetables and comfort-food flavors.

beef, barley, and sweet potato stew

prep: 40 minutes   cook: 1 hour 15 minutes   makes: 8 servings

2	pounds extra-lean beef stew meat
⅓	cup all-purpose flour
½	teaspoon ground black pepper
	Nonstick cooking spray
½	cup chopped onion (1 medium)
2	cloves garlic, minced
1	cup sliced carrots (2 medium)
2	tablespoons snipped fresh parsley
½	teaspoon dried thyme, crushed
5	cups reduced-sodium chicken broth
1	cup water
3	cups sliced fresh mushrooms (8 ounces)
2	medium potatoes, peeled and cut into 1-inch chunks (about 2 cups)*
2	small sweet potatoes, peeled and cut into 1-inch chunks (about 2 cups)*
1	cup coarsely chopped roma tomatoes (3 medium)
½	cup regular barley
1	cup frozen peas
	Fresh thyme leaves

1 Trim fat from meat. Cut meat into 1-inch pieces. In a plastic bag combine flour and pepper. Add meat pieces, at few at a time, shaking to coat. Coat a 6-quart nonstick Dutch oven with cooking spray; heat Dutch oven over medium-high heat. Add meat, half at a time; cook until brown. Remove meat from Dutch oven.

2 In the same Dutch oven cook onion and garlic over medium heat for 2 minutes. Add carrots, parsley, and dried thyme; cook and stir for 3 minutes. Add broth and the water; bring to boiling, stirring to scrape up crusty brown bits. Reduce heat.

3 Simmer, covered, for 45 minutes. Stir in mushrooms, potatoes, sweet potatoes, tomatoes, and barley. Return to boiling; reduce heat. Simmer, covered, for 30 to 45 minutes or until meat and vegetables are tender. Stir in peas; cook for 1 minute more. If desired, garnish with fresh thyme.

nutrition facts per serving: 349 cal., 9 g total fat (3 g sat. fat), 55 mg chol., 482 mg sodium, 35 g carb., 6 g dietary fiber, 33 g protein.

*tip: If desired, omit the potatoes and increase sweet potatoes to 4 cups.

southwest pork salsa stew

prep: 20 minutes   cook: 10 minutes   makes: 4 servings

12 ounces boneless pork
      loin or sirloin
      Nonstick cooking
      spray
 1   14 ounce can
      reduced-sodium
      chicken broth
 1   6-ounce can no-salt-
      added tomato paste
 ½ cup cilantro-flavor
      salsa* or regular
      salsa
 ½ teaspoon ground
      cumin
 1   medium zucchini,
      halved lengthwise
      and thinly sliced
      (1¼ cups)
 1   cup frozen shelled
      sweet soybeans
      (edamame) or baby
      lima beans
 ½ cup peeled and
      chopped mango*
      Snipped fresh cilantro
      (optional)

1 Trim fat from meat. Cut meat into bite-size strips. Lightly coat a large saucepan with cooking spray; heat saucepan over medium high heat. Add meat; cook and stir about 2 minutes or until brown.

2 Stir in broth, tomato paste, salsa, and cumin. Stir in zucchini and soybeans. Bring to boiling; reduce heat. Simmer, covered, about 10 minutes or until vegetables are tender. Top each serving with mango and, if desired, cilantro.

nutrition facts per serving: 243 cal., 7 g total fat (2 g sat. fat), 47 mg chol., 594 mg sodium, 19 g carb., 6 g dietary fiber, 26 g protein.

*tip: If you prefer, use regular salsa and stir in 2 tablespoons snipped fresh cilantro. In place of fresh mango, use refrigerated mango slices, rinsed, drained, and chopped (or use frozen chopped mango, thawed).

nutrition note

Nibbles, licks, and bites add up when sampling food during cooking, but the built-in snack here adds up in all the right ways: Enjoy the remaining mango that's not used in the stew, and you'll get some fiber, potassium, and beta-carotene.

mexican winter chili

prep: 25 minutes cook: 35 minutes makes: 4 servings

1   pound pork stew
      meat
2   tablespoons olive oil
1   large red sweet
      pepper, seeded
      and cut into ¾-inch
      pieces
1   medium poblano
      chile pepper, finely
      chopped*
1   cup chopped onion
      (1 large)
2   teaspoons
      unsweetened cocoa
      powder
1   teaspoon ground
      cumin
½   teaspoon garlic
      powder
⅛   teaspoon ground
      cinnamon
      Dash cayenne pepper
1   14-ounce can
      reduced-sodium
      chicken broth
½   cup water
1   15-ounce can
      pumpkin
¼   cup light sour cream
¼   teaspoon salt
¼   teaspoon ground
      black pepper
      Fresh cilantro leaves
      (optional)

1 Trim fat from meat. In a Dutch oven cook meat in hot oil over medium-high heat until brown. Stir in sweet pepper, poblano chile pepper, and onion; cook and stir about 5 minutes or until onion is tender. Drain off fat.

2 Stir cocoa powder, cumin, garlic powder, cinnamon, and cayenne pepper into onion mixture. Add broth and the water. Bring to boiling; reduce heat. Simmer, covered, about 30 minutes or until meat is tender.

3 Stir in pumpkin and sour cream. Return to boiling; reduce heat. Simmer, uncovered, for 5 minutes. Season with salt and black pepper. If desired, top each serving with cilantro.

nutrition facts per serving: 327 cal., 15 g total fat (4 g sat. fat), 73 mg chol., 467 mg sodium, 19 g carb., 5 g dietary fiber, 28 g protein.

*tip: Because chile peppers contain volatile oils that can burn your skin and eyes, avoid direct contact with them as much as possible. When working with chile peppers, wear plastic or rubber gloves. If your bare hands do touch the peppers, wash your hands and nails well with soap and warm water.

Toss all the ingredients into a Dutch oven and allow this stew to steam for a super easy meal.

simple seafood stew

prep: 40 minutes bake: 11 minutes oven: 450°F makes: 4 servings

1 pound fresh or frozen medium shrimp in shells and/or sea scallops

12 ounces fresh or frozen white fish fillets, such as cod, halibut, or flounder, cut into 2-inch pieces

1 tablespoon olive oil

⅓ cup chopped onion (1 small) or leek (1 medium)

2 cloves garlic, thinly sliced

¼ teaspoon crushed red pepper

½ cup chopped tomato (1 medium)

¼ cup dry white wine

1 2-inch strip orange peel*

Pinch saffron threads or ⅛ teaspoon ground turmeric

2 8-ounce bottles clam juice

2 cups water
Salt
Ground black pepper

4 thin slices crusty country bread
Olive oil

1 clove garlic, halved

2 tablespoons finely snipped fresh parsley

1 Thaw seafood and fish, if frozen. Peel and devein shrimp, if using. Rinse seafood and fish; pat dry with paper towels. Set aside. Preheat oven to 450°F.

2 In an ovenproof Dutch oven heat 1 tablespoon oil over medium heat. Add onion and sliced garlic; cook about 4 minutes or until tender.

3 Add crushed red pepper; cook for 1 minute. Add tomato, wine, orange peel, and saffron; cook for 1 minute. Add clam juice and the water. Bring to boiling; remove from heat. Add seafood and fish; sprinkle with salt and black pepper.

4 Bake, covered, for 6 to 8 minutes or until fish flakes easily when tested with a fork and shrimp and/or scallops are opaque.

5 Meanwhile, place bread slices on a baking sheet; drizzle with additional oil. Bake, uncovered, for 5 to 7 minutes or until bread is crisp and edges are golden brown. Rub surface of bread with cut sides of garlic halves.

6 Sprinkle each serving of the stew with parsley. Serve with garlic-rubbed bread.

nutrition facts per serving: 360 cal., 10 g total fat (2 g sat. fat), 209 mg chol., 788 mg sodium, 20 g carb., 2 g dietary fiber, 42 g protein.

*tip: Use a vegetable peeler to remove a thin piece of peel from the orange. Be sure to get just the colored part, not the bitter white pith underneath.

Collard greens—an excellent source of vitamins A, C, and K—give this classic Cajun favorite a delicious nutrition boost.

quick shrimp jambalaya

start to finish: 40 minutes makes: 4 to 6 servings

1 cup sliced celery
  (2 stalks)
2 teaspoons canola oil
  or vegetable oil
2 cloves garlic, minced
½ teaspoon Creole
  seasoning or Cajun
  seasoning
⅛ to ¼ teaspoon
  crushed red pepper
4 cups coarsely
  chopped fresh
  collard greens
  or kale
½ of a 16-ounce
  package (2 cups)
  frozen pepper
  and onion stir-fry
  vegetables
1 cup cubed cooked
  ham (5 ounces)
4 ounces whole fresh
  okra, cut into ½-inch
  pieces (1 cup),
  or 1 cup frozen
  cut okra
2 tablespoons water
1 14.5-ounce can no-
  salt-added stewed
  tomatoes, undrained
  and cut up
1 8.8-ounce pouch
  cooked long grain
  brown rice
8 ounces frozen peeled
  and deveined
  cooked shrimp,
  thawed

1 In a 4-quart Dutch oven cook celery in hot oil over medium heat for 5 minutes, stirring occasionally. Stir in garlic, Creole seasoning, and crushed red pepper. Stir in collard greens, stir-fry vegetables, ham, okra, and the water.

2 Bring to boiling; reduce heat. Simmer, covered, for 8 minutes, stirring occasionally. Stir in tomatoes, rice, and shrimp. Simmer, uncovered, for 5 minutes to heat through and blend flavors, stirring occasionally.

nutrition facts per serving: 286 cal., 6 g total fat (1 g sat. fat), 126 mg chol., 853 mg sodium, 34 g carb., 5 g dietary fiber, 25 g protein.

138

smoky bean chili

prep: 25 minutes cook: 10 minutes makes: 4 servings

1 large red onion, cut
   into thin wedges
1 tablespoon canola oil
4 cloves garlic, minced
2 14.5-ounce cans
   no-salt-added
   fire-roasted
   diced tomatoes,
   undrained
1 15-ounce can
   reduced-sodium
   black-eyed peas,
   rinsed and drained
1 10-ounce package
   frozen lima beans
1 cup water
1 to 2 tablespoons chili
   powder
1 tablespoon smoked
   paprika or regular
   paprika
⅛ teaspoon salt
   Shredded reduced-
   fat cheddar cheese
   (optional)

1 In a 4-quart Dutch oven cook onion in hot oil over medium heat for 8 to 10 minutes or until very tender, stirring occasionally. Stir in garlic.

2 Stir in tomatoes, black-eyed peas, lima beans, the water, chili powder, paprika, and salt. Bring to boiling; reduce heat. Simmer, covered, for 10 to 15 minutes to blend flavors. If desired, top each serving with cheese.

nutrition facts per serving: 275 cal., 5 g total fat (0 g sat. fat), 0 mg chol., 177 mg sodium, 45 g carb., 11 g dietary fiber, 13 g protein.

This soup has a sweet taste that everyone will find appealing. Use pure maple syrup for the best flavor.

sweet potato soup with nutmeg and maple syrup

prep: 30 minutes   cook: 20 minutes   makes: 4 servings

½ cup chopped onion
    (1 medium)
½ cup chopped celery
    (1 stalk)
1 clove garlic, minced
1 tablespoon butter
2 cups peeled and
    cubed sweet
    potatoes
2 cups reduced-sodium
    chicken broth
½ teaspoon ground
    nutmeg
1½ cups half-and-half or
    light cream
1 tablespoon maple
    syrup
    Sour cream (optional)
    Ground nutmeg
    (optional)

1 In a 4-quart Dutch oven cook onion, celery, and garlic in hot butter over medium heat until onion is tender, stirring occasionally. Stir in sweet potatoes, broth, and ½ teaspoon nutmeg. Bring to boiling; reduce heat. Simmer, covered, about 20 minutes or until sweet potatoes are tender. Remove from heat; cool slightly.

2 Transfer sweet potato mixture, about one-third at a time, to a blender or food processor. Cover and blend or process until smooth. Return to Dutch oven. Stir in half-and-half and maple syrup; heat through. If desired, top each serving with sour cream and additional nutmeg.

nutrition facts per serving: 233 cal., 13 g total fat (8 g sat. fat), 41 mg chol., 392 mg sodium, 24 g carb., 3 g dietary fiber, 6 g protein.

macaroni and cheese chowder

start to finish: 30 minutes makes: 4 (1⅓ cup) servings

1 10- to 12-ounce package
frozen light macaroni and
cheese (use a product
that contains less than
600 mg sodium)

1 14½-ounce can reduced-
sodium chicken broth

1 10-ounce package frozen
whole kernel corn (2 cups)

½ cup fat-free milk

¼ teaspoon ground black
pepper

2 cups chopped cooked
chicken breast (10 ounces)

⅓ cup chopped green onions

1 Prepare frozen macaroni and cheese
in the microwave oven according to
package directions.

2 In a large saucepan combine macaroni
and cheese, broth, corn, milk, and pepper.
Bring to boiling. Stir in chicken and green
onions; reduce heat. Simmer, covered, for
3 to 4 minutes or until heated through.

nutrition facts per serving: 270 cal., 5 g total fat
(2 g sat. fat), 65 mg chol., 470 mg sodium, 28 g carb.,
2 g dietary fiber, 30 g protein.

asparagus and cheese potato soup

start to finish: 35 minutes makes: 6 servings

1 cup chopped onion (1 large)

4 teaspoons canola oil

3 tablespoons all-purpose
flour

2 cups fat-free milk

1 14-ounce can reduced-
sodium chicken broth

1½ cups 1-inch pieces fresh
asparagus spears or
broccoli florets

1½ cups ½-inch cubes red-skin
potatoes

1½ cups ½-inch cubes Yukon
gold potatoes

¼ teaspoon salt

⅛ teaspoon cayenne pepper

¾ cup shredded sharp cheddar
cheese (3 ounces)

⅓ cup light sour cream

1 In a large saucepan cook onion in hot oil
over medium heat until tender, stirring
occasionally. Stir in flour. Slowly stir in milk.
Add broth, asparagus, potatoes, salt, and
cayenne pepper; cook and stir until thickened
and bubbly. Reduce heat.

2 Simmer, covered, for 10 to 12 minutes or
just until vegetables are tender, stirring
occasionally. Add cheese and sour cream,
stirring until cheese is melted.

nutrition facts per serving: 228 cal., 10 g total fat
(4 g sat. fat), 23 mg chol., 397 mg sodium, 25 g carb.,
3 g dietary fiber, 10 g protein.

Keep your resolution to eat well and enjoy hearty winter vegetables in this light and satisfying soup.

chunky lentil soup

prep: 25 minutes cook: 15 minutes makes: 6 servings

1　medium onion, cut into thin slices
1　clove garlic, minced
1　tablespoon olive oil
1　cup green (French) lentils, rinsed and drained
1　pound whole small fresh mushrooms (halve or quarter any larger mushrooms)
2　cups thinly sliced carrots (4 medium)
1　cup chopped celery (2 stalks)
¼　teaspoon salt
¼　teaspoon ground black pepper
4　cups water
1　14-ounce can vegetable broth
2　cups sliced napa or red cabbage

1 In a 4-quart saucepan or Dutch oven cook onion and garlic in hot oil over medium heat for 4 to 5 minutes or until onion is tender, stirring occasionally. Add lentils; cook and stir for 1 minute.

2 Stir in mushrooms, carrots, celery, salt, and pepper. Add the water and broth. Bring to boiling; reduce heat. Simmer, covered, for 15 to 20 minutes or until lentils are tender.

3 Top each serving with cabbage

nutrition facts per serving: 185 cal., 3 g total fat (0 g sat. fat), 0 mg chol., 408 mg sodium, 30 g carb., 13 g dietary fiber, 12 g protein.

creamy potato soup

prep: 35 minutes cook: 20 minutes makes: 6 servings

2 cups thinly sliced
    onions or leeks
1 tablespoon olive oil
2 cups milk
3 tablespoons all-
    purpose flour
4 cups reduced-sodium
    chicken broth
3 cups peeled and
    sliced Yukon gold
    potatoes
    (3 medium)
2 cups shredded
    Gruyère or baby
    Swiss cheese
    (8 ounces)
    Salt
    Ground black pepper
    Snipped fresh chives
    and/or cracked
    black pepper

1 In a 4-quart Dutch oven cook onions in hot oil over medium heat about 5 minutes or until tender, stirring occasionally. In a medium bowl stir together milk and flour. Add milk mixture to onions; cook and stir for 5 minutes. Add broth and potatoes.

2 Bring to boiling; reduce heat. Simmer, covered, about 20 minutes or until potatoes are tender. Remove from heat; cool slightly.

3 Transfer potato mixture, half at a time, to a blender or food processor. Cover and blend or process until smooth. Return to Dutch oven. Add cheese; cook and stir over medium heat just until cheese is melted. Season to taste with salt and ground pepper.

4 Sprinkle each serving with chives and/or cracked pepper.

nutrition facts per serving: 293 cal., 15 g total fat (8 g sat. fat), 41 mg chol., 588 mg sodium, 24 g carb., 1 g dietary fiber, 17 g protein.

creamy potato and asparagus soup

start to finish: 35 minutes makes: 4 servings

1¼ pounds fresh asparagus spears, trimmed

1¼ pounds potatoes, peeled and cut into ½-inch pieces

1 12-ounce can evaporated milk

1¼ cups water

½ teaspoon salt

½ teaspoon ground black pepper

6 slices bacon

1 tablespoon honey
Desired toppings, such as shredded lemon peel, snipped fresh Italian (flat-leaf) parsley, coarse salt, and/or freshly ground black pepper

1 Reserve about one-third of the asparagus for garnish. In a large saucepan combine the remaining asparagus, the potatoes, evaporated milk, the water, ½ teaspoon salt, and ½ teaspoon pepper. Bring to boiling; reduce heat. Simmer, covered, about 10 minutes or until potatoes are tender. Remove from heat; cool slightly.

2 Transfer potato mixture, half at a time, to a blender or food processor. Cover and blend or process until smooth. Return to saucepan.

3 Meanwhile, in a large skillet cook bacon over medium heat until crisp. Using a slotted spoon, remove bacon and drain on paper towels; reserve 1 tablespoon of the drippings in skillet. Coarsely chop bacon; set aside.

4 Add the reserved asparagus to the reserved drippings; cook for 5 to 6 minutes or until asparagus is crisp tender, stirring occasionally.

5 Before serving, place bacon in a microwave-safe pie plate. Drizzle with honey; cover with vented plastic wrap. Microwave on 100 percent power (high) for 30 seconds.

6 Top each serving of soup with some of the reserved asparagus, bacon, and desired toppings.

nutrition facts per serving: 356 cal., 15 g total fat (7 g sat. fat), 41 mg chol., 673 mg sodium, 43 g carb., 4 g dietary fiber, 15 g protein.

tofu-carrot soup

prep: 35 minutes   cook: 20 minutes   makes: 6 servings

3   cups sliced fresh
     mushrooms
     (8 ounces)
1   cup sliced celery
     (2 stalks)
1   medium onion, sliced
2   cloves garlic, minced
2   tablespoons
     vegetable oil
3   14-ounce cans
     reduced-sodium
     vegetable broth or
     chicken broth
4   cups sliced carrots
     (8 medium)
1   12.3-ounce package
     silken-style firm
     tofu (fresh bean
     curd), cut up
1   5-ounce can
     evaporated nonfat
     milk
1   teaspoon snipped
     fresh thyme
¼   teaspoon salt
¼   teaspoon ground
     black pepper
½   cup light sour cream
     Fresh thyme leaves
        (optional)
     Cayenne pepper
        (optional)

1 In a 4- to 6-quart Dutch oven cook mushrooms, celery, onion, and garlic in hot oil over medium heat about 5 minutes or until softened. Stir in broth and carrots. Bring to boiling; reduce heat. Simmer, covered, about 20 minutes or until vegetables are tender. Remove from heat; cool slightly.

2 Place tofu and half of the vegetable mixture in a large food processor or blender. (If you don't have a large food processor or blender, process mixture in smaller batches.) Cover and process or blend until smooth. Repeat with evaporated milk and the remaining vegetable mixture. Return pureed vegetable mixtures to Dutch oven; heat through. Stir in snipped thyme. Season to taste with salt and black pepper.

3 Top each serving with sour cream thinned with 2 to 3 teaspoons water. If desired, sprinkle with thyme leaves and cayenne pepper.

nutrition facts per serving: 185 cal., 8 g total fat (2 g sat. fat), 7 mg chol., 710 mg sodium, 20 g carb., 3 g dietary fiber, 9 g protein.

cauliflower and carrot cumin soup

prep: 30 minutes   cook: 20 minutes   makes: 6 side-dish servings

1   cup finely chopped
    onion (1 large)
2   cloves garlic, minced
2   tablespoons olive oil
3   cups small
    cauliflower florets
1½ cups coarsely
    shredded carrots
    (3 medium)
1   teaspoon ground
    cumin
2   14-ounce cans
    reduced-sodium
    chicken broth
1   cup half-and-half or
    light cream
1   tablespoon lime juice
    Salt
    Freshly ground black
    pepper

1 In a large saucepan cook onion and garlic in hot oil over medium heat about 5 minutes or until onion is tender, stirring occasionally. Stir in cauliflower, carrots, and cumin. Add broth.

2 Bring to boiling; reduce heat. Simmer, covered, about 20 minutes or until cauliflower is very tender. Remove from heat; cool slightly. Using a slotted spoon, remove 1½ cups of the vegetables and set aside.

3 Transfer the remaining mixture, half at a time, to a blender or food processor. Cover and blend or process until smooth. Return to saucepan. Stir in the reserved 1½ cups vegetables, the half-and-half, and lime juice; heat through. Season to taste with salt and pepper.

nutrition facts per serving: 140 cal., 9 g total fat (4 g sat. fat), 15 mg chol., 466 mg sodium, 11 g carb., 3 g dietary fiber, 5 g protein.

In addition to vitamin K, Swiss chard provides a bone-building mix of magnesium, manganese, and potassium.

minestrone

start to finish: 35 minutes makes: 6 side-dish servings

½ cup chopped onion
(1 medium)
1 tablespoon olive oil
2 14-ounce cans
reduced-sodium
chicken broth
1 15-ounce can
cannellini beans
(white kidney
beans), rinsed and
drained
1½ cups water
1¼ cups coarsely
chopped zucchini
(1 medium)
1 cup sliced carrots
(2 medium)
3 cloves garlic, minced
¾ cup dried multigrain
elbow macaroni
1 tablespoon snipped
fresh oregano or
1 teaspoon dried
oregano, crushed
6 cups coarsely torn
fresh Swiss chard
or 8 cups fresh baby
spinach
1 14.5-ounce can
no-salt-added
diced tomatoes,
undrained
Salt
Ground black pepper
Fresh oregano
(optional)

1 In a 5- to 6-quart Dutch oven cook onion in hot oil over medium heat until tender, stirring occasionally. Add broth, beans, the water, zucchini, carrots, and garlic.

2 Bring to boiling. Stir in macaroni and dried oregano (if using). Return to boiling; reduce heat. Simmer, covered, for 5 minutes. Stir in Swiss chard (if using). Simmer, uncovered, for 5 to 7 minutes more or until macaroni is tender but still firm, stirring occasionally.

3 Stir in tomatoes, snipped fresh oregano (if using), and spinach (if using). Remove from heat. Season to taste with salt and black pepper. If desired, garnish each serving with additional fresh oregano.

nutrition facts per serving: 162 cal., 3 g total fat (0 g sat. fat), 0 mg chol., 554 mg sodium, 30 g carb., 7 g dietary fiber, 10 g protein.

triple tomato soup

prep: 30 minutes cook: 20 minutes makes: 4 or 5 side-dish servings

1   tablespoon butter or
    olive oil
1¼ cups thinly sliced
    onion
1   28 ounce can
    whole tomatoes,
    undrained
1   14 ounce can
    reduced-sodium
    chicken broth
¾   cup dried tomatoes
    (not oil-pack)
½   cup sliced celery
    (1 stalk)
½   of a 6-ounce can
    (⅓ cup) no-salt-
    added tomato paste
2   tablespoons snipped
    fresh Italian (flat-
    leaf) parsley and/or
    regular parsley
2   to 3 teaspoons lime
    juice or lemon juice
    Snipped fresh Italian
    (flat-leaf) parsley
    and/or regular
    parsley

1 In a large saucepan heat butter over medium-low heat. Add onion; cover and cook about 10 minutes or until tender. Add canned tomatoes, broth, ½ cup of the dried tomatoes, the celery, tomato paste, and 2 tablespoons parsley. Bring to boiling; reduce heat. Simmer, covered, about 20 minutes or until celery and onion are very tender. Remove from heat; cool slightly.

2 Meanwhile, place the remaining ¼ cup dried tomatoes in a small microwave-safe bowl; add enough water to cover. Microwave on 100 percent power (high) for 1 minute. Cool about 15 minutes. Drain and snip tomatoes; set aside.

3 Transfer broth mixture, half at a time, to a blender or food processor. Cover and blend or process until nearly smooth. Return broth mixture to saucepan. Stir in lime juice; heat through.

4 Top each serving with snipped dried tomatoes and additional parsley.

nutrition facts per serving: 128 cal., 4 g total fat (2 g sat. fat), 8 mg chol., 786 mg sodium, 22 g carb., 5 g dietary fiber, 6 g protein.

Saffron gives this garden-fresh chowder a deliciously sophisticated flavor.

pepper-corn
chowder

cook: 20 minutes oven: 35 minutes makes: 6 side-dish servings

Nonstick cooking
  spray
1 cup chopped onion
  (1 large)
⅓ cup chopped leek
  (1 medium)
5 cups frozen whole
  kernel corn
2 14-ounce cans
  reduced-sodium
  chicken broth
¾ cup chopped red
  sweet pepper
  (1 medium)
⅛ teaspoon ground
  black pepper
⅛ teaspoon cayenne
  pepper
3 saffron threads
  (optional)
  Snipped fresh chives
  and/or ground black
  pepper (optional)

1 Coat a 4- to 5-quart Dutch oven with cooking spray; heat Dutch oven over medium heat. Add onion and leek; cook about 5 minutes or until onion and leek are tender, stirring occasionally. Add corn; cook about 5 minutes or until corn is softened, stirring occasionally. Add 1 can of the broth.

2 Bring to boiling; reduce heat. Simmer, covered, about 20 minutes or until corn is very tender. Remove from heat; cool slightly.

3 Transfer corn mixture, half at a time, to a blender or food processor. Cover and blend or process until nearly smooth. Return to Dutch oven.

4 Add the remaining 1 can broth, the sweet pepper, ⅛ teaspoon black pepper, cayenne pepper, and saffron (if using). Cook and stir until heated through. If desired, garnish each serving with chives and/or additional black pepper.

nutrition facts per serving: 155 cal., 1 g total fat (0 g sat. fat), 0 mg chol., 323 mg sodium, 35 g carb., 4 g dietary fiber, 7 g protein.

curried apple soup

prep: 25 minutes cook: 15 minutes makes: 4 side-dish servings

1 medium onion, thinly sliced
2 tablespoons butter or margarine
2 cups peeled and chopped cooking apples (3 medium)
1 tablespoon curry powder
3 cups chicken broth
1 cup milk
⅓ cup slivered almonds, toasted
2 tablespoons thinly sliced green onion (1)

1 In a large saucepan cook onion in hot butter over medium heat about 5 minutes or until tender, stirring occasionally. Stir in apples and curry powder. Add broth.

2 Bring to boiling; reduce heat. Simmer, uncovered, about 15 minutes or until apples are very tender. Stir in milk. Cook and stir until heated through.

3 If desired, use a potato masher to slightly mash apples. Top each serving with almonds and green onion.

nutrition facts per serving: 216 cal., 12 g total fat (5 g sat. fat), 20 mg chol., 429 mg sodium, 23 g carb., 4 g dietary fiber, 9 g protein.

sides

and

sna

6

Turn the page to find a bit of this and a bit of that—from entrée-entertaining plate pals to grab-and-go goodies.

cks

quinoa salad with
sesame vinaigrette

prep: 20 minutes **cook:** 15 minutes **makes:** 2 servings

½   cup water
¼   cup quinoa, rinsed
     and drained
 1   tablespoon rice
     vinegar
 2   teaspoons toasted
     sesame oil
⅛   teaspoon salt
⅛   teaspoon crushed red
     pepper
⅓   cup chopped red
     or yellow sweet
     pepper
⅓   cup coarsely
     shredded or thinly
     sliced carrot
⅓   cup thin bite-size
     strips zucchini
 2   tablespoons
     diagonally sliced
     green onion (1)

1 In a small saucepan combine the water
and quinoa. Bring to boiling; reduce
heat. Simmer, covered, about 15 minutes
or until water is absorbed. Remove from
heat; cool completely.

2 Meanwhile, in a small bowl whisk together
vinegar, oil, salt, and crushed red pepper.
Stir in sweet pepper, carrot, zucchini, and
green onion. Add quinoa; toss gently to coat.
If desired, cover and chill for up to 24 hours
before serving.

nutrition facts per serving: 145 cal., 6 g total fat
(1 g sat. fat), 0 mg chol., 167 mg sodium, 19 g carb.,
3 g dietary fiber, 4 g protein.

Experience perfectly cooked chard without all the fuss of a classic range-top dish.

oven-cooked
swiss chard

prep: 20 minutes bake: 20 minutes oven: 350°F makes: 6 servings

1   bunch Swiss chard
    (about 1 pound)
¼   cup golden raisins
2   tablespoons olive oil
2   tablespoons balsamic
    vinegar
¼   teaspoon salt
¼   teaspoon freshly
    ground black
    pepper
¼   cup pine nuts or
    slivered almonds,
    toasted (optional)

1 Preheat oven to 350°F. Slice Swiss chard leaves into 2-inch pieces and chop stems into ¾-inch pieces.

2 In a large bowl toss together chard, raisins, and oil. Transfer mixture to a 3-quart rectangular baking dish, mounding slightly in center if necessary. Cover dish tightly with foil.

3 Bake for 20 to 25 minutes or until chard is slightly wilted. Carefully remove foil. Add vinegar, salt, and pepper; toss gently to coat.

4 Transfer to a serving dish. If desired, sprinkle with pine nuts.

nutrition facts per serving: 79 cal., 5 g total fat (1 g sat. fat), 0 mg chol., 247 mg sodium, 9 g carb., 1 g dietary fiber, 2 g protein.

honey-and-horseradish-glazed carrots

start to finish: 20 minutes **makes:** 4 servings

1 pound carrots, sliced
  (3 cups)
1 tablespoon honey
1 tablespoon prepared
  horseradish

1 In a covered medium saucepan cook carrots in a small amount of boiling, lightly salted water for 8 to 10 minutes or until crisp-tender; drain. Return carrots to saucepan.

2 Meanwhile, in a small bowl stir together honey and horseradish. Add honey mixture to cooked carrots; toss gently to coat. Cook and stir about 1 minute more or until glazed and heated through.

nutrition facts per serving: 64 cal., 0 g total fat (0 g sat. fat), 0 mg chol., 86 mg sodium, 16 g carb., 3 g dietary fiber, 1 g protein.

double-gingered orange carrots

prep: 10 minutes **cook:** 18 minutes **makes:** 4 servings

1½ pounds baby carrots
  with tops trimmed,
  or 1 pound small to
  medium carrots
2 teaspoons olive oil
¼ cup orange juice
1 1-inch piece fresh
  ginger, peeled and
  shaved* or cut into
  very thin slices
¼ teaspoon salt
2 tablespoons chopped
  toasted hazelnuts
  (filberts)**
1 tablespoon snipped
  crystallized ginger

1 Halve baby carrots lengthwise, or quarter small to medium carrots lengthwise and cut crosswise into 3-inch pieces.

2 In a large nonstick skillet cook carrots in hot oil over medium heat for 10 minutes, stirring once. Stir in orange juice, fresh ginger, and salt. Cook, covered, for 6 to 8 minutes or until carrots are tender. Cook, uncovered, about 2 minutes more or until liquid is reduced by half.

3 To serve, sprinkle carrots with hazelnuts and crystallized ginger.

nutrition facts per serving: 109 cal., 5 g total fat (1 g sat. fat), 0 mg chol., 224 mg sodium, 16 g carb., 4 g dietary fiber, 2 g protein.

***tip:** Use a sharp vegetable peeler to thinly shave the fresh ginger.

****tip:** To toast hazelnuts, preheat oven to 350°F. Spread the nuts in a shallow baking pan. Bake for 10 to 15 minutes or until light golden brown, watching carefully and stirring once or twice so the nuts don't burn. Cool slightly. Place the nuts on a clean kitchen towel, fold towel over top, and rub vigorously to remove the skins.

Double-Gingered
Orange Carrots

creamy cauliflower and celery root

prep: 25 minutes   cook: 25 minutes   makes: 10 servings

1 large head cauliflower, cut into florets
1 medium celery root, peeled and cut into 1-inch pieces
2 cloves garlic, minced
½ cup ricotta cheese
2 tablespoons butter, melted
2 tablespoons olive oil
1 tablespoon garam masala
1 tablespoon coarse ground mustard
1 teaspoon salt
1 teaspoon cumin seeds, toasted* (optional)

1 In a covered 4-quart Dutch oven cook cauliflower, celery root, and garlic in enough boiling salted water to cover about 25 minutes or until tender; drain.

2 In a large bowl combine cheese, butter, oil, garam masala, mustard, and salt. Stir in cauliflower mixture. Transfer mixture, half at a time, to a food processor. Cover and process until smooth. Transfer to a serving platter. If desired, sprinkle with toasted cumin seeds.

nutrition facts per serving: 93 cal., 7 g total fat (3 g sat. fat), 12 mg chol., 322 mg sodium, 6 g carb., 2 g dietary fiber, 3 g protein.

*tip: To toast cumin seeds, place seeds in a small skillet. Cook over medium heat for 4 to 5 minutes or until fragrant, shaking pan occasionally.

These sweet potato fries are a lower-fat (and tasty!) alternative to traditional fries. Baking them on a foil-lined pan helps prevent overbrowning.

sweet potato fries

prep: 15 minutes bake: 20 minutes oven: 400°F makes: 6 servings

4 medium sweet
    potatoes, peeled
    (if desired)
2 tablespoons olive oil
    Salt
    Ground black pepper
    Snipped fresh parsley
    (optional)

1 Preheat oven to 400°F. Line two baking sheets with foil; set aside. Cut sweet potatoes lengthwise into ½ inch strips. Place sweet potatoes in a large bowl. Drizzle with oil. Sprinkle with salt and pepper; toss gently to coat. Arrange sweet potatoes in a single layer on prepared baking sheets.

2 Bake for 20 to 30 minutes or until golden brown, turning potatoes once halfway through baking. If desired, sprinkle with parsley.

nutrition facts per serving: 115 cal., 5 g total fat (1 g sat. fat), 0 mg chol., 145 mg sodium, 17 g carb., 3 g dietary fiber, 1 g protein.

tip: For extra flavor, try sprinkling sweet potatoes with 1 tablespoon sugar, 1 teaspoon ground cumin, and 1 teaspoon chili powder before baking.

braised cabbage with spicy croutons

prep: 10 minutes **cook:** 15 minutes **makes:** 6 to 8 servings

2 tablespoons olive oil
1 tablespoon butter
⅓ of a 12-ounce loaf baguette-style French bread, torn into coarse pieces (2 cups)
¼ teaspoon garlic powder
¼ teaspoon crushed red pepper
1 small head green cabbage, cut into 6 wedges
Salt
Ground black pepper
½ cup water
Snipped fresh parsley
Lemon wedges

1 For croutons, in an extra-large skillet heat 1 tablespoon of the oil and the butter over medium-high heat. Add bread pieces, garlic powder, and crushed red pepper; cook and stir for 3 to 5 minutes or until golden brown. Using a slotted spoon, remove croutons from skillet; cool on paper towels.

2 Add cabbage to skillet, overlapping wedges if necessary. Sprinkle with salt and pepper. Add the water. Bring to boiling; reduce heat. Simmer, covered, about 15 minutes or until cabbage is tender.

3 Arrange cabbage on a serving platter; drizzle with the remaining 1 tablespoon oil. Top with croutons and parsley and serve with lemon wedges.

nutrition facts per serving: 141 cal., 7 g total fat (2 g sat. fat), 5 mg chol., 254 mg sodium, 19 g carb., 4 g dietary fiber, 4 g protein.

roasted potato salad with chutney dressing

prep: 20 minutes   roast: 25 minutes   oven: 425°F   makes: 8 to 10 servings

3   medium potatoes, cut into ¾ - to 1-inch pieces
3   tablespoons olive oil
½   teaspoon kosher salt or salt
¼   teaspoon cayenne pepper (optional)
½   cup mango chutney
1   to 2 tablespoons lemon juice
1   teaspoon curry powder
2   cups lightly packed fresh baby spinach
    Pine nuts, toasted (optional)

1 Preheat oven to 425°F. Place potatoes in a 13×9×2-inch baking pan. Drizzle with 2 tablespoons of the oil. Sprinkle with salt and cayenne pepper (if using); toss gently to coat. Roast, uncovered, for 25 to 30 minutes or until potatoes are tender, stirring occasionally.

2 Meanwhile, for chutney dressing, snip any large pieces of fruit in chutney. In a small bowl combine chutney, the remaining 1 tablespoon oil, lemon juice, and curry powder.

3 Pour half of the chutney dressing over hot potatoes; toss gently to coat. Add spinach to hot potato mixture; toss gently to combine. If desired, sprinkle with pine nuts. Serve with the remaining chutney dressing.

nutrition facts per serving: 125 cal., 5 g total fat (1 g sat. fat), 0 mg chol., 264 mg sodium, 18 g carb., 1 g dietary fiber, 1 g protein.

Peanut oil, with its high proportion of monounsaturated fats, helps lower cholesterol.

skillet-roasted
vegetables

prep: 20 minutes **cook:** 22 minutes **makes:** 6 servings

8   ounces assorted
    baby beets
8   ounces tiny new
    potatoes and/or
    small fingerling
    potatoes, quartered
1   small sweet potato,
    peeled and cut into
    thin wedges
2   to 3 tablespoons
    peanut oil
1   cup sugar snap pea
    pods or snow pea
    pods, trimmed
    (if desired)
¼   teaspoon salt
⅛   teaspoon freshly
    ground black pepper
¼   cup snipped fresh
    cilantro or Italian
    (flat-leaf) parsley
2   tablespoons lemon
    juice
    Lemon wedges

1 Trim and halve beets; reserve ½ cup of the beet greens.

2 In a covered 12-inch skillet cook beets, potatoes, and sweet potato in hot oil over medium heat for 10 minutes, turning occasionally. Uncover and cook for 10 to 15 minutes more or until vegetables are tender and brown on all sides, turning occasionally. Add pea pods; sprinkle with salt and pepper. Cook, covered, for 2 to 3 minutes more or until pea pods are crisp-tender.

3 Add the reserved ½ cup beet greens, cilantro, and lemon juice to vegetables; toss gently to coat. Serve with lemon wedges.

nutrition facts per serving: 116 cal., 5 g total fat (1 g sat. fat), 0 mg chol., 146 mg sodium, 17 g carb., 3 g dietary fiber, 2 g protein.

nutrition note

Potatoes can be nutritional workhorses, depending on how you prepare them. Serve them skin-on and hold the fat; in return, you'll be rewarded with an abundance of potassium, niacin, magnesium, vitamin C, and fiber.

roasted potatoes and tomatoes

prep: 15 minutes **roast:** 25 minutes **oven:** 450°F **makes:** 8 servings

1 pound tiny new
   potatoes (10 to 12),
   quartered
2 tablespoons olive oil
2 teaspoons snipped
   fresh oregano or
   ½ teaspoon dried
   oregano, crushed
¼ teaspoon salt
¼ teaspoon ground
   black pepper
4 roma tomatoes,
   quartered
   lengthwise
½ cup pitted kalamata
   olives
3 cloves garlic, minced
¼ cup grated Parmesan
   cheese

1 Preheat oven to 450°F. Lightly grease a 15×10×1-inch baking pan; spread potatoes in pan. In a small bowl combine oil, oregano, salt, and pepper. Drizzle oil mixture over potatoes; toss gently to coat.

2 Roast, uncovered, for 20 minutes, stirring once. Stir in tomatoes, olives, and garlic. Roast, uncovered, for 5 to 10 minutes more or until potatoes are tender and brown on the edges and tomatoes are softened. Transfer to a serving dish. Sprinkle with cheese.

nutrition facts per serving: 102 cal., 5 g total fat (1 g sat. fat), 2 mg chol., 208 mg sodium, 11 g carb., 2 g dietary fiber, 3 g protein.

roasted root vegetables

prep: 15 minutes roast: 35 minutes oven: 425°F makes: 6 servings

8   ounces Yukon gold or round red potatoes, cut into 1-inch wedges
2   medium parsnips, peeled and cut into 1-inch pieces
2   medium carrots, peeled and cut into 1-inch pieces
1   medium sweet potato, peeled and cut into 1½-inch pieces
1   small red onion, cut into 1-inch wedges
1   tablespoon canola oil
½   teaspoon salt
2   tablespoons light mayonnaise or salad dressing
1   tablespoon Dijon-style mustard
1   tablespoon cider vinegar
1   tablespoon water
¼   teaspoon celery seeds (optional)

1 Preheat oven to 425°F. In a large roasting pan combine potatoes, parsnips, carrots, sweet potato, and red onion. Drizzle with oil. Sprinkle with salt; toss gently to coat. Roast, uncovered, for 35 to 45 minutes or until vegetables are tender and starting to brown, stirring occasionally.

2 In a small bowl stir together mayonnaise, mustard, vinegar, the water, and, if desired, celery seeds. Pour mayonnaise mixture over vegetables; toss gently to coat. Serve warm.

nutrition facts per serving: 117 cal., 4 g total fat (0 g sat. fat), 2 mg chol., 318 mg sodium, 19 g carb., 3 g dietary fiber, 2 g protein.

nutrition note

French women are known for eating well, yet maintaining their figures. Maybe one small part of their secret is their liberal use of Dijon mustard, which gives foods loads of flavor with very few calories.

smoky gouda–sauced broccoli

prep: 20 minutes **bake:** 15 minutes **oven:** 425°F **makes:** 6 servings

1¼	pounds broccoli, cut into spears
1	tablespoon butter
½	cup chopped onion (1 medium)
2	cloves garlic, minced
2	tablespoons all purpose flour
¼	teaspoon salt
⅛	teaspoon ground black pepper
1½	cups low-fat milk
¾	cup shredded smoked Gouda cheese (3 ounces)
¾	cup soft bread crumbs (1 slice)
2	teaspoons butter, melted

1 Preheat oven to 425°F. Place broccoli in a steamer basket. Place basket in a large saucepan over 1 inch of boiling water. Steam, covered, for 6 to 8 minutes or just until tender.

2 Meanwhile, for sauce, in a medium saucepan heat 1 tablespoon butter over medium heat until melted. Add onion and garlic; cook until onion is tender, stirring occasionally. Stir in flour, salt, and pepper. Gradually stir in milk; cook and stir until thickened and bubbly. Gradually add cheese, stirring until melted.

3 Transfer broccoli to an ungreased 1½ quart au gratin dish or 2-quart square baking dish. Pour sauce over broccoli. In a small bowl combine bread crumbs and 2 teaspoons melted butter; sprinkle over sauce. Bake about 15 minutes or until crumbs are golden brown.

nutrition facts per serving: 145 cal., 8 g total fat (5 g sat. fat), 23 mg chol., 429 mg sodium, 13 g carb., 2 g dietary fiber, 7 g protein.

nutrition note

Eating broccoli is all about the bones. This veggie contains calcium and vitamin C, which both help strengthen and maintain bones and teeth.

fresh corn salad with
summer herbs

prep: 20 minutes **stand:** 30 minutes **makes:** 4 servings

4   ears of corn, husks
    and silks removed
3   tablespoons snipped
    fresh herbs, such
    as chives, sage,
    oregano, cilantro,
    parsley, and/or basil
2   tablespoons chopped
    red onion or shallot
    (1 medium)
1   tablespoon olive oil
2   teaspoons red wine
    vinegar or other
    vinegar
¼   teaspoon sea salt or
    salt
⅛   teaspoon freshly
    ground black
    pepper
⅛   teaspoon crushed red
    pepper

1 Holding each ear at an angle, use a sharp
knife to cut down the length of the corn
cob, cutting off corn in planks. Place corn in a
medium bowl. Stir in herbs, onion, oil, vinegar,
salt, black pepper, and crushed red pepper.
Let stand at room temperature for 30 minutes
before serving.

nutrition facts per serving: 110 cal., 4 g total fat
(1 g sat. fat), 0 mg chol., 114 mg sodium, 18 g carb.,
3 g dietary fiber, 3 g protein.

spicy green stir-fry with peanuts

start to finish: 25 minutes **makes:** 4 servings

¼   cup cold water
1   tablespoon light
        teriyaki sauce
½   teaspoon cornstarch
2   teaspoons peanut
        oil or toasted
        sesame oil
1   teaspoon grated fresh
        ginger
½   cup lightly salted
        peanuts
⅛   teaspoon cayenne
        pepper or crushed
        red pepper
4   ounces fresh green
        beans, trimmed
        (if desired) (about
        ¾ cup)
½   of a large green or
        red sweet pepper,
        seeded and cut into
        thin bite-size strips
⅓   cup frozen shelled
        sweet soybeans
        (edamame), thawed
1   clove garlic, minced
2   baby bok choy,
        separated into
        leaves, or 3 cups
        coarsely shredded
        napa cabbage

1 For sauce, in a small bowl stir together the water, teriyaki sauce, and cornstarch; set aside.

2 Pour 1 teaspoon of the oil into a wok or large nonstick skillet; heat wok over medium-high heat. Add ginger; cook and stir for 15 seconds. Add peanuts; cook and stir for 30 seconds. Transfer peanut mixture to a small bowl. Immediately sprinkle with cayenne pepper; toss gently to coat.

3 Add the remaining 1 teaspoon oil to wok. Add green beans; cook and stir for 3 minutes. Add sweet pepper, edamame, and garlic; cook and stir for 3 to 5 minutes or until vegetables are crisp-tender. Stir sauce; add to vegetables in wok. Cook and stir until thickened and bubbly. Cook and stir for 2 minutes more. Stir in bok choy. Top with peanut mixture.

nutrition facts per serving: 130 cal., 9 g total fat (1 g sat. fat), 0 mg chol., 142 mg sodium, 8 g carb., 3 g dietary fiber, 6 g protein.

Fresh, sweet, crisp pear is tossed with walnuts for a great-tasting salad that is high in fiber and antioxidants.

pear-walnut salad

start to finish: 15 minutes **makes:** 2 servings

3 tablespoons pear
nectar
1 tablespoon seasoned
rice vinegar
2 teaspoons olive oil
⅛ teaspoon coarse
ground black
pepper
2 cups torn mixed salad
greens
½ of a medium pear,
cored and thinly
sliced (about ½ cup)
¼ of a small red onion,
thinly sliced and
separated into rings
2 tablespoons broken
walnuts, toasted

1 For vinaigrette, in a small bowl whisk together nectar, vinegar, oil, and pepper; set aside.

2 Divide mixed greens between salad plates. Top with pear, red onion, and walnuts; drizzle with vinaigrette.

nutrition facts per serving: 143 cal., 9 g total fat
(1 g sat. fat), 0 mg chol., 36 mg sodium, 15 g carb.,
3 g dietary fiber, 2 g protein.

spinach-berry salad

start to finish: 15 minutes **makes:** 8 servings

⅓ cup bottled reduced-calorie raspberry vinaigrette salad dressing

1 teaspoon finely shredded orange peel

1 tablespoon orange juice

8 cups packaged fresh baby spinach or torn mixed salad greens

3 cups sliced fresh strawberries and/or whole fresh blueberries

¼ cup coarsely chopped pecans, toasted

1 For dressing, in a small bowl stir together raspberry vinaigrette, orange peel, and orange juice; set aside

2 Divide spinach and strawberries and/or blueberries among salad plates. Drizzle with dressing and sprinkle with pecans.

nutrition facts per serving: 72 cal., 4 g total fat (0 g sat. fat), 0 mg chol., 34 mg sodium, 10 g carb., 2 g dietary fiber, 2 g protein.

sides **and snacks**

quick

lower sodium

dilled apple coleslaw

prep: 20 minutes   chill: 2 to 48 hours   makes: 12 servings

⅔   cup light mayonnaise or
     salad dressing
3   tablespoons cider vinegar
1   tablespoon snipped fresh
     dill or 1 teaspoon dried dill
½   teaspoon salt
½   teaspoon coarse ground
     black pepper
7   cups shredded green cabbage
3   cups thinly sliced apples
     (3 medium)
1   cup chopped sweet onion
     (1 large)
     Fresh dill sprigs (optional)

1 In an extra-large bowl stir together mayonnaise, vinegar, snipped or dried dill, salt, and pepper. Stir in cabbage, apples, and onion.

2 Cover and chill for 2 to 48 hours. If desired, garnish with dill sprigs.

nutrition facts per serving: 78 cal., 5 g total fat (1 g sat. fat), 5 mg chol., 195 mg sodium, 10 g carb., 2 g dietary fiber, 1 g protein.

greek vegetable salad

start to finish: 30 minutes   makes: 8 servings

2   cups chopped tomatoes
     (4 medium)
1   cup chopped cucumber
½   cup chopped yellow, red,
     and/or green sweet
     pepper (1 small)
¼   cup chopped red onion
1½   teaspoons snipped fresh
     thyme or ½ teaspoon
     dried thyme, crushed
1   teaspoon snipped fresh
     oregano or ¼ teaspoon
     dried oregano, crushed
2   tablespoons white balsamic
     vinegar or regular
     balsamic vinegar
2   tablespoons olive oil
     Leaf lettuce (optional)
½   cup crumbled reduced-fat
     feta cheese (2 ounces)

1 In a large bowl combine tomatoes, cucumber, sweet pepper, red onion, thyme, and oregano. For dressing, in a small bowl whisk together vinegar and oil. Pour dressing over vegetable mixture; toss gently to coat.

2 Line a serving bowl with lettuce (if using). Spoon vegetable mixture into serving bowl. Sprinkle with cheese.

nutrition facts per serving: 65 cal., 5 g total fat (1 g sat. fat), 3 mg chol., 120 mg sodium, 4 g carb., 1 g dietary fiber, 2 g protein.

Dilled Apple
Coleslaw

You won't believe this delicious salad fits into your slim-down plan. The lemon yogurt is key to the refreshing dressing. So much flavor, so few calories.

lightened **waldorf** salad

start to finish: 25 minutes **makes:** 6 to 8 servings

2 cups cubed fresh
pineapple or one
15.25-ounce can
pineapple chunks
(juice pack), drained

1⅓ cups coarsely
chopped apples
and/or pears
(2 medium)

½ cup thinly sliced
celery (1 stalk)

½ cup halved seedless
red grapes

2 kiwifruits, peeled,
halved lengthwise,
and sliced

⅓ cup fat-free
mayonnaise
dressing or salad
dressing

⅓ cup lemon fat-free or
low-fat yogurt

1 tablespoon honey

2 tablespoons broken
walnuts, toasted*

1 In a large bowl combine pineapple, apples and/or pears, celery, grapes, and kiwifruits.

2 For dressing, in a small bowl stir together mayonnaise dressing, yogurt, and honey. Gently fold into fruit mixture. If desired, cover and chill for up to 6 hours.

3 Before serving, stir in walnuts.

nutrition facts per serving: 147 cal., 3 g total fat (1 g sat. fat), 4 mg chol., 142 mg sodium, 29 g carb., 3 g dietary fiber, 2 g protein.

*tip: To toast walnuts, place the nuts in a small skillet. Cook over medium heat for 5 to 7 minutes or until golden brown, stirring frequently.

italian cheese twists

prep: 30 minutes bake: 10 minutes per batch oven: 400°F
makes: about 50 twists

1 cup shredded Italian
cheese blend
(4 ounces)
⅓ cup pine nuts,
toasted and finely
chopped
1 teaspoon dried Italian
seasoning, crushed
1 17.3-ounce package
(2 sheets) frozen
puff pastry sheets,
thawed
2 tablespoons butter,
melted

1 Preheat oven to 400°F. Line a baking sheet with parchment paper; set aside. In a medium bowl combine cheese, pine nuts, and Italian seasoning. Unfold one pastry sheet on a lightly floured surface. Brush with melted butter; sprinkle evenly with cheese mixture. Unfold the remaining pastry sheet and place on top of cheese mixture; press edges lightly to seal. Roll into a 14-inch square.

2 Cut in half to make two 14x7-inch rectangles. Cut each rectangle crosswise into 7x½-inch strips. Gently press down on each strip and twist two or three times. Place on the prepared baking sheet.

3 Bake for 10 to 12 minutes or until light brown and crisp. Serve warm or at room temperature. Serve same day as prepared.

nutrition facts per twist: 71 cal., 5 g total fat (2 g sat. fat), 3 mg chol., 42 mg sodium, 5 g carb., 0 g dietary fiber, 2 g protein.

sides **and snacks**

layered greek hummus

prep: 20 minutes chill: 2 to 24 hours makes: about 2½ cups

1 8-ounce package
    reduced-fat cream
    cheese, softened
1 tablespoon lemon
    juice
3 cloves garlic, minced
1 teaspoon dried Italian
    seasoning, crushed
1½ cups purchased
    hummus
1 cup chopped
    tomatoes
    (2 medium)
1 cup chopped
    cucumber
½ cup chopped pitted
    kalamata olives
½ cup crumbled
    reduced-fat feta
    cheese (2 ounces)
⅓ cup sliced green
    onions
    Reduced-fat pita
    chips, multigrain
    tortilla chips, carrot
    sticks, and/or sweet
    pepper strips

1 In a medium bowl combine cream cheese, lemon juice, garlic, and Italian seasoning. Beat with an electric mixer on medium speed until smooth.

2 Spread cream cheese mixture into the bottom of a shallow serving dish, 9-inch deep-dish pie plate, or 8-inch quiche dish. Spread hummus evenly over cream cheese mixture. Layer with tomatoes, cucumber, olives, feta cheese, and green onions. Cover and chill for 2 to 24 hours.

3 Serve dip with chips and/or vegetables.

nutrition facts per 2 tablespoons dip: 78 cal., 5 g total fat (2 g sat. fat), 9 mg chol., 168 mg sodium, 5 g carb., 1 g dietary fiber, 3 g protein.

crisp apple salsa

start to finish: 25 minutes makes: 3 cups

1 medium Granny
  Smith apple, cored
  and quartered
1 medium red cooking
  apple, cored and
  quartered
1 medium onion,
  quartered
2 fresh jalapeño chile
  peppers, seeded
  and quartered*
6 cloves garlic, minced
1 14.5-ounce can petite
  diced tomatoes,
  drained
2 tablespoons lime
  juice
1 teaspoon ground
  cumin
½ teaspoon salt
  Scoop-shape tortilla
  chips or corn chips

1 In a food processor combine apples, onion, jalapeño chile peppers, and garlic. Cover and process with several on/off pulses until chopped. (Or finely chop apples, onion, and jalapeño peppers by hand.) Transfer mixture to a serving bowl. Stir in tomatoes, lime juice, cumin, and salt.

2 If desired, cover and chill for up to 4 hours. Serve salsa with tortilla chips.

nutrition facts per 2 tablespoons salsa: 13 cal., 0 g total fat (0 g sat. fat), 0 mg chol., 83 mg sodium, 3 g carb., 1 g dietary fiber, 0 g protein.

*tip: Because chile peppers contain volatile oils that can burn your skin and eyes, avoid direct contact with them as much as possible. When working with chile peppers, wear plastic or rubber gloves. If your bare hands do touch the peppers, wash your hands and nails well with soap and warm water.

You have lots of options with these bars. You can use dried cherries or chocolate chips in place of the raisins and almonds or cashews in place of the mixed nuts.

granola bars

prep: 20 minutes **bake:** 25 minutes **oven:** 325°F **makes:** 24 bars

Nonstick cooking spray
1 cup low-fat granola
1 cup regular or quick-cooking rolled oats
½ cup mixed nuts
½ cup all-purpose flour
⅓ cup raisins
1 egg, lightly beaten
3 tablespoons packed brown sugar
3 tablespoons vegetable oil
3 tablespoons honey
½ teaspoon ground cinnamon

1 Preheat oven to 325°F. Line an 8×8×2-inch baking pan with foil, extending the foil over edges of pan. Coat foil with cooking spray; set pan aside.

2 In a large bowl combine granola, oats, nuts, flour, and raisins. In a small bowl combine egg, brown sugar, oil, honey, and cinnamon. Add honey mixture all at once to granola mixture; stir gently to coat. Press mixture evenly into the prepared baking pan.

3 Bake for 25 to 30 minutes or until light brown around the edges. Cool in pan on a wire rack. Using the edges of the foil, lift uncut bars out of pan. Cut into bars.

nutrition facts per bar: 99 cal., 4 g total fat (1 g sat. fat), 9 mg chol., 14 mg sodium, 15 g carb., 1 g dietary fiber, 2 g protein.

cranberry-orange
caramel corn

prep: 20 minutes bake: 30 minutes oven: 275°F makes: 20 (½-cup) servings

12 cups popped popcorn
1 cup dried cranberries
½ cup whole almonds
½ cup butter
½ cup packed brown sugar
¼ cup light-color corn syrup
2 tablespoons orange juice
2 teaspoons vanilla
½ teaspoon baking soda

1 Preheat oven to 275°F. Remove all unpopped kernels from popped popcorn. In an extra-large bowl combine popcorn, dried cranberries, and almonds; set aside.

2 Butter a large piece of foil; set aside. In a medium saucepan combine ½ cup butter, brown sugar, and corn syrup. Cook and stir over medium heat until butter is melted. Stir in orange juice. Bring to boiling over medium heat. Boil at a moderate, steady rate, without stirring, for 2 minutes. Remove from heat. Stir in vanilla and baking soda (mixture will foam up).

3 Pour butter mixture over popcorn mixture; stir gently to coat. Transfer to a 15×10×1-inch baking pan or shallow roasting pan. Bake for 30 minutes, stirring twice. Spread caramel corn on the prepared foil; cool.

nutrition facts per serving: 130 cal., 7 g total fat (3 g sat. fat), 12 mg chol., 68 mg sodium, 17 g carb., 1 g dietary fiber, 1 g protein.

sweet 'n' salty snack mix

start to finish: 10 minutes makes: 6 (½-cup) servings

1 cup round toasted oat cereal with nuts and honey
¾ cup fish-shape whole grain cheese crackers
½ cup honey-wheat braided pretzel twists, broken into bite-size pieces
½ cup semisweet or dark chocolate pieces

1 In a large bowl combine cereal, crackers, pretzels, and chocolate pieces.

nutrition facts per ½ cup: 129 cal., 6 g total fat (3 g sat. fat), 2 mg chol., 146 mg sodium, 20 g carb., 1 g dietary fiber, 2 g protein.

nutrition note
Keep a healthy snack at your fingertips, while keeping track of your calorie intake. Portion out snack foods into single-serving containers that can travel with you wherever you go.

Cranberry-Orange
Caramel Corn

quick

lower
sodium

178

sides **and snacks**

quick

high
fiber

fruit and veggie smoothies

start to finish: 10 minutes **makes:** 4 (about 10-ounce) servings

2 cups ice cubes
2 cups light peach-
mango fruit juice
1 medium peach,
halved and pitted
1 medium banana
2 leaves Swiss chard,
ribs removed
Mango wedges
(optional)

1 In a blender combine ice cubes, fruit juice, peach, banana, and Swiss chard. Cover and blend until smooth. Serve immediately. If desired, garnish each serving with a mango wedge.

nutrition facts per serving: 68 cal., 0 g total fat (0 g sat. fat), 0 mg chol., 41 mg sodium, 17 g carb., 1 g dietary fiber, 1 g protein.

pb and b pinwheels

start to finish: 15 minutes **makes:** 4 servings

¼ cup plain fat-free
yogurt
2 tablespoons peanut
butter
4 6-inch whole wheat
flour tortillas
¾ cup fresh raspberries
and/or chopped
fresh strawberries

1 In a small bowl stir together yogurt and peanut butter. Spread tortillas with yogurt mixture. Top with raspberries and/or strawberries; roll up tortillas.

2 Trim ends of each tortilla roll; cut roll into 1-inch slices.

nutrition facts per serving: 118 cal., 6 g total fat (1 g sat. fat), 0 mg chol., 229 mg sodium, 16 g carb., 10 g dietary fiber, 8 g protein.

make-ahead directions: Prepare as directed in Step 1. Wrap each tortilla roll in plastic wrap and chill for up to 3 hours. Serve as directed.

blue cheese–apricot bites

start to finish: 25 minutes **makes:** 16 servings

2 teaspoons butter
2 tablespoons finely
   chopped walnuts
2 teaspoons sugar
½ teaspoon finely
   snipped fresh
   rosemary or
   ¼ teaspoon dried
   rosemary, finely
   crushed
¼ cup crumbled blue
   cheese (1 ounce)
2 tablespoons cream
   cheese
16 dried apricot halves
   Snipped fresh
   rosemary (optional)

1 Line a baking sheet with foil; set aside. In a small skillet heat butter over medium heat until melted. Add walnuts and sugar; cook and stir for 2 to 3 minutes or until walnuts are light brown. Stir in ½ teaspoon rosemary. Cook and stir for 30 seconds more. Transfer nuts to the prepared baking sheet; cool.

2 Meanwhile, in a small bowl combine blue cheese and cream cheese. Beat with an electric mixer on medium speed until smooth.

3 Spoon cheese mixture onto apricot halves. Sprinkle with nut mixture. If desired, garnish with additional fresh rosemary.

nutrition facts per serving: 30 cal., 2 g total fat (1 g sat. fat), 3 mg chol., 31 mg sodium, 3 g carb., 0 g dietary fiber, 1 g protein.

crunch-coated bananas

start to finish: 20 minutes **makes:** 6 servings

⅓ cup cornflakes,
    coarsely crushed
2 tablespoons flaked
    coconut
2 tablespoons vanilla
    fat-free yogurt
2 tablespoons peanut
    butter
2 small bananas (each
    about 5 ounces or
    about 6 inches long)

1 In a small skillet combine cornflakes and coconut; cook and stir over medium heat for 2 to 3 minutes or until coconut starts to brown. Remove from heat. In a small bowl stir together yogurt and peanut butter; set aside.

2 Cut each banana into six 1-inch pieces. Spread peanut butter mixture on banana pieces. Roll pieces in cornflake mixture.

nutrition facts per serving: 78 cal., 4 g total fat (1 g sat. fat), 0 mg chol., 45 mg sodium, 11 g carb., 1 g dietary fiber, 2 g protein.

nutrition note

Step away from the screen! It's easy to overeat while watching television or working on the computer, so take a break. When snacking, slow down and savor each bite.

chicken salad
with apple slices

start to finish: 15 minutes **makes:** 6 servings

2   tablespoons light
    cream cheese
    spread with garden
    vegetables
2   tablespoons light
    mayonnaise or
    salad dressing
1   teaspoon cider
    vinegar
¼   teaspoon ground
    black pepper
9   ounces refrigerated
    cooked chicken
    breast strips, cut
    into bite size pieces
    (about 2 cups)
½   cup chopped celery
    (1 stalk)
¼   cup dried cranberries
3   cups thinly sliced
    apples (3 medium)

1 In a medium bowl combine cream cheese,
mayonnaise, vinegar, and pepper. Stir in
chicken, celery, and dried cranberries.

2 If desired, cover and chill for up to 24 hours.
Serve with apple slices.

nutrition facts per serving: 125 cal., 3 g total fat
(1 g sat. fat), 27 mg chol., 201 mg sodium, 15 g carb.,
2 g dietary fiber, 12 g protein.

Choose from this tasty
toothsome tribe—you'll
find the best friend your
fork will ever have.

meat

and
poul

7

try

beef sirloin tips with smoky pepper sauce

start to finish: 30 minutes makes: 4 servings

1¼ pounds boneless beef tri-tip steak (bottom sirloin)

½ teaspoon smoked paprika or regular paprika

1 tablespoon vegetable oil

1 12- to 16-ounce jar roasted red and/ or yellow sweet peppers

½ cup hickory- or mesquite-flavor barbecue sauce

¼ cup coarsely snipped fresh Italian (flat-leaf) parsley

1 Trim fat from meat. Cut meat into 1- to 1½-inch pieces; sprinkle with paprika. In an extra-large skillet cook meat in hot oil over medium-high heat until brown. Remove from skillet.

2 Meanwhile, drain roasted peppers, reserving liquid. Chop peppers. Measure ½ cup of the reserved liquid (if necessary, add enough water to equal ½ cup).

3 Add roasted peppers and the reserved liquid to skillet. Stir in barbecue sauce. Cook, uncovered, for 5 to 10 minutes or until mixture is slightly thickened, stirring frequently. Return meat to skillet; heat through. Sprinkle with parsley.

nutrition facts per serving: 318 cal., 16 g total fat (5 g sat. fat), 91 mg chol., 494 mg sodium, 13 g carb., 2 g dietary fiber, 30 g protein.

nutrition note

To seize the most iron out of your meat, pair it with sweet peppers. They're rich in vitamin C, which helps your body absorb iron.

skillet meat loaf

prep: 25 minutes   cook: 35 minutes   makes: 8 servings

1   egg, lightly beaten
1½ cups soft bread
     crumbs (2 slices)
⅔   cup chopped
     green onions
¼   cup milk
2   teaspoons
     Worcestershire sauce
½   teaspoon salt
½   teaspoon ground
     black pepper
⅛   teaspoon garlic
     powder
1½ pounds lean
     ground beef
1   14-ounce can
     beef broth
½   teaspoon ground sage
1   1½-pound butternut
     squash, peeled,
     seeded, and cut into
     1-inch pieces
1   pound potatoes, cut
     into 2-inch pieces

1 In a large bowl combine egg, bread crumbs, green onions, milk, Worcestershire sauce, salt, pepper, and garlic powder. Add ground beef; mix well. Divide meat mixture in half; shape into two 6x3-inch loaves.

2 Heat a large nonstick skillet over medium-high heat for 2 minutes. Place meat loaves in hot skillet; cook about 6 minutes or until brown on all sides. Drain off fat.

3 Add broth and sage to skillet; add squash and potatoes. Bring to boiling; reduce heat to medium low. Cook, covered, about 35 minutes or until temperature of the meat reaches 160°F and squash and potatoes are tender.

nutrition facts per serving: 310 cal., 14 g total fat (5 g sat. fat), 85 mg chol., 476 mg sodium, 24 g carb., 3 g dietary fiber, 20 g protein.

Flank steak is among the leanest, most flavorful cuts of beef. It takes very nicely to a teriyaki-style treatment. Serve it with hot cooked rice and a mélange of colorful sliced sweet peppers.

flank steak
teriyaki

prep: 20 minutes marinate: 4 to 24 hours broil: 17 minutes makes: 4 servings

1	pound beef flank steak
¼	cup reduced-sodium soy sauce
¼	cup chopped green onions (2)
3	tablespoons dry sherry or lower-sodium beef broth
2	tablespoons olive oil
1	clove garlic, minced
¼	teaspoon ground ginger
⅛	teaspoon ground black pepper

1 Trim fat from meat. Score both sides of meat in a diamond pattern by making shallow diagonal cuts at 1-inch intervals. Place meat in a resealable plastic bag set in a shallow dish. For marinade, in small bowl combine soy sauce, green onions, sherry, oil, garlic, ginger, and pepper. Pour marinade over meat. Seal bag; turn to coat meat. Marinate in the refrigerator for 4 to 24 hours, turning bag occasionally.

2 Preheat broiler. Drain meat, discarding marinade. Pat meat dry with paper towels. Place meat on the unheated rack of a broiler pan. Broil 3 to 4 inches from the heat for 17 to 21 minutes or until medium (160°F), turning once halfway through broiling.

3 Thinly slice steak diagonally across the grain.

nutrition facts per serving: 209 cal., 10 g total fat (3 g sat. fat), 47 mg chol., 343 mg sodium, 1 g carb., 0 g dietary fiber, 25 g protein.

chicken teriyaki: Prepare as directed, except substitute 4 skinless, boneless chicken breast halves (about 1¼ pounds total) for the flank steak. Broil chicken 4 to 5 inches from the heat for 12 to 15 minutes or until no longer pink (170°F), turning once halfway through broiling.

per serving: 200 cal., 5 g total fat (1 g sat. fat), 82 mg chol., 343 mg sodium, 1 g carb., 0 g dietary fiber, 33 g protein.

flank steak with mushrooms

prep: 25 minutes   marinate: 1 hour   broil: 17 minutes   makes: 6 servings

1½   pounds beef
        flank steak
¾   cup dry red wine
1   tablespoon
        sherry vinegar or
        red wine vinegar
1   tablespoon
        finely shredded
        orange peel
¼   teaspoon fennel
        seeds, crushed
¼   cup chopped shallots
        (2 medium)
2   cloves garlic, minced
1   tablespoon butter
3   cups sliced fresh
        cremini, oyster,
        and/or button
        mushrooms
        (8 ounces)
1   tablespoon
        cornstarch
¾   cup beef broth
       Salt
       Ground black pepper

1 Trim fat from meat. Score both sides of meat in a diamond pattern by making shallow diagonal cuts at 1-inch intervals. Place meat in a resealable plastic bag set in a shallow dish. For marinade, in small bowl combine wine, vinegar, orange peel, and fennel seeds. Pour marinade over meat. Seal bag; turn to coat meat. Marinate in the refrigerator for 1 hour, turning bag once or twice.

2 Preheat broiler. Drain meat, reserving ⅓ cup of the marinade. Place meat on the unheated rack of a broiler pan. Broil 3 to 4 inches from the heat for 17 to 21 minutes for medium (160°F), turning once halfway through broiling.

3 Meanwhile, for mushroom sauce, in a medium saucepan cook shallots and garlic in hot butter over medium heat for 2 minutes, stirring occasionally. Add mushrooms; cook and stir until tender. In a small bowl combine the ⅓ cup reserved marinade and cornstarch; stir into mushroom mixture. Add broth; cook and stir until thickened and bubbly. Cook and stir for 2 minutes more. Season to taste with salt and pepper.

4 Thinly slice meat diagonally across the grain. Serve with mushroom sauce.

nutrition facts per serving: 240 cal., 9 g total fat (4 g sat. fat), 53 mg chol., 291 mg sodium, 6 g carb., 1 g dietary fiber, 27 g protein.

steak with grapes

prep: 30 minutes broil: 15 minutes makes: 4 servings

2 tablespoons olive oil
1 large sweet onion,
   halved and
   thinly sliced
2 cups fresh button
   mushrooms,
   thickly sliced
2 cloves garlic, minced
⅔ cup beef broth
⅓ cup dry red wine or
   cranberry juice
1 cup red seedless
   grapes, halved
1 tablespoon snipped
   fresh thyme
1¼ pounds boneless beef
   top sirloin steak, cut
   1 inch thick
½ teaspoon cracked
   black pepper
¼ teaspoon sea salt
   or salt

1 Preheat broiler. For mushroom sauce, in a large nonstick skillet heat oil over medium heat. Add onion; reduce heat to medium-low. Cook, covered, for 10 to 12 minutes or just until onion is tender, stirring occasionally. Add mushrooms and garlic; cook, covered, about 5 minutes more or until onion is golden brown and mushrooms are tender, stirring occasionally.

2 Carefully stir in broth and wine. Bring to boiling; reduce heat. Boil gently, uncovered, about 6 minutes or until liquid is slightly reduced. Stir in grapes and thyme. Remove from heat; cover and keep warm.

3 Meanwhile, trim fat from meat. Cut meat into four serving-size pieces; sprinkle with pepper and salt. Place meat on the unheated rack of a broiler pan. Broil 3 to 4 inches from the heat for 15 to 17 minutes for medium-rare (145°F) or 20 to 22 minutes for medium (160°F), turning once halfway through broiling. Serve meat with mushroom sauce.

nutrition facts per serving: 277 cal., 7 g total fat (2 g sat. fat), 67 mg chol., 336 mg sodium, 16 g carb., 2 g dietary fiber, 34 g protein.

grilled steak fajitas

prep: 25 minutes grill: 20 minutes makes: 4 servings

3 green, yellow, and/or red sweet peppers, seeded and cut into strips
1 medium onion, sliced
1 tablespoon olive oil
1½ teaspoons fajita seasoning
1 clove garlic, minced
1 pound boneless beef top sirloin steak, cut 1 inch thick
4 8-inch whole wheat flour tortillas
Salsa (optional)
Sour cream (optional)

1 Fold a 36×18-inch piece of heavy foil in half to make an 18-inch square. Place sweet peppers and onion in the center of foil. Drizzle with oil; sprinkle with ½ teaspoon of the fajita seasoning and the garlic. Bring up two opposite edges of foil; seal with a double fold. Fold the remaining ends to completely enclose vegetables, leaving space for steam to build; set aside.

2 Trim fat from meat. Sprinkle the remaining 1 teaspoon fajita seasoning evenly over both sides of meat; rub in with your fingers.

3 For a charcoal grill, place meat and vegetable packet on the rack of an uncovered grill directly over medium coals. Grill until meat is desired doneness and vegetables are tender, turning once halfway through grilling. Allow 14 to 18 minutes for medium rare (145°F) or 18 to 22 minutes for medium (160°F); for vegetables, allow about 20 minutes. (For a gas grill, preheat grill. Reduce heat to medium. Place meat and vegetable packet on grill rack over heat. Cover and grill as above.)

4 Meanwhile, stack tortillas and wrap in foil. While meat and vegetables are grilling, add tortilla packet to grill. Grill about 10 minutes or until heated through.

5 Cut meat into thin bite-size strips. Divide meat among tortillas; top with vegetables. Roll up tortillas. If desired, serve with salsa and sour cream.

nutrition facts per serving: 333 cal., 12 g total fat (3 g sat. fat), 69 mg chol., 454 mg sodium, 22 g carb., 12 g dietary fiber, 33 g protein.

chicken with olives

prep: 25 minutes cook: 13 minutes makes: 4 servings

4   skinless, boneless
    chicken breast
    halves (about
    1¼ pounds total)
1   tablespoon olive oil
1   medium onion, sliced
2   cloves garlic, minced
1   15-ounce can
    no-salt-added
    crushed tomatoes
1   5.75-ounce jar
    sliced pitted green
    olives, drained
1   2.25-ounce can
    sliced pitted ripe
    olives, drained
2   tablespoons
    finely shredded
    lemon peel
1   tablespoon
    drained capers
1   teaspoon dried
    oregano, crushed
    Fresh Italian (flat-leaf)
    parsley sprigs

1 In a large skillet cook chicken in hot oil over medium-high heat about 5 minutes or until brown, turning once. Remove chicken from skillet; set aside. Add onion to skillet; cook over medium heat for 8 to 10 minutes or until tender and light brown, stirring occasionally and adding garlic for the last 1 minute of cooking.

2 Stir in tomatoes, olives, lemon peel, capers, and oregano. Return chicken to skillet. Bring to boiling; reduce heat. Simmer, covered, for 13 to 15 minutes or until chicken is no longer pink (170°F).

3 Serve chicken with tomato mixture. Garnish with parsley sprigs.

nutrition facts per serving: 315 cal., 13 g total fat (2 g sat. fat), 82 mg chol., 957 mg sodium, 13 g carb., 5 g dietary fiber, 36 g protein.

roasted **cranberry** chicken

prep: 25 minutes bake: 20 minutes oven: 375°F makes: 4 servings

8   small bone-in
     chicken thighs
     (2 to 2¼ pounds
     total), skinned
¼   teaspoon salt
¼   teaspoon ground
     black pepper
     Nonstick
     cooking spray
¾   cup low-calorie
     cranberry juice
¾   cup fresh or frozen
     cranberries
4   teaspoons packed
     brown sugar
2   sprigs fresh thyme
¼   teaspoon salt
     Fresh thyme leaves
     and/or rosemary
     sprigs

1 Preheat oven to 375°F. Sprinkle chicken with ¼ teaspoon salt and pepper. Coat an extra-large ovenproof skillet with cooking spray; heat skillet over medium-high heat. Place chicken, meaty sides down, in hot skillet; cook about 5 minutes or until brown, turning once. Transfer skillet to oven. Bake about 20 minutes or until chicken is no longer pink (180°F).

2 Meanwhile, for sauce, in a small saucepan combine cranberry juice, cranberries, brown sugar, thyme sprigs, and ¼ teaspoon salt. Bring to boiling; reduce heat. Simmer, uncovered, for 15 to 20 minutes or until slightly thickened. Discard thyme sprigs.

3 Serve chicken with sauce. Garnish with thyme leaves and/or rosemary sprigs.

nutrition facts per serving: 187 cal., 5 g total fat (1 g sat. fat), 107 mg chol., 383 mg sodium, 9 g carb., 1 g dietary fiber, 26 g protein.

spinach chicken breast rolls

prep: 30 minutes bake: 50 minutes stand: 10 minutes
oven: 375°F makes: 4 servings

4   skinless, boneless
    chicken breast
    halves (about
    1¼ pounds total)
1   egg white
1   cup shredded part-
    skim mozzarella
    cheese (4 ounces)
½   of a 10-ounce
    package frozen
    chopped spinach,
    thawed and
    well drained
⅓   cup low-fat cottage
    cheese, drained
1¼ cups (about ½ of
    26-ounce jar) light,
    reduced-sodium
    seasoned
    spaghetti sauce
2   tablespoons no-salt-
    added tomato paste
6   ounces dried
    multigrain or whole
    wheat spaghetti,
    cooked according
    to package
    directions and
    drained (optional)

1 Preheat oven to 375°F. Place each chicken breast half between two pieces of plastic wrap. Using the flat side of a meat mallet, pound chicken lightly until about ¼ inch thick. Remove plastic wrap.

2 For filling, in a small bowl combine egg white, ½ cup of the mozzarella cheese, the spinach, and cottage cheese. Spoon filling onto chicken, spreading to within ½ inch of the edges. Starting from a short end, roll up chicken. Place chicken rolls, seam sides down, in an ungreased 2-quart rectangular baking dish. For sauce, in a medium bowl stir together spaghetti sauce and tomato paste; spoon over chicken.

3 Bake, covered, for 25 minutes. Sprinkle with the remaining ½ cup mozzarella cheese. Bake, uncovered, about 25 minutes more or until chicken is no longer pink (170°F) and cheese is light brown. Let stand for 10 minutes before serving. If desired, serve with hot cooked spaghetti.

nutrition facts per serving: 332 cal., 9 g total fat (4 g sat. fat), 103 mg chol., 416 mg sodium, 15 g carb., 3 g dietary fiber, 46 g protein.

Lean chicken is a good way to get protein without excessive saturated fat.

blackened chicken with avocado salsa

start to finish: 25 minutes oven: 375°F makes: 4 servings

- 4 skinless, boneless chicken breast halves (about 1¼ pounds total)
- 2 teaspoons blackened steak seasoning
- 2 tablespoons olive oil
- 2 tablespoons rice vinegar
- ¼ teaspoon ground cumin
- ⅛ teaspoon salt
   Dash ground black pepper
- 1 avocado, seeded, peeled, and chopped
- ⅔ cup chopped fresh or refrigerated papaya
- ⅓ cup chopped red sweet pepper
- ¼ cup snipped fresh cilantro
   Fresh cilantro sprigs (optional)

1 Preheat oven to 375°F. Lightly sprinkle both sides of chicken with steak seasoning. In a large ovenproof skillet heat 1 tablespoon of the oil over medium heat. Add chicken; cook until brown, turning once. Transfer skillet to oven. Bake about 15 minutes or until chicken is no longer pink (170°F.)

2 Meanwhile, for salsa, in a large bowl whisk together the remaining 1 tablespoon oil, vinegar, cumin, salt, and black pepper. Stir in avocado, papaya, sweet pepper, and ¼ cup cilantro.

3 Serve chicken with salsa. If desired, garnish with cilantro sprigs.

nutrition facts per serving: 293 cal., 14 g total fat (2 g sat. fat), 82 mg chol., 513 mg sodium, 7 g carb., 3 g dietary fiber, 33 g protein.

almond-
crusted chicken

start to finish: 30 minutes makes: 4 servings

4   skinless, boneless
     chicken breast
     halves (1 to
     1¼ pounds total)
1   egg, lightly beaten
2   tablespoons
     buttermilk
½   cup finely chopped
     almonds
½   cup panko (Japanese-
     style bread crumbs)
     or fine dry bread
     crumbs
2   teaspoons snipped
     fresh rosemary
¼   teaspoon salt
1   tablespoon peanut oil
     or canola oil
2   tablespoons chopped
     shallot (1 medium)
8   cups fresh spinach
     leaves
¼   teaspoon salt
     Freshly ground black
     pepper
     Fresh mint leaves
     (optional)

1 Place each chicken breast half between two pieces of plastic wrap. Using the flat side of a meat mallet, pound chicken lightly until ¼ to ½ inch thick. Remove plastic wrap.

2 In a shallow dish combine egg and buttermilk. In another shallow dish combine almonds, panko, rosemary, and ¼ teaspoon salt. Dip chicken into egg mixture, then into almond mixture to coat.

3 In a 12-inch nonstick skillet cook chicken, half at a time if necessary, in hot oil over medium heat for 4 to 6 minutes or until no longer pink, turning once. Remove chicken, reserving drippings in skillet. Cover chicken and keep warm.

4 Add shallot to the reserved drippings; cook for 3 to 5 minutes or just until tender, stirring frequently. Add spinach and ¼ teaspoon salt; cook about 1 minute or just until spinach is wilted, tossing frequently. Serve chicken with wilted spinach. Sprinkle with pepper and, if desired, garnish with mint.

nutrition facts per serving: 276 cal., 11 g total fat (1 g sat. fat), 66 mg chol., 456 mg sodium, 11 g carb., 3 g dietary fiber, 33 g protein.

grilled chicken with
watermelon salsa

prep: 35 minutes   chill: 1 hour   grill: 12 minutes   makes: 6 servings

2	cups seeded and chopped watermelon
½	cup chopped cucumber
½	cup chopped orange or yellow sweet pepper (1 small)
¼	cup fresh or frozen corn kernels
2	tablespoons snipped fresh cilantro
1	to 2 fresh jalapeño chile peppers, seeded and chopped*
1	tablespoon finely chopped red onion
1	teaspoon finely shredded lime peel
¼	cup lime juice
1	teaspoon packed brown sugar
¼	teaspoon salt
¼	teaspoon crushed red pepper
6	skinless, boneless chicken breast halves (about 2 pounds total)
1	teaspoon lemon-pepper seasoning
1	tablespoon vegetable oil
	Halved lime slices (optional)

1 For salsa, in a medium bowl combine watermelon, cucumber, sweet pepper, corn, cilantro, jalapeño chile peppers, and red onion. In a small bowl combine ½ teaspoon of the lime peel, 2 tablespoons of the lime juice, the brown sugar, salt, and crushed red pepper. Add to watermelon mixture; toss gently to coat. Cover and chill for 1 hour to let flavors blend.

2 Sprinkle chicken with lemon-pepper seasoning. In a small bowl combine the remaining ½ teaspoon lime peel, the remaining 2 tablespoons lime juice, and the oil.

3 For a charcoal grill, grill chicken on the rack of an uncovered grill directly over medium coals for 12 to 15 minutes or until chicken is no longer pink (170°F), turning once halfway through grilling and brushing with oil mixture during the last 2 minutes of grilling. (For a gas grill, preheat grill. Reduce heat to medium. Place chicken on grill rack over heat. Cover and grill as above.) Serve chicken with salsa and, if desired, lime slices.

nutrition facts per serving: 221 cal., 4 g total fat (1 g sat. fat), 88 mg chol., 360 mg sodium, 9 g carb., 1 g dietary fiber, 36 g protein.

*tip: Because chile peppers contain volatile oils that can burn your skin and eyes, avoid direct contact with them as much as possible. When working with chile peppers, wear plastic or rubber gloves. If your bare hands do touch the peppers, wash your hands and nails well with soap and warm water.

golden grilled chicken thighs with apricots

prep: 25 minutes   marinate: 2 to 4 hours   grill: 12 minutes   makes: 4 servings

1	pound skinless, boneless chicken thighs
	Salt
	Ground black pepper
½	cup apricot nectar
6	tablespoons apricot preserves
¼	cup snipped fresh mint
1	tablespoon olive oil
1	tablespoon sherry vinegar
½	teaspoon curry powder
1	clove garlic, minced
4	medium apricots, halved and pitted
¼	cup chopped pistachio nuts
¼	cup chopped green onions (2)
1	tablespoon Dijon-style mustard
1	teaspoon olive oil
½	teaspoon mustard seeds
¼	teaspoon salt

1 Sprinkle chicken with salt and pepper. Place chicken in a resealable plastic bag set in a shallow dish. For marinade, in a small bowl combine ¼ cup of the nectar, 2 tablespoons of the preserves, 2 tablespoons of the mint, 1 tablespoon oil, vinegar, curry powder, and garlic. Pour marinade over chicken. Seal bag; turn to coat chicken. Marinate in the refrigerator for 2 to 4 hours, turning bag once or twice. Drain chicken, discarding marinade.

2 For a charcoal grill, grill chicken on the rack of an uncovered grill directly over medium coals for 12 to 15 minutes or until chicken is no longer pink (180°F), turning once halfway through grilling. (For a gas grill, preheat grill. Reduce heat to medium. Place chicken on grill rack over heat. Cover and grill as above.)

3 While chicken is grilling, add apricots, cut sides down, to grill. Grill about 5 minutes or until light grill marks appear.

4 For sauce, in a small bowl combine the remaining ¼ cup nectar, the remaining 4 tablespoons preserves, the remaining 2 tablespoons mint, 3 tablespoons of the pistachios, the green onions, mustard, 1 teaspoon oil, mustard seeds, and ¼ teaspoon salt. Serve chicken and apricots with sauce and sprinkle with the remaining 1 tablespoon pistachios.

nutrition facts per serving: 348 cal., 13 g total fat (2 g sat. fat), 94 mg chol., 504 mg sodium, 33 g carb., 2 g dietary fiber, 25 g protein.

Peanuts have a hefty amount of vitamin E and omega-3 fats, which help keep LDL cholesterol low.

chicken with **pretzels** and **couscous**

prep: 15 minutes bake: 10 minutes oven: 425°F makes: 6 servings

Nonstick cooking
spray
1 cup pretzel sticks
⅔ cup unsalted peanuts
¼ to ½ teaspoon
crushed red pepper
(optional)
½ cup refrigerated or
frozen egg product,
thawed, or 2 eggs,
lightly beaten
1 14- to 16-ounce
package chicken
breast tenderloins
1 16-ounce package
frozen sweet
pepper and onion
stir-fry vegetables
½ cup reduced-sodium
chicken broth
½ cup couscous
2 tablespoons seasoned
rice vinegar
1 tablespoon canola oil
1 recipe Dipping Sauce

1 Preheat oven to 425°F. Line a 15x10x1-inch baking pan with foil. Coat foil with cooking spray; set pan aside. In a food processor* combine pretzels, ½ cup of the peanuts, and the crushed red pepper (if using). Cover and process until chopped. Transfer mixture to a plastic bag.

2 Pour egg product into a shallow dish. Dip chicken, a few pieces at a time, into egg product, allowing excess to drip off. Add to pretzel mixture in bag, shaking to coat. Arrange chicken in the prepared baking pan. Bake for 10 to 15 minutes or until no longer pink (170°F).

3 Meanwhile, in a large saucepan combine stir-fry vegetables and broth. Bring to boiling. Stir in couscous; remove from heat. Let stand, covered, for 5 minutes. Chop the remaining peanuts. Stir chopped peanuts, vinegar, and oil into couscous mixture.

4 Serve chicken with couscous mixture and Dipping Sauce.

nutrition facts per serving: 336 cal., 12 g total fat (2 g sat. fat), 39 mg chol., 344 mg sodium, 31 g carb., 4 g dietary fiber, 26 g protein.

dipping sauce: In a small bowl combine ⅓ cup plain low-fat yogurt, 2 tablespoons yellow mustard, and 2 teaspoons honey. Makes about ½ cup.

*tip: If you do not have a food processor, place pretzels in a large resealable plastic bag; seal bag and use a rolling pin or meat mallet to crush pretzels. Chop ½ cup of the peanuts and add to crushed pretzels in bag.

lemon chicken
stir-fry

start to finish: 25 minutes makes: 4 servings

¾ cup reduced-sodium
   chicken broth

3 tablespoons lemon
   juice

1 tablespoon
   cornstarch

1 tablespoon reduced
   sodium soy sauce

2 tablespoons
   vegetable oil

1 16-ounce package
   frozen stir-fry
   vegetables (any
   blend)

1 pound skinless,
   boneless chicken
   breast halves, cut
   into thin bite-size
   strips

2 cups hot cooked
   brown rice
   Reduced-sodium soy
   sauce (optional)

1 For sauce, in a small bowl stir together broth, lemon juice, cornstarch, and 1 tablespoon soy sauce; set aside.

2 In a large skillet heat 1 tablespoon of the oil over medium-high heat. Add stir-fry vegetables; cook and stir for 5 to 7 minutes or until crisp-tender. Remove from skillet.

3 Add the remaining 1 tablespoon oil to skillet; add half of the chicken. Cook and stir for 2 to 3 minutes or until chicken is no longer pink. Remove from skillet. Repeat with the remaining chicken (add more oil if necessary). Return all of the chicken to skillet; push from center of skillet

4 Stir sauce, add to center of skillet. Cook and stir until thickened and bubbly. Return vegetables to skillet; stir all ingredients together to coat with sauce. Cook and stir for 1 to 2 minutes more or until heated through. Serve with hot cooked rice. If desired, pass additional soy sauce.

nutrition facts per serving: 350 cal., 9 g total fat (1 g sat. fat), 66 mg chol., 351 mg sodium, 33 g carb., 4 g dietary fiber, 32 g protein.

edamame-chicken stir-fry

start to finish: 30 minutes makes: 4 servings

3   tablespoons hoisin
    sauce
1   tablespoon rice
    vinegar
1   tablespoon reduced-
    sodium soy sauce
¼   teaspoon crushed red
    pepper
1   tablespoon olive oil or
    canola oil
2   teaspoons grated
    fresh ginger
1   cup diagonally sliced
    carrots (2 medium)
2   cups broccoli florets
1   cup fresh or
    frozen shelled
    sweet soybeans
    (edamame), thawed
8   ounces skinless,
    boneless chicken
    breast halves, cut
    into thin bite-size
    strips
1   8.8-ounce pouch
    cooked long grain
    brown rice

1 For sauce, in a small bowl stir together
hoisin sauce, vinegar, soy sauce, and
crushed red pepper; set aside.

2 Pour 2 teaspoons of the oil into a wok
or large nonstick skillet; heat wok over
medium-high heat. Add ginger; cook and stir
for 15 seconds. Add carrots; cook and stir for
1 minute. Add broccoli and edamame; cook
and stir for 4 to 5 minutes or until vegetables
are crisp-tender. Remove vegetables from wok.

3 Add the remaining 1 teaspoon oil to
wok. Add chicken; cook and stir for 2 to
3 minutes or until chicken is no longer pink.
Return vegetables to wok. Add sauce; stir all
ingredients together to coat with sauce. Cook
and stir until heated through.

4 Meanwhile, heat rice according to package
directions. Serve chicken mixture over rice.

nutrition facts per serving: 312 cal., 9 g total fat
(1 g sat. fat), 33 mg chol., 299 mg sodium, 35 g carb.,
5 g dietary fiber, 23 g protein.

chicken lo mein

start to finish: 45 minutes makes: 6 servings

6   tablespoons reduced-
    sodium soy sauce
1   tablespoon rice
    vinegar
4   teaspoons sugar
12 ounces skinless,
    boneless chicken
    breast halves, cut
    into bite-size strips
10 ounces dried Chinese
    egg noodles or
    linguine
⅓   cup reduced-sodium
    chicken broth
2   teaspoons cornstarch
1   tablespoon vegetable
    oil
1   tablespoon sesame
    oil
4   cloves garlic, minced
½   cup shredded carrot
    (1 medium)
1   cup chopped bok
    choy
4   green onions, cut into
    thin 2-inch strips

1 For marinade, in a medium bowl combine 2 tablespoons of the soy sauce, the vinegar, and 2 teaspoons of the sugar. Add chicken; toss gently to coat. Cover and marinate at room temperature for 20 minutes or in the refrigerator for 1 hour. Drain chicken, discarding marinade.

2 Meanwhile, cook noodles according to package directions; drain. Rinse with cold water; drain again. For sauce, in a small bowl stir together the remaining 4 tablespoons soy sauce, the remaining 2 teaspoons sugar, the broth, and cornstarch; set aside.

3 Pour vegetable oil and sesame oil into a wok or large nonstick skillet; heat wok over medium-high heat. Add garlic; cook and stir for 30 seconds. Add carrot; cook and stir for 2 minutes. Add bok choy and green onions; cook and stir for 2 minutes more. Remove vegetables from wok.

4 Add chicken to wok (add more vegetable oil if necessary); cook and stir for 3 to 4 minutes or until no longer pink. Push from center of wok. Stir sauce; add to center of wok. Cook and stir until thickened and bubbly. Add cooked noodles and vegetables; stir all ingredients together to coat with sauce. Cook until heated through, stirring occasionally.

nutrition facts per serving: 326 cal., 7 g total fat (1 g sat. fat), 73 mg chol., 615 mg sodium, 42 g carb., 2 g dietary fiber, 22 g protein.

beef or pork lo mein: Prepare as directed, except substitute 12 ounces boneless beef sirloin steak or lean boneless pork for the chicken and cook for 2 to 3 minutes or until slightly pink in center.

per serving: 339 cal., 9 g total fat (2 g sat. fat), 64 mg chol., 617 mg sodium, 42 g carb., 2 g dietary fiber, 22 g protein.

shrimp lo mein: Prepare as directed, except substitute 12 ounces fresh or frozen peeled and deveined shrimp, thawed, for the chicken and cook shrimp about 3 minutes or until opaque.

per serving: 324 cal., 8 g total fat (1 g sat. fat), 126 mg chol., 657 mg sodium, 43 g carb., 2 g dietary fiber, 21 g protein.

spicy wild mushroom and chicken stroganoff

start to finish: 30 minutes makes: 6 servings

1 8-ounce carton fat-free sour cream
2 tablespoons all-purpose flour
2 tablespoons tomato paste
1 tablespoon Worcestershire sauce
½ cup beef broth
2 teaspoons finely chopped canned chipotle peppers in adobo sauce*
2 tablespoons olive oil
6 cups sliced assorted fresh mushrooms, such as cremini, oyster, stemmed shiitake, and/or button (1 pound)
1 medium sweet onion, halved and thinly sliced
½ teaspoon seasoned salt
¼ teaspoon ground black pepper
⅛ teaspoon paprika
1 pound skinless, boneless chicken breast halves, cut into bite-size pieces
3 cups hot cooked noodles
   Snipped fresh parsley (optional)

1 In a small bowl combine ⅔ cup of the sour cream, the flour, tomato paste, and Worcestershire sauce. Stir in broth and chipotle chile peppers; set aside.

2 In an extra-large skillet heat 1 tablespoon of the oil over medium-high heat. Add mushrooms and onion; cook until onion is tender and most of the liquid is evaporated, stirring frequently. Meanwhile, in a medium bowl combine seasoned salt, black pepper, and paprika. Add chicken; toss gently to coat. Add the remaining 1 tablespoon oil to skillet. Add chicken; cook and stir until chicken is no longer pink.

3 Add sour cream mixture to skillet; cook and stir until thickened and bubbly. Reduce heat; cook and stir for 2 minutes more.

4 Serve chicken mixture over hot cooked noodles. Top with the remaining sour cream and, if desired, garnish with parsley.

nutrition facts per serving: 314 cal., 7 g total fat (1 g sat. fat), 70 mg chol., 394 mg sodium, 36 g carb., 3 g dietary fiber, 26 g protein.

*tip: Because chile peppers contain volatile oils that can burn your skin and eyes, avoid direct contact with them as much as possible. When working with chile peppers, wear plastic or rubber gloves. If your bare hands do touch the peppers, wash your hands and nails well with soap and warm water.

Multigrain pasta, spinach, and reduced-fat cheese provide a beneficial boost to this one-dish meal.

chicken, macaroni, and cheese

start to finish: 35 minutes   makes: 5 servings

1½ cups packaged dried multigrain or regular elbow macaroni
   Nonstick cooking spray
12 ounces skinless, boneless chicken breast halves, cut into 1-inch pieces
¼ cup finely chopped onion
1 6.5-ounce container light semisoft cheese with garlic and herb
1⅔ cups fat-free milk
1 tablespoon all-purpose flour
¾ cup shredded reduced-fat cheddar cheese (3 ounces)
2 cups packaged fresh baby spinach
1 cup cherry tomatoes, quartered

1 Cook macaroni according to package directions, except do not add any salt to the water; drain.

2 Meanwhile, coat a large nonstick skillet with cooking spray; heat skillet over medium-high heat. Add chicken and onion; cook for 4 to 6 minutes or until chicken is no longer pink and onion is tender, stirring frequently. (If onion browns too quickly, reduce heat to medium.) Remove skillet from heat. Stir in semisoft cheese until melted.

3 In a medium bowl whisk together milk and flour until smooth. Add to chicken mixture; cook and stir over medium heat until thickened and bubbly. Reduce heat to low. Stir in cheddar cheese until melted. Add cooked macaroni; cook and stir for 1 to 2 minutes or until heated through. Stir in spinach and tomatoes. Serve immediately.

nutrition facts per serving: 369 cal., 12 g total fat (7 g sat. fat), 85 mg chol., 393 mg sodium, 33 g carb., 4 g dietary fiber, 33 g protein.

grilled spiced chicken
kabobs

prep: 25 minutes   marinate: 1 to 24 hours   grill: 8 minutes
makes: 4 servings

1 tablespoon paprika
1 tablespoon olive oil
2 teaspoons garlic powder
2 teaspoons dried thyme, crushed
2 teaspoons dried oregano, crushed
1 teaspoon salt
1 teaspoon Asian chili sauce
1 to 1¼ pounds skinless, boneless chicken breast halves, cut into 1-inch pieces
12 to 16 baby pattypan squash or 2 small yellow summer squash, cut into chunks
Olive oil (optional)

1 For marinade, in a large bowl combine paprika, 1 tablespoon oil, garlic powder, thyme, oregano, salt, and chili sauce. Add chicken and squash; toss gently to coat. Cover and marinate in the refrigerator for 1 to 24 hours, tossing once or twice.

2 If using wooden skewers, soak in water for at least 30 minutes; drain before using. On eight 8-inch skewers thread chicken and squash, leaving ¼ inch between pieces.

3 For a charcoal grill, grill kabobs on the rack of an uncovered grill directly over medium coals for 8 to 10 minutes or until chicken is no longer pink, turning occasionally to brown evenly. (For a gas grill, preheat grill. Reduce heat to medium. Place kabobs on grill rack over heat. Cover and grill as above.) If desired, drizzle kabobs with additional oil before serving.

nutrition facts per serving: 174 cal., 5 g total fat (1 g sat. fat), 66 mg chol., 672 mg sodium, 4 g carb., 1 g dietary fiber, 27 g protein.

nutrition note

Enjoy the sweet life—with no sugar added! Grilling veggies brings out their natural flavor and sweetness without the extra calories.

chicken sausage with bow ties and sweet peppers

start to finish: 25 minutes makes: 4 to 6 servings

8 ounces dried farfalle pasta (bow ties) or rigatoni pasta

12 ounces sweet Italian or apple-flavor cooked chicken sausage links, cut into 1-inch pieces

2 medium red and/or yellow sweet peppers, seeded and cut into 1-inch pieces

½ cup lower-sodium beef broth or reduced-sodium chicken broth

¼ cup snipped fresh basil or Italian (flat-leaf) parsley

¼ cup finely shredded Parmigiano-Reggiano cheese or Parmesan cheese (1 ounce)

1 In a Dutch oven cook pasta according to package directions; drain. Return pasta to hot Dutch oven; cover and keep warm.

2 Meanwhile, in a large skillet cook sausage and sweet peppers over medium heat about 8 minutes or until sausage is brown, stirring occasionally.

3 Stir broth into sausage mixture. Bring to boiling; reduce heat. Simmer, uncovered, for 5 minutes. Add sausage mixture and basil to cooked pasta; toss gently to coat. Sprinkle each serving with cheese.

nutrition facts per serving: 378 cal., 10 g total fat (4 g sat. fat), 29 mg chol., 630 mg sodium, 48 g carb., 3 g dietary fiber, 24 g protein.

turkey-spinach toss

start to finish: 20 minutes makes: 4 servings

2   turkey breast
    tenderloins (about
    1 pound total)
¼   teaspoon coarse
    ground black pepper
2   tablespoons butter
2   ounces thinly sliced
    cooked ham, cut
    into bite-size strips
½   cup orange juice
2   9- to 10-ounce
    packages fresh
    spinach
    Salt
    Coarse ground
    black pepper
    Orange wedges
    (optional)

1 Split turkey tenderloins in half horizontally. Sprinkle turkey with ¼ teaspoon pepper. In an extra-large skillet heat butter over medium-high heat until melted. Add turkey; cook about 12 minutes or until no longer pink (165°F), turning once. Remove from skillet; cover and keep warm.

2 Add ham to hot skillet; cook and stir for 1 to 2 minutes or until ham is heated through and starting to crisp. Using a slotted spoon, remove ham from skillet. Add orange juice to skillet; bring to boiling. Add spinach, half at a time, if necessary; cook about 1 minute or just until spinach starts to wilt.

3 Using tongs, remove spinach from skillet and divide among dinner plates. Sprinkle with salt and additional pepper. Slice turkey; arrange turkey and ham on spinach. Drizzle with any orange juice remaining in skillet. If desired, serve with orange wedges.

nutrition facts per serving: 244 cal., 8 g total fat (4 g sat. fat), 94 mg chol., 528 mg sodium, 9 g carb., 3 g dietary fiber, 34 g protein.

turkey tetrazzini

prep: 30 minutes bake: 25 minutes stand: 5 minutes oven: 400°F
makes: 4 servings

Nonstick cooking
  spray
4 ounces dried whole
  wheat spaghetti
2 cups sliced fresh
  cremini, stemmed
  shiitake, or button
  mushrooms
¾ cup chopped red
  and/or green
  sweet pepper
1 cup fat-free milk
3 tablespoons
  all-purpose flour
1 12-ounce can
  evaporated
  fat-free milk
½ teaspoon instant
  chicken bouillon
  granules
¼ teaspoon salt
⅛ teaspoon ground
  black pepper
1 cup chopped cooked
  turkey or chicken
  breast (5 ounces)
½ cup finely shredded
  Parmesan cheese
  (2 ounces)
2 tablespoons snipped
  fresh parsley

1 Preheat oven to 400°F. Lightly coat a 2-quart square baking dish with cooking spray; set aside. In a large saucepan cook spaghetti according to package directions, except omit any oil and salt; Add mushrooms and sweet pepper for the last 3 to 5 minutes of cooking; drain in a colander.

2 In the same saucepan whisk together 1 cup milk and flour until smooth. Stir in evaporated milk, bouillon granules, salt, and black pepper; cook and stir over medium heat until thickened and bubbly. Stir in spaghetti mixture, turkey, ¼ cup of the cheese, and the parsley. Transfer to prepared baking dish.

3 Bake, covered, for 20 to 25 minutes or just until heated through. Sprinkle with the remaining ¼ cup cheese. Bake, uncovered, for 5 minutes more. Let stand for 5 minutes before serving.

nutrition facts per serving: 347 cal., 4 g total fat (2 g sat. fat), 41 mg chol., 562 mg sodium, 51 g carb., 5 g dietary fiber, 29 g protein.

make-ahead directions: Prepare as directed through Step 2. Cover and chill for 2 to 24 hours. To serve, bake as directed, except increase the first baking time to 25 to 30 minutes.

This dish provides the heartiness and good flavor of Thanksgiving favorites—cranberries, turkey, apple cider, and pecans.

turkey-cranberry
fried rice

start to finish: 25 minutes makes: 4 servings

1 pound uncooked
   ground turkey
   breast
½ cup chopped celery
   (1 stalk)
½ cup chopped onion
   (1 medium)
1 8.8-ounce pouch
   cooked long grain
   and wild rice
½ cup apple cider or
   apple juice
⅓ cup dried cranberries
½ teaspoon dried
   thyme, crushed
⅓ cup chopped pecans,
   toasted
¼ teaspoon salt
¼ teaspoon ground
   black pepper

1 In an extra-large skillet cook ground turkey, celery, and onion over medium heat until turkey is no longer pink and vegetables are tender, using a wooden spoon to break up meat as it cooks. Drain off fat.

2 Meanwhile, heat cooked rice according to package directions.

3 Stir rice, apple cider, dried cranberries, and thyme into turkey mixture; cook and stir until liquid is absorbed. Stir in pecans. Season with salt and pepper.

nutrition facts per serving: 337 cal., 9 g total fat (1 g sat. fat), 55 mg chol., 434 mg sodium, 34 g carb., 2 g dietary fiber, 29 g protein.

nutrition note

When buying ground turkey, look for the word "breast" on the label. Other products may contain high-fat dark meat, while ground turkey breast contains white meat only.

chili-ginger turkey
meatballs in tomato sauce

prep: 30 minutes cook: 10 minutes makes: 6 servings

1   medium onion, cut up
2   to 3 fresh serrano
      chile peppers,
      seeded and finely
      chopped*
2   tablespoons snipped
      fresh cilantro
1   tablespoon grated
      fresh ginger
1   egg yolk
1½ cups soft whole
      wheat bread
      crumbs (2 slices)
½   teaspoon salt
¼   teaspoon ground
      black pepper
1½ pounds uncooked
      ground turkey
      breast
2   tablespoons
      canola oil
1   large onion, cut into
      thin wedges
2   cloves garlic, minced
1   15-ounce can no-salt-
      added tomato sauce
¼   cup water
1   teaspoon sugar
¼   teaspoon salt
¼   teaspoon ground
      black pepper
3   cups hot cooked rice

1 In a food processor combine cut up onion, 1 to 2 of the serrano peppers, the cilantro, and ginger. Cover and process until finely chopped. Transfer to a large bowl. Stir in egg yolk, bread crumbs, ½ teaspoon salt, and ¼ teaspoon black pepper. Add ground turkey; mix well. Shape turkey mixture into 1½-inch meatballs.

2 In an extra-large skillet cook meatballs in hot oil over medium heat until brown. Remove meatballs, reserving drippings in skillet. Add onion wedges and garlic to the reserved drippings; cook for 5 minutes, stirring frequently.

3 Stir in tomato sauce, the water, sugar, ¼ teaspoon salt, ¼ teaspoon black pepper, and the remaining 1 to 2 serrano peppers. Bring to boiling, reduce heat. Stir in meatballs. Cook, covered, for 10 to 15 minutes or until meatballs are no longer pink (165°F). Serve over hot cooked rice.

nutrition facts per serving: 340 cal., 7 g total fat (1 g sat. fat), 90 mg chol., 414 mg sodium, 36 g carb., 3 g dietary fiber, 31 g protein.

*tip: Because chile peppers contain volatile oils that can burn your skin and eyes, avoid direct contact with them as much as possible. When working with chile peppers, wear plastic or rubber gloves. If your bare hands do touch the peppers, wash your hands and nails well with soap and warm water.

caramelized pork with melon

start to finish: 25 minutes makes: 4 servings

3½ cups peeled, seeded, and chopped cantaloupe (1 small)
¼ cup orange juice
3 tablespoons hoisin sauce
⅓ cup sliced green onions
4 bone-in pork center-cut loin chops, cut ½ inch thick
Salt
Ground black pepper
1 tablespoon vegetable oil
Shredded napa cabbage (optional)

1 In a food processor or blender combine 2 cups of the cantaloupe and the orange juice. Cover and process or blend until smooth. Transfer ½ cup of the pureed mixture to a small bowl; stir in hoisin sauce.

2 Press the remaining pureed mixture through a fine-mesh sieve, reserving juice and discarding solids. In a medium bowl combine the remaining 1½ cups cantaloupe, the strained juice, and green onions; set aside.

3 Trim fat from chops. Sprinkle chops lightly with salt and pepper. Remove 2 tablespoons of the hoisin mixture; brush over both sides of chops. In an extra-large skillet heat oil over medium heat. Add chops; cook for 6 to 8 minutes or until slightly pink in center (160°F), turning once. Remove from skillet.

4 Add the remaining hoisin mixture to skillet; cook and stir until heated through. Spoon warm hoisin mixture onto dinner plates. Top with chops.

5 Add cantaloupe mixture to skillet; cook and stir until warm. Spoon over chops. If desired, serve with cabbage.

nutrition facts per serving: 327 cal., 10 g total fat (2 g sat. fat), 117 mg chol., 452 mg sodium, 19 g carb., 2 g dietary fiber, 39 g protein.

grilled pork and pineapple

start to finish: 20 minutes makes: 4 servings

4 boneless pork top loin
   chops, cut ¾ inch
   thick
¼ teaspoon salt
¼ teaspoon ground
   black pepper
1 6-ounce carton plain
   fat-free yogurt
⅓ cup low-sugar orange
   marmalade
1 fresh pineapple,
   peeled, cored, and
   cut crosswise into
   ½-inch slices
2 tablespoons coarsely
   chopped toasted
   pecans
1 tablespoon fresh
   thyme leaves

1 Trim fat from chops. Sprinkle both sides with salt and pepper. In a small bowl combine yogurt and 2 tablespoons of the marmalade; set aside.

2 For a charcoal grill, grill chops on the rack of an uncovered grill directly over medium coals for 4 minutes. Turn chops; add pineapple to grill. Brush chops and pineapple with the remaining marmalade. Grill for 3 to 5 minutes more or until chops are slightly pink in center (160°F) and pineapple has light grill marks, turning pineapple once halfway through grilling.

3 Arrange chops and pineapple on dinner plates. Top with yogurt mixture; sprinkle with pecans and thyme.

nutrition facts per serving: 295 cal., 5 g total fat (2 g sat. fat), 94 mg chol., 242 mg sodium, 28 g carb., 2 g dietary fiber, 35 g protein

nutrition note

When it comes to meat, portion control is in the palm of your hand. Take a look! Visually, your palm is about the size of a reasonable portion of meat, which is 4 ounces uncooked, or 3 ounces cooked.

pork chops pizziola

prep: 20 minutes   cook: 30 minutes   makes: 4 servings

4   bone-in pork rib or
    loin chops, cut
    ½ inch thick
1   tablespoon canola oil
1   tablespoon snipped
    fresh oregano or
    1 teaspoon dried
    oregano, crushed
2   cloves garlic, minced
1   14.5-ounce can
    no-salt-added
    diced tomatoes,
    undrained
¼   cup dry red wine
    or low-sodium
    tomato juice
1   tablespoon tomato
    paste
    Small fresh oregano
    leaves and/or
    snipped fresh
    oregano (optional)

1 Trim fat from chops. In a large skillet cook chops in hot oil over medium-high heat until brown on both sides. Remove from skillet.

2 Add dried oregano (if using) and garlic to skillet; cook and stir for 15 seconds. Stir in tomatoes, wine, and tomato paste. Bring to boiling. Return chops to skillet; reduce heat. Simmer, covered, for 30 minutes.

3 Transfer chops to a serving dish. Skim off any fat from tomato mixture. Stir 1 tablespoon snipped fresh oregano (if using) into tomato mixture. If desired, cook, uncovered, for 1 to 2 minutes more or until mixture reaches desired consistency, stirring occasionally. Serve chops with tomato mixture. If desired, sprinkle with additional fresh oregano.

nutrition facts per serving: 210 cal., 10 g total fat (3 g sat. fat), 58 mg chol., 130 mg sodium, 7 g carb., 2 g dietary fiber, 19 g protein.

If pressed for time, piercing the tenderloin in several places with a fork will allow marinade to work its magic more quickly.

roasted pork tenderloin with
blackberry sauce

prep: 20 minutes marinate: 2 to 5 hours roast: 30 minutes
stand: 10 minutes oven: 425°F makes: 6 servings

1   1½ -pound pork
     tenderloin
¼   cup blackberry
     preserves, melted
     and cooled
¼   cup dry white wine
     or apple juice
2   tablespoons balsamic
     vinegar
2   tablespoons olive oil
2   tablespoons Dijon-
     style mustard
3   cloves garlic, minced
1   teaspoon soy sauce
1   teaspoon finely
     shredded orange
     peel
½   teaspoon snipped
     fresh rosemary
     Shredded orange peel
     (optional)

1 Trim fat from meat. Place meat in a resealable plastic bag set in a shallow dish. For marinade, in a small bowl combine preserves, wine, vinegar, oil, mustard, garlic, soy sauce, 1 teaspoon orange peel, and rosemary. Pour marinade over meat. Seal bag; turn to coat meat. Marinate in the refrigerator for 2 to 5 hours, turning bag occasionally.

2 Preheat oven to 425°F. Drain meat, reserving marinade. Place meat on a rack in a shallow roasting pan. Roast for 30 to 40 minutes or until meat is done (155°F). Remove from oven. Cover with foil; let stand for 10 minutes before serving. (Temperature of the meat after standing should be 160°F.)

3 Meanwhile, for sauce, in a small saucepan bring the reserved marinade to boiling; reduce heat. Simmer, uncovered, about 5 minutes or until desired consistency.

4 Slice meat. Serve meat with sauce. If desired, garnish with additional orange peel.

nutrition facts per serving: 221 cal., 7 g total fat (1 g sat. fat), 74 mg chol., 244 mg sodium, 11 g carb., 0 g dietary fiber, 24 g protein.

cranberry-pear
pork tenderloin

prep: 30 minutes roast: 25 minutes stand: 10 minutes oven: 425°F
makes: 4 servings

1   cup Chardonnay, other dry white wine, or cranberry juice
¾   cup chicken broth
⅓   cup dried cranberries
1   tablespoon honey
6   inches stick cinnamon
2   sprigs fresh thyme
¼   teaspoon salt
⅛   to ¼ teaspoon ground black pepper
2   small pears, peeled, cored, and sliced
1   1-pound pork tenderloin
1   tablespoon olive oil
1   tablespoon snipped fresh rosemary
1   tablespoon snipped fresh thyme
¼   teaspoon salt
⅛   teaspoon ground black pepper

1 Preheat oven to 425°F. For sauce, in a medium saucepan combine Chardonnay, broth, dried cranberries, honey, cinnamon, thyme sprigs, ¼ teaspoon salt, and ⅛ to ¼ teaspoon pepper. Bring to boiling; reduce heat. Simmer, covered, for 10 minutes. Remove and discard cinnamon and thyme sprigs. Add pears. Simmer, uncovered, for 5 minutes more. Transfer mixture to a food processor. Cover and process until smooth.

2 Meanwhile, trim fat from meat. Brush meat with oil. Sprinkle with rosemary, snipped thyme, ¼ teaspoon salt, and ⅛ teaspoon pepper. Place on a rack in a shallow roasting pan.

3 Roast for 25 to 35 minutes or until meat is done (155°F). Remove from oven. Cover with foil; let stand for 10 minutes. (Temperature of the meat after standing should be 160°F.) Slice meat. Serve meat with sauce.

nutrition facts per serving: 287 cal., 6 g total fat (1 g sat. fat), 74 mg chol., 535 mg sodium, 24 g carb., 3 g dietary fiber, 24 g protein.

pork medallions in
cream sauce

start to finish: 25 minutes makes: 4 servings

1 pound pork
    tenderloin
½ teaspoon garlic salt
½ teaspoon coarse
    ground black
    pepper
¼ teaspoon onion
    powder
¼ teaspoon dried
    thyme, crushed
2 tablespoons olive oil
2 tablespoons finely
    chopped shallot
    (1 medium)
¼ cup dry vermouth
⅓ cup half-and-half or
    light cream
1 tablespoon honey
    mustard
⅓ cup reduced-sodium
    chicken broth
¼ cup finely chopped
    red sweet pepper
2 cups hot cooked
    noodles or pasta
    (optional)

1 Trim fat from meat. Cut meat crosswise into 1-inch slices. Place meat, cut sides up, on a baking sheet or tray. Press each slice with the palm of your hand to make an even ½-inch thickness. In a small bowl combine garlic salt, pepper, onion powder, and thyme; sprinkle over both sides of meat.

2 In a 12-inch skillet cook meat in hot oil over medium high heat for 4 to 6 minutes or until meat is slightly pink in center (160°F), turning once. Remove from skillet.

3 Add shallot to skillet; cook and stir for 30 seconds. Carefully add vermouth; cook and stir until vermouth is nearly evaporated. Add half-and-half. Bring to simmering. Stir in mustard (mixture may appear curdled). Return meat to skillet; add broth and sweet pepper. Return to simmering; cook, uncovered, about 2 minutes or until sauce is slightly thickened, stirring occasionally.

4 Serve meat with sauce and, if desired, hot cooked noodles.

nutrition facts per serving: 242 cal., 12 g total fat (3 g sat. fat), 81 mg chol., 260 mg sodium, 4 g carb., 0 g dietary fiber, 25 g protein.

pork loin with
parsnips and pears

start to finish: 25 minutes makes: 4 servings

1 pound boneless pork top loin roast
¼ teaspoon salt
¼ teaspoon ground black pepper
3 tablespoons Pickapeppa sauce or Worcestershire sauce
1 tablespoon olive oil
3 to 4 small parsnips, peeled and sliced
2 pears, cored and sliced and/or chopped
½ cup pear nectar or apple juice
Snipped fresh Italian (flat-leaf) parsley (optional)

1 Trim fat from meat. Cut meat into ½-inch slices; sprinkle lightly with salt and black pepper. Brush with some of the Pickapeppa sauce.

2 In a 12-inch skillet cook meat in hot oil over medium heat until brown on both sides. Transfer meat to a plate, reserving drippings in skillet. Cover meat and keep warm.

3 Add parsnips and pears to the reserved drippings; cook about 5 minutes or until parsnips are crisp-tender, stirring occasionally. Stir in the remaining Pickapeppa sauce and pear nectar; return meat to skillet. Cook about 5 minutes or until meat is slightly pink in center (160°F). Divide meat, parsnips, and pears among dinner plates.

4 For sauce, bring nectar mixture to boiling; reduce heat. Boil gently, uncovered, until slightly thickened. Pour sauce over meat, parsnips, and pears. If desired, sprinkle with parsley.

nutrition facts per serving: 311 cal., 11 g total fat (3 g sat. fat), 62 mg chol., 293 mg sodium, 28 g carb., 4 g dietary fiber, 26 g protein.

gingered pork
skewers with orange couscous

prep: 20 minutes grill: 18 minutes
makes: 4 servings

1 pound pork tenderloin or pork sirloin roast
⅛ teaspoon ground black pepper
⅓ cup orange juice or lemon juice
2 tablespoons honey
2 teaspoons grated fresh ginger or ½ teaspoon ground ginger
2 oranges, cut into wedges
1 cup reduced-sodium chicken broth
1 teaspoon finely shredded orange peel
⅔ cup whole wheat couscous
2 tablespoons snipped fresh mint

1 If using wooden skewers, soak in water for at least 30 minutes, drain before using. Trim fat from meat. Cut meat into 1½-inch pieces. Sprinkle with pepper. Thread meat onto four 6-inch skewers, leaving ¼ inch between pieces. In a small bowl combine juice, honey, and ginger; set aside.

2 For a charcoal grill, grill meat skewers on the greased rack of an uncovered grill directly over medium coals for 18 to 20 minutes or until meat is slightly pink in center and juices run clear, turning occasionally to brown evenly and brushing with lemon mixture during the last 3 minutes of grilling. (For a gas grill, preheat grill. Reduce heat to medium. Place meat skewers on greased grill rack over heat. Cover and grill as above.)

3 While meat skewers are grilling, add orange wedges to grill. Grill for 4 to 5 minutes or until heated through and grill marks appear, turning once halfway through grilling.

4 Meanwhile, in a medium saucepan combine broth and orange peel. Bring to boiling. Stir in couscous; remove from heat. Let stand, covered, for 5 minutes. Fluff with a fork; stir in mint.

5 Remove meat from skewers. Serve meat and orange wedges with couscous.

nutrition facts per serving: 350 cal., 5 g total fat (1 g sat. fat), 74 mg chol., 200 mg sodium, 49 g carb., 6 g dietary fiber, 30 g protein.

fish and

sea

8

Make waves at the dinner table by serving up some of the seas' most delicious and healthful foods.

food

This recipe has double benefits: Catfish is low in fat, and the use of sweet potatoes in place of some of the white potatoes boosts vitamins.

catfish and potato wedges

prep: 20 minutes bake: 14 minutes oven: 450°F makes: 4 servings

1 pound fresh or frozen skinless catfish fillets
  Nonstick cooking spray
1 teaspoon chili powder or paprika
½ teaspoon salt
¼ teaspoon dried dillweed
¼ teaspoon ground black pepper
2 small sweet potatoes (10 ounces total)
1 medium Yukon gold potato
1 tablespoon canola oil
⅓ cup buttermilk
⅔ cup panko (Japanese-style bread crumbs)
2 cloves garlic, minced
  Fresh dill sprigs (optional)
  Malt vinegar (optional)

1 Thaw fish, if frozen. Rinse fish; pat dry with paper towels. Cut into four to eight serving-size pieces. Measure thickness of fish; set aside. Preheat oven to 450°F. Line two baking sheets with foil; lightly coat with cooking spray. Set aside. In a small bowl combine chili powder, salt, dill, and pepper; set aside.

2 Scrub sweet and Yukon gold potatoes; cut into ½-inch thick wedges. In a bowl toss potato wedges with oil to coat. Sprinkle with ½ teaspoon of the chili powder mixture; toss to coat. Arrange potatoes in a single layer on one of the prepared baking sheets. Bake potatoes for 10 minutes.

3 Meanwhile, pour buttermilk into a shallow dish. In another shallow dish combine panko, garlic, and the remaining chili powder mixture.

4 Dip fish pieces in buttermilk, turning to coat and allowing excess to drip off. Dip in panko mixture to coat all sides. Place fish on second baking sheet. Lightly coat fish with cooking spray.

5 Bake, uncovered, for 4 to 6 minutes per ½-inch thickness of fish or until fish begins to flake when tested with fork and potatoes are tender. If desired, sprinkle fish with fresh dill and serve with malt vinegar.

nutrition facts per serving: 317 cal., 13 g total fat (2 g sat. fat), 54 mg chol., 449 mg sodium, 28 g carb., 3 g dietary fiber, 22 g protein.

pan-seared tilapia with black bean salsa

prep: 10 minutes chill: 15 minutes cook: 4 minutes to 6 minutes per ½-inch thickness makes: 4 servings

4 6 ounce fresh or frozen skinless tilapia, cod, orange roughy, or flounder fillets, ½ to ¾ inch thick

2 teaspoons salt-free lemon-pepper seasoning

1 15-ounce can reduced-sodium black beans, rinsed and drained

1 small papaya, halved, seeded, and cubed

¼ cup finely chopped red onion

1 small fresh jalapeño chile pepper, seeded and chopped

1 teaspoon finely shredded lime peel

1 tablespoon lime juice

2 tablespoons olive oil

1 Thaw fish, if frozen. Rinse fish; pat dry with paper towels. Sprinkle both sides of fish with lemon-pepper seasoning.

2 For salsa, in a medium bowl combine beans, papaya, red onion, jalapeño chile pepper, lime peel, and lime juice. Cover and chill about 15 minutes or until ready to serve.

3 In a very large skillet heat oil over medium heat. Add fish; cook for 4 to 6 minutes or until fish begins to flake when tested with fork, turning once halfway through cooking.

4 To serve, stir salsa and spoon over fish just before serving.

nutrition facts per serving: 329 cal., 10 g total fat (2 g sat. fat), 85 mg chol., 103 mg sodium, 21 g carb., 6 g dietary fiber, 40 g protein.

224

pan-fried fish with peppers and pecans

start to finish: 25 minutes makes: 4 servings

1   pound fresh or frozen
    thin white fish
    fillets, such as trout,
    tilapia, or catfish
    (skinned, if desired)

⅓   cup all-purpose flour

¼   teaspoon salt

¼   cup butter or
    margarine

1   tablespoon packed
    brown sugar

¼   cup chopped pecans

½   of a red sweet
    pepper, seeded and
    cut into strips

⅛   teaspoon cayenne
    pepper

1   tablespoon lime juice
    Green onions, sliced

1 Thaw fish, if frozen. Rinse fish; pat dry with paper towels. If necessary, cut fish into four serving-size pieces; set aside. In a shallow dish combine flour and salt. Dip fish into flour mixture to coat.

2 In a large skillet heat 2 tablespoons of the butter over medium-high heat. Add fish in a single layer; reduce heat to medium. Cook for 6 to 8 minutes or until golden and fish begins to flake when tested with fork, turning once halfway through cooking. Remove fish from skillet; cover and keep warm.

3 Wipe out skillet. Add the remaining 2 tablespoons of the butter; melt over medium heat. Add brown sugar, stirring until sugar dissolves. Stir in pecans, sweet pepper, and cayenne pepper. Cook and stir over medium heat for 3 to 4 minutes or until pecans are lightly toasted and pepper strips are just tender. Remove from heat. Stir in lime juice.

4 To serve, spoon pecan mixture over fish and top with green onions.

nutrition facts per serving: 363 cal., 23 g total fat (10 g sat. fat), 97 mg chol., 269 mg sodium, 14 g carb., 1 g dietary fiber, 26 g protein.

grilled bass with
lemon and herbs

prep: 15 minutes grill: 4 minutes to 6 minutes per ½-inch thickness
makes: 4 servings

1   pound fresh or
    frozen striped bass,
    rockfish, or other
    fish fillets, ½ to
    ¾ inch thick
2   teaspoons olive oil
¼   teaspoon salt
⅛   teaspoon ground
    black pepper
2   tablespoons snipped
    fresh Italian (flat-
    leaf) parsley
1   tablespoon snipped
    fresh basil and/or
    chives
2   teaspoons finely
    shredded lemon
    peel
1   teaspoon snipped
    fresh rosemary

1 Thaw fish, if frozen. Rinse fish; pat dry with paper towels. Cut into four serving-size pieces. Brush both sides of fish with oil; sprinkle with salt and pepper. Measure thickness of fish.

2 For charcoal grill, place fish on the greased rack of uncovered grill directly over medium coals. Grill for 4 to 6 minutes per ½-inch thickness of fish or until fish begins to flake easily when tested with fork, carefully turning fish once halfway through grilling. (For gas grill, preheat grill. Reduce heat to medium. Place fish on a greased grill rack over heat; cover. Grill as above.)

3 In a small bowl combine parsley, basil, lemon peel, and rosemary. Sprinkle parsley mixture over fish.

nutrition facts per serving: 131 cal., 5 g total fat (1 g sat. fat), 90 mg chol., 225 mg sodium, 0 g carb., 0 g dietary fiber, 20 g protein.

lime fish tacos with salsa verde

prep: 20 minutes broil: 4 minutes to 6 minutes per ½-inch thickness
makes: 4 servings

1 pound fresh or frozen cod or orange roughy fillets
1 medium lime
1 tablespoon olive oil
⅛ teaspoon salt
⅛ teaspoon ground black pepper
½ cup green salsa
1 to 2 tablespoons snipped fresh cilantro
8 6-inch corn tortillas
½ cup shredded Monterey Jack cheese (2 ounces)
Radishes, thinly sliced (optional)

1 Thaw fish, if frozen. Preheat broiler. Cut lime in half. Squeeze one lime half to get 1 tablespoon juice. Cut the remaining lime half into wedges; set wedges aside. In a small bowl combine lime juice, oil, salt, and pepper.

2 Rinse fish; pat dry with paper towels. Measure thickness of fish. Brush fish with lime juice mixture. Place fish on the greased unheated rack of a broiler pan. Tuck under any thin edges. Broil 4 inches from heat or until fish begins to flake when tested with a fork. Allow 4 to 6 minutes per ½-inch thickness of fish, turning once if fish is 1 inch thick or more.

3 Meanwhile, stir together salsa and cilantro. To serve, flake fish and divide among corn tortillas. Top with salsa mixture and sprinkle with shredded cheese. If desired, garnish with radish slices. Serve with lime wedges.

nutrition facts per serving: 302 cal., 10 g total fat (4 g sat. fat), 61 mg chol., 406 mg sodium, 26 g carb., 4 g dietary fiber, 27 g protein.

nutrition note

Next time you crave tacos, give ground beef a pass and upgrade to fish—it's a good protein source, yet low in saturated fat. If cod isn't available, substitute another mild finfish.

mediterranean halibut and squash

prep: 10 minutes   cook: 15 minutes   microwave: 20 minutes

makes: 4 servings

1   pound fresh or frozen halibut fillets or steaks, about 1 inch thick

¼   teaspoon salt

¼   teaspoon ground black pepper

1   3- to 3½-pound spaghetti squash

¼   teaspoon salt

¼   cup water

½   cup chopped onion (1 medium)

2   cloves garlic, minced

1   tablespoon olive oil

2   cups sliced fresh mushrooms

1   14.5-ounce can no-salt-added diced tomatoes with basil, garlic, and oregano

¼   cup pitted kalamata or Greek black olives, chopped

¼   cup snipped fresh Italian (flat-leaf) parsley

1 Thaw fish, if frozen. Rinse fish; pat dry with paper towels. Cut into four serving-size pieces, if necessary. Season with salt and pepper.

2 Halve squash lengthwise; discard seeds. (Wrap and store one squash portion in the refrigerator for another use.) Sprinkle remaining squash portion with ¼ teaspoon salt. Place squash, cut side down, in a 2-quart microwave-safe baking dish with the water; cover with plastic wrap, turning back corner of wrap to allow steam to escape. Microwave on 100 percent power (high) for 20 to 22 minutes or until tender, turning once. Cool slightly. Using a fork, scrape stringy squash pulp from shell; cover and keep warm.

3 Meanwhile, for tomato sauce, in a large skillet cook onion and garlic in hot oil for 2 minutes. Add mushrooms; cook and stir until tender. Stir in undrained tomatoes, olives, and parsley. Bring to boiling; reduce heat. Place fish on top of sauce; cook, covered, for 8 to 12 minutes or until fish begins to flake when tested with fork.

4 To serve, divide squash among dinner plates. Top with fish and tomato sauce.

nutrition facts per serving: 268 cal., 8 g total fat (1 g sat. fat), 36 mg chol., 513 mg sodium, 22 g carb., 8 g dietary fiber, 28 g protein.

steamed cod with gingery mushrooms

prep: 15 minutes   cook: 4 minutes to 6 minutes per ½-inch thickness
makes: 4 servings

1 pound fresh or frozen
   cod, tilapia, or other
   fish fillets, about
   ½ inch thick
½ teaspoon ground
   ginger
¼ teaspoon salt
¼ teaspoon ground
   black pepper
1 tablespoon finely
   chopped fresh
   ginger
2 teaspoons canola oil
8 ounces fresh shiitake
   mushrooms,
   stemmed and
   halved
1 large red sweet
   pepper, seeded and
   cut into rings
½ cup sliced green
   onions (4)
¼ cup dry white wine
   or reduced-sodium
   chicken broth
⅔ cup reduced-sodium
   chicken broth
   Thin strips green
   onion
   Very thin slices fresh
   ginger

1 Thaw fish, if frozen. Rinse fish; pat dry with paper towels. In a bowl combine the ½ teaspoon ground ginger, salt, and black pepper. Sprinkle on fish; set aside.

2 In a skillet cook and stir 1 tablespoon chopped ginger in hot oil over medium-high heat for 15 seconds. Add mushrooms, sweet pepper, and ½ cup sliced green onions; cook about 5 minutes or until mushrooms are tender, stirring occasionally. Remove skillet from heat; add wine. Return to heat; cook and stir until wine is almost evaporated.

3 Add chicken broth; bring to boiling. Place seasoned fish on vegetables in skillet; reduce heat. Simmer, covered, until fish begins to flake when tested with fork. Allow 4 to 6 minutes per ½-inch thickness of fish.

4 To serve, top fish and vegetables with thin green onion strips and sliced ginger. Spoon cooking liquid over fish and vegetables.

nutrition facts per serving: 155 cal., 4 g total fat (0 g sat. fat), 48 mg chol., 308 mg sodium, 6 g carb., 2 g dietary fiber, 23 g protein.

grilled halibut with corn and pepper relish

prep: 45 minutes grill: 8 minutes makes: 4 servings

4 5- to 6-ounce fresh or frozen halibut steaks, cut 1 inch thick
   Kosher salt
   Ground black pepper
3 tablespoons olive oil
1 tablespoon snipped fresh Italian (flat-leaf) parsley
1 tablespoon snipped fresh oregano
1½ cups fresh or frozen corn kernels
1 cup finely chopped sweet red pepper
1 cup finely chopped sweet green pepper
2 cloves garlic, minced
¼ teaspoon kosher salt
⅛ teaspoon cayenne pepper
½ cup chopped tomato (1 medium)
¼ cup finely chopped red onion
3 tablespoons snipped fresh Italian (flat-leaf) parsley
1 tablespoon white wine vinegar
   Fresh oregano (optional)

1 Thaw fish, if frozen. Rinse fish; pat dry with paper towels. Sprinkle both sides of fish with salt and black pepper. In a small bowl combine 1 tablespoon of the olive oil, 1 tablespoon parsley, and 1 tablespoon oregano. Rub over both sides of fish; set aside.

2 In a large skillet heat 1 tablespoon of the oil over medium-high heat. Add corn; cook about 4 minutes or until corn begins to brown, stirring often. Add sweet peppers; cook and stir for 2 minutes more. Stir in garlic, ¼ teaspoon salt, and cayenne pepper; cook and stir for 1 minute more. Remove from the heat; cool slightly.

3 For a charcoal grill, place fish on the greased rack of an uncovered grill directly over medium coals. Grill for 8 to 12 minutes or until fish begins to flake when tested with a fork, carefully turning fish once halfway through grilling. (For a gas grill, preheat grill. Reduce heat to medium. Place fish on greased grill rack over heat. Cover and grill as directed.)

4 Meanwhile, for relish, in a medium bowl combine corn mixture, tomato, red onion, 3 tablespoons parsley, vinegar, and the remaining 1 tablespoon oil; toss to combine.

5 To serve, place fish on four dinner plates. Top each with ½ cup relish. (Cover and chill the remaining 2 cups relish for up to 3 days.) If desired, garnish with additional fresh oregano.

nutrition facts per serving: 282 cal., 12 g total fat (2 g sat. fat), 45 mg chol., 283 mg sodium, 13 g carb., 2 g dietary fiber, 32 g protein.

crispy almond fish with potato crisps

prep: 20 minutes bake: 4 minutes to 6 minutes per ½-inch thickness
oven: 450°F makes: 4 servings

Nonstick cooking
  spray
1 pound fresh or frozen
  skinless cod fish
  fillets, ¾ inch thick
¼ cup all-purpose flour
2 egg whites, lightly
  beaten
2 tablespoons fat-free
  milk
¼ cup fine dry bread
  crumbs
¼ cup finely chopped
  almonds
1 teaspoon snipped
  fresh thyme
2 tablespoons canola
  oil
1 recipe Potato Crisps
  Snipped fresh chives
  (optional)

1 Preheat oven to 450°F. Lightly coat a 9x9x2-inch baking pan with cooking spray; set aside. Thaw fish, if frozen. Rinse fish; pat dry with paper towels. Cut into four serving-size pieces, if necessary. Measure thickness of fish.

2 Place flour in a shallow dish or small bowl. In a second shallow dish whisk together egg white and milk. In a third shallow dish combine bread crumbs, almonds, and thyme. Coat both sides of fish with flour. Dip fish in the egg mixture; dip in bread crumb mixture to coat all sides.

3 Place fish in prepared pan. Drizzle with oil. Bake, uncovered, for 4 to 6 minutes per ½-inch thickness of fish or until fish begins to flake when tested with a fork. Serve fish immediately with Potato Crisps. If desired, sprinkle potatoes with snipped fresh chives.

nutrition facts per serving: 252 cal., 11 g total fat (1 g sat. fat), 49 mg chol., 142 mg sodium, 13 g carb., 1 g dietary fiber, 25 g protein.

potato crisps: Preheat oven to 450°F. Line a large baking sheet with foil. Coat foil with nonstick cooking spray. Cut 2 medium white- and/or yellow-fleshed potatoes or sweet potatoes (6 to 8 ounces each) into ⅛-inch-thick lengthwise slices. Arrange the potato slices in a single layer on the baking sheet. Coat potato slices with nonstick cooking spray. Sprinkle with ¼ teaspoon garlic salt. Bake for 15 to 20 minutes or until the potatoes are light brown and crisp. (If any slices brown more quickly than others, remove from baking sheet and keep warm.) Makes 4 servings.

nutrition facts per serving: 47 cal., 0 g total fat (0 g sat. fat), 0 mg chol., 64 mg sodium, 11 g carb., 1 g dietary fiber, 1 g protein.

Low in saturated fats, tilapia take well to a wide variety of flavors.

tilapia puttanesca
start to finish: 30 minutes makes: 4 servings

1 pound fresh or frozen
   skinless tilapia or
   other fish fillets
⅛ teaspoon salt
½ medium red onion,
   cut in wedges
1 tablespoon olive oil
1 14.5-ounce can
   diced tomatoes,
   undrained
2 cloves garlic, minced
2 teaspoons dried
   oregano, crushed
¼ teaspoon crushed red
   pepper
¼ cup pitted kalamata
   olives
1 tablespoon capers,
   drained (optional)
2 tablespoons coarsely
   snipped fresh
   Italian (flat-leaf)
   parsley
   Fresh oregano
   (optional)

1 Thaw fish, if frozen. Rinse fish; pat dry with paper towels. Sprinkle with salt; set aside.

2 For sauce, in a large skillet cook red onion in hot oil over medium heat about 8 minutes or until tender, stirring occasionally. Stir in tomatoes, garlic, oregano, and crushed red pepper. Bring to boiling; reduce heat. Simmer, uncovered, for 5 minutes.

3 Add olives and capers (if using) to sauce. Top with fish. Return to boiling; reduce heat. Cook, covered, for 6 to 10 minutes or until fish begins to flake when tested with fork. Remove fish to serving platter. Simmer sauce, uncovered, for 1 to 2 minutes more or until thickened.

4 To serve, spoon sauce over fish. Sprinkle with parsley. If desired, garnish with fresh oregano.

nutrition facts per serving: 182 cal., 6 g total fat (1 g sat. fat), 56 mg chol., 431 mg sodium, 8 g carb., 2 g dietary fiber, 24 g protein.

tuna and fruit salsa

start to finish: 25 minutes makes: 4 servings

4   5- to 6-ounce fresh or
    frozen tuna steaks,
    1-inch thick
2   medium fresh
    peaches, halved
    and pitted
2   tablespoons olive oil
    Salt
    Cracked black pepper
2   tablespoons apricot
    preserves
1   tablespoon vinegar
½   cup fresh raspberries
⅓   cup thinly bias-sliced
    green onions
    (about 3)

1 Thaw fish, if frozen. Rinse fish; pat dry
with paper towels. Lightly brush fish steaks
and peach halves with oil; sprinkle with
salt and pepper.

2 In a large skillet cook fish and peach halves
over medium-high heat for 5 minutes.
Remove peaches; set aside. Turn fish over; cook
for 6 to 7 minutes more or until fish begins to
flake when tested with fork. Remove fish to a
serving platter; cover to keep warm.

3 Coarsely chop peach halves. In a medium
microwave-safe bowl microwave
apricot preserves on 100 percent (high) for
15 seconds. Stir in vinegar; gently fold in
raspberries and peaches.

4 To serve, top fish with fruit mixture with
fish. Sprinkle with green onions.

nutrition facts per serving: 333 cal., 14 g total fat
(3 g sat. fat), 54 mg chol., 133 mg sodium, 17 g carb.,
3 g dietary fiber, 34 g protein.

thai tuna toss

start to finish: 25 minutes makes: 4 servings

6   cups shredded napa
     or Chinese cabbage
12   ounces cooked tuna,*
     broken into chunks,
     or two 6-ounce cans
     very low-sodium
     chunk white tuna,
     drained
1   medium red or yellow
     sweet pepper, cut
     into thin strips
1   cup fresh snow pea
     pods, trimmed and
     halved crosswise
¼   cup sliced green
     onions (2)
½   cup rice vinegar
1   tablespoon sugar
1   tablespoon reduced-
     sodium soy sauce
1   teaspoon toasted
     sesame oil
¼   teaspoon ground
     ginger
⅛   to ¼ teaspoon
     crushed red pepper
2   tablespoons chopped
     cashews

1 In a very large bowl combine cabbage, tuna, sweet pepper, pea pods, and green onions. Toss gently to combine.

2 For dressing, in a screw-top jar combine rice vinegar, sugar, soy sauce, sesame oil, ginger, and crushed red pepper. Cover and shake well.

3 Pour dressing over cabbage mixture; toss gently to coat. Serve immediately or cover and chill for up to 12 hours. Sprinkle with cashews before serving.

nutrition facts per serving: 268 cal., 9 g total fat (2 g sat. fat), 43 mg chol., 205 mg sodium, 14 g carb., 3 g dietary fiber, 30 g protein.

*tip: For cooked tuna, purchase 1 pound frozen tuna steaks, 1 inch thick. Thaw fish. Rinse fish; pat dry with paper towels. Place fish on the greased unheated rack of a broiler pan. Broil 4 inches from the heat for 8 to 12 minutes or until fish begins to flake when tested with fork, turning fish once halfway through cooking. Use right away or freeze for later use. Makes about 12 ounces cooked fish.

sicilian tuna with capers

prep: 10 minutes marinate: 15 minutes broil: 8 minutes makes: 4 servings

4   4- to 5-ounce fresh or
    frozen tuna steaks,
    1 inch thick
2   tablespoons red wine
    vinegar
1   tablespoon snipped
    fresh dill or
    1 teaspoon dried
    dillweed
2   teaspoons olive oil
¼   teaspoon salt
⅛   teaspoon cayenne
    pepper
    Nonstick cooking
    spray
½   cup chopped tomato
    (1 medium)
1   tablespoon capers,
    rinsed and drained
1   tablespoon chopped
    pitted ripe olives
1   clove garlic, minced

1 Thaw fish, if frozen. Rinse fish; pat dry with paper towels.

2 For marinade, in a shallow dish combine vinegar, dill, oil, salt, and half of the cayenne pepper. Add fish to marinade in dish, turning to coat fish. Cover; marinate in the refrigerator for 15 minutes.

3 Preheat broiler. Lightly coat the unheated rack of a broiler pan with cooking spray. In a small bowl combine tomato, drained capers, olives, garlic, and the remaining cayenne pepper.

4 Drain fish, reserving marinade. Place fish on prepared rack. Broil 4 inches from the heat for 8 to 12 minutes or until fish begins to flake when tested with fork, turning once and brushing with reserved marinade halfway through cooking.

5 To serve, top tuna with tomato mixture.

nutrition facts per serving: 151 cal., 4 g total fat (0 g sat. fat), 51 mg chol., 271 mg sodium, 1 g carb., 0 g dietary fiber, 27 g protein.

pacific
northwest paella

start to finish: 45 minutes makes: 6 servings

1¼ pounds fresh or
    frozen skinless
    salmon fillet, about
    1 inch thick
4 slices apple wood–
    smoked bacon
3 cups sliced fresh
    cremini or button
    mushrooms
    (8 ounces)
1 cup chopped onion
    (1 large)
2 cloves garlic, minced
2½ cups reduced-sodium
    chicken broth
1 cup uncooked long
    grain white rice
2 teaspoons snipped
    fresh thyme or
    ½ teaspoon dried
    thyme, crushed
¼ teaspoon cracked
    black pepper
1 pound fresh asparagus,
    trimmed and cut into
    1-inch pieces, or one
    10-ounce package
    frozen cut asparagus,
    thawed
⅓ cup chopped roma
    tomato (1 medium)

1 Thaw fish, if frozen. In a large deep skillet
or paella pan cook bacon over medium
heat until crisp, turning occasionally. Drain
bacon on paper towels, reserving drippings in
skillet. Crumble bacon; set aside.

2 Add mushrooms, onion, and garlic to
reserved drippings in skillet; cook about
5 minutes or until the onion is tender, stirring
occasionally. Stir in broth, uncooked rice, and
thyme. Bring to boiling; reduce heat. Simmer,
covered, for 10 minutes.

3 Meanwhile, rinse fish; pat dry with paper
towels. Cut fish into 1-inch pieces. Sprinkle
with pepper.

4 Place fish pieces and asparagus on top
of rice mixture. Simmer, covered, for
10 to 12 minutes more or until fish begins to
flake when tested with a fork and asparagus is
crisp-tender.

5 To serve, sprinkle with tomato and
crumbled bacon before serving.

nutrition facts per serving: 320 cal., 10 g total fat
(3 g sat. fat), 56 mg chol., 569 mg sodium, 31 g carb.,
2 g dietary fiber, 27 g protein.

salmon potato scramble

start to finish: 25 minutes makes: 6 servings

1   pound fresh or frozen
     skinless salmon
     fillets, about ¾ inch
     thick
2   tablespoons butter or
     margarine
2   cups frozen diced
     hash brown
     potatoes, thawed
¾   cup chopped green
     sweet pepper
     (1 medium)
2   to 3 teaspoons Old
     Bay seasoning
6   eggs, lightly beaten
⅓   cup water

1 Thaw fish, if frozen. Rinse fish; pat dry
with paper towels. In a covered 12-inch
skillet cook fish in a small amount of boiling
water for 6 to 9 minutes or until fish begins to
flake when tested with fork. Remove fish from
skillet; discard liquid. Using a fork, break fish
into large chunks.

2 Wipe skillet with paper towels. Add
butter; melt over medium-high heat.
Add potatoes, sweet pepper, and Old Bay
seasoning; cook for 5 to 10 minutes or until
potatoes start to brown, stirring occasionally.

3 In a medium bowl combine eggs and the
water; pour over potato mixture. Cook over
medium heat, without stirring, until mixture
starts to set on the bottom and around edges.
Using a spatula or large spoon, lift and fold
the partially cooked egg mixture so that the
uncooked portion flows underneath. Continue
cooking for 2 to 3 minutes or until egg mixture
is cooked through, but is still glossy and
moist. Gently stir in cooked fish; heat through.
Immediately remove from heat and serve.

nutrition facts per serving: 294 cal., 17 g total fat
(6 g sat. fat), 266 mg chol., 396 mg sodium, 12 g carb.,
1 g dietary fiber, 23 g protein.

nutrition note
*The American Heart Association
recommends eating at least two
servings of fish per week, especially
fatty fish with a high omega-3
content. Fortunately, these include
salmon, tuna, and mackerel—some
of the tastiest fish around.*

pepper jelly and soy glazed salmon

prep: 30 minutes marinate: 1 hour grill: 15 minutes makes: 8 servings

1   2-pound fresh or
    frozen skinless
    salmon fillet, about
    1 inch thick
⅔   cup green jalapeño
    jelly
⅓   cup sliced green
    onions (about 3)
⅓   cup rice vinegar
⅓   cup reduced-sodium
    soy sauce
1   tablespoon grated
    fresh ginger
2   teaspoons toasted
    sesame oil
3   cloves garlic, minced
¼   teaspoon crushed red
    pepper
¼   cup snipped fresh
    cilantro
¼   cup sliced fresh
    jalapeño chile
    peppers* and/or
    sliced green onions

1 Thaw fish, if frozen. Rinse fish; pat dry with paper towels. For marinade, in a small saucepan melt jelly over low heat; remove from heat. Stir in ⅓ cup green onions, rice vinegar, soy sauce, ginger, oil, garlic, and crushed red pepper. Place salmon in a shallow dish and pour marinade over fish. Cover; marinate in the refrigerator for 1 to 2 hours, turning fish occasionally. Remove salmon from marinade, reserving marinade.

2 For a charcoal grill, arrange medium-hot coals around edge of grill. Test for medium heat in center of grill. Place fish on a greased piece of foil. Place fish on foil in center of the grill. Cover; grill for 15 to 18 minutes or until fish begins to flake when tested with fork. (For a gas grill, preheat grill. Reduce heat to medium. Adjust for indirect cooking. Grill as above.) Remove fish from grill.

3 Meanwhile, for sauce, in a small saucepan bring the reserved marinade to boiling; reduce heat. Simmer, uncovered, for 10 to 15 minutes or until liquid is reduced to ½ cup.

4 To serve, drizzle sauce over fish. Sprinkle fish with cilantro and jalapeño chile peppers and/or additional green onions.

nutrition facts per serving: 334 cal., 16 g total fat (4 g sat. fat), 62 mg chol., 428 mg sodium, 20 g carb., 0 g dietary fiber, 24 g protein.

*tip: Because chile peppers contain volatile oils that can burn your skin and eyes, avoid direct contact with them as much as possible. When working with chile peppers, wear plastic or rubber gloves. If your bare hands do touch the peppers, wash your hands and nails well with soap and warm water.

chile-dusted salmon with pineapple-jicama salsa

prep: 25 minutes grill: 4 minutes to 6 minutes per ½-inch thickness
makes: 4 servings

4   6-ounce fresh or
    frozen salmon
    steaks, ½ to 1 inch
    thick
2   teaspoons chili
    powder
½   teaspoon salt
1½ cups chopped fresh
    pineapple
1   cup chopped, peeled
    jicama
½   cup chopped red
    onion
1   large Anaheim chile
    pepper, seeded and
    finely chopped*
3   tablespoons snipped
    fresh cilantro
3   tablespoons lime
    juice

1 Thaw fish, if frozen. Rinse fish; pat dry with paper towels. Sprinkle both sides of fish steaks with chili powder and salt. Measure thickness of fish. Cover and chill in the refrigerator.

2 For pineapple salsa, in a medium bowl combine pineapple, jicama, red onion, Anaheim chile pepper, cilantro, and lime juice. Mix well and let stand at room temperature while grilling fish.

3 For a charcoal grill, place fish on the greased rack of an uncovered grill directly over medium coals. Grill for 4 to 6 minutes per ½-inch thickness of fish or until fish begins to flake easily when tested with a fork, carefully turning fish once halfway through grilling. (For a gas grill, preheat grill. Reduce heat to medium. Place fish on a greased grill rack over heat. Cover and grill as above.)

4 Serve fish immediately with pineapple salsa.

nutrition facts per serving: 367 cal., 19 g total fat (4 g sat. fat), 100 mg chol., 408 mg sodium, 14 g carb., 3 g dietary fiber, 35 g protein.

*tip: Because chile peppers contain volatile oils that can burn your skin and eyes, avoid direct contact with them as much as possible. When working with chile peppers, wear plastic or rubber gloves. If your bare hands do touch the peppers, wash your hands and nails well with soap and warm water.

shrimp scampi

start to finish: 20 minutes makes: 4 servings

1½   pounds fresh or
       frozen large shrimp
6   ounces dried whole
       wheat or plain
       linguine
1   tablespoon olive oil
3   cloves garlic, minced
2   tablespoons dry
       white wine or
       reduced-sodium
       chicken broth
1   tablespoon butter
⅛   teaspoon salt
1   tablespoon snipped
       fresh chives and/or
       parsley

1 Thaw shrimp, if frozen. Peel and devein
shrimp, leaving the tails intact if desired.
Rinse shrimp; pat dry with paper towels.
Set aside.

2 Cook pasta according to package
directions; drain. Return pasta to pan;
cover and keep warm.

3 Meanwhile, in a large skillet heat oil and
garlic over medium-high heat. Add shrimp;
cook and stir for 2 to 4 minutes or until shrimp
are opaque. Transfer shrimp to a serving platter
using a slotted spoon.

4 Remove skillet from heat. Add wine, butter,
and salt to the skillet. Return skillet to
heat; cook and stir over medium heat for 1 to
2 minutes to loosen any browned bits and to
melt butter.

5 To serve, divide pasta among four serving
plates. Top with shrimp. Pour butter
mixture over shrimp and sprinkle with chives
and/or parsley.

nutrition facts per serving: 320 cal., 9 g total fat
(3 g sat. fat), 180 mg chol., 236 mg sodium, 34 g carb.,
5 g dietary fiber, 28 g protein.

parmesan crusted shrimp with napoli sauce

prep: 25 minutes bake: 10 minutes oven: 400°F makes: 4 servings

1 pound fresh or frozen large shrimp
1 tablespoon butter
1 tablespoon olive oil
3 cloves garlic, minced
2⅓ cups chopped roma tomatoes, chopped (about 5 medium)
1 medium fresh poblano chile pepper, halved, seeded, and chopped* (about ⅔ cup)
1 tablespoon honey
1 teaspoon paprika
¼ cup thinly sliced green onions (2)
2 tablespoons finely shredded Parmesan cheese
1 tablespoon snipped fresh oregano
¼ teaspoon salt
¼ teaspoon ground black pepper
Nonstick cooking spray
½ cup fine dry bread crumbs
½ cup finely shredded Parmesan cheese
2 egg whites, beaten

1 Thaw shrimp, if frozen. Peel and devein shrimp; remove tails. Rinse shrimp; pat dry with paper towels. Set aside.

2 Preheat oven to 400°F. For tomato sauce, in a large skillet heat butter, oil, and garlic over medium-high heat. Add tomatoes, poblano chile pepper, honey, and paprika. Bring to boiling; reduce heat. Simmer, uncovered, about 10 minutes or until most of liquid is evaporated. Stir in green onions, 2 tablespoons Parmesan cheese, and oregano. Season to taste with salt and black pepper.

3 Meanwhile, coat the bottom of a 15x10x1-inch baking pan with cooking spray; set aside. In a shallow dish combine bread crumbs and ½ cup Parmesan cheese. Place egg whites in another shallow dish. Dip shrimp in egg whites; coat shrimp with bread crumb mixture. Arrange shrimp in the prepared pan.

4 Bake for 10 minutes or until shrimp are opaque. To serve, divide tomato sauce among four plates; top with shrimp.

nutrition facts per serving: 345 cal., 13 g total fat (5 g sat. fat), 189 mg chol., 692 mg sodium, 24 g carb., 2 g dietary fiber, 33 g protein.

*tip: Because chile peppers contain volatile oils that can burn your skin and eyes, avoid direct contact with them as much as possible. When working with chile peppers, wear plastic or rubber gloves. If your bare hands do touch the peppers, wash your hands and nails well with soap and warm water.

grilled shrimp and pineapple skewers

prep: 30 minutes grill: 8 minutes makes: 4 servings

1 pound fresh or frozen jumbo shrimp
½ of a fresh pineapple
½ cup water
6 tablespoons orange marmalade
1 tablespoon soy sauce
1 8.8-ounce pouch cooked long grain rice
¼ cup snipped fresh cilantro

1 Thaw shrimp, if frozen. Peel and devein shrimp. Rinse shrimp; pat dry with paper towels. Thread shrimp onto four skewers.* Cut pineapple crosswise into four slices; if desired, core pineapple. Cut each slice into quarters, making 16 small wedges. Thread wedges onto four additional skewers.*

2 For sauce, in a small saucepan combine the water, 4 tablespoons of the marmalade, and the soy sauce. Brush some of the sauce onto shrimp and pineapple wedges. Reserve remaining sauce.

3 For charcoal grill, place skewers on rack of an uncovered grill directly over medium coals. Grill for 8 to 10 minutes or until shrimp are opaque and pineapple is heated through, carefully turning skewers once halfway through grilling. (For gas grill, preheat grill. Reduce heat to medium. Place shrimp on grill rack over heat; cover. Grill as above.) Remove from grill; cover to keep warm.

4 Heat rice according to package directions. Transfer rice to a serving bowl; stir in the remaining 2 tablespoons marmalade and the cilantro. Bring the remaining sauce to boiling.

5 Immediately serve shrimp and pineapple skewers with the hot rice and sauce.

nutrition facts per serving: 322 cal., 3 g total fat (0 g sat. fat), 172 mg chol., 451 mg sodium, 49 g carb., 2 g dietary fiber, 25 g protein.

*tip: If using wooden skewers, soak in water for at least 30 minutes before threading on shrimp and pineapple. Drain before using.

orzo with shrimp in
yogurt-chive sauce

start to finish: 30 minutes makes: 4 servings

1 Thaw shrimp, if frozen. Peel and devein shrimp. Rinse shrimp; pat dry with paper towels. Set aside.

8	ounces fresh or frozen medium shrimp
1	cup dried orzo
¼	cup snipped dried tomatoes (not oil-packed)
2	tablespoons canola oil
1½	cups coarsely chopped zucchini or yellow summer squash
1	cup coarsely chopped onion
2	cloves garlic, minced
¼	cup reduced-sodium chicken broth
½	cup plain lowfat yogurt
2	tablespoons snipped fresh chives
¼	teaspoon salt
¼	teaspoon freshly ground black pepper
2	tablespoons finely shredded Parmesan cheese

2 Cook pasta according to package directions, adding dried tomatoes to pasta for the last 2 minutes of cooking; drain. Set aside.

3 Meanwhile, in a large skillet cook shrimp in hot oil for 2 to 3 minutes or until shrimp are just opaque. Remove shrimp from skillet with a slotted spoon; set aside.

4 Add zucchini, onion, and garlic to same skillet; cook and stir for 3 to 4 minutes or until onion is just tender. Stir in shrimp, broth, and pasta mixture; heat through. Remove skillet from heat. Stir in yogurt and chives until combined. Season with salt and pepper. Sprinkle each serving with cheese.

nutrition facts per serving: 348 cal., 10 g total fat (2 g sat. fat), 90 mg chol., 409 mg sodium, 43 g carb., 3 g dietary fiber, 22 g protein.

caribbean edamame and shrimp

start to finish: 25 minutes makes: 4 servings

- 8 ounces fresh or frozen large shrimp
- ½ teaspoon Jamaican jerk seasoning
- 0 ounces dried multigrain penne pasta
- 1 cup frozen shelled sweet soybeans (edamame)
- 1 tablespoon canola oil
- 1 to 2 medium fresh jalapeño chile peppers, sliced and seeded*
- ⅓ cup tequila lime liquid meat marinade
- 1 mango, seeded, peeled, and sliced
- 2 tablespoons snipped fresh cilantro
  Lime wedges

1 Thaw shrimp, if frozen. Peel and devein shrimp, leaving the tails intact if desired. Rinse shrimp; pat dry with paper towels. In a medium bowl toss shrimp with jerk seasoning; set aside.

2 Cook pasta according to package directions, adding edamame to pasta for the last 3 minutes of cooking; drain. Return pasta mixture to pan; cover and keep warm.

3 Meanwhile, in a large skillet heat oil over medium-high heat. Add shrimp and jalapeño chile pepper; cook for 2 to 4 minutes or until shrimp are opaque, turning shrimp once and stirring chile pepper slices. Stir in meat marinade; remove skillet from heat.

4 Divide pasta mixture among four serving plates. Top with shrimp mixture, mango, and cilantro. Serve with lime wedges.

nutrition facts per serving: 356 cal., 8 g total fat (1 g sat. fat), 86 mg chol., 794 mg sodium, 48 g carb., 6 g dietary fiber, 24 g protein.

*tip. Because chile peppers contain volatile oils that can burn your skin and eyes, avoid direct contact with them as much as possible. When working with chile peppers, wear plastic or rubber gloves. If your bare hands do touch the peppers, wash your hands and nails well with soap and warm water.

meatless

ent

9

Do It once or twice a week. Making meatless meals—especially fabulously filling ones like these—a part of your regimen is good for your body as well as your pocketbook.

rées

pasta with garden vegetables

start to finish: 25 minutes   makes: 4 servings

8   ounces dried penne,
    rotini, or medium
    shell pasta
¼   cup olive oil
½   to 1 cup snipped
    fresh herbs and/or
    chopped leafy
    greens
½   cup chopped fresh or
    canned tomatoes
½   cup chopped yellow
    sweet pepper
    (1 small)
⅓   cup shaved and/or
    crumbled cheese,
    such as Parmigiano-
    Reggiano, feta,
    Gorgonzola, or
    Grana Padano
¼   teaspoon salt
¼   teaspoon ground
    black pepper

1 Cook pasta according to package
directions; drain. Return pasta to hot pan.
Pour oil over pasta; toss gently to coat.

2 Stir in herbs and/or greens, tomatoes, and
sweet pepper. Sprinkle each serving with
cheese, salt, and black pepper.

nutrition facts per serving: 383 cal., 17 g total fat
(4 g sat. fat), 6 mg chol., 306 mg sodium, 46 g carb.,
3 g dietary fiber, 12 g protein.

nutrition note

*Herbs not only add flavor, but they
can pad the nutritional bottom line,
too. Served in large amounts, as they
are here, parsley, basil, chives, and
cilantro brim with vitamin A.*

summertime tortellini

prep: 20 minutes   chill: 2 to 24 hours   stand: 10 minutes   makes: 4 servings

1   9-ounce package
    refrigerated
    cheese tortellini
8   ounces fresh green
    beans, trimmed and
    cut diagonally into
    1-inch pieces
1   to 1½ teaspoons
    finely shredded
    lemon peel
3   tablespoons
    lemon juice
1   teaspoon Dijon-style
    mustard
½   teaspoon sugar
1   clove garlic, minced
¼   teaspoon salt
1¼ cups yellow sweet
    pepper cut into
    ½-inch pieces
    (1 large)
2   tablespoons olive oil
½   cup cubed part-skim
    mozzarella cheese
    (2 ounces)
½   cup sliced green
    onions (4)
2   tablespoons pine
    nuts or chopped
    almonds, toasted

1 In a large saucepan cook tortellini according to package directions, adding green beans for the last 5 minutes of cooking; drain. Rinse tortellini mixture with cold water; drain again.

2 Meanwhile, for dressing, in a screw-top jar combine lemon peel, lemon juice, mustard, sugar, garlic, and salt. Cover and shake well. Chill until ready to serve.

3 In a large bowl combine cooked tortellini mixture and sweet pepper. Drizzle with oil; toss gently to coat. Cover and chill for 2 to 24 hours.

4 Before serving, stir cheese, green onions, and nuts into tortellini mixture. Shake dressing. Pour dressing over tortellini mixture; toss gently to coat. Let stand for 10 minutes before serving.

nutrition facts per serving: 363 cal., 16 g total fat (4 g sat. fat), 30 mg chol., 503 mg sodium, 41 g carb., 3 g dietary fiber, 16 g protein.

fresh-herb pasta
primavera
start to finish: 35 minutes makes: 6 servings

8 ounces dried
   multigrain or whole
   wheat penne or
   mostaccioli pasta
3 cups assorted fresh
   vegetables, such
   as red sweet
   pepper strips, sugar
   snap pea pods,
   asparagus pieces,
   and/or carrot strips
1 cup halved cherry
   tomatoes
½ cup reduced-sodium
   chicken broth
3 tablespoons all-
   purpose flour
½ teaspoon salt
1¼ cups low-fat milk
¼ cup dry sherry or
   reduced-sodium
   chicken broth
¾ cup finely shredded
   Parmesan or Asiago
   cheese (3 ounces)
½ cup lightly packed
   fresh basil, coarsely
   snipped
4 teaspoons snipped
   fresh thyme
   or oregano
⅓ cup sliced green
   onions (optional)

1 In a 4-quart Dutch oven cook pasta according to package directions, adding the 3 cups assorted vegetables for the last 2 minutes of cooking; drain. Return pasta mixture to hot Dutch oven. Add cherry tomatoes.

2 In a medium saucepan whisk together broth, flour, and salt until smooth. Gradually stir in milk and sherry; cook and stir over medium heat until thickened and bubbly. Cook and stir for 2 minutes more. Remove from heat; stir in cheese, basil, and thyme.

3 Add cheese mixture to pasta mixture; stir gently to coat. If desired, sprinkle each serving with green onions.

nutrition facts per serving: 253 cal., 5 g total fat (3 g sat. fat), 12 mg chol., 496 mg sodium, 41 g carb., 6 g dietary fiber, 13 g protein.

asian noodle slaw

start to finish: 25 minutes makes: 4 servings

6 ounces dried multigrain spaghetti or soba (buckwheat noodles)

⅓ cup peanut sauce

⅓ cup carrot juice

1 tablespoon canola oil

1 tablespoon finely chopped, peeled fresh ginger

1 16-ounce package shredded broccoli (broccoli slaw mix)

¾ cup shredded carrots

1 Cook pasta according to package directions; drain. Return pasta to hot pan. Using kitchen scissors, snip pasta into small pieces; cover and keep warm. For sauce, in a small bowl whisk together peanut sauce and carrot juice; set aside.

2 Pour oil into a wok or large nonstick skillet; heat wok over medium-high heat. Add ginger; cook and stir for 15 seconds. Add broccoli slaw and carrots; cook and stir for 1 minute.

3 Add sauce to wok; stir all ingredients together to coat with sauce. Cook and stir about 2 minutes more or until heated through. Add pasta; toss gently to coat. Serve warm.

nutrition facts per serving: 285 cal., 7 g total fat (1 g sat. fat), 0 mg chol., 318 mg sodium, 45 g carb., 7 g dietary fiber, 12 g protein.

beefy asian noodle slaw: Thinly slice 12 ounces boneless beef sirloin steak across the grain into bite-size strips. Prepare as directed through Step 2. Remove vegetables from wok. Add meat to wok; cook and stir for 2 to 3 minutes or until slightly pink in center. Continue as directed in Step 3, returning vegetables to wok with sauce.

per serving: 397 cal., 11 g total fat (3 g sat. fat), 43 mg chol., 366 mg sodium, 48 g carb., 8 g dietary fiber, 29 g protein.

254

orzo risotto
with roasted vegetables

start to finish: 45 minutes   roast: 25 minutes   oven: 425°F   makes: 4 servings

Nonstick cooking spray
½   of a 2-pound butternut squash, peeled, seeded, and cut into ¾- to 1-inch pieces
⅛   teaspoon ground black pepper
3   cups halved fresh button or cremini mushrooms (8 ounces)
1   large onion, cut into thin wedges
1   tablespoon snipped fresh rosemary or oregano or 1 teaspoon dried rosemary or oregano, crushed
1   tablespoon olive oil
2   14-ounce cans reduced-sodium chicken broth
1⅓   cups dried whole wheat orzo pasta (rosamarina)
2   cloves garlic, minced
¼   cup coarsely chopped walnuts, toasted
¼   cup crumbled feta cheese (1 ounce) (optional)

1 Preheat oven to 425°F. Coat a 15x10x1-inch baking pan with cooking spray. Place squash in pan; sprinkle with pepper. Roast, covered, for 10 minutes. Add mushrooms, onion, and rosemary. Drizzle with oil; toss gently to coat. Roast, uncovered, for 15 to 20 minutes more or until vegetables are tender and light brown, stirring once or twice.

2 Meanwhile, in a medium saucepan bring broth to boiling; reduce heat. Cover and keep broth simmering. Coat a large skillet with cooking spray; heat skillet over medium heat. Add orzo and garlic; cook and stir for 2 to 3 minutes or until orzo is light brown.

3 Slowly add ½ cup of the broth to orzo mixture, stirring constantly. Continue to cook and stir over medium heat until broth is absorbed. Add another ½ cup of the broth to orzo mixture, stirring constantly. Continue to cook and stir until broth is absorbed. Add the remaining broth, ½ cup at a time, stirring constantly until broth is absorbed. (This should take about 15 minutes total.)

4 Add roasted vegetables and walnuts to orzo mixture; stir gently to combine. If desired, sprinkle each serving with cheese.

nutrition facts per serving: 385 cal., 9 g total fat (1 g sat. fat), 0 mg chol., 471 mg sodium, 64 g carb., 6 g dietary fiber, 15 g protein.

Kids will dive into these pasta shell "bowls" filled with cheesy vegetables.

broccoli-and-cheese-
stuffed shells

prep: 25 minutes bake: 15 minutes oven: 350°F makes: 4 or 5 servings

16 dried jumbo
     pasta shells
2 cups chopped
     broccoli florets
1 tablespoon water
1 15 ounce carton light
     ricotta cheese
½ cup shredded part-
     skim mozzarella
     cheese (2 ounces)
⅔ cup pasta sauce
2 tablespoons
     shredded part-skim
     mozzarella cheese

1 Preheat oven to 350°F. Cook pasta shells according to package directions; drain. Rinse with cold water; drain again.

2 Meanwhile, for filling, in a medium microwave-safe bowl combine broccoli and the water. Cover with waxed paper. Microwave on 100 percent power (high) for 2 minutes; drain. Stir ricotta cheese and ½ cup mozzarella cheese into cooked broccoli. Spoon filling into shells.

3 Arrange filled shells in an ungreased 2-quart rectangular baking dish. Spoon pasta sauce over shells; sprinkle with 2 tablespoons mozzarella cheese. Bake, uncovered, about 15 minutes or until heated through.

nutrition facts per serving: 389 cal., 9 g total fat (4 g sat. fat), 37 mg chol., 348 mg sodium, 54 g carb., 3 g dietary fiber, 22 g protein.

nutrition note
Go meatless now and then to tap into health benefits enjoyed by vegetarians. They tend to have lower cholesterol and body mass index (BMI) than avid meat eaters.

tortellini-vegetable
bake

prep: 30 minutes bake: 30 minutes oven: 350°F makes: 8 servings

2 9-ounce packages
   refrigerated whole
   wheat cheese
   tortellini
1½ cups fresh sugar snap
   pea pods, trimmed
   and halved
   crosswise (if desired)
½ cup thinly sliced
   carrot (1 medium)
1 tablespoon butter
1 cup sliced fresh
   mushrooms
⅓ cup reduced-sodium
   vegetable broth
2 teaspoons all-purpose
   flour
1½ teaspoons dried
   oregano, crushed
½ teaspoon garlic salt
½ teaspoon ground
   black pepper
1 cup fat-free milk
1 8-ounce package
   reduced-fat cream
   cheese (Neufchâtel),
   cubed and softened
1 tablespoon lemon juice
1 cup halved and/or
   quartered red and/
   or yellow cherry
   tomatoes
½ cup coarsely chopped
   red or green sweet
   pepper (1 small)
2 tablespoons grated
   Parmesan cheese

1 Preheat oven to 350°F. Cook tortellini according to package directions, adding sugar snap peas and carrot for the last 1 minute of cooking; drain.

2 Meanwhile, in a 12-inch skillet heat butter over medium heat until melted. Add mushrooms; cook about 5 minutes or until mushrooms are tender, stirring occasionally. Remove from skillet.

3 In a screw-top jar combine broth, flour, oregano, garlic salt, and black pepper. Cover and shake until smooth; add to same skillet. Add milk; cook and stir over medium heat until thickened and bubbly. Add cream cheese; cook and stir until smooth. Remove from heat; stir in lemon juice.

4 Stir tortellini mixture, mushrooms, tomatoes, and sweet pepper into cream cheese mixture. Transfer to an ungreased 3-quart rectangular baking dish. Bake, covered, about 30 minutes or until heated through. Sprinkle with Parmesan cheese.

nutrition facts per serving: 333 cal., 15 g total fat (7 g sat. fat), 66 mg chol., 516 mg sodium, 34 g carb., 6 g dietary fiber, 15 g protein.

cheese manicotti with roasted pepper sauce

prep: 30 minutes   bake: 25 minutes   stand: 10 minutes   oven: 350°F
makes: 4 servings

8   dried manicotti shells
    Nonstick cooking
    spray
1   cup chopped fresh
    mushrooms
¾   cup shredded carrots
3   to 4 cloves garlic,
    minced
1   cup light ricotta cheese
    or low-fat cream-
    style cottage cheese
¾   cup shredded reduced-
    fat mozzarella
    cheese (3 ounces)
2   eggs, lightly beaten
¼   cup grated
    Parmesan cheese
2   teaspoons dried Italian
    seasoning, crushed
1   14.5-ounce can no-
    salt-added diced
    tomatoes with basil,
    garlic, and oregano,
    undrained
1   cup roasted red sweet
    peppers, drained
    and chopped

1 Preheat oven to 350°F. Cook manicotti shells according to package directions; drain. Rinse with cold water; drain again.

2 Meanwhile, for filling, coat a large nonstick skillet with cooking spray; heat skillet over medium heat. Add mushrooms, carrots, and garlic; cook for 3 to 5 minutes or just until vegetables are tender, stirring occasionally. Remove from heat; cool slightly. Stir in ricotta cheese, ½ cup of the mozzarella cheese, the eggs, Parmesan cheese, and Italian seasoning. Spoon filling into shells.

3 For sauce, place tomatoes in a blender or food processor. Cover and blend or process until smooth. Stir in roasted peppers. Spread about ⅓ cup of the sauce in the bottom of each of four ungreased 12- to 16-ounce individual baking dishes or a 2-quart rectangular baking dish. Arrange filled manicotti shells in baking dishes, overlapping shells slightly if necessary. Pour the remaining sauce over shells.

4 Bake, covered, for 20 to 25 minutes for individual baking dishes, 35 to 40 minutes for large baking dish, or until heated through. Sprinkle with the remaining ¼ cup mozzarella cheese. Bake, uncovered, for 5 minutes more. Let stand for 10 minutes before serving.

nutrition facts per serving: 377 cal., 13 g total fat (7 g sat. fat), 140 mg chol., 370 mg sodium, 43 g carb., 9 g dietary fiber, 22 g protein.

moroccan chickpeas
and couscous

start to finish: 25 minutes makes: 6 servings

1½ cups water
1 cup whole
   wheat couscous
¾ cup sliced green
   onions (6)
4 cloves garlic, minced
1 tablespoon olive oil
1 tablespoon grated
   fresh ginger
1 teaspoon ground
   cumin
¼ teaspoon ground
   black pepper
¼ teaspoon ground
   turmeric
¼ teaspoon ground
   nutmeg
⅛ teaspoon salt
2 15-ounce cans no-
   salt-added garbanzo
   beans (chickpeas),
   rinsed and drained
½ cup pimiento-stuffed
   or jalapeño-stuffed
   green olives,
   coarsely chopped
½ cup coarsely snipped
   dried apricots
⅓ cup snipped fresh
   Italian (flat-leaf)
   parsley

1 In a small saucepan bring the water to boiling. Stir in couscous. Remove from heat; let stand, covered, for 5 minutes.

2 Meanwhile, in a large saucepan cook green onions and garlic in hot oil over medium heat about 3 minutes or until green onions are tender, stirring occasionally. Stir in ginger, cumin, pepper, turmeric, nutmeg, and salt; cook and stir for 1 minute. Add beans, olives, and dried apricots; cook and stir until heated through.

3 Fluff couscous with a fork; stir in parsley. Serve bean mixture over couscous.

nutrition facts per serving: 343 cal., 6 g total fat (1 g sat. fat), 0 mg chol., 231 mg sodium, 60 g carb., 12 g dietary fiber, 14 g protein.

Quinoa (KEEN-wah) is a nutrient-packed grain as versatile as rice. When combined with barley and vegetables, it elevates this stuffed pepper dish to tantalizing heights.

peppers stuffed with quinoa and spinach

prep: 35 minutes   bake: 45 minutes   oven: 400°F   makes: 6 servings

1   14-ounce can
     reduced-sodium
     vegetable broth
¼   cup quick-cooking
     barley
¼   cup quinoa, rinsed
     and drained
2   tablespoons olive oil
½   cup chopped onion
     (1 medium)
2   cloves garlic, minced
2   cups sliced fresh
     mushrooms
1   14.5-ounce can
     no-salt-added
     diced tomatoes,
     undrained
½   of a 10-ounce
     package frozen
     chopped spinach,
     thawed and well
     drained
¼   teaspoon salt
¼   teaspoon ground
     black pepper
1   cup shredded
     Monterey Jack
     cheese with
     jalapeño peppers
     or Monterey Jack
     cheese (4 ounces)
3   large red sweet
     peppers
¼   teaspoon salt
¼   teaspoon ground
     black pepper

1 Preheat oven to 400°F. In a medium saucepan bring broth to boiling. Stir in barley and quinoa. Return to boiling; reduce heat. Simmer, covered, about 12 minutes or until tender. Drain, reserving cooking liquid.

2 Meanwhile, in a large skillet heat oil over medium-high heat. Add onion and garlic; cook and stir for 2 minutes. Add mushrooms; cook and stir for 4 to 5 minutes or until mushrooms and onion are tender. Stir in tomatoes, spinach, ¼ teaspoon salt, and ¼ teaspoon black pepper. Stir in quinoa mixture and ½ cup of the cheese.

3 Cut sweet peppers in half lengthwise; remove seeds and membranes. Lightly sprinkle insides of peppers with additional salt and black pepper. Fill pepper halves with quinoa mixture. Place filled pepper halves in an ungreased 3-quart rectangular baking dish. Pour the reserved cooking liquid into baking dish around peppers.

4 Bake, covered, for 35 minutes. Sprinkle with the remaining ½ cup cheese. Bake, uncovered, about 10 minutes more or until sweet peppers are crisp-tender and cheese is light brown.

nutrition facts per serving: 345 cal., 17 g total fat (7 g sat. fat), 30 mg chol., 798 mg sodium, 36 g carb., 8 g dietary fiber, 15 g protein.

couscous and squash

start to finish: 30 minutes makes: 4 servings

¼ cup lime juice
3 tablespoons olive oil
½ teaspoon salt
½ teaspoon ground cumin
½ teaspoon ground black pepper
2 small zucchini and/or yellow summer squash
1 small head cauliflower, trimmed
1 small red onion
1½ cups water
1 cup couscous
1 teaspoon finely shredded lime peel
Snipped fresh parsley (optional)

1 In a small bowl whisk together lime juice, oil, salt, cumin, and pepper; set aside.

2 Cut zucchini lengthwise into ½-inch-thick slices. Cut cauliflower crosswise into four equal slices. Cut red onion crosswise into ½-inch-thick slices. Brush vegetable slices with some of the oil mixture.

3 For a charcoal grill, grill vegetables on the rack of an uncovered grill directly over medium coals until crisp-tender, carefully turning vegetables once with a wide spatula halfway through grilling. Allow 5 to 6 minutes for zucchini and 10 to 12 minutes for cauliflower and onion. (For a gas grill, preheat grill. Reduce heat to medium. Place vegetables on grill rack over heat. Cover and grill as above.)

4 Meanwhile, in a small saucepan bring the water to boiling. Stir in couscous and lime peel. Remove from heat; let stand, covered, for 5 minutes. Fluff couscous with a fork.

5 To serve, drizzle vegetables and couscous with the remaining oil mixture. If desired, sprinkle with parsley.

nutrition facts per serving: 311 cal., 11 g total fat (2 g sat. fat), 0 mg chol., 335 mg sodium, 46 g carb., 6 g dietary fiber, 9 g protein.

nutty meatless loaf

prep: 30 minutes bake: 35 minutes stand: 15 minutes oven: 350°F
makes: 8 servings

Nonstick cooking
   spray
3   cups water
1¼ cups red or yellow
   lentils, rinsed and
   drained
1   cup shredded carrots
   (2 medium)
¾ cup snipped dried
   apricots and/or
   golden raisins
½ cup chopped onion
   (1 medium)
½ cup chopped celery
   (1 stalk)
1½ teaspoons garam
   masala or
   2 teaspoons
   Jamaican jerk
   seasoning
2   cloves garlic, minced
1   tablespoon
   vegetable oil
3   eggs, lightly beaten
1½ cups cooked brown
   rice
¾ cup pecans, toasted
   and chopped
½ cup mango chutney
1   teaspoon salt
¼ cup chopped red
   sweet pepper
¼ cup peeled and
   chopped mango
Fresh cilantro leaves
   (optional)

1 Preheat oven to 350°F. Lightly coat a 9- or 9½-inch deep-dish pie plate with cooking spray; set aside. In a medium saucepan combine the water and lentils. Bring to boiling; reduce heat. Simmer, covered, for 10 to 15 minutes or until lentils are tender; drain.

2 Meanwhile, in a medium skillet cook carrots, dried apricots and/or raisins, onion, celery, garam masala, and garlic in hot oil over medium heat about 5 minutes or until onion is tender, stirring occasionally.

3 In a large bowl combine eggs, cooked rice, ⅔ cup of the pecans, ¼ cup of the chutney, and the salt. Stir in cooked lentils and carrot mixture. Press mixture firmly into the prepared pie plate. Bake for 25 minutes.

4 For topping, in a small bowl combine the remaining pecans, the remaining ¼ cup chutney, sweet pepper, and mango. Spoon topping over lentil loaf.

5 Bake about 10 minutes more or until topping is heated through and temperature of loaf registers 160°F. If desired, sprinkle with cilantro. Let stand for 15 minutes before cutting into wedges.

nutrition facts per serving: 347 cal., 12 g total fat (1 g sat. fat), 79 mg chol., 471 mg sodium, 49 g carb., 13 g dietary fiber, 13 g protein.

tomato-artichoke
focaccia

prep: 40 minutes   rise: 1 hour 15 minutes   bake: 25 minutes   oven: 450°F
makes: 6 servings

3½   to 4 cups all-purpose
      flour
  1   package active
      dry yeast
  1   teaspoon salt
1¼   cups warm water
      (120°F to 130°F)
  2   tablespoons olive oil
  ¼   cup cornmeal
      Nonstick cooking
      spray
1¼   pounds roma
      tomatoes and/or
      green or yellow
      tomatoes, thinly
      sliced
  1   14-ounce can
      artichoke hearts,
      drained and
      quartered
  1   tablespoon olive oil
  1   tablespoon snipped
      fresh rosemary or
      1 teaspoon dried
      rosemary, crushed
  1   small red onion, very
      thinly sliced and
      separated into rings
  4   cloves garlic, cut into
      thin slivers or slices

1 In a large bowl combine 1½ cups of the flour, the yeast, and salt. Add the warm water and 2 tablespoons oil. Beat with an electric mixer on low speed for 30 seconds, scraping side of bowl constantly. Beat on high speed for 3 minutes. Using a wooden spoon, stir in cornmeal and as much of the remaining flour as you can.

2 Turn dough out onto a lightly floured surface. Knead in enough of the remaining flour to make a moderately soft dough that is smooth and elastic (3 to 5 minutes total). Shape dough into a ball. Place in a lightly greased bowl, turning once to grease surface. Cover and let rise in a warm place until double in size (45 to 60 minutes).

3 Punch dough down; cover and let rest for 10 minutes. Lightly coat a 15x10x1-inch baking pan with cooking spray. Place dough in the prepared baking pan. Gently pull and stretch dough into a 15x8-inch rectangle, being careful not to overwork dough.

4 Lightly coat dough with cooking spray. Cover loosely with plastic wrap; let dough rise in a warm place until nearly double in size (about 30 minutes). Meanwhile, arrange tomato slices and artichoke quarters on a double thickness of paper towels; let stand for 15 minutes. Change paper towels as necessary so all of the excess liquid is absorbed from tomatoes and artichokes.

5 Preheat oven to 450°F. Using your fingers, press deep indentations, 1½ to 2 inches apart, in dough. Brush dough with 1 tablespoon oil; sprinkle with rosemary. Arrange tomatoes, artichokes, red onion, and garlic evenly on top of dough.

6 Bake about 25 minutes or until golden brown. Transfer to a wire rack; cool. Cut into rectangles. Serve warm or at room temperature.

nutrition facts per serving: 394 cal., 8 g total fat (2 g sat. fat), 0 mg chol., 620 mg sodium, 70 g carb., 6 g dietary fiber, 10 g protein.

summer ratatouille tart

prep: 50 minutes   bake: 25 minutes   stand: 20 minutes   oven: 400°F/350°F
makes: 6 servings

½   of a 15-ounce
    package (1 crust)
    rolled refrigerated
    unbaked piecrust
¼   cup chopped
    yellow onion
2   cloves garlic, minced
1   tablespoon olive oil
4   cups peeled and
    cubed eggplant
    (1 small)
1¼ cups sliced zucchini
    (1 medium)
¾   cup sweet red pepper
    cut into bite-size
    pieces (1 medium)
1½ cups peeled and
    chopped tomatoes
    (3 medium)
½   teaspoon sea salt
    or salt
½   teaspoon dried
    herbes de Provence
    or Italian
    seasoning, crushed
½   teaspoon ground
    black pepper
8   ounces fresh
    asparagus spears,
    trimmed and cut
    into 2-inch pieces
¼   cup finely shredded
    Parmesan cheese
    (1 ounce)

1 Preheat oven to 400°F. Let piecrust stand according to package directions. Line the bottom and side of a 9- to 10-inch tart pan that has a removable bottom with piecrust. Line piecrust with foil. Bake for 10 minutes. Remove foil; bake for 5 minutes more. Cool on a wire rack. Reduce oven temperature to 350°F.

2 Meanwhile, in a large saucepan cook onion and garlic in hot oil over medium heat about 3 minutes or until onion is tender, stirring occasionally. Add eggplant, zucchini, and half of the sweet pepper; cook and stir about 10 minutes or until vegetables are tender. Stir in tomatoes, salt, herbes de Provence, and black pepper. Simmer, covered, for 10 minutes. Simmer, uncovered, about 10 minutes more or until mixture is thickened and most of the liquid is evaporated.

3 Spoon vegetable mixture into the partially baked tart shell. Bake for 10 minutes. Top with the remaining sweet pepper and the asparagus. Bake for 15 minutes more. Sprinkle with cheese. Let stand for 20 minutes before serving.

nutrition facts per serving: 237 cal., 13 g total fat (4 g sat. fat), 6 mg chol., 344 mg sodium, 27 g carb 4 g dietary fiber, 4 g protein.

meatless **entrées**

grilled eggplant parmesan

prep: 20 minutes grill: 10 minutes makes: 2 servings

4 ¾-inch-thick slices
   eggplant
¼ teaspoon salt
¼ teaspoon ground
   black pepper
1 tablespoon balsamic
   vinegar
2 teaspoons olive oil
1 teaspoon snipped
   fresh thyme
1 clove garlic, minced
2 tablespoons finely
   shredded Parmesan
   cheese
2 tablespoons
   finely shredded
   mozzarella cheese
1 medium roma tomato,
   cut into ½-inch-
   thick slices
¼ cup reduced-sodium
   tomato pasta sauce,
   warmed
   Snipped fresh thyme
   (optional)

1 Sprinkle eggplant with salt and pepper. In a small bowl combine vinegar, oil, 1 teaspoon thyme, and garlic; brush on both sides of eggplant.

2 For a charcoal grill, grill eggplant on the rack of an uncovered grill directly over medium coals for 10 to 12 minutes or until tender, turning once halfway through grilling and topping with Parmesan and mozzarella cheeses for the last 3 minutes of grilling. (For a gas grill, preheat grill. Reduce heat to medium. Place eggplant on grill rack over heat. Cover and grill as above.)

3 While eggplant is grilling, add tomato slices to grill. Grill about 3 minutes or until heated through and grill marks appear, turning once halfway through grilling.

4 Serve eggplant slices with pasta sauce and tomato slices. If desired, garnish with additional thyme.

nutrition facts per serving: 153 cal., 9 g total fat (3 g sat. fat), 7 mg chol., 436 mg sodium, 13 g carb., 5 g dietary fiber, 6 g protein.

Looking for a way to sneak some vegetables into your kids diets? This pizza makes it easy—and kids will clamor for it.

deep-dish garden vegetable pizza

prep: 30 minutes bake: 20 minutes oven: 400°F makes: 6 servings

1 egg, lightly beaten
1 8.5-ounce package corn muffin mix
⅓ cup all-purpose flour
3 tablespoons skim milk
1 tablespoon dried Italian seasoning, crushed
1 cup shredded carrots (2 medium)
1 cup fresh or frozen corn kernels, thawed
1 cup chopped red or green sweet pepper
⅔ cup seeded and chopped roma tomatoes (2 medium)
1 fresh jalapeño chile pepper, seeded and finely chopped*
1 tablespoon snipped fresh oregano
¼ cup bottled Italian salad dressing
1½ cups finely shredded reduced-fat Italian cheese blend (6 ounces)
1 tablespoon snipped fresh Italian (flat-leaf) parsley

1 Preheat oven to 400°F. Generously grease a 13x9x2-inch baking pan; set aside. In a medium bowl combine egg, corn muffin mix, flour, milk, and Italian seasoning. Turn dough out onto a well-floured surface. Knead for 10 to 12 strokes or until easy to handle (dough will be soft). Using floured hands, pat dough into the prepared baking pan.

2 Sprinkle carrots, corn, sweet pepper, tomatoes, jalapeño chile pepper, and oregano over dough. Drizzle with Italian dressing; sprinkle with cheese.

3 Bake about 20 minutes or until a toothpick inserted near the center comes out clean. Sprinkle with parsley.

nutrition facts per serving: 355 cal., 13 g total fat (4 g sat. fat), 50 mg chol., 695 mg sodium, 46 g carb., 2 g dietary fiber, 14 g protein.

*tip: Because chile peppers contain volatile oils that can burn your skin and eyes, avoid direct contact with them as much as possible. When working with chile peppers, wear plastic or rubber gloves. If your bare hands do touch the peppers, wash your hands and nails well with soap and warm water.

cheesy red pepper pizza

prep: 15 minutes   bake: 15 minutes   oven: 425°F   makes: 4 servings

Nonstick cooking
    spray
1   13.8-ounce package
    refrigerated pizza
    dough
1   tablespoon olive oil
1   cup shredded
    mozzarella cheese
    (4 ounces)
2   medium roma
    tomatoes, thinly
    sliced
½   cup sliced roasted
    yellow and/or red
    sweet pepper
2   tablespoons shredded
    fresh spinach
    (optional)
¼   teaspoon coarse
    ground black
    pepper
2   tablespoons snipped
    fresh basil

1 Preheat oven to 425°F. Coat a 12-inch pizza pan with cooking spray. Press pizza dough into the prepared pan, building up edge. Brush crust with oil. Bake for 10 minutes.

2 Remove crust from oven. Sprinkle with cheese. Arrange tomatoes, roasted sweet pepper, and spinach (if using) on crust. Sprinkle with black pepper.

3 Bake for 5 to 10 minutes more or until cheese is bubbly. Sprinkle with basil

nutrition facts per serving: 364 cal., 12 g total fat (4 g sat. fat), 18 mg chol., 718 mg sodium, 50 g carb., 2 g dietary fiber, 16 g protein.

thai bulgur salad

prep: 25 minutes cook: 15 minutes makes: 4 servings

1 cup water
½ cup bulgur
2 cups frozen shelled sweet soybeans (edamame), thawed
1 cup red sweet pepper cut into thin bite-size strips (1 medium)
½ cup coarsely shredded carrot (1 medium)
½ cup thinly sliced, quartered red onion
2 tablespoons snipped fresh cilantro
4 cups packaged fresh spinach leaves
1 recipe Thai Peanut Dressing
¼ cup chopped peanuts (optional)

1 In a medium saucepan bring the water to boiling; stir in bulgur. Return to boiling; reduce heat. Simmer, covered, about 15 minutes or until bulgur is tender and most of the liquid is absorbed. Drain if necessary. Transfer to a large bowl. Stir in soybeans, sweet pepper, carrot, red onion, and cilantro.

2 Divide spinach among salad bowls or dinner plates. Top with bulgur mixture; drizzle with Thai Peanut Dressing. If desired, sprinkle with peanuts.

nutrition facts per serving: 313 cal., 12 g total fat (2 g sat. fat), 0 mg chol., 436 mg sodium, 36 g carb., 10 g dietary fiber, 19 g protein.

thai peanut dressing: In a small saucepan combine ⅓ cup water; ¼ cup reduced-fat creamy peanut butter; 2 tablespoons reduced-sodium soy sauce; 1 teaspoon sugar; 1 clove garlic, minced; ¼ teaspoon ground ginger; and ⅛ teaspoon crushed red pepper. Cook, whisking constantly, over medium-low heat about 3 minutes or until smooth and slightly thickened (mixture will appear curdled at first, but will become smooth as it is whisked over the heat). Makes ⅔ cup.

nutrition note

Bulgur can usually be found in the health-food aisles of the supermarket. Or, head to health-food stores, where it's often available in bulk containers, allowing you to buy just the amount you need for a recipe.

cheesy
eggplant burgers
prep: 15 minutes grill: 6 minutes makes: 6 servings

1   teaspoon garlic
    powder
½   teaspoon ground
    black pepper
⅛   teaspoon salt
½   cup seeded and
    chopped tomato
    (1 medium)
2   tablespoons olive oil
1   tablespoon snipped
    fresh oregano
2   teaspoons snipped
    fresh thyme
2   teaspoons cider
    vinegar
6   ½-inch slices
    eggplant
4   to 5 ounces sliced
    smoked Gouda
    cheese
6   ½-inch slices whole
    grain baguette-
    style French bread,
    toasted

1 In a small bowl combine garlic powder,
pepper, and salt. In another small bowl
combine half of the garlic powder mixture, the
tomato, 1 tablespoon of the oil, the oregano,
thyme, and vinegar; set aside.

2 Brush both sides of eggplant slices with
the remaining 1 tablespoon oil. Sprinkle
with the remaining garlic powder mixture.

3 For a charcoal grill, grill eggplant on the
rack of an uncovered grill directly over
medium coals for 6 to 8 minutes or just until
tender and golden brown, turning once
halfway through grilling and topping with
cheese for the last 2 minutes of grilling. (For a
gas grill, preheat grill. Reduce heat to medium.
Place eggplant on grill rack over heat. Cover
and grill as above.)

4 Serve eggplant slices on toasted bread
slices with tomato mixture.

nutrition facts per serving: 201 cal., 11 g total fat
(4 g sat. fat), 17 mg chol., 506 mg sodium, 19 g carb.,
4 g dietary fiber, 7 g protein.

black bean chipotle
burgers

prep: 35 minutes   chill: 1 hour   cook: 10 minutes   makes: 4 servings

1   15-ounce can no-salt-
     added black beans,
     rinsed and drained
1   cup baked corn chips,
     finely crushed
     (about ½ cup
     crushed)
½   cup cooked
     brown rice
½   cup frozen whole
     kernel corn, thawed
¼   cup finely chopped
     red onion
¼   cup chunky salsa
½   to 1 teaspoon finely
     chopped canned
     chipotle pepper in
     adobo sauce*
1   clove garlic, minced
½   teaspoon ground
     cumin
1   tablespoon olive oil
     Shredded green
     cabbage
4   tostada shells, heated
     according to
     package directions
     Radish slices
     Fresh cilantro leaves
     Light sour cream
     (optional)
     Chunky salsa
     (optional)
     Lime wedges
     (optional)

1 In a medium bowl mash half of the beans
with a fork or potato masher. Stir in the
remaining beans, corn chips, cooked rice, corn,
red onion, ¼ cup salsa, chipotle pepper, garlic,
and cumin.

2 Shape bean mixture into four ¾-inch-thick
patties. Place patties on a plate; cover and
chill for at least 1 hour before cooking.

3 Brush both sides of patties with oil. In a
12-inch skillet or large griddle cook patties
over medium heat about 10 minutes or until
heated through, turning once.

4 Place some shredded cabbage on each
tostada shell; top with burgers, radish,
and cilantro. If desired, serve with sour cream,
additional salsa, and lime wedges.

nutrition facts per burger: 399 cal, 11 g total fat
(2 g sat. fat), 0 mg chol., 245 mg sodium, 43 g carb.,
8 g dietary fiber, 9 g protein.

*tip: Because chile peppers contain volatile oils
that can burn your skin and eyes, avoid direct
contact with them as much as possible. When
working with chile peppers, wear plastic or rubber
gloves. If your bare hands do touch the peppers,
wash your hands and nails well with soap and
warm water.

broiling directions: Preheat broiler. Place patties on the
unheated rack of a broiler pan. Broil about 4 inches from the heat
about 10 minutes or until heated through, turning once halfway
through broiling.

tomato-edamame
grilled cheese
prep: 20 minutes   roast: 15 minutes   oven: 425°F   makes: 4 sandwiches

1   garlic bulb
1   teaspoon canola oil
1   12-ounce package
     frozen shelled sweet
     soybeans (edamame)
¼   cup lemon juice
¼   cup water
½   teaspoon salt
½   teaspoon ground
     cumin
⅓   cup snipped fresh
     Italian (flat-leaf)
     parsley
8   slices whole
     grain bread
4   ounces reduced-fat
     Monterey Jack
     cheese, thinly sliced
1   tomato, thinly sliced

1 Preheat oven to 425°F. Cut off the top
½ inch of garlic bulb to expose ends of
individual cloves. Leaving garlic bulb whole,
remove any loose, papery outer layers. Place
bulb, cut side up, in a custard cup. Drizzle with
oil. Cover with foil; roast about 15 minutes or
until garlic feels soft when squeezed; cool.

2 Meanwhile, cook soybeans according to
package directions; drain. Rinse with cold
water; drain again.

3 Squeeze three of the garlic cloves from
bulb into a food processor. (Wrap and chill
the remaining garlic cloves for another use.)
Add cooked soybeans, lemon juice, the water,
salt, and cumin to garlic in food processor.
Cover and process until smooth. Transfer to a
small bowl; stir in parsley.

4 Spread one side of each bread slice with
2 tablespoons of the soybean mixture.
(Cover and chill the remaining 1 cup mixture
for another use.) Layer four of the bread slices
with cheese and tomato slices. Top with
the remaining four bread slices, spread
sides down.

5 Heat a nonstick griddle or large skillet over
medium-high heat. Add sandwiches; cook
until bread is toasted and cheese is melted,
turning once.

nutrition facts per sandwich: 332 cal., 12 g total fat
(4 g sat. fat), 20 mg chol., 685 mg sodium, 38 g carb.,
11 g dietary fiber, 22 g protein.

baked bean and corn chimichangas

prep: 25 minutes bake: 10 minutes oven: 425°F makes: 6 servings

Nonstick cooking
  spray
6 10-inch whole wheat
    flour tortillas
½ cup chopped onion
    (1 medium)
1 15-ounce can no-salt-
    added black beans,
    rinsed and drained
1 8.75-ounce can
    reduced-sodium
    whole kernel corn,
    rinsed and drained
1 cup green salsa or
    red salsa
½ cup chopped tomato
    (1 medium)
¼ cup snipped fresh
    cilantro
¾ cup shredded
    reduced-fat
    Monterey Jack
    cheese (3 ounces)

1 Preheat oven to 425°F. Coat a baking sheet with cooking spray; set aside. Stack tortillas and wrap in foil. Bake about 5 minutes or until warm and softened.

2 Meanwhile, for filling, coat a large skillet with cooking spray; heat skillet over medium heat. Add onion, cook about 5 minutes or until tender, stirring occasionally. Add beans. Using a fork or potato masher, mash beans slightly. Stir in corn, ½ cup of the salsa, and the tomato; heat through. Stir in cilantro.

3 To assemble, spoon about ½ cup of the filling onto each tortilla, spooning filling just below the center. Fold bottom edge of each tortilla up and over filling. Fold in opposite sides, roll up from the bottom. If necessary, secure with wooden toothpicks. Place filled tortillas, seam sides down, on the prepared baking sheet. Coat top and sides of the filled tortillas with cooking spray.

4 Bake for 10 to 12 minutes or until tortillas are golden brown and crisp. To serve, sprinkle chimichangas with cheese and top with the remaining ½ cup salsa.

nutrition facts per serving: 325 cal., 10 g total fat (3 g sat. fat), 10 mg chol., 916 mg sodium, 47 g carb., 9 g dietary fiber, 15 g protein.

mushroom and
poblano enchiladas

start to finish: 30 minutes   makes: 4 servings

1   tablespoon
     vegetable oil
3   cups sliced fresh
     cremini mushrooms
     (8 ounces)
6   ounces firm, tub-style
     tofu (fresh bean
     curd), drained and
     cut into cubes
1   small fresh poblano
     chile pepper,
     stemmed, seeded,
     and cut into strips*
1   teaspoon ground
     cumin
½   teaspoon salt
1   cup shredded
     reduced-fat cheddar
     cheese (4 ounces)
¼   cup light sour cream
8   6-inch corn tortillas
     Chopped tomatoes
     (optional)
     Sliced green onions
     (optional)

1 Preheat broiler. For filling, in a large skillet heat oil over medium heat. Add mushrooms, tofu, poblano chile pepper, cumin, and salt; cook for 8 to 10 minutes or until mushrooms and pepper are tender, stirring occasionally. Remove from heat. Stir in ½ cup of the cheese and the sour cream.

2 Lightly grease a 3-quart rectangular baking dish; set aside. Stack tortillas and wrap in damp paper towels. Microwave on 100 percent power (high) about 30 seconds or until warm and softened. Spoon filling onto tortillas; roll up and place in the prepared baking dish. Sprinkle with the remaining ½ cup cheese.

3 Broil 4 to 5 inches from the heat for 1 to 2 minutes or until cheese is melted. If desired, top with tomatoes and green onions.

nutrition facts per serving: 292 cal., 13 g total fat (5 g sat. fat), 20 mg chol., 549 mg sodium, 30 g carb., 4 g dietary fiber, 16 g protein.

*tip: Because chile peppers contain volatile oils that can burn your skin and eyes, avoid direct contact with them as much as possible. When working with chile peppers, wear plastic or rubber gloves. If your bare hands do touch the peppers, wash your hands and nails well with soap and warm water.

nutrition note

Soy products such as tofu make winning switch-ins for meat. A complete protein, soy contains all the essential amino acids, yet has less fat and cholesterol than meat products.

meatless **entrées**

gingered vegetable–tofu
stir-fry

start to finish: 45 minutes makes: 4 servings

¾ cup water
¼ cup dry sherry, dry
    white wine, or
    chicken broth
3 tablespoons reduced-
    sodium soy sauce
1 tablespoon cornstarch
½ teaspoon sugar
1 tablespoon olive oil
2 teaspoons grated
    fresh ginger
1 pound fresh
    asparagus spears,
    trimmed and
    cut into 1-inch
    pieces (2½ cups),
    or one 10-ounce
    package frozen cut
    asparagus, thawed
    and well drained
1 medium yellow
    summer squash,
    halved lengthwise
    and sliced (1¼ cups)
¼ cup sliced green
    onions (2)
1 10.5-ounce package
    extra-firm, tub-style
    tofu (fresh bean
    curd), drained
    and cut into
    ½-inch cubes
⅓ cup chopped
    toasted almonds
2 cups hot cooked
    brown rice

1 For sauce, in a small bowl stir together the water, sherry, soy sauce, cornstarch, and sugar; set aside.

2 Pour oil into a wok or large skillet; heat wok over medium-high heat. Add ginger (add more oil if necessary during cooking); cook and stir for 15 seconds. Add fresh asparagus (if using) and squash; cook and stir for 3 minutes. Add thawed asparagus (if using) and green onions; cook and stir about 1½ minutes more or until asparagus is crisp-tender. Remove vegetables from wok.

3 Add tofu to wok; cook and stir carefully for 2 to 3 minutes or until light brown. Remove from wok. Stir sauce; add to wok. Cook and stir until thickened and bubbly. Return cooked vegetables and tofu to wok; stir all ingredients together to coat with sauce. Cook, covered, about 1 minute more or until heated through. Stir in almonds. Serve over hot cooked rice.

nutrition facts per serving: 288 cal., 10 g total fat (1 g sat. fat), 0 mg chol., 432 mg sodium, 35 g carb., 5 g dietary fiber, 12 g protein.

big batch vegetarian lentil chili

prep: 15 minutes   cook: 35 minutes   makes: 12 servings

4   14.5-ounce cans
     no-salt-added
     diced tomatoes,
     undrained
2   15-ounce cans no-
     salt-added red
     kidney beans,
     rinsed and drained
3   cups water
2   cups red lentils,
     rinsed and drained
1   12-ounce package
     frozen chopped
     green sweet
     peppers
1   12-ounce package
     frozen chopped
     onions
¼   cup chili powder
2   tablespoons garlic
     powder
1   8-ounce can no-salt-
     added tomato sauce
1   6-ounce can no-salt-
     added tomato paste
⅛   teaspoon ground
     black pepper
2   cups shredded
     reduced-fat cheddar
     cheese (8 ounces)
     Tortilla chips
     (optional)

1 In an 8-quart Dutch oven combine tomatoes, beans, the water, lentils, sweet peppers, onions, chili powder, and garlic powder. Bring to boiling; reduce heat. Simmer, covered, for 30 minutes, stirring occasionally.

2 Stir in tomato sauce, tomato paste, and black pepper. Simmer, covered, about 5 minutes more or until heated through. Sprinkle each serving with cheese and, if desired, serve with tortilla chips.

nutrition facts per serving: 314 cal., 7 g total fat (4 g sat. fat), 20 mg chol., 752 mg sodium, 47 g carb., 19 g dietary fiber, 21 g protein.

tip: Store any leftovers in a covered container in the refrigerator for up to 3 days or in the freezer for up to 3 months.

bubbly cass

10

Lift the lid on the amazing aromas and terrific tastes of oven-baked goodness. This caboodle of casseroles will lighten more than just your mood.

casseroles

Reduced-fat cheese and light sour cream join other healthful ingredients in this spiced-up casserole.

mexican beef bake with cilantro-lime cream

prep: 25 minutes **bake:** 33 minutes **oven:** 350°F **makes:** 6 servings

1⅓ cups dried multigrain rotini pasta or elbow macaroni
12 ounces extra-lean ground beef
2 cloves garlic, minced
1 15-ounce can black beans or pinto beans, rinsed and drained
1 14.5-ounce can no-salt-added diced tomatoes, undrained
¾ cup picante sauce or salsa
1 teaspoon dried oregano, crushed
½ teaspoon ground cumin
½ teaspoon chili powder
½ cup shredded reduced-fat Colby and Monterey Jack cheese (2 ounces)
⅓ cup light sour cream
3 tablespoons sliced green onions
2 teaspoons coarsely snipped fresh cilantro (optional)
½ teaspoon finely shredded lime peel
Lime wedges (optional)

1 Preheat oven to 350°F. In a large saucepan cook pasta according to package directions; drain. Return pasta to hot saucepan; set aside.

2 Meanwhile, in a large skillet cook meat and garlic until meat is brown, using a wooden spoon to break up meat as it cooks. Drain off fat.

3 Stir meat into pasta in saucepan. Stir in beans, tomatoes, picante sauce, oregano, cumin, and chili powder. Transfer mixture to an ungreased 1½- or 2-quart baking dish or casserole.

4 Bake, covered, about 30 minutes or until heated through. Sprinkle with cheese. Bake, uncovered, about 3 minutes more or until cheese is melted.

5 Meanwhile, in a small bowl stir together sour cream, 2 tablespoons of the green onions, the cilantro (if using), and lime peel. Serve beef mixture with sour cream mixture, the remaining 1 tablespoon green onions, and, if desired, lime wedges.

nutrition facts per serving: 283 cal., 10 g total fat (4 g sat. fat), 45 mg chol., 520 mg sodium, 29 g carb., 7 g dietary fiber, 23 g protein.

Serve this recipe when you crave classic comfort food but want more nutrients and fiber than are present in refined wheat pasta.

chicken caesar lasagna

prep: 35 minutes **bake:** 50 minutes **stand:** 15 minutes **oven:** 325°F
makes: 9 servings

9 dried whole wheat or regular lasagna noodles

2 10-ounce containers refrigerated light Alfredo sauce

3 tablespoons lemon juice

½ teaspoon cracked black pepper

3 cups chopped, cooked chicken breast*

1 10-ounce package frozen chopped spinach, thawed and well drained

1 cup bottled roasted red sweet peppers, drained and chopped
Nonstick cooking spray

¾ cup shredded Italian blend cheese (3 ounces)

1 Preheat oven to 325°F. Cook lasagna noodles according to package directions; drain. Rinse with cold water; drain again. Meanwhile, in a large bowl combine Alfredo sauce, lemon juice, and black pepper. Stir in chicken, spinach, and roasted sweet peppers.

2 Lightly coat a 3-quart rectangular baking dish with cooking spray. Arrange three of the noodles in bottom of dish. Top with one-third of the chicken mixture. Repeat layers twice. Bake, covered, for 45 to 55 minutes or until heated through. Sprinkle with cheese. Bake, uncovered, about 5 minutes more or until cheese is melted. Let stand for 15 minutes before serving.

nutrition facts per serving: 268 cal., 10 g total fat (6 g sat. fat), 68 mg chol., 557 mg sodium, 20 g carb., 2 g dietary fiber, 24 g protein.

*****tip:** For chopped cooked chicken, season 2 pounds skinless, boneless chicken breast halves with ¼ teaspoon salt and ⅛ teaspoon ground black pepper. Heat 1 tablespoon olive oil in skillet over medium-high heat. Reduce heat to medium. Add chicken. Cook, uncovered, for 8 to 12 minutes or until no longer pink (170°F), turning once halfway through cooking. Cool chicken slightly before chopping.

chicken and tortillas with tomatillo sauce

prep: 40 minutes **bake:** 30 minutes **oven:** 350°F **makes:** 8 servings

1 pound skinless, boneless chicken thighs
1 teaspoon salt
2½ pounds fresh tomatillos, husked and quartered*
3 cloves garlic, halved
2 fresh jalapeño chile peppers, stemmed, seeded, and cut up**
1½ cups reduced-fat shredded Mexican-style four-cheese blend (6 ounces)
½ of an 8-ounce package reduced-fat cream cheese, softened
1½ teaspoons chili powder
Nonstick cooking spray
8 8-inch flour tortillas
Cherry tomatoes, quartered (optional)
Fresh snipped cilantro (optional)

1 Preheat oven to 350°F. In a large saucepan combine chicken thighs and enough cold water to cover; add ½ teaspoon of the salt. Bring to boiling; reduce heat to medium low. Simmer, covered, about 15 minutes or until chicken is tender. Using a slotted spoon, transfer chicken to a large bowl; cool. When chicken is cool enough to handle, use two forks to shred meat; set aside.

2 Meanwhile, bring a large saucepan of water to boiling. Add tomatillos and cook for 3 minutes; drain. Transfer tomatillos to a food processor or blender. Add the remaining ½ teaspoon salt, the garlic, and jalapeño chile peppers. Cover and process or blend until smooth.

3 In a medium bowl combine shredded cheese, cream cheese, and chili powder.

4 Coat a 3-quart rectangular baking dish with cooking spray. Spoon one-third of the tomatillo mixture into the prepared baking dish. Lay two of the tortillas over the tomatillo mixture. Top with half of the chicken and half of the cheese mixture. Top with another two tortillas, another one-third of the tomatillo mixture, and two more tortillas. Top with the remaining chicken and the remaining cheese mixture. Top with the remaining two tortillas and the remaining tomatillo mixture. Cover with foil.

5 Bake, covered, about 30 minutes or until heated through and bubbly around the edges. If desired, top with cherry tomatoes and cilantro.

nutrition facts per serving: 359 cal., 14 g total fat (5 g sat. fat), 71 mg chol., 807 mg sodium, 36 g carb., 3 g dietary fiber, 24 g protein.

*tip: If you can't find fresh tomatillos, use 5 cups quartered canned tomatillos. Do not cook. Combine in food processor as directed in Step 2. Continue as directed.

**tip: Because chile peppers contain volatile oils that can burn your skin and eyes, avoid direct contact with them as much as possible. When working with chile peppers, wear plastic or rubber gloves. If your bare hands do touch the peppers, wash your hands and nails well with soap and warm water.

Offer up a variety of toppings and let everyone take their pick.

chicken taco casserole

prep: 25 minutes **bake:** 30 minutes **stand:** 5 minutes **oven:** 350°F
makes: 6 servings

Nonstick cooking
   spray
12 ounces chicken
   breast strips for
   stir-frying
2 cloves garlic, minced
1 teaspoon chili
   powder
2 teaspoons canola oil
1 medium onion,
   halved and
   thinly sliced
¾ cup chopped red or
   green sweet pepper
   (1 medium)
1 10-ounce package
   frozen chopped
   spinach, thawed
   and well drained
1½ cups salsa
4 6-inch corn
   tortillas, torn
¾ cup reduced-fat
   shredded Monterey
   Jack cheese
   (3 ounces)
½ cup cherry tomatoes,
   quartered or
   chopped (optional)
½ of an avocado,
   seeded, peeled, and
   chopped (optional)
Baked tortilla chips
   or broken taco
   shells (optional)

1 Preheat oven to 350°F. Coat a large nonstick skillet with cooking spray; heat skillet over medium-high heat. In a medium bowl toss together chicken, garlic, and chili powder. Add to hot skillet; cook for 4 to 6 minutes or until chicken is no longer pink, stirring frequently. Remove chicken from skillet; set aside.

2 Add oil to hot skillet. Add onion and sweet pepper; cook over medium heat about 5 minutes or until tender, stirring occasionally. Stir in spinach.

3 Coat a 2-quart square baking dish with cooking spray. Spread about ½ cup of the salsa in the baking dish. Top with half of the tortilla pieces, half of the chicken mixture, and half of the vegetable mixture. Pour half of the remaining salsa over the vegetables and top with half of the cheese. Repeat layers once, except do not top with the remaining cheese.

4 Bake, covered, for 30 to 35 minutes or until heated through. Sprinkle with the remaining cheese. Let stand for 5 minutes before serving. If desired, garnish with cherry tomatoes, avocado, and/or tortilla chips.

nutrition facts per serving: 196 cal., 6 g total fat (2 g sat. fat), 43 mg chol., 544 mg sodium, 15 g carb., 4 g dietary fiber, 20 g protein.

greek chicken and
pita casserole

prep: 20 minutes   **bake:** 20 minutes   **oven:** 350°F   **makes:** 6 servings

4   cups chopped cooked chicken or turkey

3   medium zucchini, halved lengthwise and cut into ½-inch pieces (4 cups)

1   10.75-ounce can reduced-fat and reduced-sodium condensed cream of chicken soup

½   cup chopped red onion (1 medium)

½   cup reduced-sodium chicken broth

1½ teaspoons Greek seasoning*

2   cloves garlic, minced

2   6-inch pita bread rounds, cut into bite-size wedges

Nonstick cooking spray

1   cup chopped roma tomatoes (3 medium)

1   cup crumbled reduced-fat feta cheese (4 ounces)

⅓   cup pitted kalamata olives, cut up

1 Preheat oven to 350°F. In a large bowl combine chicken, zucchini, cream of chicken soup, red onion, broth, 1 teaspoon of the Greek seasoning, and the garlic. Transfer mixture to an ungreased 3-quart rectangular baking dish.

2 Coat pita wedges with cooking spray; sprinkle with the remaining ½ teaspoon Greek seasoning. Sprinkle pita wedges, tomatoes, cheese, and olives on top of chicken mixture. Bake about 20 minutes or until heated through.

nutrition facts per serving: 354 cal., 12 g total fat (4 g sat. fat), 94 mg chol., 884 mg sodium, 24 g carb., 3 g dietary fiber, 36 g protein.

*tip: If you can't find Greek seasoning, make your own by combining 2 teaspoons dried oregano, 1½ teaspoons onion powder, 1½ teaspoons garlic powder, 1 teaspoon dried parsley flakes, 1 teaspoon ground black pepper, ½ teaspoon ground cinnamon, and ½ teaspoon ground nutmeg. Store in an airtight container for up to 2 months. Makes about 2 tablespoons.

To adapt this homey, one-dish meal to fit into a healthy diet, we decreased the chicken and took advantage of reduced-fat soup, fat-free milk, and light mayonnaise.

chicken supreme
casserole
prep: 30 minutes **bake:** 40 minutes **stand:** 10 minutes **oven:** 350°F
makes: 4 servings

6	cups water
1⅓	cups dried bow-tie or rotini pasta (6 ounces)
1	16-ounce package frozen sweet pepper and onion stir-fry vegetables
1	10.75-ounce can reduced-fat and reduced-sodium condensed cream of chicken soup
1¼	cups fat-free milk
3	tablespoons light mayonnaise or salad dressing
1	teaspoon salt-free lemon-pepper seasoning
1	cup cubed cooked chicken breast*
	French bread, cut into chunks and toasted (optional)
	Cracked black pepper (optional)

1 Preheat oven to 350°F. In a large saucepan bring the water to boiling. Add pasta; reduce heat. Simmer, uncovered, for 6 minutes, stirring occasionally. Stir in frozen vegetables. Return to boiling; reduce heat. Simmer, uncovered, for 3 to 5 minutes more or until pasta is tender but still firm; drain. Rinse with cold water; drain again. Set aside.

2 In a large bowl stir together cream of chicken soup, milk, mayonnaise, and lemon-pepper seasoning. Stir in chicken and pasta mixture. Transfer mixture to a 2-quart square baking dish.

3 Bake, covered, for 30 minutes. Stir mixture. Bake, uncovered, for 10 to 15 minutes more or until mixture is heated through and bubbly. Let stand for 10 minutes before serving. If desired, top with French bread pieces and cracked black pepper.

nutrition facts per serving: 359 cal., 7 g total fat (1 g sat. fat), 40 mg chol., 441 mg sodium, 51 g carb., 3 g dietary fiber, 22 g protein.

*tip: Since using a packaged, cooked chicken product will increase the sodium, it is best to cook your own chicken breasts to use in this recipe. You may grill, roast, or poach the chicken.

Hand over the cookie cutters and let the kids create their own toppers by cutting into purchased pie crust.

quick chicken potpie

prep: 25 minutes **bake:** 20 minutes
stand: 10 minutes **oven:** 400°F
makes: 6 servings

1 rolled refrigerated
   unbaked piecrust
   (½ of a 15-ounce
   package)
1 pound chicken breast
   strips for stir-frying
2 tablespoons butter
⅓ cup all-purpose flour
½ teaspoon snipped
   fresh thyme
   or oregano
¼ teaspoon ground
   black pepper
2½ cups reduced-sodium
   chicken broth
1½ cups packed coarsely
   shredded carrots or
   carrots cut into bite
   size strips
1½ cups frozen peas
   Milk (optional)
   Coarse salt (optional)

1 Preheat oven to 400°F. Let piecrust stand according to package directions. Meanwhile, cut up any large chicken pieces. In a large skillet melt butter over medium heat. Add chicken; cook for 5 to 6 minutes or until chicken is light brown and no longer pink, stirring frequently. Stir in flour, thyme, and pepper. Add broth all at once. Stir in carrots. Cook and stir over medium heat until thickened and bubbly. Stir in frozen peas; heat through. Cover and keep warm while preparing piecrust cutouts.

2 For topper, unroll piecrust on a lightly floured surface. Cut rounds from pastry to fit on top of six ungreased 10-ounce custard cups or individual casseroles (4 to 4½ inches), rerolling scraps, if necessary. Using 1- to 2-inch desired-shape cutters, cut shapes from center of each pastry round. Spoon chicken mixture into custard cups. Arrange piecrust rounds on top of custard cups. If desired, brush cutout shapes with milk and sprinkle with coarse salt. Arrange one or two cutouts on top of each potpie.

3 Place custard cups in a 15x10x1-inch baking pan. Bake about 20 minutes or until topper is golden brown and mixture is bubbly. Let stand for 10 minutes before serving.

nutrition facts per serving: 345 cal., 14 g total fat (6 g sat. fat), 57 mg chol., 516 mg sodium, 30 g carb., 3 g dietary fiber, 22 g protein.

creamy chicken–broccoli bake

prep: 30 minutes bake: 55 minutes oven: 350°F makes: 12 servings

Nonstick cooking
  spray
10 ounces dried
  medium noodles
1½ pounds skinless,
  boneless chicken
  breasts, cut into
  bite-size pieces
3 cups sliced
  fresh mushrooms
1 cup sliced green
  onions (8)
¾ cup chopped red
  sweet pepper
  (1 medium)
1 tablespoon vegetable
  oil (optional)
2 10.75-ounce cans
  condensed cream of
  broccoli soup
2 8-ounce cartons light
  sour cream
⅓ cup reduced-sodium
  chicken broth
2 teaspoons dry
  mustard
¼ teaspoon ground
  black pepper
1 16-ounce package
  frozen chopped
  broccoli, thawed
  and drained
½ cup fine dry bread
  crumbs
2 tablespoons butter,
  melted
Diagonally sliced
  green onions
  (optional)

1 Preheat oven to 350°F. Coat a 3-quart rectangular baking dish with cooking spray; set aside.

2 Cook noodles according to package directions; drain. Rinse with cold water; drain again.

3 Meanwhile, coat a large skillet with cooking spray; heat over medium heat. Add chicken to hot skillet; cook and stir about 3 minutes or until chicken is no longer pink. Transfer chicken to a large bowl.

4 Add mushrooms, 1 cup green onions, and sweet pepper to skillet (add 1 tablespoon vegetable oil if necessary); cook and stir until vegetables are tender.

5 Transfer vegetables to bowl with chicken. Stir in cream of broccoli soup, sour cream, broth, mustard, and black pepper. Gently stir in cooked noodles and broccoli.

6 Spoon chicken mixture into prepared dish. In a small bowl combine bread crumbs and melted butter; sprinkle over chicken mixture. Bake, covered, for 30 minutes. Bake, uncovered, about 25 minutes more or until heated through. If desired, garnish with additional green onions.

nutrition facts per serving: 301 cal., 10 g total fat (5 g sat. fat), 73 mg chol., 452 mg sodium, 32 g carb., 3 g dietary fiber, 22 g protein.

Enjoy chicken and stuffing without the fuss.

chicken and stuffing
bake

prep: 25 minutes **bake:** 35 minutes **stand:** 5 minutes **oven:** 350°F
makes: 8 servings

1 cup water
1 cup chopped red
   sweet pepper
½ cup chopped onion
   (1 medium)
½ cup uncooked long
   grain rice
1 8-ounce package
   herb-seasoned
   stuffing mix
2 cups water
4 cups diced cooked
   chicken or turkey
   (about 1¼ pounds)
3 eggs, lightly beaten
1 10.75-ounce can
   reduced-fat and
   reduced-sodium
   condensed cream of
   chicken soup
½ cup light sour cream
¼ cup fat-free milk
2 teaspoons dry sherry
   (optional)

1 In a medium saucepan bring the 1 cup water to boiling. Stir in sweet pepper, onion, and rice. Reduce heat to low. Simmer, covered, about 20 minutes or until rice and vegetables are tender and water is absorbed.

2 Preheat oven to 350°F. Grease a 3-quart casserole; set aside. In a large bowl combine stuffing mix and the 2 cups water. Stir in chicken, eggs, and half of the cream of chicken soup. Stir in cooked rice mixture. Spread in prepared baking dish. Bake for 35 to 40 minutes or until heated through.

3 Meanwhile, for sauce, in a small saucepan stir together the remaining soup, the sour cream, and milk. Cook over low heat until heated through, stirring occasionally. Stir in sherry (if using).

4 Let casserole stand for 5 minutes before serving. Serve chicken mixture with sauce.

nutrition facts per serving: 367 cal., 10 g total fat (3 g sat. fat), 149 mg chol., 664 mg sodium, 38 g carb., 3 g dietary fiber, 28 g protein.

curried rice and turkey
casserole

prep: 20 minutes **bake:** 35 minutes **stand:** 10 minutes **oven:** 375°F
makes: 4 servings

Nonstick cooking
   spray
1 pound turkey breast
   tenderloins or
   skinless, boneless
   chicken breast
   halves, cut
   crosswise into
   ½-inch-thick slices
2 cups uncooked
   instant brown rice
1 14-ounce can
   reduced-sodium
   chicken broth
½ cup sliced green
   onions (4)
⅓ cup dried cranberries
¼ cup apricot
   spreadable fruit
1 tablespoon reduced-
   sodium soy sauce
1 teaspoon curry
   powder
Sliced green onions
   (optional)

1 Preheat oven to 375°F. Coat a large nonstick skillet with cooking spray; heat over medium-high heat. Cook turkey slices in hot skillet for 5 to 6 minutes or until brown, turning once to brown evenly. Remove from skillet; set aside.

2 In a medium bowl combine rice, broth, ½ cup green onions, cranberries, 1 tablespoon of the spreadable fruit, the soy sauce, and curry powder. Spread evenly in an ungreased 2-quart rectangular baking dish. Top with turkey slices.

3 Bake, covered, for 35 to 40 minutes or until turkey is no longer pink and rice is tender. Spread the remaining 3 tablespoons spreadable fruit over turkey. Let stand, covered, for 10 minutes before serving. If desired, sprinkle with additional green onions.

nutrition facts per serving: 333 cal., 2 g total fat (0 g sat. fat), 70 mg chol., 431 mg sodium, 47 g carb., 3 g dietary fiber, 33 g protein.

nutrition note

Sear a golden-brown crust onto your chicken, without loading on the fat—brown it in a skillet using nonstick spray. Finish the dish in the oven for moist results.

The pizza dough goes on top of saucy ingredients in this topsy-turvy dish.

crisscross pizza
casserole

prep: 30 minutes **bake:** 30 minutes **stand:** 10 minutes **oven:** 350°F
makes: 8 servings

1½   cups thin strips
        yellow, red, and/
        or green sweet
        peppers (2 medium)
½   cup chopped onion
        (1 medium)
1   tablespoon olive oil
1   medium zucchini
        (8 ounces), halved
        lengthwise and
        sliced
2   cloves garlic, minced
2   14.5-ounce cans no-
        salt-added diced
        tomatoes, drained
5   cooked chicken
        sausage links
        (about 12 ounces
        total), halved
        lengthwise
        and sliced
1   teaspoon dried Italian
        seasoning, crushed
¼   teaspoon ground
        black pepper
1   13.8-ounce package
        refrigerated
        pizza dough
2   cups shredded
        mozzarella cheese
        (8 ounces)
¼   cup grated Parmesan
        cheese
        Snipped fresh
        rosemary (optional)

1 Preheat oven to 350°F. Grease a 2-quart rectangular baking dish; set aside. In a large skillet cook and stir sweet peppers and onion in hot oil over medium-high heat for 5 minutes. Add zucchini and garlic; cook for 5 minutes more, stirring occasionally.

2 Add tomatoes, sausage, ½ teaspoon of the Italian seasoning, and the black pepper to mixture in skillet. Bring to boiling; boil gently, uncovered, for 5 to 7 minutes or until most of the liquid has evaporated.

3 Meanwhile, unroll pizza dough onto a lightly floured surface. Using a knife or pastry wheel, cut pizza dough into strips.

4 Remove skillet from heat. Stir in 1 cup of the mozzarella cheese and the Parmesan cheese. Spoon tomato-cheese mixture into the prepared baking dish. Top with the remaining 1 cup mozzarella cheese. Arrange pizza dough strips on top of casserole in a lattice pattern. Sprinkle with the remaining ½ teaspoon Italian seasoning. Bake about 30 minutes or until crust is brown and filling is bubbly. Let stand for 10 minutes before serving. If desired, garnish with rosemary.

nutrition facts per serving: 323 cal., 15 g total fat (6 g sat. fat), 54 mg chol., 660 mg sodium, 29 g carb., 3 g dietary fiber, 21 g protein.

dijon lentil and sausage casserole

prep: 40 minutes **bake:** 35 minutes **oven:** 400°F **makes:** 8 servings

1   14-ounce can reduced-sodium chicken broth
1   cup water
8   ounces fresh green beans, trimmed and cut into 2-inch pieces
2   medium parsnips, peeled and cut into ½-inch slices
3   medium shallots, halved
8   ounces smoked cooked turkey sausage, chopped
1¼ cups red lentils, rinsed and drained
⅓   cup dry white wine or reduced-sodium chicken broth
2   tablespoons Dijon-style mustard
2   teaspoons snipped fresh thyme
4   cloves garlic, minced
1½ cups coarse soft whole wheat bread crumbs
1   tablespoon canola oil
¼   cup snipped fresh Italian parsley
2   teaspoons finely shredded lemon peel
    Lemon slices, halved (optional)
    Fresh Italian (flat-leaf) parsley sprig (optional)

1 Preheat oven to 400°F. In a large saucepan combine broth and the water. Bring to boiling. Add green beans, parsnips, and shallots. Return to boiling; reduce heat. Simmer, covered, for 8 to 10 minutes or just until vegetables are tender. Remove from heat. Stir in sausage and lentils. In a small bowl combine wine, mustard, thyme, and 2 of the garlic cloves; stir into sausage mixture.

2 Transfer sausage mixture to an ungreased 2-quart casserole. Bake, covered, for 25 to 30 minutes or just until lentils are tender.

3 Meanwhile, in a medium bowl toss together bread crumbs and oil. Sprinkle over sausage mixture. Bake, uncovered, about 10 minutes more or until mixture is heated through and crumbs are lightly browned.

4 In a small bowl combine the snipped parsley, lemon peel, and the remaining two cloves garlic. Sprinkle over casserole. If desired, garnish with lemon slices and parsley sprig.

nutrition facts per serving: 236 cal., 5 g total fat (1 g sat. fat), 20 mg chol., 577 mg sodium, 31 g carb., 12 g dietary fiber, 15 g protein.

High-fiber whole grain pasta, Italian-style turkey sausage, and part-skim mozzarella cheese stand in for more traditional— but less healthful— ingredients.

baked sausage and mushroom rotini

prep: 40 minutes **bake:** 30 minutes **oven:** 350°F **makes:** 6 servings

3½ cups dried whole grain rotini or penne pasta

12 ounces uncooked Italian turkey sausage links (casings removed), uncooked ground turkey, or lean ground beef

1 8-ounce package sliced fresh mushrooms

½ cup chopped onion (1 medium)

2 cloves garlic, minced

2 14.5-ounce cans no-salt-added diced tomatoes with basil, garlic, and oregano, undrained

1 6-ounce can no-salt-added tomato paste

⅓ cup water

¼ teaspoon crushed red pepper

¼ cup shredded part-skim mozzarella cheese (1 ounce)

¼ cup finely shredded Parmesan cheese

1 Preheat oven to 350°F. Lightly grease a 3-quart casserole; set aside. Cook pasta according to package directions; drain well.

2 Meanwhile, in a 4-quart Dutch oven cook sausage, mushrooms, onion, and garlic over medium heat until sausage is brown and vegetables are tender, using a wooden spoon to break up meat as it cooks. Drain off fat. Add cooked pasta, tomatoes, tomato paste, the water, and red pepper flakes to sausage mixture in Dutch oven, stirring until combined. Transfer pasta mixture to prepared casserole.

3 Bake, covered, for 20 minutes. Sprinkle with mozzarella cheese and Parmesan cheese. Bake, uncovered, about 10 minutes more or until heated through.

nutrition facts per serving: 349 cal., 14 g total fat (4 g sat. fat), 34 mg chol., 303 mg sodium, 40 g carb., 10 g dietary fiber, 16 g protein.

pork casserole with mushrooms and kale

prep: 25 minutes **bake:** 30 minutes **stand:** 10 minutes **oven:** 350°F
makes: 6 servings

Nonstick cooking
   spray
1   pound lean boneless
    pork, cut into thin
    bite-size strips
2   cups sliced fresh
    mushrooms
½   cup chopped onion
    (1 medium)
2   tablespoons canola
    oil or olive oil
¼   cup all-purpose flour
½   teaspoon salt
½   teaspoon dried sage,
    crushed
¼   teaspoon ground
    black pepper
2   cups fat-free milk
4   cups chopped,
    stemmed kale or
    Swiss chard
2   cups cooked wild rice
1   tablespoon finely
    shredded lemon
    peel

1 Preheat oven to 350°F. Coat a very large skillet with cooking spray; heat skillet over medium-high heat. Add pork to hot skillet; cook and stir for 2 to 4 minutes or until slightly pink in center. Remove pork from skillet; set aside.

2 Add mushrooms, onion, and oil to the same skillet; cook about 5 minutes or until mushrooms are tender, stirring occasionally. Stir in flour, salt, sage, and pepper. Add milk all at once; cook and stir until thickened and bubbly. Stir in pork, kale, cooked wild rice, and lemon peel.

3 Spoon mixture into an ungreased 1½- to 2-quart baking dish. Bake for 30 to 35 minutes or until heated through. Let stand for 10 minutes before serving.

nutrition facts per serving: 285 cal., 10 g total fat (2 g sat. fat), 49 mg chol., 305 mg sodium, 27 g carb., 3 g dietary fiber, 24 g protein.

Similar to corn grits, polenta pairs well with sausage. Instant polenta makes this dish even easier to put together.

polenta and sausage
casseroles

prep: 30 minutes **bake:** 25 minutes **oven:** 350°F **makes:** 6 servings

10	ounces hot Italian sausage (casings removed if present)
1½	cups chopped red sweet peppers (2 medium)
1½	cups chopped green sweet peppers (2 medium)
½	cup chopped onion (1 medium)
1	clove garlic, thinly sliced
½	teaspoon dried Italian seasoning, crushed
1	14.5-ounce can no-salt-added stewed tomatoes, drained
⅛	teaspoon ground black pepper
2	tablespoons instant polenta
4	cups water
¼	teaspoon salt
1⅓	cups instant polenta
½	cup grated Parmesan cheese

1 Preheat oven to 350°F. Grease six 8- to 10-ounce ramekins or individual casseroles; set aside. For filling, heat a large skillet over medium-high heat. Add sausage; cook about 5 minutes or until brown, using a wooden spoon to break up meat as it cooks. Drain off fat.

2 Add sweet peppers, onion, garlic, and Italian seasoning to sausage in skillet. Reduce heat to medium; cook for 5 minutes more. Stir in tomatoes and the black pepper; cook for 3 minutes more.

3 Remove skillet from heat. Stir in the 2 tablespoons instant polenta.

4 For polenta mixture, in a medium saucepan bring the water and salt to boiling. Add the 1⅓ cups instant polenta to the boiling water in a thin stream, stirring constantly. Reduce heat to medium; cook and stir polenta about 3 minutes or until medium-soft. Remove from heat. Stir in ⅓ cup of the cheese.

5 Divide sausage mixture among prepared ramekins. Top with about ½ cup polenta mixture. Sprinkle with the remaining cheese.

6 Bake, uncovered, for 25 minutes.

nutrition facts per serving: 462 cal., 13 g total fat (6 g sat. fat), 38 mg chol., 493 mg sodium, 63 g carb., 10 g dietary fiber, 7 g sugar, 17 g protein.

Something fishy is going on top of this tuna-noodle casserole that will lure all family members into gobbling it up.

tuna and green bean bake

prep: 35 minutes **bake:** 25 minutes **oven:** 350°F **makes:** 6 servings

4   ounces dried medium noodles

3   tablespoons panko (Japanese-style bread crumbs)

1   tablespoon butter, melted (optional)

10   ounces fresh green beans, trimmed and cut into 2-inch pieces

1   cup sliced fresh mushrooms

¾   cup chopped red or green sweet pepper (1 medium)

½   cup chopped onion

½   cup sliced celery

½   cup water

2   cloves garlic, minced

1   10.75-ounce can reduced-fat and reduced-sodium condensed cream of mushroom soup

½   cup fat-free milk

½   cup cubed reduced-fat American or process Swiss cheese (2 ounces)

2   4.5-ounce cans very low sodium chunk white tuna in spring water, drained and flaked

Fish-shape crackers (optional)

1 Preheat oven to 350°F. Cook noodles according to package directions; drain and set aside.

2 Meanwhile, if desired, in a small bowl toss panko with butter; set aside.

3 In a large saucepan combine green beans, mushrooms, sweet pepper, onion, celery, the water, and garlic. Bring to boiling; reduce heat. Simmer, covered, about 5 minutes or until vegetables are tender.

4 Stir in cream of mushroom soup and milk into vegetable mixture; cook and stir until heated through. Remove from heat. Add cheese, stirring until melted. Stir in cooked noodles and tuna.

5 Spoon mixture into an ungreased 2-quart casserole. If desired, sprinkle panko mixture around outside edge of casserole. Bake for 25 to 30 minutes or until tuna mixture is bubbly and panko mixture is golden brown. If desired, top with fish-shape crackers.

nutrition facts per serving: 228 cal., 6 g total fat (2 g sat. fat), 49 mg chol., 403 mg sodium, 27 g carb., 3 g dietary fiber, 18 g protein.

Get to know fontina, one of Italy's great cheeses. Its mild, buttery, and slightly nutty taste makes it the perfect cheese for most any use. This cheese has excellent meltability.

crab, spinach, and pasta with fontina

prep: 25 minutes **bake:** 30 minutes **stand:** 10 minutes **oven:** 375°F
makes: 6 servings

2   cups dried bow tie
    pasta (8 ounces)
1   26-ounce jar reduced-
    sodium tomato-base
    pasta sauce
2   6-ounce cans
    crabmeat, drained,
    flaked, and cartilage
    removed
1   10-ounce package
    frozen chopped
    spinach, thawed
    and well drained
1   cup shredded fontina
    cheese (4 ounces)

1 Preheat oven to 375°F. Lightly grease a 2-quart square baking dish; set aside. Cook pasta according to package directions; drain.

2 Meanwhile, in a large bowl combine pasta sauce, crabmeat, spinach, and ½ cup of the cheese. Add cooked pasta; toss gently to combine. Transfer mixture to the prepared baking dish. Sprinkle with the remaining ½ cup cheese.

3 Bake for 30 to 35 minutes or until mixture is bubbly around edges and cheese is lightly browned. Let stand for 10 minutes before serving.

nutrition facts per serving: 368 cal., 12 g total fat (4 g sat. fat), 94 mg chol., 740 mg sodium, 41 g carb., 4 g dietary fiber, 23 g protein.

seafood enchiladas

prep: 1 hour **stand:** 45 minutes **bake:** 25 minutes **oven:** 350°F
makes: 10 enchiladas

2   to 3 dried ancho chile
    peppers or mulato
    chile peppers
12 ounces chopped
    cooked shrimp;**
    12 ounces chopped
    cooked crabmeat;
    two 6-ounce
    packages frozen
    peeled cooked
    shrimp, thawed
    and chopped; or
    12 ounces frozen
    crabmeat, thawed
    and flaked
2   cups shredded
    Chihuahua cheese
    or Monterey Jack
    cheese
10 6-inch corn tortillas
½   cup chopped onion
    (1 medium)
1   tablespoon olive oil
⅓   cup all-purpose flour
¼   teaspoon salt
¼   teaspoon ground
    black pepper
3   cups milk

make-ahead directions:
Prepare filling as directed
in Step 1. Cover and chill
in the refrigerator for up
to 24 hours. Continue
as directed in Steps 2
through 5.

1 For filling, cut ancho chile peppers open; discard stems and seeds.* Place ancho chile peppers in a small bowl and cover with boiling water. Let stand for 45 to 60 minutes to soften; drain well. Cut one of the chile peppers into thin slivers; cut the remaining chile pepper(s) into small pieces. Set chile slivers aside to use as a garnish. In a medium bowl combine shrimp, 1½ cups of the cheese, and the chile pieces. Set filling aside.

2 Preheat oven to 350°F. Stack tortillas and wrap tightly in foil. Bake about 10 minutes or until heated through.

3 Spoon about ¼ cup of the filling onto each tortilla near one end; roll up. Place filled tortillas, seam sides down, in an ungreased 3-quart rectangular baking dish.

4 For sauce, in a medium saucepan cook and stir onion in hot oil over medium heat until tender. Stir in flour, salt, and black pepper. Add milk all at once; cook and stir until thickened and bubbly. Pour sauce over filled tortillas.

5 Bake, covered, about 20 minutes or until heated through. Sprinkle with the remaining ½ cup cheese. Place chile slivers diagonally across enchiladas. Bake about 5 minutes more or until cheese is melted.

nutrition facts per enchilada: 241 cal., 11 g total fat (6 g sat. fat), 92 mg chol., 334 mg sodium, 19 g carb., 0 g dietary fiber, 17 g protein.

*tip: Because chile peppers contain volatile oils that can burn your skin and eyes, avoid direct contact with them as much as possible. When working with chile peppers, wear plastic or rubber gloves. If your bare hands do touch the peppers, wash your hands and nails well with soap and warm water.

**tip: For 12 ounces cooked shrimp, purchase 1½ pounds fresh or frozen raw shrimp in the shell. Thaw shrimp, if frozen. Peel and devein shrimp. Rinse shrimp; pat dry with paper towels. In a large saucepan combine 5 cups water and ½ teaspoon salt; bring to boiling. Add shrimp; cook for 1 to 3 minutes or until shrimp are opaque, stirring occasionally. Rinse under cold water; drain.

cajun shrimp and corn bread casserole

prep: 35 minutes **bake:** 15 minutes **stand:** 5 minutes **oven:** 400°F
makes: 6 servings

1 pound fresh or frozen
   large shrimp in shells
1 teaspoon Cajun
   seasoning
1½ cups coarsely
   chopped green
   and/or red sweet
   peppers (2 medium)
1 cup sliced celery
   (2 stalks)
½ cup chopped onion
   (1 medium)
1 tablespoon canola oil
2 cloves garlic, minced
1 15-ounce can black-
   eye peas, rinsed
   and drained
1 14.5-ounce can no-
   salt-added stewed
   tomatoes, undrained
   and cut up
1 recipe Corn Bread
   Dumplings
   Snipped fresh
   parsley (optional)

1 Thaw shrimp, if frozen. Preheat oven to
400°F. Peel and devein shrimp, leaving tails
intact (if desired). Rinse shrimp; pat dry with
paper towels. In a large bowl combine shrimp
and ½ teaspoon of the Cajun seasoning; toss
gently to coat. Set aside.

2 In a 10-inch cast-iron skillet or large
ovenproof skillet cook sweet peppers,
celery, and onion in hot oil over medium-high
heat for 5 to 7 minutes or until vegetables are
tender, stirring frequently. Add shrimp and
garlic; cook and stir for 2 to 3 minutes or until
shrimp are opaque.

3 Stir in black-eye peas, tomatoes, and the
remaining ½ teaspoon Cajun seasoning.
Spread mixture in an even layer. Drop Corn
Bread Dumplings into eight mounds on top of
shrimp mixture.

4 Bake for 15 to 18 minutes or until a
toothpick inserted in centers of dumplings
comes out clean. Let stand for 5 minutes
before serving. If desired, sprinkle with parsley.

nutrition facts per serving: 336 cal., 10 g total fat
(1 g sat. fat), 122 mg chol., 496 mg sodium, 42 g carb.,
6 g dietary fiber, 21 g protein.

corn bread dumplings: In a medium bowl stir
together ¾ cup all-purpose flour, ⅓ cup yellow
cornmeal, 1 tablespoon sugar, 1¼ teaspoons
baking powder, and ¼ teaspoon salt. In a small
bowl beat 1 egg with a fork; stir in ¼ cup fat-free
milk and 2 tablespoons canola oil. Add egg
mixture all at once to flour mixture; stir just until
moistened. Makes 8 dumplings

Take potstickers out of the appetizer category and serve them up for dinner in a vegetable-filled casserole with a spicy sauce.

asian vegetables and potstickers

prep: 35 minutes **bake:** 40 minutes **oven:** 350°F **makes:** 6 servings

2 9- to 13-ounce packages frozen shrimp, pork, or chicken potstickers
1 16-ounce package frozen Asian-blend stir-fry vegetables with sugar snap pea pods, thawed
1 8-ounce can sliced water chestnuts, drained
1 tablespoon finely chopped peeled fresh ginger
1 14-ounce can lower-sodium beef broth
2 tablespoons cornstarch
2 tablespoons reduced sodium soy sauce
2 tablespoons honey
1 teaspoon Chinese-style hot mustard
1 tablespoon sesame seeds, toasted
   Chile oil (optional)

1 Preheat oven to 350°F. Cook potstickers according to package directions; drain, if necessary. Place potstickers in an ungreased 2½-quart casserole. Stir in vegetables, water chestnuts, and ginger; set aside.

2 In a medium saucepan combine broth, cornstarch, soy sauce, honey, and mustard; cook and stir over medium heat until thickened and bubbly. Pour broth mixture over potstickers in casserole.

3 Bake, covered, for 40 to 45 minutes or until heated through. Sprinkle with sesame seeds. If desired, serve with chile oil.

nutrition facts per serving: 272 cal., 5 g total fat (1 g sat. fat), 12 mg chol., 751 mg sodium, 46 g carb., 3 g dietary fiber, 9 g protein.

baked mexican macaroni and cheese

prep: 30 minutes **bake:** 30 minutes **stand:** 5 minutes **oven:** 350°F
makes: 8 servings

6	ounces dried whole wheat elbow macaroni (1½ cups)
2	tablespoons butter
2	tablespoons all-purpose flour
1¼	cups half-and-half or light cream
2	cups reduced-fat shredded cheddar cheese (8 ounces)
1	1.25-ounce envelope reduced-sodium taco seasoning mix
1	15-ounce can no-salt-added black beans, rinsed and drained
1	14.5-ounce can no-salt-added diced tomatoes, drained
¾	cup chopped green sweet pepper (1 medium)
¾	cup chopped red sweet pepper (1 medium)
½	cup chopped red onion (1 medium)
½	cup chunky salsa
½	cup sliced green onions (4)
1	medium avocado, seeded, peeled, and chopped (optional)
1	lime, cut into wedges (optional)

1 Preheat oven to 350°F. Grease a 3-quart rectangular baking dish; set aside. Cook macaroni according to package directions; drain. Transfer to a very large bowl; set aside.

2 In a medium saucepan melt butter over low heat. Whisk in flour until smooth. Add half-and-half. Increase heat to medium; whisk constantly until mixture is boiling. Boil gently for 2 minutes, whisking frequently. Remove from heat. Stir in 1½ cups of the cheese and the taco seasoning mix. Pour over macaroni in bowl.

3 Add beans, tomatoes, sweet peppers, red onion, and salsa to macaroni mixture in bowl. Stir to combine. Transfer mixture to the prepared baking dish. Sprinkle with green onions and the remaining ½ cup cheese.

4 Bake about 30 minutes or until heated through. Let stand for 5 minutes before serving. If desired, sprinkle with avocado and serve with lime wedges.

nutrition facts per serving: 317 cal., 13 g total fat (8 g sat. fat), 37 mg chol., 660 mg sodium, 36 g carb., 6 g dietary fiber, 16 g protein.

Broccoli and mushrooms kick up the nutrition profile in this cheesy number.

loaded macaroni and cheese

prep: 25 minutes **bake:** 30 minutes **stand:** 10 minutes **oven:** 375°F
makes: 6 servings

2 cups dried elbow
   macaroni (8 ounces)
1 cup low-fat
   cottage cheese
½ of an 8-ounce
   package (4 ounces)
   reduced-fat cream
   cheese, softened
1 tablespoon yellow
   mustard
½ teaspoon ground
   black pepper
¼ teaspoon salt
   Dash bottled hot
   pepper sauce
2 cups cooked broccoli
   florets
1 cup sliced fresh
   mushrooms
½ cup finely chopped
   onion (1 medium)
1 cup shredded
   mozzarella cheese
   (4 ounces)
1 cup shredded
   cheddar cheese
   (4 ounces)
¼ cup freshly grated
   Parmesan cheese

1 Preheat oven to 375°F. Cook macaroni according to package directions; drain. Grease a 2-quart square baking dish; set aside.

2 In a large bowl combine cottage cheese, cream cheese, mustard, black pepper, salt, and hot pepper sauce; mix well. Stir in broccoli, mushrooms, and onion. Stir in mozzarella cheese and ¼ cup of the cheddar cheese. Gently stir in cooked macaroni. Transfer mixture to prepared baking dish.

3 Bake, covered, for 20 minutes. Sprinkle with the remaining ¾ cup cheddar cheese and the Parmesan cheese. Bake, uncovered, about 10 minutes more or until cheese is melted. Let stand for 10 minutes before serving.

nutrition facts per serving: 380 cal., 17 g total fat (10 g sat. fat), 48 mg chol., 650 mg sodium, 35 g carb., 3 g dietary fiber, 24 g protein.

You won't even miss the corned beef in this meatless casserole that tastes just like a Reuben sandwich.

cabbage swiss bread pudding

prep: 25 minutes   **bake:** 35 minutes   **stand:** 10 minutes   **oven:** 300°F/375°F
makes: 6 to 8 servings

6 cups cubed light-color rye bread (6 ounces)
4 cups coarsely chopped red and/or green cabbage
½ cup chopped onion (1 medium)
2 tablespoons olive oil
2 tablespoons balsamic vinegar
4 cloves garlic, minced
2 teaspoons caraway seeds
2 cups refrigerated or frozen egg product, thawed, or 8 eggs, lightly beaten
1½ cups fat-free milk
1½ cups reduced-fat shredded Swiss cheese (6 ounces)
½ teaspoon salt
¼ teaspoon ground black pepper
Thousand Island salad dressing (optional)

1 Preheat oven to 300°F. Grease a 2-quart rectangular baking dish; set aside. Spread bread cubes in a 15x10x1-inch baking pan. Bake about 10 minutes or until lightly toasted, stirring once. Cool in pan on a wire rack. Increase oven temperature to 375°F.

2 In a large skillet cook cabbage and onion in hot oil over medium heat about 10 minutes or until cabbage is crisp-tender, stirring occasionally. Stir in vinegar, garlic, and caraway seeds. Cook for 1 minute more. Remove from heat.

3 In a large bowl combine eggs, milk, 1 cup of the cheese, the salt, and pepper. Stir in bread cubes and cabbage mixture. Transfer to the prepared baking dish.

4 Bake for 30 minutes. Top with the remaining ½ cup cheese. Bake about 5 minutes more or until a knife inserted near the center comes out clean. Let stand for 10 minutes before serving. If desired, serve with Thousand Island salad dressing.

nutrition facts per serving: 295 cal., 12 g total fat (4 g sat. fat), 21 mg chol., 691 mg sodium, 26 g carb., 3 g dietary fiber, 22 g protein.

Season this baked pasta dish with a bit of hot sauce for extra kick.

baked penne
florentine

prep: 30 minutes **bake:** 30 minutes **stand:** 10 minutes **oven:** 375°F
makes: 6 servings

8 ounces dried
   multigrain or whole
   wheat penne pasta
1 10-ounce package
   frozen chopped
   spinach, thawed
   and well drained
½ cup chopped onion
   (1 medium)
¼ cup vegetable broth
2 cloves garlic, minced
½ cup raw cashews
1¾ cups water
1 15- to 16-ounce can
   Great Northern
   beans, navy beans,
   or cannellini beans
   (white kidney
   beans), rinsed and
   drained
2 teaspoons lemon juice
½ teaspoon dry mustard
¼ teaspoon salt
¼ teaspoon ground
   black pepper
½ cup soft whole wheat
   bread crumbs

1 Preheat oven to 375°F. Cook pasta according to package directions; drain. Return to hot pan. Add spinach; toss to combine. Set aside.

2 In a small saucepan combine onion, broth, and garlic. Bring to boiling; reduce heat. Simmer, uncovered, about 5 minutes or until onion is tender. Remove from heat; set aside.

3 Place cashews in a food processor. Cover and process until finely ground. Add half of the water; blend until smooth. Add onion mixture, beans, lemon juice, mustard, salt, and pepper. Cover and process until smooth. Transfer to a medium bowl and stir in the remaining water. Stir bean mixture into pasta mixture. Transfer to an ungreased 2-quart casserole. Sprinkle with bread crumbs.

4 Bake about 30 minutes or until crumbs are toasted. Let stand for 10 minutes before serving.

nutrition facts per serving: 315 cal., 8 g total fat (1 g sat. fat), 0 mg chol., 198 mg sodium, 53 g carb., 10 g dietary fiber, 15 g protein.

Pass salsa and light sour cream as optional toppings with this chile pepper dish.

chiles rellenos casserole

prep: 20 minutes **bake:** 15 minutes **stand:** 5 minutes **oven:** 450°F
makes: 4 servings

2   large fresh poblano
    chile peppers or
    fresh Anaheim chile
    peppers (8 ounces)
1   cup reduced-fat
    shredded Mexican-
    style four-cheese
    blend or shredded
    Monterey Jack
    cheese with
    jalapeño chile
    peppers (4 ounces)
½   cup crumbled Cotija
    cheese (2 ounces)
3   eggs, lightly beaten
¼   cup fat-free milk
⅓   cup all-purpose flour
½   teaspoon baking
    powder
¼   teaspoon cayenne
    pepper
⅛   teaspoon salt

1 Preheat oven to 450°F. Grease a 2-quart square baking dish; set aside. Quarter the poblano chile peppers, removing seeds, stems, and veins.* Immerse peppers in boiling water for 3 minutes; drain. Invert peppers onto paper towels to drain well. Place the peppers, cut sides up, in prepared baking dish. Top with Mexican-style cheese and Cotija cheese.

2 In a medium bowl combine eggs and milk. Add flour, baking powder, cayenne pepper, and salt. Beat with a rotary beater until smooth (or place in a food processor or blender; cover and process or blend until smooth). Pour egg mixture over chile peppers and cheeses.

3 Bake about 15 minutes or until a knife inserted into the center of the egg mixture comes out clean. Let stand for 5 minutes before serving.

nutrition facts per serving: 252 cal., 14 g total fat (5 g sat. fat), 189 mg chol., 386 mg sodium, 16 g carb., 1 g dietary fiber, 19 g protein.

*****tip:** Because chile peppers contain volatile oils that can burn your skin and eyes, avoid direct contact with them as much as possible. When working with chile peppers, wear plastic or rubber gloves. If your bare hands do touch the peppers, wash your hands and nails well with soap and warm water.

With barley, bulgur, black beans, and a lentil soup base, this aromatic meatless bake is as flavorful as it is nutritious.

vegetable casserole with barley and bulgur

prep: 15 minutes **bake:** 1 hour 15 minutes **stand:** 5 minutes **oven:** 350°F
makes: 4 servings

1   14.5- to 18.5-ounce
    can ready-to-serve
    lentil soup
1   15-ounce can no-salt-
    added black beans,
    rinsed and drained
1   cup sliced carrots
    (2 medium)
1   cup small fresh
    mushrooms,
    quartered
1   cup frozen whole
    kernel corn
½   cup regular barley
½   cup water
⅓   cup bulgur
¼   cup chopped onion
½   teaspoon ground
    black pepper
½   cup reduced-fat
    shredded cheddar
    cheese (2 ounces)

1 Preheat oven to 350°F. In a large bowl combine lentil soup, beans, carrots, mushrooms, corn, barley, the water, bulgur, onion, and pepper. Transfer to an ungreased 2-quart casserole.

2 Bake, covered, about 1¼ hours or until barley and bulgur are tender, stirring twice. Stir again; sprinkle with cheese. Let stand, covered, about 5 minutes or until cheese is melted.

nutrition facts per serving: 366 cal., 5 g total fat (2 g sat. fat), 0 mg chol., 310 mg sodium, 66 g carb., 15 g dietary fiber, 20 g protein.

nutrition note
Black beans pack fiber, but they get bonus points for their punch of potassium, too. One-half cup contains 370 mg of this nutrient, which can help lower blood pressure.

Quinoa (KEEN-wah), a sweet and slightly nutty whole grain, is packed with protein.

artichoke-quinoa bake

prep: 30 minutes **bake:** 45 minutes **oven:** 375°F **makes:** 6 servings

1½ cups water
¾ cup red and/or regular quinoa
⅓ cup chopped onion (1 small)
1 clove garlic, minced
1 tablespoon olive oil
1 14-ounce can quartered artichoke hearts, drained
½ cup finely shredded Asiago cheese (2 ounces)
2 eggs
1 cup milk
2 teaspoons snipped fresh oregano
¼ teaspoon coarsely ground black pepper
⅛ teaspoon salt
¼ cup crumbled feta cheese (1 ounce)
1 medium tomato, cut into wedges
   Fresh oregano (optional)

1 Preheat oven to 375°F. Lightly grease a 2-quart casserole; set aside. In a medium saucepan bring the water to boiling. Stir in quinoa. Return to boiling; reduce heat. Simmer, covered, about 10 minutes or until the water is absorbed. Uncover and let quinoa cool to room temperature.

2 In a large skillet cook onion and garlic in hot oil over medium heat about 5 minutes or until tender. Remove from heat. Stir in cooked quinoa, artichoke hearts, and Asiago cheese.

3 In a medium bowl combine eggs, milk, the 2 teaspoons oregano, pepper, and salt. Stir into artichoke mixture. Transfer to prepared casserole, spreading evenly. Sprinkle with feta cheese. Bake about 45 minutes or until the mixture is set in center and a knife inserted near the center comes out clean. Garnish with tomato wedges and, if desired, additional oregano.

nutrition facts per serving: 220 cal., 10 g total fat (4 g sat. fat), 88 mg chol., 460 mg sodium, 21 g carb., 4 g dietary fiber, 11 g protein.

three cheese manicotti

prep: 30 minutes **bake:** 40 minutes **stand:** 10 minutes **oven:** 350°F
makes: 10 to 12 servings

20	dried manicotti shells
2⅓	cups light ricotta cheese (24 ounces)
2	cups shredded part-skim mozzarella cheese (8 ounces)
½	cup refrigerated or frozen egg product, thawed, or 2 eggs
⅓	cup grated Romano cheese or Asiago cheese
¼	cup snipped fresh parsley
¼	teaspoon ground black pepper
4	cups reduced-sodium light tomato-basil pasta sauce
	Snipped fresh parsley (optional)

1 Preheat oven to 350°F. Cook manicotti shells according to package directions; drain. For filling, in a large bowl combine ricotta cheese, 1 cup of the mozzarella cheese, the eggs, Romano cheese, the ¼ cup parsley, and pepper.

2 Spread 1 cup of the pasta sauce in the bottom of an ungreased 3-quart rectangular baking dish. Spoon about 3 tablespoons of the filling into each cooked manicotti shell and place in the dish. Spoon the remaining pasta sauce evenly over filled shells.

3 Bake for 35 to 40 minutes or until heated through. Sprinkle with the remaining 1 cup mozzarella cheese. Bake about 5 minutes more or until cheese is melted. Let stand for 10 minutes before serving. If desired, sprinkle with additional parsley.

nutrition facts per serving: 328 cal., 12 g total fat (5 g sat. fat), 36 mg chol., 586 mg sodium, 38 g carb., 3 g dietary fiber, 20 g protein.

make-ahead directions: Prepare as directed through Step 2. Cover with plastic wrap and chill for 2 to 24 hours. To serve, preheat oven to 350°F. Remove plastic wrap. Bake for 40 to 45 minutes or until heated through. Sprinkle with the remaining 1 cup mozzarella cheese. Bake about 5 minutes more or until cheese is melted. Let stand for 10 minutes before serving. If desired, sprinkle with additional parsley.

artichoke-basil lasagna

prep: 45 minutes **bake:** 40 minutes **stand:** 15 minutes **oven:** 350°F
makes: 8 servings

9   dried whole grain
    lasagna noodles
2   8- or 9-ounce
    packages frozen
    artichoke hearts,
    thawed and
    well drained
¼   cup pine nuts
4   cloves garlic, minced
1   tablespoon olive oil
1   15-ounce carton light
    ricotta cheese
1½ cups reduced-fat
    shredded Italian
    blend cheeses
    or part-skim
    mozzarella cheese
    (6 ounces)
1   cup snipped fresh
    basil or 4 teaspoons
    dried basil, crushed
1   egg
¼   teaspoon salt
1   cup reduced-sodium
    chicken broth
¼   cup all-purpose flour
2   cups fat-free milk
    Chopped fresh
      tomato (optional)
    Snipped fresh parsley
      (optional)

1 Preheat oven to 350°F. Cook lasagna noodles according to package directions; drain. Rinse with cold water; drain again. Set aside.

2 In a large skillet cook artichokes, pine nuts, and garlic in hot oil over medium heat about 5 minutes or until artichokes, nuts, and garlic start to brown, stirring frequently. Transfer to a large bowl. Stir in ricotta cheese, ½ cup of the Italian blend cheese, ½ cup of the fresh basil or 1 tablespoon of the dried basil, the egg, and salt.

3 For sauce, in a medium saucepan whisk together chicken broth and flour until smooth. Stir in milk. Cook and stir over medium heat until sauce is slightly thickened and bubbly. Remove from heat. Stir in the remaining ½ cup fresh basil or 1 teaspoon dried basil.

4 Pour 1 cup of the sauce into a 3-quart rectangular baking dish. Top with three of the cooked lasagna noodles. Spoon one-third of the ricotta mixture (about 1⅓ cups) over noodles in dish; carefully spread evenly over the noodles. Top with one-third of the remaining sauce (about ⅔ cup). Sprinkle with ⅓ cup of the remaining Italian blend cheese. Repeat layers twice more, beginning with the lasagna noodles and ending with the Italian blend cheese.

5 Bake about 40 minutes or until heated through and top is lightly browned. Let stand for 15 minutes before serving. If desired, top with tomato and parsley.

nutrition facts per serving: 330 cal., 12 g total fat (5 g sat. fat), 52 mg chol., 431 mg sodium, 35 g carb., 8 g dietary fiber, 21 g protein.

slow

COO

11

Give yourself a (toned
and trim) leg up on
busy night dinners.
With just a smidgeon
of forward thinking,
you'll open the door
to deliciousness that is
ready when you are.

ker

so-easy pepper steak

prep: 15 minutes   cook: 9 to 10 hours (low) or 4½ to 5 hours (high)
makes: 6 servings

2 pounds boneless beef
round steak, cut
¾ to 1 inch thick

½ teaspoon salt

¼ teaspoon ground
black pepper

1 14.5-ounce can
Cajun-, Mexican-,
or Italian-style
stewed tomatoes,
undrained

½ of a 6-ounce can
(⅓ cup) tomato
paste

½ teaspoon bottled
hot pepper sauce
(optional)

1 16-ounce package
frozen pepper
and onion stir-fry
vegetables

4 cups hot cooked
whole wheat pasta
(optional)

1 Trim fat from meat. Cut meat into six
serving-size portions. Sprinkle meat with
salt and black pepper. Place meat in a 3½- or
4-quart slow cooker.

2 In a medium bowl combine tomatoes,
tomato paste, and hot pepper sauce (if
using). Pour over meat in cooker. Top with
frozen vegetables.

3 Cover and cook on low-heat setting for
9 to 10 hours or on high-heat setting for
4½ to 5 hours. If desired, serve over hot
cooked pasta.

nutrition facts per serving: 258 cal., 6 g total fat
(2 g sat. fat), 83 mg chol., 644 mg sodium, 12 g carb.,
2 g dietary fiber, 37 g protein.

Here it is—the meat loaf topped with ketchup and brown-sugar beloved by generations. Note that you'll need a large oval slow cooker for this recipe—it makes two loaves.

classic meat loaf

prep: 30 minutes   cook: 7 to 8 hours (low) or 3½ to 4 hours (high)
makes: 12 servings

3   eggs, lightly beaten
¾   cup milk
2   cups soft bread crumbs
1   cup finely chopped onion (1 large)
2   teaspoons salt
½   teaspoon ground black pepper
1½ pounds lean ground beef
1½ pounds ground pork
½   cup ketchup
¼   cup packed brown sugar
2   teaspoons dry mustard

1 In a large bowl combine eggs and milk. Stir in bread crumbs, onion, salt, and pepper. Add ground beef and pork; mix well. Shape meat mixture into two 5-inch round loaves.

2 Tear off two 18 inch square pieces of heavy foil. Cut each into thirds. Fold each piece of foil in half lengthwise to make strips. Crisscross three of the strips and place one meat loaf in the center of the foil strips. Bringing up strips, transfer meat loaf and foil to a 6- to 7-quart oval slow cooker (leave foil strips under loaf). Repeat with the remaining three foil strips and meat loaf.

3 Cover and cook on low-heat setting for 7 to 8 hours or on high-heat setting for 3½ to 4 hours. Using the foil strips, transfer meat loaves to a serving platter; discard foil strips.

4 For glaze, in a small bowl combine ketchup, brown sugar, and dry mustard. Spread glaze over meat loaves.

nutrition facts per serving: 239 cal., 11 g total fat (5 g sat. fat), 116 mg chol., 617 mg sodium, 13 g carb., 0 g dietary fiber, 20 g protein.

tip: If you want to store one of the meat loaves, place the loaf in an airtight container. Seal and chill for up to 3 days or freeze for up to 3 months. If frozen, thaw in the refrigerator overnight before using.

Is your pot roast in need of a makeover? Here kicky Moroccan seasonings ramp up the slow-cooker standby. Couscous makes a quick accompaniment.

moroccan-spiced beef

prep: 25 minutes   cook: 9 to 10 hours (low) or 4½ to 5 hours (high)
makes: 6 servings

1   1½ - to 2-pound boneless beef chuck pot roast
1½   teaspoons curry powder
1   teaspoon ground cumin
¾   teaspoon salt
⅛   teaspoon ground black pepper
Dash cayenne pepper
1   medium onion, cut into thin wedges
1   14.5-ounce can no-salt-added diced tomatoes, undrained
½   cup lower-sodium beef broth
3   cups hot cooked couscous

1 Trim fat from meat; set meat aside. In a small bowl stir together curry powder, cumin, salt, black pepper, and cayenne pepper. Sprinkle mixture evenly over meat; rub in with your fingers.

2 Place onion in a 3½ - or 4-quart slow cooker; add meat. Pour tomatoes and broth over meat.

3 Cover and cook on low-heat setting for 9 to 10 hours or on high-heat setting for 4½ to 5 hours.

4 Using a slotted spoon, remove meat from cooker. Skim fat from tomato mixture. To serve, spoon tomato mixture over meat and hot cooked couscous.

nutrition facts per serving: 205 cal., 3 g total fat (1 g sat. fat), 45 mg chol., 410 mg sodium, 24 g carb., 3 g dietary fiber, 20 g protein.

Add a jar of beef gravy to a slow-cooker meat recipe and you get a smooth sauce that's the perfect consistency for topping mashed potatoes or noodles.

mushroom-and-onion-sauced
round steak

prep: 20 minutes   cook: 8 to 10 hours (low) or 4 to 5 hours (high)
makes: 8 servings

2   pounds boneless beef
     round steak, cut
     ¾ inch thick
1   tablespoon vegetable
     oil
2   medium onions,
     sliced
3   cups sliced fresh
     mushrooms
     (8 ounces)
1   12-ounce jar beef
     gravy
1   1.25-ounce envelope
     mushroom gravy
     mix
4   cups hot mashed
     potatoes or cooked
     noodles (optional)

1 Trim fat from meat. Cut meat into eight serving-size portions. In a large skillet cook meat, half at a time, in hot oil over medium-high heat until brown on both sides. Drain off fat.

2 Place onions in a 3½- or 4-quart slow cooker. Add meat and mushrooms. In a small bowl combine beef gravy and mushroom gravy mix; pour over mixture in cooker.

3 Cover and cook on low-heat setting for 8 to 10 hours or on high-heat setting for 4 to 5 hours. To serve, spoon mushroom mixture over meat and, if desired, hot mashed potatoes.

nutrition facts per serving: 194 cal., 7 g total fat (2 g sat. fat), 57 mg chol., 479 mg sodium, 7 g carb., 1 g dietary fiber, 24 g protein.

beef stew with
red wine gravy

prep: 30 minutes   cook: 12 to 14 hours (low) or 6 to 7 hours (high)
makes: 6 servings

2 pounds boneless beef
   chuck roast
¼ cup all-purpose flour
2 teaspoons dried
   Italian seasoning,
   crushed
1 teaspoon salt
½ teaspoon freshly
   ground black
   pepper
2 tablespoons olive oil
2 large onions, cut into
   thin wedges
8 ounces carrots,
   halved or quartered
   lengthwise and
   cut up
8 ounces parsnips,
   peeled, quartered
   lengthwise, and cut
   up
8 ounces Jerusalem
   artichokes
   (sunchokes), peeled
   and coarsely
   chopped
1 cup Cabernet
   Sauvignon or beef
   broth
½ cup beef broth
¼ cup tomato paste
3 cups hot cooked
   noodles (optional)
   Golden raisins,
   chopped roma
   tomatoes, and/or
   red wine vinegar or
   balsamic vinegar

1 Trim fat from meat. Cut meat into 1-inch pieces. In a plastic bag combine flour, Italian seasoning, salt, and pepper. Add meat pieces, a few at a time, shaking to coat. In a large skillet cook meat, half at a time (add more oil during cooking if necessary), in hot oil over medium-high heat until brown. Drain off fat.

2 In a 4½- to 6-quart slow cooker combine onions, carrots, parsnips, and artichokes; add meat. Pour wine and broth over meat.

3 Cover and cook on low-heat setting for 12 to 14 hours or on high-heat setting for 6 to 7 hours. Stir in tomato paste. If desired, serve over hot cooked noodles. Top each serving with raisins, tomatoes, and/or vinegar.

nutrition facts per serving: 215 cal., 4 g total fat (1 g sat. fat), 64 mg chol., 405 mg sodium, 7 g carb., 1 g dietary fiber, 26 g protein.

espresso-braised beef

prep: 20 minutes   cook: 8 to 9 hours (low) or 4 to 4½ hours (high)
makes: 6 servings

1½   pounds boneless beef
     chuck roast
3   medium carrots, cut
     into 1 inch pieces
1   medium turnip,
     peeled and cut into
     1-inch pieces
1   large onion, cut into
     wedges
⅔   cup dry red wine
2   tablespoons no-salt-
     added tomato paste
1   tablespoon instant
     espresso coffee
     powder or coffee
     crystals
1   teaspoon packed
     brown sugar
1   teaspoon dried
     thyme, crushed
½   teaspoon salt
¼   teaspoon ground
     black pepper
1   24-ounce package
     refrigerated mashed
     sweet potatoes
     Salt (optional)
     Coarse ground black
     pepper (optional)

1 Trim fat from meat. Cut meat into 1-inch pieces. In a 3½- or 4-quart slow cooker combine carrots, turnip, and onion; add meat. In a medium bowl whisk together wine, tomato paste, coffee powder, brown sugar, thyme, ½ teaspoon salt, and ¼ teaspoon pepper. Pour wine mixture over meat.

2 Cover and cook on low-heat setting for 8 to 9 hours or on high-heat setting for 4 to 4½ hours.

3 Before serving, prepare mashed sweet potatoes according to package directions. Serve meat mixture with sweet potatoes. If desired, sprinkle with additional salt and coarse pepper.

nutrition facts per serving: 308 cal., 9 g total fat (4 g sat. fat), 66 mg chol., 410 mg sodium, 26 g carb., 4 g dietary fiber, 26 g protein

Suit your taste by adjusting the amount of smoky-flavored chipotle peppers.

beef and chipotle
burritos

prep: 25 minutes cook: 8 to 9 hours (low) or 4 to 4½ hours (high)
makes: 8 servings

2½ pounds boneless beef round steak, cut ¾ inch thick

2 14.5-ounce cans no-salt-added diced tomatoes, undrained

1 medium onion, cut into thin wedges

2 to 3 canned chipotle peppers in adobo sauce, chopped

2 cloves garlic, minced

1 teaspoon dried oregano, crushed

¼ teaspoon salt

¼ teaspoon ground cumin

8 8-inch whole wheat flour tortillas, warmed

1 cup shredded reduced-fat cheddar cheese (4 ounces) (optional)

1 recipe Pico de Gallo Salsa (optional)

1 Trim fat from meat. Cut meat into six pieces. Place meat in a 3½- or 4-quart slow cooker. Add tomatoes, onion, chipotle peppers, garlic, oregano, salt, and cumin.

2 Cover and cook on low-heat setting for 8 to 9 hours or on high-heat setting for 4 to 4½ hours.

3 Remove meat from cooker, reserving cooking liquid. Using two forks, pull meat apart into shreds. Using a slotted spoon, remove tomatoes and onion from cooker; set aside. Stir enough of the reserved cooking liquid into meat to moisten. Discard any remaining cooking liquid.

4 To serve, spoon ½ cup of the meat just below the center of each warm tortilla. Top each with about 3 tablespoons of the tomatoes and onion. If desired, top with cheese and Pico de Gallo Salsa. Roll up tortillas.

nutrition facts per serving: 361 cal., 11 g total fat (4 g sat. fat), 86 mg chol., 540 mg sodium, 22 g carb., 12 g dietary fiber, 40 g protein.

*tip: Because chile peppers contain volatile oils that can burn your skin and eyes, avoid direct contact with them as much as possible. When working with chile peppers, wear plastic or rubber gloves. If your bare hands do touch the peppers, wash your hands and nails well with soap and warm water.

pico de gallo salsa: In a small bowl combine 1 cup finely chopped tomatoes (2 medium), 2 tablespoons finely chopped onion, 2 tablespoons snipped fresh cilantro, and 1 fresh serrano chile pepper, seeded and finely chopped.* Stir in ½ cup peeled and chopped jicama and ¼ cup thin radish strips. Cover and chill for several hours before serving. Makes about 1¾ cups.

italian chicken

prep: 15 minutes   cook: 5 to 5 hours 30 minutes (low)   makes: 8 servings

1 15-ounce can no-salt-
    added pinto beans,
    rinsed and drained

1 14.5-ounce can no-
    salt-added diced
    tomatoes with basil,
    garlic, and oregano,
    undrained

1 9-ounce package
    frozen artichoke
    hearts

1 4-ounce can (drained
    weight) sliced
    mushrooms,
    drained

1 1.4-ounce envelope
    vegetable soup mix

8 skinless, boneless
    chicken breast
    halves (about
    2 pounds total)

1 10.75-ounce can
    reduced-sodium
    condensed cream
    of chicken soup

⅓ cup bottled Italian
    salad dressing

1 In a 5- to 6-quart slow cooker combine beans, tomatoes, artichokes, mushrooms, and vegetable soup mix; add chicken. In a medium bowl stir together soup and salad dressing; pour over chicken, spreading evenly.

2 Cover and cook on low-heat setting for 5 to 5½ hours.

3 Using tongs or a slotted spoon, transfer chicken to dinner plates. Stir artichoke mixture in cooker; spoon over chicken.

nutrition facts per serving: 276 cal., 5 g total fat (1 g sat. fat), 69 mg chol., 798 mg sodium, 22 g carb., 8 g dietary fiber, 32 g protein.

Hoisin sauce is thick and dark. Slow cooking gives the chicken plenty of time to absorb the sauce's sweet and spicy flavors.

simple hoisin chicken

prep: 15 minutes   cook: 4 to 5 hours (low) or 2½ hours (high) + 30 minutes (high)
makes: 6 servings

Nonstick cooking
spray
12 bone-in chicken
thighs (3½ to
4 pounds total),
skinned
2 tablespoons quick-
cooking tapioca
⅛ teaspoon salt
⅛ teaspoon ground
black pepper
½ cup hoisin sauce
1 16-ounce package
frozen broccoli
stir-fry vegetables
3 cups hot cooked rice

1 Coat the inside of a 3½- or 4-quart slow cooker with cooking spray. Place chicken in the prepared cooker; sprinkle with tapioca, salt, and pepper. Pour hoisin sauce over chicken.

2 Cover and cook on low-heat setting for 4 to 5 hours or on high-heat setting for 2½ hours.

3 If using low-heat setting, turn to high-heat setting. Stir in frozen vegetables. Cover and cook for 30 to 45 minutes more or just until vegetables are tender. Serve over hot cooked rice.

nutrition facts per serving: 345 cal., 6 g total fat (2 g sat. fat), 115 mg chol., 537 mg sodium, 37 g carb., 3 g dietary fiber, 32 g protein.

slow **cooker**

slow-cooked
moroccan
chicken

prep: 20 minutes   cook: 8 to 10 hours (low) or 4 to 5 hours (high)
makes: 4 servings

8   ounces baby carrots
      with tops, trimmed
8   bone-in chicken
      thighs (2¼ to
      2½ pounds total),
      skinned
1   14-ounce can
      reduced-sodium
      chicken broth
½   cup coarsely chopped
      onion (1 medium)
½   cup pitted dried
      plums (prunes)
1¼ teaspoons curry
      powder
½   teaspoon salt
½   teaspoon ground
      cinnamon
      Fresh Italian (flat-
      leaf) parsley sprigs
      (optional)

1 Cut any large carrots in half lengthwise.
In a 4- to 5-quart slow cooker combine
carrots, chicken, broth, onion, dried plums,
curry powder, salt, and cinnamon.

2 Cover and cook on low-heat setting for
8 to 10 hours or on high-heat setting for
4 to 5 hours.

3 Use a slotted spoon to serve chicken
mixture. Spoon some of the cooking liquid
over each serving. If desired, garnish with
parsley.

nutrition facts per serving: 255 cal., 6 g total fat
(1 g sat. fat), 115 mg chol., 691 mg sodium, 22 g carb.,
4 g dietary fiber, 30 g protein.

cacciatore-style
drumsticks

prep: 25 minutes   cook: 6 to 7 hours (low) or 3 to 3½ hours (high) + 15 minutes (high)
makes: 6 to 8 servings

2   cups sliced fresh
      mushrooms
2   medium onions, cut
      into wedges
1   cup sliced celery
      (2 stalks)
1   cup chopped carrots
      (2 medium)
1   cup green sweet
      pepper strips
      (1 medium)
4   cloves garlic, minced
8   chicken drumsticks
      (about 2 pounds
      total), skinned
1   14-ounce can
      reduced-sodium
      chicken broth
2   tablespoons quick-
      cooking tapioca
1   teaspoon salt
1   teaspoon dried
      oregano, crushed
½   teaspoon ground
      black pepper
1   14.5-ounce can
      no-salt-added
      diced tomatoes,
      undrained
½   of a 6-ounce can
      (⅓ cup) no-salt-
      added tomato paste
3   to 4 cups hot cooked
      fettuccine or rice
      (optional)

1 In a 4- to 5-quart slow cooker combine mushrooms, onions, celery, carrots, sweet pepper, and garlic; add chicken. In a medium bowl combine broth, tapioca, salt, oregano, and black pepper; pour over chicken.

2 Cover and cook on low-heat setting for 6 to 7 hours or on high heat setting for 3 to 3½ hours. Transfer chicken to a serving platter; cover and keep warm.

3 If using low-heat setting, turn to high-heat setting. Stir in tomatoes and tomato paste. Cover and cook for 15 minutes more.

4 To serve, spoon tomato mixture over chicken and, if desired, hot cooked fettuccine.

nutrition facts per serving: 245 cal., 5 g total fat (1 g sat. fat), 105 mg chol., 713 mg sodium, 18 g carb., 4 g dietary fiber, 32 g protein.

chicken and
mushrooms

prep: 25 minutes   cook: 8 to 9 hours (low) or 4 to 4½ hours (high)
makes: 4 servings

2   cups sliced fresh
     mushrooms
1   14.5-ounce can no-salt-
     added diced tomatoes
     with basil, garlic, and
     oregano, undrained
1   cup red sweet pepper
     cut into bite-size strips
     (1 medium)
1   medium onion, thinly
     sliced
¼   cup dry red wine
     or lower-sodium
     beef broth
2   tablespoons quick-
     cooking tapioca
2   tablespoons balsamic
     vinegar
3   cloves garlic, minced
2   to 2½ pounds meaty
     chicken pieces (breast
     halves, thighs, and
     drumsticks), skinned
¼   teaspoon salt
¼   teaspoon paprika
¼   teaspoon ground black
     pepper
2   cups hot cooked noodles
     or other pasta

1 In a 5- to 6-quart slow cooker combine mushrooms, tomatoes, sweet pepper, onion, wine, tapioca, vinegar, and garlic; add chicken. In a small bowl combine salt, paprika, and black pepper; sprinkle over chicken.

2 Cover and cook on low-heat setting for 8 to 9 hours or on high-heat setting for 4 to 4½ hours.

3 To serve, spoon tomato mixture over chicken and hot cooked noodles.

nutrition facts per serving: 427 cal., 9 g total fat (2 g sat. fat), 92 mg chol., 278 mg sodium, 44 g carb., 10 g dietary fiber, 38 g protein.

nutrition note

As a general rule, either one cup of raw vegetables or ½ cup cooked equals one serving of veggies. With this recipe, you'll get two servings of vegetable in one hearty dish.

Great-tasting ribs with just five ingredients? Chipotle chiles make it happen. These flavor-charged babies are actually jalapeño peppers that have been dried and smoked; here, they lend a nice balance of sweet and hot flavors to the meat.

chipotle baby back ribs

prep: 15 minutes broil: 10 minutes cook: 6 to 7 hours (low) or 3 to 3½ hours (high) + 15 minutes (high) makes: 8 servings

3 pounds pork loin back ribs or meaty pork spareribs

¾ cup no-salt-added tomato sauce

½ cup barbecue sauce

2 canned chipotle peppers in adobo sauce, finely chopped*

2 tablespoons cornstarch

2 tablespoons cold water

Shredded cabbage with carrot (coleslaw mix) and/ or thinly sliced fresh jalapeño chile peppers* (optional)

1 Preheat broiler. Cut ribs into two-rib portions. Place ribs on the unheated rack of a broiler pan. Broil about 6 inches from the heat about 10 minutes or until brown, turning once halfway through broiling.**

2 Place ribs in a 4- to 5-quart slow cooker. For sauce, in a medium bowl combine tomato sauce, barbecue sauce, and chipotle peppers; pour over ribs.

3 Cover and cook on low-heat setting for 6 to 7 hours or on high-heat setting for 3 to 3½ hours.

4 Transfer ribs to a serving platter, reserving sauce in cooker. Cover ribs and keep warm. Skim fat from sauce.

5 If using low-heat setting, turn to high-heat setting. In a small bowl combine cornstarch and the water; stir into sauce. Cover and cook about 15 minutes more or until sauce is thickened. Spoon sauce over ribs and, if desired, serve with coleslaw mix and/or jalapeño chile peppers.

nutrition facts per serving: 286 cal., 8 g total fat (3 g sat. fat), 91 mg chol., 526 mg sodium, 10 g carb., 1 g dietary fiber, 40 g protein.

*tip: Because chile peppers contain volatile oils that can burn your skin and eyes, avoid direct contact with them as much as possible. When working with chile peppers, wear plastic or rubber gloves. If your bare hands do touch the peppers, wash your hands and nails well with soap and warm water.

**tip: Broiling will make the ribs less fatty. But you may omit this step, if you prefer.

Treat your guests to a succulent pork roast draped with a golden herbed fruit sauce. The 15-minute standing time makes the tender meat easier to slice.

herbed apricot pork roast

prep: 20 minutes   cook: 6 to 7 hours (low) or 3 to 3½ hours (high)
stand: 15 minutes   makes: 8 servings

1   3-pound boneless
      pork top loin roast
      (double loin, tied)
      Salt
      Ground black pepper
1   10-ounce jar apricot
      spreadable fruit
⅓   cup finely chopped
      onion (1 small)
2   tablespoons Dijon-
      style mustard
1   tablespoon brandy
1   teaspoon finely
      shredded lemon
      peel
1   teaspoon snipped
      fresh rosemary
1   teaspoon snipped
      fresh sage
1   teaspoon snipped
      fresh thyme
¼   teaspoon ground
      black pepper
2   tablespoons cold
      water
4   teaspoons cornstarch
      Fresh apricot wedges
      (optional)
      Fresh rosemary, sage,
      and/or thyme sprigs
      (optional)

1 Trim fat from meat. Sprinkle meat with salt and pepper. Place meat in a 4- to 5-quart slow cooker. In a medium bowl combine spreadable fruit, onion, mustard, brandy, lemon peel, 1 teaspoon rosemary, sage, and thyme, and ¼ teaspoon pepper; pour over meat.

2 Cover and cook on low-heat setting for 6 to 7 hours or on high-heat setting for 3 to 3½ hours. Remove meat from cooker. Cover loosely with foil and let stand for 15 minutes.

3 Meanwhile, for sauce, in a medium saucepan combine the water and cornstarch. Carefully add spreadable fruit mixture from cooker; cook and stir over medium heat until thickened and bubbly. Cook and stir for 2 minutes more.

4 Slice meat; serve meat with sauce. If desired, garnish with fresh apricots and herb sprigs.

nutrition facts per serving: 314 cal., 7 g total fat (2 g sat. fat), 107 mg chol., 247 mg sodium, 21 g carb., 0 g dietary fiber, 38 g protein.

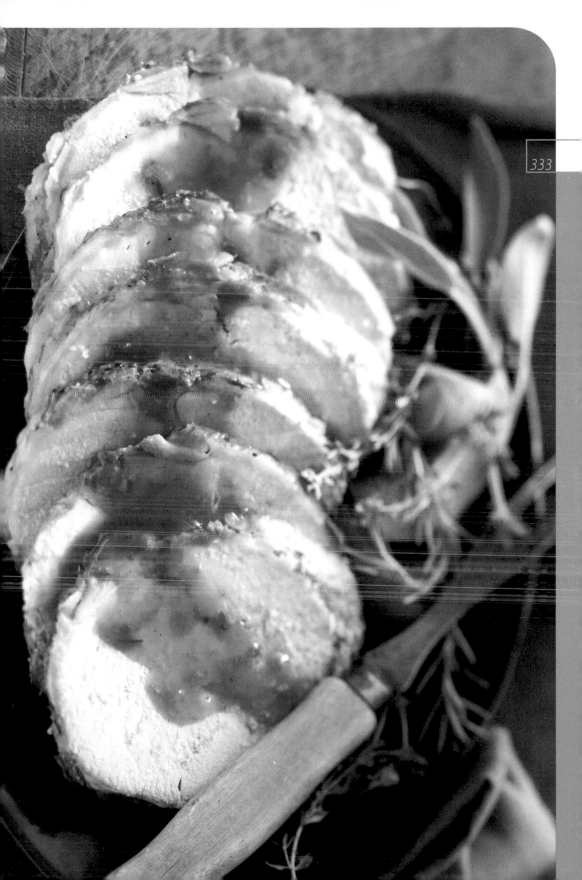

Shredded meat is a welcome change from sliced roast. This slow cooker method makes it especially tender.

shredded pork salad

prep: 20 minutes   cook: 8 to 10 hours (low) or 4 to 5 hours (high)
makes: 6 servings

1   2-pound boneless
    pork shoulder roast
2   large onions,
    quartered
1   cup water
3   fresh jalapeño chile
    peppers, cut up*
8   cloves garlic, minced
2   teaspoons ground
    coriander
2   teaspoons ground
    cumin
2   teaspoons dried
    oregano, crushed
½   teaspoon salt
½   teaspoon ground
    black pepper
12 butterhead (Boston or
    Bibb) lettuce leaves
¾   cup salsa
    Fresh oregano sprigs
    (optional)

1 Trim fat from meat. If necessary, cut meat to fit into a 3½- or 4-quart slow cooker. Place meat in the cooker. Add onions, the water, jalapeño chile peppers, garlic, coriander, cumin, dried oregano, salt, and black pepper.

2 Cover and cook on low-heat setting for 8 to 10 hours or on high-heat setting for 4 to 5 hours.

3 Remove meat from cooker; discard cooking liquid. Using two forks, pull meat apart into shreds. Spoon warm meat onto lettuce leaves. Top with salsa. If desired, garnish with fresh oregano.

nutrition facts per serving: 278 cal., 12 g total fat (4 g sat. fat), 102 mg chol., 402 mg sodium, 10 g carb., 3 g dietary fiber, 32 g protein.

*tip: Because chile peppers contain volatile oils that can burn your skin and eyes, avoid direct contact with them as much as possible. When working with chile peppers, wear plastic or rubber gloves. If your bare hands do touch the peppers, wash your hands and nails well with soap and warm water.

chili-style
vegetable pasta

prep: 20 minutes   cook: 5 to 6 hours (low) or 2½ to 3 hours (high)
makes: 6 servings

2   14.5-ounce cans
    no salt-added
    diced tomatoes,
    undrained
1   15-ounce can no-salt-
    added garbanzo
    beans (chickpeas),
    rinsed and drained
1   15-ounce can no-salt-
    added red kidney
    beans, rinsed and
    drained
1   8-ounce can no-salt-
    added tomato sauce
1   cup finely chopped
    onion (1 large)
1   cup chopped green
    or yellow sweet
    pepper
2   to 3 teaspoons chili
    powder
2   cloves garlic, minced
½   teaspoon dried
    oregano, crushed
⅛   teaspoon cayenne
    pepper
8   ounces dried whole
    wheat and/or
    vegetable wagon
    wheel macaroni
½   cup shredded
    reduced-fat cheddar
    cheese (2 ounces)

1 In a 3½- or 4-quart slow cooker combine tomatoes, garbanzo beans, kidney beans, tomato sauce, onion, sweet pepper, chili powder, garlic, oregano, and cayenne pepper.

2 Cover and cook on low-heat setting for 5 to 6 hours or on high-heat setting for 2½ to 3 hours.

3 Before serving, cook macaroni according to package directions; drain. Serve bean mixture over hot cooked macaroni. Sprinkle with cheese.

nutrition facts per serving: 353 cal., 4 g total fat (1 g sat. fat), 7 mg chol., 164 mg sodium, 63 g carb., 14 g dietary fiber, 17 g protein.

nutrition note
Getting your recommended 25 grams of fiber each day may sound like a challenge, but eating kidney beans gives you a swift step toward the goal. One-half cup contains 7 grams of fiber.

We only exaggerate slightly when we say this great-tasting chili is so easy you could do it in your sleep. It really is super-easy.

in-your-sleep chili

prep: 15 minutes   cook: 4 to 6 hours (low) or 2 to 3 hours (high)
makes: 6 servings

1 pound lean ground beef
1 cup chopped onion (1 large)
2 15-ounce cans reduced-sodium chili beans in chili gravy, undrained
1 14.5-ounce can no-salt-added fire roasted diced tomatoes, undrained
1 11.5-ounce can hot-style vegetable juice
   Sliced green onions, sour cream, and/or shredded cheddar cheese (optional)

1 In a large skillet cook ground beef and onion over medium-high heat until meat is brown, using a wooden spoon to break up meat as it cooks. Drain off fat.

2 Transfer meat mixture to a 3½- or 4-quart slow cooker. Stir in beans in gravy, tomatoes and chiles, and vegetable juice.

3 Cover and cook on low-heat setting for 4 to 6 hours on high-heat setting for 2 to 3 hours.

4 If desired, top each serving with green onions, sour cream, and/or cheese.

nutrition facts per serving: 272 cal., 6 g total fat (2 g sat. fat), 47 mg chol., 238 mg sodium, 30 g carb., 7 g dietary fiber, 24 g protein.

chicken and noodles

prep: 20 minutes   cook: 7 hours (low) or 3 hours (high) + 1 hour (high)
stand: 5 minutes   makes: 8 servings

3   medium carrots, cut
    into 1-inch pieces
2   medium parsnips,
    peeled and cut into
    1-inch pieces
2   stalks celery, cut into
    1 inch pieces
1   cup pearl onions* or
    frozen small whole
    onions
3   whole chicken legs
    (drumstick and
    thigh) (about
    3 pounds total),
    skinned
2   cloves garlic, minced
½   teaspoon salt
½   teaspoon dried
    thyme, crushed
½   teaspoon dried sage,
    crushed
¼   teaspoon ground
    black pepper
2   14-ounce cans
    reduced-sodium
    chicken broth
¼   cup dry sherry or
    reduced-sodium
    chicken broth
1   12-ounce package
    frozen egg noodles
¾   cup frozen peas
    Fresh sage leaves
    (optional)

1 In a 5- to 6-quart slow cooker combine carrots, parsnips, celery, and onions; add chicken. Sprinkle with garlic, salt, dried thyme, sage, and pepper. Pour broth and sherry over chicken.

2 Cover and cook on low heat setting for 7 hours or on high-heat setting for 3 hours. Stir in noodles. If using low-heat setting, turn to high-heat setting. Cover and cook for 1 to 1½ hours more or until noodles are tender.

3 Remove chicken from cooker. Using two forks, remove chicken from bones, pulling meat apart into shreds; discard bones. Stir shredded chicken into broth mixture. Stir in peas. Cover and let stand for 5 minutes. If desired, garnish each serving with fresh sage.

nutrition facts per serving: 301 cal., 5 g total fat (1 g sat. fat), 127 mg chol., 497 mg sodium, 35 g carb., 4 g dietary fiber, 26 g protein.

*tip: If using pearl onions, in a small saucepan cook the onions in enough boiling water to cover for 1 minute; drain. Rinse with cold water; drain again. Cut off root ends and slip off peels.

slow cooker indian chicken stew

prep: 15 minutes   cook: 8 to 10 hours (low) or 4 to 5 hours (high)
makes: 8 servings

Nonstick cooking
spray
2   pounds skinless,
boneless chicken
thighs, cut into
1-inch pieces
½   cup chopped onion
(1 medium)
5   teaspoons curry
powder
2   teaspoons ground
ginger
3   cloves garlic, minced
½   teaspoon salt
¼   teaspoon ground
black pepper and/or
cayenne pepper
2   15-ounce cans no-
salt-added garbanzo
beans (chickpeas),
rinsed and drained
2   14.5-ounce cans
no-salt-added
diced tomatoes,
undrained
1   cup reduced-sodium
chicken broth
1   bay leaf
2   tablespoons lime
juice
Fresh Italian (flat-
leaf) parsley sprigs
(optional)

1 Lightly coat the inside of a 6-quart slow cooker with cooking spray. Place chicken, onion, curry powder, ginger, garlic, salt, and pepper in cooker; toss to coat. Stir in beans, tomatoes, broth, and bay leaf.

2 Cover and cook on low-heat setting for 8 to 10 hours or on high-heat setting for 4 to 5 hours. Remove and discard bay leaf.

3 Stir lime juice into chicken mixture. If desired, garnish each serving with parsley

nutrition facts per serving: 265 cal., 6 g total fat (1 g sat. fat), 94 mg chol., 508 mg sodium, 23 g carb., 6 g dietary fiber, 30 g protein.

turkey and squash chili

prep: 25 minutes   cook: 10 to 12 hours (low) or 5 to 6 hours (high)
makes: 6 servings

1   pound turkey breast
    tenderloin, cut into
    1-inch pieces
1   28-ounce can
    no-salt-added
    diced tomatoes,
    undrained
1   15-ounce can no-salt-
    added black beans,
    rinsed and drained
1   8-ounce can no-salt-
    added tomato sauce
1   cup peeled and cubed
    butternut squash or
    pumpkin
½   cup chopped onion
    (1 medium)
½   cup frozen whole
    kernel corn
½   cup dried cranberries
½   cup reduced-sodium
    chicken broth
1   fresh jalapeño chile
    pepper, seeded and
    finely chopped*
1   tablespoon chili
    powder
1   clove garlic, minced
    Reduced-sodium
    chicken broth
    (optional)
2   cups shredded fresh
    spinach leaves
1   cup shredded
    Monterey Jack
    cheese with
    jalapeño peppers
    (4 ounces)

1 In a 5-quart slow cooker combine turkey, tomatoes, beans, tomato sauce, squash, onion, corn, dried cranberries, ½ cup broth, jalapeño chile pepper, chili powder, and garlic.

2 Cover and cook on low-heat setting for 10 to 12 hours or on high-heat setting for 5 to 6 hours.

3 If necessary, stir in additional broth to reach desired consistency. Before serving, stir in spinach. Sprinkle each serving with cheese.

nutrition facts per serving: 338 cal., 7 g total fat (4 g sat. fat), 67 mg chol., 333 mg sodium, 41 g carb., 9 g dietary fiber, 31 g protein.

*tip: Because chile peppers contain volatile oils that can burn your skin and eyes, avoid direct contact with them as much as possible. When working with chile peppers, wear plastic or rubber gloves. If your bare hands do touch the peppers, wash your hands and nails well with soap and warm water.

Slices of mushrooms, slivers of bok choy, and chunks of turkey mingle in a soy- and ginger-flavored broth, giving stir-fry flavors to this savory soup.

asian turkey and rice
soup

prep: 25 minutes cook: 7 to 8 hours (low) or 3½ to 4 hours (high) + 10 minutes (high) makes: 6 servings

1 pound turkey breast tenderloin or skinless, boneless chicken breast halves, cut into 1-inch pieces

2 14-ounce cans reduced-sodium chicken broth

2 cups sliced fresh shiitake or button mushrooms

1½ cups water

2 medium carrots, cut into thin bite-size strips (1 cup)

½ cup chopped onion (1 medium)

2 tablespoons reduced-sodium soy sauce

2 teaspoons grated fresh ginger

4 cloves garlic, minced

1½ cups sliced bok choy

1 cup uncooked instant brown rice

¾ cup chow mein noodles (optional)

1 In a 3½- or 4-quart slow cooker combine turkey, broth, mushrooms, the water, carrots, onion, soy sauce, ginger, and garlic.

2 Cover and cook on low-heat setting for 7 to 8 hours or on high-heat setting for 3½ to 4 hours.

3 If using low-heat setting, turn to high-heat setting. Stir in bok choy and rice. Cover and cook for 10 to 15 minutes more or until rice is tender. If desired, top each serving with chow mein noodles.

nutrition facts per serving: 166 cal., 2 g total fat (0 g sat. fat), 45 mg chol., 572 mg sodium, 15 g carb., 2 g dietary fiber, 22 g protein.

Poblano peppers are mild to medium-hot. They're long and deep green with an irregular bell-pepper shape. Remove the membranes and seeds for the mildest flavor.

poblano pork stew

prep: 35 minutes cook: 7½ hours to 8 hours (low) or 3½ to 4 hours (high) + 15 minutes (high) makes: 8 servings

1½ pounds boneless pork shoulder roast
1 tablespoon vegetable oil
1½ pounds tiny new potatoes, quartered
2 cups chopped onions (2 large)
1 10-ounce package frozen whole kernel corn
3 poblano chile peppers, seeded and cut into 1-inch pieces,* or 2 small green sweet peppers, seeded and cut into 1-inch pieces
1 fresh jalapeño chile pepper, seeded and chopped*
6 cloves garlic, minced
1 teaspoon salt
½ teaspoon dried oregano, crushed
1 14-ounce can reduced-sodium chicken broth
3 medium zucchini, halved lengthwise and cut into ½-inch pieces (about 4 cups)
¼ cup snipped fresh cilantro or parsley
Fresh jalapeño chile pepper, seeded and cut into thin strips* (optional)
Lime wedges (optional)

1 Trim fat from meat. Cut meat into 1-inch pieces. In a large skillet cook meat, half at a time, in hot oil over medium-high heat until brown. Drain off fat.

2 In a 5- to 6-quart slow cooker combine potatoes, onions, frozen corn, poblano chile peppers, chopped jalapeño pepper, garlic, salt, and oregano; add meat. Pour broth over mixture in cooker.

3 Cover and cook on low-heat setting for 7½ to 8 hours or on high-heat setting for 3½ to 4 hours.

4 If using low-heat setting, turn to high-heat setting. Stir in zucchini. Cover and cook for 15 minutes more. Stir in cilantro.

5 If desired, top each serving with jalapeño chile pepper strips and serve with lime wedges.

nutrition facts per serving: 276 cal., 7 g total fat (2 g sat. fat), 51 mg chol., 483 mg sodium, 33 g carb., 4 g dietary fiber, 22 g protein.

*tip: Because chile peppers contain volatile oils that can burn your skin and eyes, avoid direct contact with them as much as possible. When working with chile peppers, wear plastic or rubber gloves. If your bare hands do touch the peppers, wash your hands and nails well with soap and warm water.

butternut squash soup with thai gremolata

prep: 25 minutes cook: 4 to 5 hours (low) or 2 to 2½ hours (high)
makes: 4 to 6 servings

2 pounds butternut squash, peeled, seeded, and cut into 1-inch pieces
2 cups reduced-sodium chicken broth
1 14-ounce can unsweetened coconut milk
¼ cup finely chopped onion
1 tablespoon packed brown sugar
1 tablespoon fish sauce or soy sauce
½ to 1 teaspoon Asian chili sauce, such as sriracha, or crushed red pepper
2 tablespoons lime juice
1 recipe Thai Gremolata
Lime wedges (optional)

1 In a 3½- or 4-quart slow cooker combine squash, broth, coconut milk, onion, brown sugar, fish sauce, and Asian chili sauce.

2 Cover and cook on low-heat setting for 4 to 5 hours or on high-heat setting for 2 to 2½ hours.

3 Using an immersion blender, carefully blend squash mixture until completely smooth. (Or use a food processor or blender to process mixture in batches until completely smooth or a potato masher to mash mixture until nearly smooth.) Stir in lime juice.

4 Top each serving with Thai Gremolata. If desired, serve with lime wedges.

nutrition facts per serving: 284 cal., 15 g total fat (5 g sat. fat), 0 mg chol., 677 mg sodium, 36 g carb., 6 g dietary fiber, 8 g protein.

thai gremolata: In a small bowl stir together ½ cup snipped fresh basil or cilantro, ½ cup chopped peanuts, and 1 tablespoon finely shredded lime peel. Makes about 1 cup.

make-ahead me

12

Become a culinary Cub Scout by being prepared. Spending a few weekend hours whipping up a few dishes that will earn you a badge for togetherness during the week.

als

wine-braised brisket
with onions

prep: 30 minutes **chill:** overnight **slow cook:** 10 to 12 hours (low) or 5 to 6 hours (high) **makes:** 8 to 10 servings

1   3- to 3½-pound boneless beef brisket
½   teaspoon salt
½   teaspoon freshly ground black pepper
1½ cups dry red wine
1   14-ounce can lower-sodium beef broth
10 ounces fresh mushrooms, sliced
2   large onions, cut in wedges
3   sprigs fresh thyme or ½ teaspoon dried thyme, crushed
1   bay leaf
1   tablespoon bottled minced garlic

to serve brisket:
¼   teaspoon salt
¼   teaspoon freshly ground black pepper

1 Pat the brisket dry with paper towels. Trim fat from meat. Sprinkle meat with ½ teaspoon salt and ½ teaspoon pepper. If necessary, cut brisket to fit into a 5- to 6-quart slow cooker. Place meat in removable liner of slow cooker. Pour wine and broth evenly over brisket.

2 Top with mushrooms, onions, thyme, bay leaf, and garlic. Cover and chill in the refrigerator overnight.

3 Remove from refrigerator. Place liner in slow cooker. Cover and cook on low-heat setting for 10 to 12 hours or on high-heat setting for 5 to 6 hours.

4 To serve, carefully remove brisket from slow cooker and slice across the grain. If desired, for sauce, transfer cooking liquid to a large saucepan. Bring to boiling; reduce heat. Simmer, uncovered, until desired consistency; serve with brisket. Sprinkle brisket with ¼ teaspoon salt and ¼ teaspoon pepper.

nutrition facts per serving: 329 cal., 13 g total fat (4 g sat. fat), 105 mg chol., 449 mg sodium, 7 g carb., 1 g dietary fiber, 37 g protein.

baked penne with meat sauce

prep: 30 minutes **freeze:** up to 1 month **thaw:** 24 to 48 hours
bake: 55 minutes **oven:** 350°F **makes:** two 6-serving casseroles

1 pound dried penne
   pasta
2 14.5-ounce cans no-
   salt-added diced
   tomatoes with
   basil and oregano,
   undrained
1 6-ounce can no-salt-
   added tomato paste
⅔ cup water
⅔ cup tomato juice
1 teaspoon sugar
1 teaspoon dried
   oregano, crushed
½ teaspoon salt
½ teaspoon ground
   black pepper
2 pounds extra-lean
   ground beef
1 cup chopped onion
   (1 large)
½ cup sliced pitted ripe
   olives

to serve one casserole:
1 cup shredded
   reduced-fat
   mozzarella cheese
   (4 ounces)

1 Cook pasta according to package directions; drain well. Set aside.

2 Meanwhile, in a medium bowl stir together tomatoes, tomato paste, the water, tomato juice, sugar, oregano, salt, and pepper; set aside.

3 In a large skillet cook ground beef and onion over medium heat until meat is brown and onion is tender, using a wooden spoon to break up meat as it cooks. Drain off fat. Stir tomato mixture into meat mixture in skillet. Bring to boiling; reduce heat. Simmer, covered, for 10 minutes. Stir in cooked pasta and olives.

4 Divide the pasta mixture between two 3-quart casseroles. Cover with plastic wrap; cover with heavy foil. Seal, label, and freeze for up to 1 month.

5 To serve, thaw one casserole in the refrigerator for 24 to 48 hours. Preheat oven to 350°F. Remove plastic wrap; cover with foil. Bake about 55 minutes or until heated through, carefully stirring once. Sprinkle with cheese. Bake, uncovered, about 5 minutes more or until cheese melts.

nutrition facts per serving: 322 cal., 7 g total fat (3 g sat. fat), 53 mg chol., 334 mg sodium, 39 g carb., 7 g dietary fiber, 25 g protein.

nutrition note
There's no need to cut fat entirely—just keep it in check. A little goes a long way to add flavor and moistness, so look for ground beef that's 95% to 98% lean.

The bit of bittersweet chocolate in this chili keeps the heat of the chili seasoning in check and adds richness.

make-ahead
game day chili

prep: 25 minutes **stand:** 30 minutes **slow cook:** 6 to 7 hours (low) or 3 to 3½ hours (high) **chill:** overnight **heat:** 1 to 2 hours (high) **makes:** 8 servings

1½ pounds extra-lean ground beef
1 cup chopped onion (1 large)
1 cup sliced celery (2 stalks)
1 recipe Chili Seasoning Puree
1 28-ounce can no-salt-added diced tomatoes, undrained
1 14-ounce can lower-sodium beef broth
1½ cups pitted dried plums (prunes) or raisins, chopped
1½ cups water
1 6-ounce can no-salt-added tomato paste
2 tablespoons smoked paprika
2 teaspoons ground coriander
1 teaspoon crushed red pepper
¼ to ½ teaspoon ground cloves

1 In a 6-quart Dutch oven cook ground beef, onion, and celery over medium-high heat until meat is brown and onion is tender, using a wooden spoon to break up meat as it cooks. Drain off fat.

2 Transfer meat mixture to a 5- to 6-quart slow cooker. Stir in Chili Seasoning Puree, tomatoes, broth, dried plums, the water, tomato paste, paprika, coriander, crushed red pepper, and cloves.

3 Cover and cook on low-heat setting for 6 to 7 hours or on high-heat setting for 3 to 3½ hours; cool slightly. Transfer chili to a storage container.

4 Cover and chill in the refrigerator overnight.

5 To serve, return chili to slow cooker. Cover and reheat on high-heat setting for 1 to 2 hours or until heated through, stirring occasionally. Before serving, stir in chocolate.

nutrition facts per serving: 291 cal., 6 g total fat (3 g sat. fat), 53 mg chol., 264 mg sodium, 40 g carb., 7 g dietary fiber, 23 g protein

to serve chili:
1 ounce bittersweet chocolate, chopped

*****tip:** Because chile peppers contain volatile oils that can burn your skin and eyes, avoid direct contact with them as much as possible. When working with chile peppers, wear plastic or rubber gloves. If your bare hands do touch the peppers, wash your hands and nails well with soap and warm water.

chili seasoning puree: In a small bowl combine 2 dried ancho, mulato, or pasilla chile peppers and enough boiling water to cover. Let stand for 30 minutes; drain well. Remove stems and seeds from peppers.* In a food processor or blender combine the drained chile peppers, ¾ cup beef broth, 5 pitted dried plums (prunes), and 1 fresh jalapeño chile pepper, seeded and chopped.* Cover and process or blend until smooth.

beefy tortilla casserole

prep: 25 minutes chill: 2 to 24 hours bake: 40 minutes stand: 10 minutes
oven: 350°F makes: 6 to 8 servings

1 pound extra-lean
   ground beef
½ cup chopped onion
   (1 medium)
1 4-ounce can diced
   green chile peppers,
   undrained
1½ teaspoons chili
    powder
1 teaspoon ground
   cumin
1 8-ounce carton light
   sour cream
2 tablespoons all-
   purpose flour
¼ teaspoon garlic
   powder
8 6-inch corn tortillas
1 8-ounce can tomato
   sauce

to serve casserole:
1 cup reduced-fat
   shredded cheddar
   cheese (4 ounces)

1 Lightly grease a 2-quart rectangular baking dish; set aside. In a large skillet cook ground beef and onion until meat is brown and onion is tender, using a wooden spoon to break up meat as it cooks. Drain off fat. Stir green chile peppers, chili powder, and cumin into meat mixture in skillet. Cook for 1 minute more; set aside.

2 In a small bowl combine sour cream, flour, and garlic powder; set aside.

3 Place half of the tortillas in bottom of the prepared baking dish, overlapping as necessary. Top evenly with half of the meat mixture. Spoon half of the sour cream mixture over meat mixture in small mounds; spread to an even layer. Top with half of the tomato sauce. Repeat layers.

4 Cover baking dish with plastic wrap. Chill in the refrigerator for 2 to 24 hours.

5 To serve, preheat oven to 350°F. Remove plastic wrap; cover with foil. Bake for 35 minutes. Sprinkle with cheese. Bake, uncovered, about 5 minutes more or until heated through and cheese is melted. Let stand for 10 minutes before serving.

nutrition facts per serving: 316 cal., 13 g total fat (7 g sat. fat), 71 mg chol., 489 mg sodium, 25 g carb., 4 g dietary fiber, 26 g protein.

beef-bean burritos

prep: 25 minutes **chill:** overnight **bake:** 35 minutes
oven: 350°F **makes:** 8 burritos

Nonstick cooking
   spray
8 8-inch flour tortillas
8 ounces lean ground
   beef
1 cup chopped onion
   (1 large)
2 cloves garlic, minced
1 15-ounce can black
   beans or pinto
   beans, rinsed and
   drained
½ cup salsa
2 teaspoons chili
   powder
Several dashes
   bottled hot pepper
   sauce
¾ cup shredded
   cheddar cheese
   (3 ounces)

to serve burritos:
¼ cup shredded
   cheddar cheese
   (1 ounce)
1½ cups shredded fresh
   spinach
1½ cups shredded
   lettuce
Salsa (optional)
Sour cream (optional)

1 Preheat oven to 350°F. Line a 15×10×1-inch baking pan with foil. Lightly coat foil with cooking spray; set aside. Stack tortillas; wrap in foil. Bake for 10 minutes to soften. Meanwhile, for filling, in a large skillet cook ground beef, onion, and garlic until meat is brown and onion is tender, using a wooden spoon to break up meat as it cooks. Drain off fat. Stir beans, ½ cup salsa, chili powder, and hot pepper sauce into meat mixture in skillet.

2 Spoon about ½ cup of the filling onto each tortilla and top with 1 tablespoon of the cheese. Fold bottom edge up and over filling. Fold in opposite sides. Roll up, tucking in sides. Secure with wooden toothpicks. Arrange tortillas, seam sides down, in prepared baking pan.

3 Cover baking pan with plastic wrap; cover with foil. Chill in the refrigerator overnight. Cover and chill the remaining cheese until needed.

4 To serve, preheat oven to 350°F. Remove plastic wrap; cover with foil. Bake for 30 to 40 minutes or until heated through. Sprinkle with the remaining cheese. Bake, uncovered, about 5 minutes more or until cheese is melted. Serve burritos on a bed of spinach and lettuce. If desired, serve with additional salsa and sour cream.

nutrition facts per burrito: 300 cal., 11 g total fat (4 g sat. fat), 33 mg chol., 539 mg sodium, 36 g carb., 3 g dietary fiber, 17 g protein.

bean-and-beef enchilada casserole

prep: 25 minutes **chill:** overnight **bake:** 35 minutes **oven:** 350°F
makes: 6 servings

Nonstick cooking
  spray
8 ounces extra-lean
  ground beef
½ cup chopped onion
  (1 medium)
1 teaspoon chili powder
½ teaspoon ground
  cumin
1 15-ounce can no-salt-
  added pinto beans,
  rinsed and drained
1 4-ounce can diced
  green chile peppers,
  undrained
1 8-ounce carton light
  sour cream
2 tablespoons all-
  purpose flour
¼ teaspoon garlic
  powder
8 6-inch corn tortillas
1 10-ounce can
  enchilada sauce

to serve casserole:
1 cup reduced-fat
  shredded cheddar
  cheese (4 ounces)
  Snipped fresh cilantro
  (optional)

1 Lightly coat a 2-quart rectangular baking dish with cooking spray; set aside. In a large skillet cook ground beef and onion over medium-high heat until meat is brown and onion is tender, using a wooden spoon to break up meat as it cooks. Drain off fat. Stir chili powder and cumin into the meat mixture in skillet. Stir pinto beans and green chile peppers into meat mixture in skillet. Remove from heat.

2 In a small bowl stir together sour cream, flour, and garlic powder; set aside.

3 Place half of the tortillas in bottom of the prepared baking dish, overlapping as necessary. Top evenly with half of the meat mixture. Spoon half of the sour cream mixture over meat mixture in small mounds; spread to an even layer. Top with half of the enchilada sauce. Repeat layers.

4 Cover baking dish with plastic wrap. Chill in the refrigerator overnight.

5 To serve, preheat oven to 350°F. Remove plastic wrap; cover with foil. Bake about 30 minutes or until heated through. Sprinkle with cheese. Bake, uncovered, about 5 minutes more or until cheese is melted. If desired, sprinkle with cilantro.

nutrition facts per serving: 333 cal., 12 g total fat (6 g sat. fat), 47 mg chol., 484 mg sodium, 35 g carb., 6 g dietary fiber, 21 g protein.

When using a low-fat meat, help keep burgers juicy by avoiding overcooking them. Check the doneness with an instant-read thermometer inserted through the side of the patty.

veggie-filled hamburgers

prep: 25 minutes **freeze:** up to 3 months **thaw:** overnight **grill:** 11 minutes
makes: 4 servings

2 tablespoons fat-free milk
½ cup finely shredded carrot (1 medium)
¼ cup thinly sliced green onions (2)
¼ cup soft whole wheat bread crumbs
¼ teaspoon garlic salt
¼ teaspoon dried Italian seasoning, crushed
Dash ground black pepper
12 ounces extra-lean ground beef or uncooked ground turkey breast or chicken breast

to serve burgers:
4 whole wheat hamburger buns, split and toasted
1 recipe Curry Mustard (optional)
4 lettuce leaves
4 to 8 slices tomato
½ cup sliced zucchini

1 In a medium bowl stir together milk, carrot, green onions, bread crumbs, garlic salt, Italian seasoning, and pepper. Add the ground meat; mix well. Shape the mixture into four ½-inch-thick patty.

2 Place patties in a single layer in a freezer container. Seal, label, and freeze for up to 3 months.

3 To serve, thaw in the refrigerator overnight. For a charcoal grill, grill patties on the rack of an uncovered grill directly over medium coals for 11 to 14 minutes or until done (160°F for beef or 165°F for turkey or chicken), turning once halfway through grilling. (For a gas grill, preheat grill. Reduce heat to medium. Place patties on grill rack over heat. Cover and grill as above.)

4 If desired, spread bun bottoms with Curry Mustard. Top with patties lettuce leaves, tomato, zucchini, and bun tops

nutrition facts per serving: 254 cal., 6 g total fat (2 g sat. fat), 55 mg chol., 350 mg sodium, 27 g carb., 3 g dietary fiber, 24 g protein.

curry mustard: In a small bowl stir together ¼ cup Dijon-style mustard and ½ teaspoon curry powder. Makes ¼ cup.

Accompany this south-of-the-border inspired dish with a salad of tossed greens embellished with tomato wedges and tossed with a reduced-fat dressing.

creamy chicken enchiladas

prep: 40 minutes **freeze:** up to 3 months **thaw:** overnight **bake:** 40 minutes
stand: 5 minutes **oven:** 350°F **makes:** 6 servings

8 ounces skinless, boneless chicken breast halves
⅔ cup reduced-sodium chicken broth
¼ teaspoon ground black pepper
1 10-ounce package frozen chopped spinach, thawed and well drained
2 tablespoons thinly sliced green onion (1)
1 8-ounce tub light cream cheese
2 tablespoons all-purpose flour
¼ teaspoon salt
¼ teaspoon ground cumin
¼ cup fat-free milk
1 4-ounce can diced green chile peppers, drained

to serve enchiladas:
  Nonstick cooking spray
6 7-inch flour tortillas
¾ cup salsa
½ cup shredded reduced-fat cheddar or Monterey Jack cheese (2 ounces)
  Thinly sliced green onions (optional)
  Snipped fresh cilantro (optional)

1 In a large skillet combine chicken, broth, and black pepper. Bring to boiling; reduce heat. Simmer, covered, for 12 to 14 minutes or until chicken is no longer pink (170°F). Drain well; cool slightly. When cool enough to handle, use two forks to pull chicken apart into bite-size pieces; set aside.

2 For filling, in a large bowl combine chicken, spinach, and the 2 tablespoons green onion. In a small bowl combine cream cheese, flour, salt, and cumin. Stir in milk and green chile peppers. Stir cream cheese mixture into chicken mixture.

3 Transfer filling to a freezer container. Seal, label, and freeze for up to 3 months.

4 To serve, thaw filling in refrigerator overnight. Preheat oven to 350°F. Coat a 2-quart rectangular baking dish with cooking spray; set aside. Divide filling among the tortillas. Roll up tortillas. Place tortillas, seam sides down, in the prepared baking dish. Cover with foil.

5 Bake for 20 minutes. Pour salsa over enchiladas and sprinkle with cheese. Bake, uncovered, about 20 minutes more or until heated through and cheese is melted. Let stand for 5 minutes before serving. If desired, sprinkle with additional green onions and/or cilantro.

nutrition facts per serving: 274 cal., 11 g total fat (6 g sat. fat), 47 mg chol., 803 mg sodium, 25 g carb., 3 g dietary fiber, 20 g protein.

spanish chicken casserole

prep: 30 minutes chill: 6 to 24 hours bake: 55 minutes oven: 350°F
makes: 4 or 5 servings

1	5-ounce package saffron-flavor yellow rice mix
½	cup frozen peas
2	cups shredded cooked chicken
1½	cups salsa
¼	cup sliced pimento-stuffed green olives or pitted ripe olives
1	teaspoon ground cumin

to serve casserole:

1	tablespoon snipped fresh cilantro

1 Grease a 2-quart rectangular baking dish; set aside. Prepare rice according to package directions. Stir in frozen peas. Spread rice mixture in prepared baking dish. Top with chicken. In a medium bowl combine salsa, olives, and cumin. Pour over chicken.

2 Cover dish with plastic wrap. Chill in the refrigerator for 6 to 24 hours.

3 To serve, preheat oven to 350°F. Remove plastic wrap. Cover baking dish with foil. Bake about 55 minutes or until heated through. Sprinkle with cilantro.

nutrition facts per serving: 359 cal., 12 g total fat (5 g sat. fat), 78 mg chol., 1285 mg sodium, 36 g carb., 6 g dietary fiber, 5 g sugar, 26 g protein.

parmesan chicken and broccoli

prep: 30 minutes freeze: up to 3 months thaw: 24 to 48 hours bake: 1 hour
oven: 350°F makes: three 4-serving casseroles

2   cups uncooked
    converted rice
1   cup chopped onion
    (1 large) or sliced
    green onions (8)
2   tablespoons butter
2½ teaspoons dried
    Italian seasoning,
    crushed
2   tablespoons
    vegetable oil
2   pounds skinless,
    boneless chicken
    breast halves, cut
    into bite-size strips
3   cloves garlic, minced
1   24-ounce package
    frozen cut broccoli
    (6 cups)
2   10.75-ounce cans
    reduced-fat and
    reduced-sodium
    condensed cream
    of mushroom soup
    or cream of chicken
    soup
1   cup water
1   cup chopped tomato
    (2 medium)
⅔   cup grated Parmesan
    cheese
    Salt
    Ground black pepper

1 Cook rice according to package directions; remove from heat. Stir in half of the onion, the butter, and 1 teaspoon of the Italian seasoning. Divide the rice mixture among three 2-quart baking dishes or casseroles; set aside.

2 In a very large skillet heat oil over medium heat. Add the remaining onion, the remaining 1½ teaspoons Italian seasoning, the chicken, and garlic; cook and stir for 4 to 6 minutes or until chicken is no longer pink. Remove from heat. Stir in frozen broccoli, soup, the water, tomato, and cheese. Season to taste with salt and pepper.

3 Spoon chicken mixture over rice in dishes. Cover casseroles or baking dishes with freezer wrap; cover with heavy foil. Seal, label, and freeze for up to 3 months.

4 To serve, thaw one casserole in the refrigerator for 24 to 48 hours (mixture may still be icy). Preheat oven to 350°F. Remove freezer wrap; cover with foil. Bake for 30 minutes. Bake, uncovered, about 30 minutes more or until heated through.

nutrition facts per serving: 302 cal., 8 g total fat (2 g sat. fat), 55 mg chol., 402 mg sodium, 34 g carb., 2 g dietary fiber, 24 g protein.

nutrition note
Cooking tomatoes pumps up their natural health benefits by increasing lycopene, a powerful antioxidant.

Keep these family-pleasing chicken "sandwiches" in the freezer and take out as many as you need for tomorrow's lunch.

chicken-spinach calzones

prep: 40 minutes   **cool:** 30 minutes   **freeze:** up to 3 months   **thaw:** overnight
bake: 20 minutes + 12 minutes   **oven:** 375°F/350°F   **makes:** 12 calzones

Nonstick cooking
   spray
1 pound cooked chicken
   breast or turkey
   breast, chopped
   (about 3 cups)
2½ cups coarsely chopped
   fresh spinach
1½ cups shredded part-
   skim mozzarella
   cheese (6 ounces)
½ cup no-salt-added
   tomato sauce
1 teaspoon dried Italian
   seasoning, crushed
1 clove garlic, minced
2 13.8-ounce packages
   (each for 1 crust)
   refrigerated pizza
   dough
   Fat-free milk
   Grated Parmesan
   or Romano cheese
   (optional)

to serve calzones:
   No-salt-added tomato
   sauce or pizza sauce,
   warmed (optional)

1 Preheat oven to 375°F. Lightly coat two large baking sheets with cooking spray; set aside. In a large bowl combine chicken, spinach, mozzarella cheese, ½ cup tomato sauce, Italian seasoning, and garlic. On a lightly floured surface, roll out one package of the pizza dough to a 15×10-inch rectangle. Cut rectangle in half lengthwise and then in thirds crosswise to make six 5-inch squares.

2 Place about ⅓ cup of the chicken mixture onto half of each square, spreading to within about ½ inch of edges. Moisten edges of dough with water and fold over, forming a triangle or rectangle. Pinch or press with a fork to seal edges. Prick tops of calzones with a fork; brush with milk. Place on a prepared baking sheet. Repeat with remaining dough and chicken mixture.

3 If desired, sprinkle calzones with Parmesan cheese. Bake about 20 minutes or until golden. Transfer to wire racks; cool for 30 minutes.

4 Transfer calzones to an ungreased baking sheet. Cover loosely with plastic wrap; freeze until firm. Transfer to freezer containers. Seal, label, and freeze for up to 3 months.

5 To serve, thaw desired number of calzones in the refrigerator overnight. Preheat oven to 350°F. Lightly grease a baking sheet. Arrange calzones on prepared baking sheet. Bake calzones for 12 to 15 minutes or until heated through. If desired, serve with warmed tomato sauce.

nutrition facts per calzone: 270 cal., 6 g total fat (2 g sat. fat), 41 mg chol., 483 mg sodium, 32 g carb., 1 g dietary fiber, 21 g protein.

Get a head start on the salad preparations by purchasing a roasted chicken from the supermarket. Buy the mushrooms already sliced and you'll save additional preparation time.

savory chicken salad

prep: 30 minutes **freeze:** up to 3 months **thaw:** 24 to 48 hours
makes: 4 servings

1   2- to 2¼-pound
     purchased roasted
     chicken
1   pound sliced fresh
     mushrooms
1   tablespoon olive oil
⅓   cup dried tomato
     pesto
3   tablespoons white
     or regular balsamic
     vinegar

to serve salad:
½   cup grape tomatoes
1   5-ounce package
     mixed salad greens
     (about 8 cups)
     Shaved Parmesan
     cheese (optional)

1 Remove and chop enough meat from the chicken to make 2 cups. (Save any remaining chicken for another use.)

2 In a large skillet cook mushrooms in hot oil over medium heat about 10 minutes or until tender, stirring occasionally. Remove from heat. Stir in tomato pesto and vinegar. Add chicken; stir gently to combine.

3 Transfer to a freezer container. Seal, label, and freeze for up to 3 months.

4 To serve, thaw chicken mixture in refrigerator for 24 to 48 hours. Stir tomatoes into chicken mixture. Line a platter with salad greens and top with chicken mixture. If desired, top with shaved cheese.

nutrition facts per serving: 264 cal., 12 g total fat (3 g sat. fat), 61 mg chol., 216 mg sodium, 12 g carb., 3 g dietary fiber, 29 g protein.

Make and freeze this soup in the summer using produce from the garden. On cold winter days, heat it on the stove for a ready-made healthful meal.

barley-vegetable
chicken soup

prep: 1 hour **freeze:** up to 3 months **thaw:** overnight **cook:** 10 minutes
makes: 8 servings

8 cups reduced-sodium chicken broth

½ cup regular barley

1 to 1¼ pounds skinless, boneless chicken breast halves, cut into ¾-inch pieces

1½ cups sliced celery (3 stalks)

1½ cups sliced carrots (3 medium)

½ cup chopped onion (1 medium)

¼ cup snipped fresh parsley or 2 tablespoons dried parsley flakes

1 tablespoon snipped fresh sage or rosemary or 1 teaspoon dried sage or rosemary, crushed

¼ teaspoon ground black pepper

1 cup chopped yellow, green, and/or red sweet pepper (2 small)

to serve soup:
Fresh sage leaves (optional)

1 In a 4-quart Dutch oven bring broth to boiling; add barley. Return to boiling; reduce heat. Simmer, covered, for 30 minutes.

2 Add chicken, celery, carrots, onion, dried parsley (if using), sage, and black pepper. Return to boiling; reduce heat. Simmer, covered, about 15 minutes or until chicken is no longer pink and vegetables are tender. Stir in sweet pepper and fresh parsley (if using). Cool.

3 Transfer mixture to freezer container(s). Seal, label, and freeze for up to 3 months.

4 To serve, thaw in the refrigerator overnight (soup may still be a little icy). Place soup in a 4-quart Dutch oven. Cook over medium heat for 10 to 15 minutes or until heated through, stirring occasionally. If desired, garnish with fresh sage leaves.

nutrition facts per serving: 137 cal., 1 g total fat (0 g sat. fat), 33 mg chol., 631 mg sodium, 14 g carb., 3 g dietary fiber, 18 g protein.

spicy skillet pork chops

prep: 35 minutes **freeze:** up to 3 months **thaw:** 24 to 48 hours **cook:** 10 minutes **makes:** two 4-serving containers

3 cups frozen whole kernel corn

2 10-ounce cans chopped tomatoes and green chile peppers, undrained

4 cloves garlic, minced

1 teaspoon ground cumin

½ teaspoon bottled hot pepper sauce

8 boneless pork loin chops, cut ¾ inch thick (about 3 pounds total)

1 teaspoon chili powder

1 tablespoon vegetable oil

2 medium onions, cut into thin wedges

to serve one container:
Light sour cream (optional)

1 In a medium bowl combine frozen corn, tomatoes, garlic, cumin, and hot pepper sauce; set aside.

2 Trim fat from chops. Sprinkle all sides of chops with chili powder. In an extra-large skillet heat oil over medium-high heat. Add chops; cook about 4 minutes or until brown, turning once. Remove chops from skillet; set aside.

3 Reduce heat to medium. Add onions to drippings in skillet; cook and stir for 3 minutes. Stir corn mixture into onions. Place chops on top of corn mixture. Bring to boiling; reduce heat. Simmer, covered, for 10 to 12 minutes or until juices run clear (160°F).

4 Remove skillet from heat; cool slightly. Divide chops and corn mixture between two large freezer containers. Seal, label, and freeze for up to 3 months.

5 To serve, thaw one container in the refrigerator for 24 to 48 hours. Transfer mixture to a large skillet. Cook, covered, over medium-low heat until heated through. If desired, top with sour cream.

nutrition facts per serving: 316 cal., 9 g total fat (2 g sat. fat), 107 mg chol., 368 mg sodium, 19 g carb., 2 g dietary fiber, 41 g protein.

lime-and-herb-stuffed pork loin

prep: 40 minutes   **chill:** overnight   **grill:** 1 hour   **stand:** 15 minutes
makes: 8 to 10 servings

1   cup loosely packed fresh Italian (flat-leaf) parsley leaves
1   cup loosely packed fresh cilantro leaves
3   tablespoons olive oil
1   tablespoon finely shredded lime peel
3   large cloves garlic, minced
1   2½- to 3-pound boneless pork top loin roast (single loin)
¼   teaspoon ground black pepper

1 Snip 2 tablespoons of the parsley and 2 tablespoons of the cilantro. In a small bowl combine the snipped herbs, 1 tablespoon of the oil, ½ teaspoon of the lime peel, and 1 clove of the garlic; set aside.

2 Trim fat from meat. Butterfly the meat by making a lengthwise cut down the center of the meat, cutting to within ½ inch of the other side. Spread open. Place knife in the V of the cut. Cutting horizontally to the cut surface and away from the center, cut to within ½ inch of the other side of the meat. Repeat on the opposite side of the V. Spread meat open.

3 Brush meat with the remaining 2 tablespoons oil. Sprinkle with pepper and the remaining parsley, cilantro, lime peel, and garlic. Starting from a long side, roll up meat into a spiral. Using 100-percent-cotton kitchen string, tie meat roll at 2-inch intervals. Spread the snipped herb mixture over the outside of meat roll. Transfer to a storage container.

4 Cover and chill in the refrigerator overnight.

5 To serve, for a charcoal grill, arrange medium-hot coals around a drip pan. Test for medium heat above pan. Place meat on grill rack over drip pan. Cover and grill for 1 to 1½ hours or until meat is done (150°F). Add more coals as needed to maintain temperature. (For a gas grill, preheat grill. Reduce heat to medium. Adjust for indirect cooking. Grill as above.) Remove meat from grill.

6 Cover meat with foil; let stand for 15 minutes before slicing. (Temperature of the meat after standing should be 160°F.) Remove and discard string. Slice meat.

nutrition facts per serving: 231 cal., 14 g total fat (4 g sat. fat), 73 mg chol., 67 mg sodium, 1 g carb., 1 g dietary fiber, 23 g protein.

ham-asparagus strata

prep: 25 minutes   **chill:** 2 to 24 hours   **bake:** 1 hour   **stand:** 10 minutes
oven: 325°F   **makes:** 6 servings

4   English muffins, torn or cut into bite-size pieces (4 cups)
2   cups low-sodium cubed cooked ham (10 ounces)
2   cups cut up cooked fresh asparagus or broccoli
1   cup shredded Swiss cheese (4 ounces)
4   eggs, beaten
¼   cup light sour cream
1¼   cups fat-free milk
2   tablespoons finely chopped onion
1   tablespoon Dijon-style mustard
⅛   teaspoon ground black pepper

1 Grease a 2-quart square baking dish. Spread half of the muffin pieces in the prepared baking dish. Top with ham, asparagus, and cheese. Top with the remaining muffin pieces.

2 In a medium bowl whisk together eggs and sour cream. Stir in milk, onion, mustard, and pepper. Pour over layers in dish.

3 Cover with plastic wrap. Chill in the refrigerator for 2 to 24 hours.

4 To serve, preheat oven to 325°F. Remove plastic wrap. Bake for 60 to 65 minutes or until cooked through (170°F). Let stand for 10 minutes before serving.

nutrition facts per serving: 319 cal., 13 g total fat (6 g sat. fat), 188 mg chol., 1028 mg sodium, 24 g carb., 2 g dietary fiber, 25 g protein.

nutrition note

Make it easy to pass by that drive-through on your way home from work. Get the week's meals planned advance, including a few make-ahead dishes like this one.

pork mole

prep: 35 minutes **stand:** 45 minutes **chill:** 4 to 24 hours **roast:** 30 minutes
oven: 375°F **makes:** 4 to 6 servings

high fiber

4   dried ancho and/or pasilla chile peppers
1   6-inch white corn tortilla, cut into strips
2   tablespoons slivered almonds
2   tablespoons pumpkin seeds
¼   teaspoon cumin seeds
½   cup chopped onion (1 medium)
1½ teaspoons bottled minced garlic
1   tablespoon vegetable oil
1   cup chopped tomato
½ to ⅔ cup chicken broth
¼   cup raisins
2   tablespoons unsweetened cocoa powder
1   tablespoon packed brown sugar
⅛   teaspoon salt
1   1-pound pork tenderloin

to serve mole:
   Hot cooked rice (optional)

*tip: Because chile peppers contain volatile oils that can burn your skin and eyes, avoid direct contact with them as much as possible. When working with chile peppers, wear plastic or rubber gloves. If your bare hands do touch the peppers, wash your hands and nails well with soap and warm water.

1 For mole, remove stems and seeds from peppers.* In small bowl combine peppers and enough warm water to cover. Let stand for 30 minutes; drain, discarding liquid.

2 Heat a large skillet over medium heat for 1 minute. Add tortilla strips, almonds, pumpkin seeds, and cumin seeds; cook and stir for 2 to 3 minutes or until lightly toasted. Transfer mixture to blender or food processor; set aside.

3 In the same skillet cook and stir onion and garlic in hot oil over medium high heat for 3 to 4 minutes or until onion is tender. Stir in tomato; heat through. Reserve ¼ cup of the broth for the sauce. Add ¼ cup of the remaining broth to almond mixture in blender or food processor. Add drained peppers, onion mixture, raisins, cocoa powder, brown sugar, and salt. Cover and blend or process until smooth. If necessary, add enough of the remaining broth to make a smooth paste.

4 Trim fat from meat. Butterfly meat by making a lengthwise cut down the center of the meat, cutting to within ½ inch of the other side. Spread open. Place knife in the V of the cut. Cutting horizontally to the cut surface and away from the center, cut to within ½ inch of the other side of the meat. Repeat on the opposite side of the V. Spread meat open. Place meat between two pieces of plastic wrap. Working from center to edges, pound lightly with the flat side of a meat mallet until ½ inch thick. Remove plastic wrap.

5 Spread meat with about ⅓ cup of the mole. Starting from long side, roll up meat into a spiral.

6 Wrap meat in plastic wrap and chill in the refrigerator for 4 to 24 hours. Cover and chill the remaining mole and the reserved chicken broth in the refrigerator until needed.

7 To serve, preheat oven to 375°F. Place meat on rack in shallow roasting pan. Insert an ovenproof meat thermometer into center of roast. Roast for 30 to 40 minutes or until thermometer registers 155°F. Cover loosely with foil; let stand for 15 minutes before slicing. (The temperature of the meat after standing should be 160°F.)

8 Meanwhile, for sauce, in a small saucepan combine the reserved ¼ cup broth and the remaining mole. Cook and stir over low heat about 5 minutes or until sauce is heated through. Slice meat; serve with sauce and, if desired, hot cooked rice.

nutrition facts per serving: 345 cal., 13 g total fat (2 g sat. fat), 73 mg chol., 473 mg sodium, 30 g carb., 6 g dietary fiber, 30 g protein.

pork and potato stack

prep: 45 minutes   roast: 25 minutes   stand: 10 minutes   chill: 2 to 24 hours
oven: 425°F   makes: 6 servings

1   1-pound pork
    tenderloin*
¼   teaspoon salt
¼   teaspoon ground
    black pepper
1   pound Yukon gold or
    other yellow-flesh
    potatoes
1   cup frozen sweet
    soybeans (edamame)
1   medium zucchini
    or yellow summer
    squash
1   recipe Creamy
    Walnut-Garlic
    Vinaigrette
1   cup frozen whole
    kernel corn, thawed
½   cup sliced green
    onions (4)

to serve stack:
    Shredded and/or
    shaved carrots
    (optional)
    Fresh tarragon and
    thyme (optional)

1 Preheat oven to 425°F. Place pork on rack in roasting pan; sprinkle with salt and pepper. Roast for 25 to 35 minutes or until an instant-read thermometer inserted in center registers 155°F. Cover; let stand for 10 minutes. Cut pork into bite-size pieces.

2 Meanwhile, cut potatoes into ¼-inch-thick slices. In a covered large saucepan cook potatoes and soybeans in boiling water for 5 to 8 minutes or until potatoes are tender; drain.

3 Cut zucchini into 1½- to 2-inch-long sections. Slice sections lengthwise into planks; set aside.

4 Lightly grease a 2-quart baking dish. Layer half of the potatoes and soybeans in the prepared baking dish. Drizzle with ⅓ cup of the Creamy Walnut-Garlic Vinaigrette. Arrange zucchini in an even layer over top; drizzle with ⅓ cup of the Creamy Walnut-Garlic Vinaigrette. Evenly arrange pork and the remaining potatoes and soybeans over zucchini; drizzle with another ⅓ cup of the Creamy Walnut-Garlic Vinaigrette. In a small bowl combine corn, green onions, and the remaining Creamy Walnut-Garlic Vinaigrette; spoon over layers in baking dish.

5 Cover with plastic wrap. Chill in the refrigerator for 2 to 24 hours to allow flavors to blend.

6 To serve, remove plastic wrap. If desired, top with carrots and tarragon and thyme.

nutrition facts per serving: 308 cal., 14 g total fat (2 g sat. fat), 49 mg chol., 576 mg sodium, 24 g carb., 4 g dietary fiber, 23 g protein.

creamy walnut-garlic vinaigrette: In a food processor combine ¼ cup refrigerated or frozen egg product, thawed; ¼ cup white wine vinegar; 1 teaspoon Dijon-style mustard; 1 teaspoon snipped fresh tarragon or thyme or ¼ teaspoon dried tarragon or thyme, crushed; 1 teaspoon salt; ¼ teaspoon ground black pepper; and 3 cloves garlic, quartered. With food processor running, gradually add 3 tablespoons olive oil through feed tube. Process until mixture is slightly thickened. Stir in ⅓ cup finely chopped toasted walnuts. Makes about 1¼ cups.

horseradish
ham-potato bake

prep: 20 minutes **chill:** 4 to 24 hours **bake:** 55 minutes **stand:** 5 minutes
oven: 350°F **makes:** 8 servings

Nonstick cooking
    spray
1 28-ounce package
    frozen diced hash
    brown potatoes
    with onions and
    peppers
1½ cups diced cooked
    ham (about
    8 ounces)
1 cup shredded Swiss
    cheese (4 ounces)
⅓ cup finely chopped
    red onion
5 eggs, lightly beaten
1½ cups fat-free milk
3 tablespoons
    horseradish mustard
½ teaspoon salt
¼ teaspoon ground
    black pepper
    Chopped green
    onions (optional)
1 recipe Horseradish
    Sour Cream

1 Coat a 3-quart rectangular baking dish with cooking spray. Arrange potatoes evenly in the bottom of prepared dish. Sprinkle with ham, cheese, and red onion.

2 In a medium bowl whisk together eggs, milk, mustard, salt, and pepper. Pour egg mixture over potato mixture.

3 Cover with plastic wrap. Chill in the refrigerator for 4 to 24 hours.

4 To serve, preheat oven to 350°F. Remove plastic wrap. Bake for 55 to 60 minutes or until a knife inserted near center comes out clean. Let stand for 5 minutes before serving. If desired, sprinkle with green onions. Serve with Horseradish Sour Cream.

nutrition facts per serving: 251 cal., 12 g total fat (5 g sat. fat), 165 mg chol., 654 mg sodium, 21 g carb., 2 g dietary fiber, 16 g protein.

horseradish sour cream: In a small bowl stir together ½ cup light sour cream, 1 to 2 tablespoons horseradish mustard, and 1 tablespoon snipped fresh chives. Makes about ⅔ cup.

mexican-style
pork pot roast

prep: 35 minutes stand: 30 minutes marinate: 8 to 24 hours
slow cook: 8 to 10 hours (low) or 4 to 5 hours (high) makes: 6 servings

3 dried ancho chile
    peppers
3 dried guajillo
    chile peppers
    (1½ ounces)
⅓ cup orange juice
3 tablespoons lime juice
1 tablespoon cider
    vinegar
4 cloves garlic
1 teaspoon salt
1 teaspoon dried
    Mexican oregano
    or dried regular
    oregano, crushed
½ teaspoon dried
    thyme, crushed
¼ teaspoon ground
    cinnamon
¼ teaspoon ground
    allspice
¼ teaspoon ground
    cloves
1 2½-pound boneless
    pork shoulder roast
1 large red onion,
    sliced
½ cup reduced-sodium
    chicken broth

to serve roast:
1½ cups shredded
      lettuce
¾ cup chopped
      tomatoes
¾ cup sliced radishes
6 8-inch flour tortillas

1 On a dry griddle or in a dry skillet toast ancho and guajillo chile peppers over medium-high heat about 1 minute or until fragrant, turning frequently.

2 Remove and discard stems and seeds from chile peppers*; break peppers into pieces. Place pepper pieces in a medium bowl. Pour enough boiling water over to cover peppers. Cover and let stand for 30 minutes; drain.

3 For marinade, in a blender or food processor combine soaked peppers, orange juice, lime juice, vinegar, garlic, salt, oregano, thyme, cinnamon, allspice, and cloves. Cover and blend or process until smooth.

4 Trim excess fat from meat. Spread marinade evenly over the meat. Wrap meat in plastic wrap. Place in a shallow dish and marinate in the refrigerator for 8 to 24 hours.

5 Place red onion in a 3½- or 4-quart slow cooker. Unwrap meat. Place meat and any excess marinade on top of onion. Pour broth around meat. Cover and cook on low-heat setting for 8 to 10 hours or on high-heat setting for 4 to 5 hours.

6 To serve, using a slotted spoon, transfer meat and onion to a platter. Skim excess fat from juices in cooker. Break meat into large chunks; return meat and onion to juices in cooker. Serve with lettuce, tomatoes, radishes, and tortillas.

nutrition facts per serving: 468 cal., 11 g total fat (3 g sat. fat), 113 mg chol., 799 mg sodium, 41 g carb., 3 g dietary fiber, 50 g protein.

*tip: Because chile peppers contain volatile oils that can burn your skin and eyes, avoid direct contact with them as much as possible. When working with chile peppers, wear plastic or rubber gloves. If your bare hands do touch the peppers, wash your hands and nails well with soap and warm water.

stuffed fish
with couscous

prep: 25 minutes stand: 5 minutes chill: 4 to 24 hours bake: 40 minutes
oven: 350°F makes: 4 servings

4 4-ounce fresh or
   frozen skinless sole
   or flounder fillets,
   about ½ inch thick
1 cup water
¼ teaspoon salt
1 cup couscous
¼ teaspoon salt
⅛ teaspoon ground
   black pepper
¾ cup herb-seasoned
   croutons, coarsely
   crushed
⅓ cup shredded
   zucchini
¼ cup basil pesto
2 tablespoons grated
   Parmesan cheese
½ cup chopped tomato
   (1 medium)
2 tablespoons snipped
   fresh basil

to serve fish:
   Chopped tomato
   (optional)
   Fresh basil (optional)

1 Thaw fish, if frozen. In a small saucepan bring the water and ¼ teaspoon salt to boiling. Stir in couscous. Cover, remove from heat. Let stand for 5 minutes. Fluff with a fork. Cool while preparing fish.

2 Rinse fish; pat dry with paper towels. Season with ¼ teaspoon salt and pepper. In a small bowl stir together croutons, zucchini, pesto, and cheese.

3 Spoon one-fourth of the crouton mixture onto the widest end of each fillet. Roll up each into a spiral; secure rolls with wooden toothpicks. Stir ½ cup tomato and 2 tablespoons basil into couscous. Spread couscous into a 2-quart baking dish. Top couscous with fish rolls.

4 Cover baking dish with plastic wrap. Chill in the refrigerator for 4 to 24 hours.

5 To serve, preheat oven to 350°F. Remove plastic wrap. Cover baking dish with foil. Bake for 40 to 50 minutes or until fish flakes easily when tested with a fork and filling is heated through. If desired, garnish with additional chopped tomato and fresh basil.

nutrition facts per serving: 389 cal., 10 g total fat (3 g sat. fat), 60 mg chol., 658 mg sodium, 44 g carb., 4 g dietary fiber, 29 g protein.

Lasagna never tasted so good. This version is packed with plenty of vegetables—broccoli, sweet pepper, and two kinds of squash. Add two kinds of fat-reduced cheeses, and you have a main dish that's easy on the fat and calories.

garden vegetables lasagna

prep: 45 minutes **freeze:** up to 3 months **thaw:** 48 hours **bake:** 1 hour
stand: 10 minutes **oven:** 375°F **makes:** 8 servings

Nonstick cooking
   spray
9 dried white or whole
   grain lasagna
   noodles
3 cups broccoli florets
1 red sweet pepper,
   seeded and cut into
   bite-size strips
1¼ cups sliced zucchini
   (1 medium)
1¼ cups sliced yellow
   summer squash
   (1 medium)
2 15-ounce cartons
   light ricotta cheese
½ cup snipped
   fresh basil or
   1 tablespoon dried
   basil, crushed
1 tablespoon snipped
   fresh thyme or
   1 teaspoon dried
   thyme, crushed
3 cloves garlic, minced
½ teaspoon salt
¼ teaspoon ground
   black pepper
¼ teaspoon bottled hot
   pepper sauce
2 cups shredded part-
   skim mozzarella
   cheese (8 ounces)
Shredded fresh basil
   (optional)

1 Lightly coat a 3-quart rectangular baking dish with cooking spray; set aside. In a 4-quart Dutch oven cook lasagna noodles according to package directions; drain. Drain noodles; rinse with cold water. Drain well.

2 Place a steamer basket in the same Dutch oven. Add water to just below bottom of steamer basket. Bring to boiling. Add broccoli, sweet pepper, zucchini, and yellow summer squash. Reduce heat. Cover and steam for 6 to 8 minutes or until vegetables are crisp-tender. Remove from heat.

3 In a large bowl combine ricotta cheese, snipped basil, thyme, garlic, salt, black pepper, and hot pepper sauce. Layer three of the cooked noodles in the prepared baking dish. Spread with one-third of the ricotta cheese mixture. Top with one-third of the vegetable mixture and ⅔ cup of the mozzarella cheese. Repeat layers twice.

4 Cover baking dish with plastic wrap; cover with heavy foil. Seal, label, and freeze for up to 3 months.

5 To serve, thaw lasagna in the refrigerator for 48 hours. Preheat oven to 375°F. Remove plastic wrap; cover with foil. Bake lasagna for 1 to 1¼ hours or until heated through. Let stand, covered, on a wire rack for 10 minutes before serving. If desired, sprinkle with shredded basil.

nutrition facts per serving: 293 cal., 9 g total fat (6 g sat. fat), 44 mg chol., 428 mg sodium, 30 g carb., 3 g dietary fiber, 20 g protein.

miraculous

make

13

Indulge yourself. The fat and calories in this anthology of comfort food favorites and restaurant-style classics have been whittled down to make you happy—not hippy.

overs

Here, sloppy joes, a favorite Saturday lunch or quick weeknight dinner, get a Tex-Mex makeover! Hint: Choose hotter or milder salsa, depending on how high up on the heat scale you want to go!

spicy beef sloppy joes

prep: 20 minutes   slow cook: 8 to 10 hours (low) or 4 to 5 hours (high)
makes: 16 servings

2   pounds lean ground beef
2   16-ounce jars salsa
3   cups sliced fresh mushrooms (8 ounces)
1½   cups shredded carrots (3 medium)
1½   cups finely chopped red and/or green sweet peppers (2 medium)
⅓   cup no-salt-added tomato paste
2   teaspoons dried basil, crushed
1   teaspoon dried oregano, crushed
¼   teaspoon salt
¼   teaspoon cayenne pepper
4   cloves garlic, minced
16   kaiser rolls, split and toasted

1 In a large skillet cook beef over medium heat until brown, using a wooden spoon to break up meat as it cooks. Drain off fat. In a 5- or 6-quart slow cooker stir together cooked beef, salsa, mushrooms, carrots, sweet peppers, tomato paste, basil, oregano, salt, cayenne pepper, and garlic.

2 Cover and cook on low-heat setting for 8 to 10 hours or on high-heat setting for 4 to 5 hours.

3 Serve meat mixture in toasted kaiser rolls.

nutrition facts per serving: 280 cal., 6 g total fat (2 g sat. fat), 35 mg chol., 739 mg sodium, 37 g carb., 3 g dietary fiber, 20 g protein.

classic french dips

prep: 20 minutes slow cook: 9 to 10 hours (low) or 4½ to 5 hours (high)
makes: 6 servings

1 large sweet onion, such as Vidalia, Maui, or Walla Walla, cut into ¼-inch slices and separated into rings (1 cup)

1 2- to 2½-pound fresh beef brisket or boneless beef bottom round roast

2 cloves garlic, minced

1 teaspoon dried thyme, marjoram, or oregano, crushed

½ teaspoon ground black pepper

1 14-ounce can lower-sodium beef broth

2 tablespoons Worcestershire sauce

1 16-ounce loaf whole grain baguette-style bread, cut crosswise into 6 pieces, halved lengthwise, and toasted, or 6 whole grain hoagie buns, split and toasted

1 Place onion in a 3½- to 5-quart slow cooker. Trim fat from beef. If necessary, cut beef to fit cooker. Place beef on top of onion. Sprinkle with garlic, thyme, and pepper. Pour broth and Worcestershire sauce over all.

2 Cover and cook on low-heat setting for 9 to 10 hours for brisket or 8 to 9 hours for bottom round or on high-heat setting for 4½ to 5 hours for brisket or 4 to 4½ hours for bottom round.

3 Transfer meat to a cutting board; thinly slice across the grain, removing any visible fat as you slice. Using a slotted spoon, remove onion from cooker. Divide sliced brisket and onion among bread bottoms and top with remaining bread pieces. Skim fat from cooking juices in cooker; pass juices for dipping sandwiches.

nutrition facts per serving: 339 cal., 7 g total fat (2 g sat. fat), 45 mg chol., 453 mg sodium, 39 g carb., 9 g dietary fiber, 33 g protein

miraculous **makeovers**

philly steak sandwiches

prep: 20 minutes broil: 17 minutes makes: 4 servings

1 12-ounce boneless beef top sirloin steak, cut 1 inch thick

½ teaspoon garlic pepper seasoning
Nonstick cooking spray

2 medium red and/ or green sweet peppers, seeded and cut into thin strips

1 large onion, thinly sliced and separated into rings

4 whole wheat frankfurter buns, split

½ cup shredded reduced-fat cheddar or reduced-fat Monterey Jack cheese (2 ounces)

1 Preheat broiler. Trim fat from steak. Sprinkle steak with garlic pepper seasoning. Place seasoned steak on the unheated rack of a broiler pan. Broil 3 to 4 inches from heat until desired doneness. Allow 15 to 17 minutes for medium rare (145°F) or 20 to 22 minutes for medium (160°F).

2 Meanwhile, coat a very large nonstick skillet* with cooking spray. Heat skillet over medium heat. Add sweet peppers and onion; cook, covered, for 5 minutes. Cook, uncovered, about 5 minutes more or just until tender, stirring occasionally.

3 Place buns split side up on a large baking sheet. Broil 4 to 5 inches from the heat for 1 to 2 minutes or until lightly toasted. Remove bun tops from baking sheet; set aside. Slice steak into bite-size strips. Divide steak strips and sweet pepper mixture among bun bottoms. Sprinkle with cheese. Broil 4 to 5 inches from the heat for 1 to 2 minutes or until cheese is melted. Top with bun tops.

nutrition facts per serving: 320 cal., 12 g total fat (5 g sat. fat), 52 mg chol., 414 mg sodium, 29 g carb., 4 g dietary fiber, 25 g protein.

*tip: If you do not have a very large nonstick skillet, use a large nonstick skillet and cook sweet peppers and onions separately.

turkey pizza burgers

prep: 20 minutes grill: 14 minutes makes: 4 burgers

1 egg, beaten
¼ cup quick-cooking
    rolled oats
4 teaspoons snipped
    fresh oregano
⅛ teaspoon salt
⅛ teaspoon ground
    black pepper
1 pound uncooked
    ground turkey breast
4 ½-ounce slices
    provolone cheese
½ cup low-sodium
    tomato-base pasta
    sauce
4 whole wheat
    hamburger buns,
    toasted

1 In a medium bowl combine egg, rolled oats, half of the oregano, the salt, and pepper. Add ground turkey breast; mix well. Shape turkey mixture into four ¾-inch-thick patties.

2 For a charcoal grill, grill patties on the rack of an uncovered grill directly over medium coals for 14 to 18 minutes or until no longer pink (165°F),* turning once halfway through grilling and topping each burger with a cheese slice for the last 1 minute of grilling. (For a gas grill, preheat grill. Reduce heat to medium. Place burgers on grill rack over heat. Cover and grill as above.)

3 Meanwhile, in a small saucepan cook pasta sauce over low heat until heated though.

4 Place burgers on bun bottoms. Top with pasta sauce, the remaining oregano, and bun tops.

nutrition facts per burger: 354 cal., 9 g total fat (3 g sat. fat), 133 mg chol., 487 mg sodium, 28 g carb., 3 g dietary fiber, 38 g protein.

*tip: The internal color of a burger is not a reliable doneness indicator. A turkey patty cooked to 165°F is safe, regardless of color. To measure the doneness of a patty, insert an instant-read thermometer through the side of the patty to a depth of 2 to 3 inches.

nutrition note

You love burgers, but hate what they do to your aim to eat well. Here, with high-flavor and lean protein ingredients, you can end this love-hate relationship once and for all.

378

chicken caesar salad

start to finish: 25 minutes makes: 4 servings

12 ounces skinless, boneless chicken breast halves
1 teaspoon vegetable oil
½ teaspoon salt
¼ teaspoon ground black pepper
6 cups torn romaine lettuce and/or assorted lettuce leaves
1 cup plain croutons
8 cherry tomatoes, quartered
8 whole ripe olives
4 teaspoons grated Parmesan cheese
1 recipe Caesar Dressing

1 Heat a grill pan over medium-high heat. Brush chicken with oil. Sprinkle chicken with salt and pepper. Cook chicken on grill pan for 12 to 15 minutes or until chicken is no longer pink (170°F), turning once. Transfer chicken to a cutting board; cut into bite-size pieces.

2 Meanwhile, place lettuce in a serving bowl. Top with chicken, croutons, tomatoes, and olives. Sprinkle with cheese. Drizzle with Caesar Dressing.

nutrition facts per serving: 303 cal., 19 g total fat (3 g sat. fat), 53 mg chol., 619 mg sodium, 11 g carb., 3 g dietary fiber, 2 g sugar, 23 g protein.

broiling directions: Preheat broiler. Place chicken on the unheated rack of a broiler pan. Broil 4 to 5 inches from heat for 12 to 15 minutes or until chicken is no longer pink (170°F), turning once.

caesar dressing: In a small bowl whisk together 1 tablespoon lemon juice; 1½ teaspoons light mayonnaise or salad dressing; 1 teaspoon red wine vinegar; ⅛ teaspoon salt; ⅛ teaspoon Dijon-style mustard; ½ of a small clove garlic, minced; and dash ground black pepper. Gradually add ¼ cup olive oil in a slow, steady stream, whisking constantly until well mixed. Whisk in 1 tablespoon grated Parmesan cheese.

chicken fettuccine alfredo

start to finish: 30 minutes makes: 6 servings

6 ounces dried whole wheat fettuccine
12 ounces fresh green beans or 1 pound fresh asparagus, trimmed and cut into 1- to 2-inch pieces
1 small onion, halved and thinly sliced
1 tablespoon olive oil
12 ounces skinless, boneless chicken breast halves, cut into bite-size strips
3 cloves garlic, minced
1 10-ounce container refrigerated light Alfredo pasta sauce
¼ cup chicken broth
½ teaspoon dried thyme, crushed
Cracked black pepper

1 In a 4-quart saucepan cook fettuccine according to package directions, except do not add any salt. Add green beans for the last 5 to 6 minutes of cooking or the asparagus for the last 2 minutes of cooking. Drain; return pasta mixture to hot saucepan.

2 Meanwhile, in a covered large nonstick skillet cook onion in hot oil over medium heat for 7 to 8 minutes or until starting to brown, stirring occasionally. Add chicken and garlic; cook, uncovered, for 4 to 6 minutes more or until chicken is no longer pink and onion is very tender, stirring frequently. Reduce heat to low. Add Alfredo sauce, broth, and thyme; cook and stir until heated through.

3 Add chicken mixture to cooked fettuccine; toss to coat. Sprinkle with pepper.

nutrition facts per serving: 276 cal., 8 g total fat (3 g sat. fat), 45 mg chol., 354 mg sodium, 31 g carb., 2 g dietary fiber, 22 g protein.

chicken cacciatore

prep: 30 minutes   cook: 30 minutes   makes: 6 servings

6   small bone-in chicken
    breast halves,
    skinned (about
    2½ pounds total)
1   tablespoon olive oil
8   ounces fresh
    mushrooms, sliced
    (about 3 cups)
1   medium onion, sliced
1   clove garlic, minced
1   14.5-ounce can
    diced tomatoes,
    undrained
1   6-ounce can tomato
    paste
½   cup dry white wine
1   teaspoon dried Italian
    seasoning, crushed
½   teaspoon salt
⅛   teaspoon ground
    black pepper
6   ounces dried
    multigrain or whole
    grain fettuccine or
    linguine, cooked
    according to
    package directions
2   tablespoons small
    fresh basil leaves

1 In a very large skillet brown chicken on all
sides in hot oil over medium heat, turning
to brown evenly. Remove chicken, reserving
drippings in skillet. Set chicken aside.

2 Add mushrooms, onion, and garlic to
drippings in skillet; cook and stir about
5 minutes or just until vegetables are tender.
Return chicken to skillet.

3 In a medium bowl combine tomatoes,
tomato paste, wine, Italian seasoning, salt,
and pepper. Pour over chicken in skillet. Bring
to boiling; reduce heat. Simmer, covered, for
30 to 35 minutes or until chicken is no longer
pink (170°F), turning once halfway through
cooking. Serve over hot cooked pasta. Sprinkle
with basil.

nutrition facts per serving: 311 cal., 4 g total fat
(1 g sat. fat), 68 mg chol., 427 mg sodium, 33 g carb.,
6 g dietary fiber, 34 g protein.

Cut into these cornmeal-coated chicken rolls and discover a lusciously gooey mix of cheese, cilantro, and chile pepper.

poblano
chicken bundles

prep: 30 minutes cook: 20 minutes
makes: 4 servings

4 6-ounce skinless, boneless chicken breast halves
2 tablespoons snipped fresh cilantro
4 2½×½-inch sticks reduced-fat Monterey Jack cheese (1½ to 2 ounces total)
12 2½×½-inch strips fresh poblano chile pepper (1 large pepper) or 3 large jalapeño chile peppers, quartered and seeded*
⅓ cup yellow cornmeal
1 teaspoon chili powder
¼ teaspoon salt
1 egg white, lightly beaten
1 tablespoon water
1 tablespoon canola oil or olive oil
½ cup pico de gallo or salsa (optional)
  Snipped fresh cilantro (optional)

1 Place each chicken breast half between two pieces of plastic wrap. Using the flat side of a meat mallet, pound chicken until about ⅛ inch thick. Remove plastic wrap.

2 Divide the 2 tablespoons cilantro evenly among chicken pieces. Place a cheese stick and three poblano chile pepper strips or jalapeno chile pepper quarters across the center of each chicken piece. Fold in sides; roll up from bottom. Secure with wooden toothpicks.

3 In a shallow dish combine cornmeal, chili powder, and salt. In another shallow dish combine egg white and the water. Dip chicken bundles into egg white mixture, turning to coat. Dip into cornmeal mixture, turning to coat.

4 In a large nonstick skillet heat oil over medium heat. Add chicken bundles, seam sides down; cook about 10 minutes or until browned on all sides, turning occasionally. Reduce heat to medium low; cook, covered, for 10 to 12 minutes more or until no longer pink (170°F), turning once. If desired, serve with pico de gallo and sprinkle with additional snipped cilantro.

nutrition facts per serving: 301 cal., 8 g total fat (2 g sat. fat), 106 mg chol., 350 mg sodium, 11 g carb., 1 g dietary fiber, 44 g protein.

*tip: Because chile peppers contain volatile oils that can burn your skin and eyes, avoid direct contact with them as much as possible. When working with chile peppers, wear plastic or rubber gloves. If your bare hands do touch the peppers, wash your hands and nails well with soap and warm water.

crispy chicken parmesan

prep: 25 minutes bake: 15 minutes oven: 425°F makes: 4 servings

Olive oil nonstick
  cooking spray
¼ cup refrigerated or
  frozen egg product,
  thawed, or 2 egg
  whites, lightly
  beaten
1 tablespoon water
1 clove garlic, minced
1 cup bran cereal
  flakes, crushed
  (about ½ cup
  crushed)
¼ cup grated Parmesan
  cheese
1 teaspoon dried Italian
  seasoning, crushed
1 pound chicken breast
  tenderloins
4 ounces dried
  multigrain or whole
  grain spaghetti
1 cup 1-inch pieces
  eggplant, peeled if
  desired
1½ cups no-sugar-added
  light tomato-basil
  pasta sauce
1 cup torn fresh
  spinach leaves
½ cup chopped roma
  tomatoes
  Fresh basil leaves
  (optional)

1 Preheat oven to 425°F. Line a 15×10×1-inch baking pan with foil; lightly coat foil with cooking spray. Set baking pan aside. In a shallow dish combine egg, the water, and garlic. In another shallow dish combine crushed bran flakes, cheese, and Italian seasoning.

2 Dip chicken pieces, one at a time, in egg mixture, turning to coat evenly and allowing excess to drip off. Dip chicken pieces in cereal mixture, turning to coat evenly. Place chicken pieces in a single layer in the prepared baking pan. Coat tops of chicken pieces with cooking spray. Bake for 15 to 20 minutes or until chicken is no longer pink (170°F).

3 Meanwhile, cook spaghetti according to package directions; drain. Keep warm. Coat a medium saucepan with cooking spray; heat saucepan over medium heat. Add eggplant; cook about 5 minutes or until tender, stirring occasionally. Add pasta sauce; heat through. Stir in spinach and tomatoes.

4 Divide spaghetti among four serving plates. Top with eggplant mixture and chicken pieces. If desired, garnish with basil.

nutrition facts per serving: 240 cal., 4 g total fat (1 g sat. fat), 4 mg chol., 464 mg sodium, 42 g carb., 10 g dietary fiber, 13 g protein.

*tip: If you are making Eggplant Parmesan, 1 medium eggplant should be just enough for the eight ½-inch-thick slices and the 1 cup pieces for the sauce.

eggplant parmesan: Prepare as directed, except substitute eight ½-inch-thick slices eggplant* for the chicken. Bake for 15 to 20 minutes or until eggplant is tender and golden.

per serving: 239 cal., 2 g total fat (1 g sat. fat), 4 mg chol., 475 mg sodium, 44 g carb., 10 g dietary fiber, 13 g protein.

Love wings? We've got a heart-healthy way to make these popular appetizers (don't worry, they taste just as good). Our zesty wings recipe includes blue cheese, garlic powder, vinegar, and hot pepper sauce for kick.

buffalo chicken wings with blue cheese dressing

prep: 25 minutes **broil:** 15 minutes **makes:** 8 servings

24	chicken drummettes*
¼	cup bottled hot pepper sauce
2	teaspoons cider vinegar
½	teaspoon garlic powder
½	teaspoon ground ginger
¾	cup fat-free sour cream
½	cup crumbled blue cheese (2 ounces)
2	tablespoons chopped green onion (1)
1	tablespoon white wine vinegar
1	tablespoon lemon juice
1	teaspoon sugar
	Carrot and celery sticks

1 Preheat broiler; arrange rack 4 to 5 inches from heat. To skin chicken, grasp the edge of the skin with a paper towel and pull it away from the drummette. In a large bowl combine 2 tablespoons of the hot pepper sauce, 1 teaspoon of the cider vinegar, the garlic powder, and ginger. Add skinned drummettes; toss to coat drummettes.

2 Arrange drummettes on the unheated rack of a broiler pan. Broil 4 to 5 inches from heat for 15 to 20 minutes or until chicken is tender and no longer pink, turning once. Drizzle chicken with the remaining 2 tablespoons hot pepper sauce and 1 teaspoon cider vinegar.

3 Meanwhile, for blue cheese dressing, in a small bowl combine sour cream, blue cheese, green onion, white wine vinegar, lemon juice, and sugar. Serve dressing with drummettes and carrot and celery sticks.

nutrition facts per 3 drummettes plus 2 tablespoons dressing: 112 cal., 4 g total fat (2 g sat. fat), 24 mg chol., 216 mg sodium, 10 g carb., 2 g dietary fiber, 9 g protein.

*tip: If you can't find chicken drummettes, start with 12 chicken wings. Cut off the wing tips; discard or save for making chicken stock. Cut wings at joints to form 24 pieces.

buffalo
chicken tenders

prep: 30 minutes bake: 10 minutes oven: 425°F makes: 6 servings

Nonstick cooking
spray
1¼ ounces reduced-fat
shredded wheat
crackers, broken
(½ cup)
1 ounce honey wheat
pretzel rods, broken
(½ cup)
¼ teaspoon cayenne
pepper
2 eggs
¼ cup fat-free milk
1⅛ pounds chicken
breast tenderloins
⅓ cup light mayonnaise
or salad dressing
¼ cup crumbled blue
cheese (1 ounce)
1 clove garlic, minced
½ recipe Buffalo Sauce
Celery sticks
(optional)

1 Preheat oven to 425°F. Line a 15×10×1-inch baking pan with foil; coat foil with cooking spray. Set baking pan aside. Place crackers in a food processor. Cover and process until coarsely ground. Add pretzels to food processor. Cover and process until pretzels are coarsely ground. Transfer cracker mixture to a shallow dish; stir in cayenne pepper. In another shallow dish whisk together eggs and 2 tablespoons of the milk.

2 Dip chicken into egg mixture, allowing excess to drip off. Dip chicken into crumb mixture, turning to coat. Arrange chicken in prepared pan. Lightly coat breaded chicken with cooking spray. Bake for 10 to 15 minutes or until no longer pink (170°F).

3 Meanwhile, for blue cheese dip, in a small bowl stir together mayonnaise, blue cheese, the remaining 2 tablespoons milk, and the garlic. Serve chicken tenderloins with blue cheese dip and Buffalo Sauce. If desired, serve with celery sticks.

nutrition facts per 2½ tablespoons Buffalo Sauce and 1 tablespoon blue cheese dip: 265 cal., 10 g total fat (2 g sat. fat), 145 mg chol., 444 mg sodium, 12 g carb., 1 g dietary fiber, 31 g protein.

buffalo sauce: In a small saucepan stir together one 8-ounce can tomato sauce, ¼ cup cider vinegar, 2 tablespoons water, 2 teaspoons packed brown sugar, 1½ teaspoons bottled hot pepper sauce, ½ teaspoon dry mustard, ¼ teaspoon celery seeds, and ⅛ teaspoon salt. Bring to boiling; reduce heat. Simmer, uncovered, for 8 to 10 minutes or until mixture is reduced to 1 cup, stirring occasionally. Use immediately or cool, cover, and store in the refrigerator for up to 1 week. Makes 1 cup.

oven-fried chicken

prep: 20 minutes   bake: 45 minutes   oven: 375°F   makes: 4 to 6 servings

1 egg, lightly beaten
3 tablespoons milk
1¼ cups crushed cornflakes or finely crushed rich round crackers (about 35 crackers)
1 teaspoon dried thyme, crushed
½ teaspoon paprika
¼ teaspoon salt
⅛ teaspoon ground black pepper
2 tablespoons butter or margarine, melted
2½ to 3 pounds meaty chicken pieces (breast halves, thighs, and drumsticks)

1 Preheat oven to 375°F. Grease a 15×10×1-inch baking pan. In a small bowl combine egg and milk. For coating, in a shallow dish combine crushed cornflakes, thyme, paprika, salt, and pepper; stir in melted butter. Set aside. Skin chicken. Dip chicken pieces, one at a time, into egg mixture, turning to coat. Dip chicken in cornflake mixture, turning to coat.

2 Arrange chicken in prepared pan, bone sides down, so the pieces aren't touching. Sprinkle chicken pieces with any remaining cornflake mixture so they are generously coated.

3 Bake for 45 to 55 minutes or until chicken is no longer pink (170°F for breasts; 180°F for thighs and drumsticks). Do not turn chicken pieces while baking.

nutrition facts per serving: 223 cal., 7 g total fat (3 g sat. fat), 124 mg chol., 290 mg sodium, 11 g carb., 0 g dietary fiber, 28 g protein.

oven-fried parmesan chicken: Prepare as directed, except omit the thyme and salt and reduce the crushed cornflakes to ½ cup. For coating, combine cornflakes; ½ cup grated Parmesan cheese; 1 teaspoon dried oregano, crushed; the paprika; and pepper. Stir in melted butter.

per serving: 227 cal., 9 g total fat (5 g sat. fat), 130 mg chol., 245 mg sodium, 5 g carb., 0 g dietary fiber, 30 g protein.

Turkey and sweet potatoes make this casserole a bit healthier than the classic shepherd's pie.

turkey and sweet potato shepherd's pies

prep: 40 minutes bake: 20 minutes oven: 375°F makes: 4 servings

1½ pounds sweet potatoes, peeled and cut into 2-inch pieces
2 cloves garlic, halved
¼ cup fat-free milk
½ teaspoon salt
12 ounces uncooked ground turkey breast
½ cup chopped onion (1 medium)
1¼ cups coarsely chopped zucchini (1 medium)
1 cup chopped carrots (2 medium)
½ cup frozen whole kernel corn
¼ cup water
1 8-ounce can no-salt-added tomato sauce
2 tablespoons Worcestershire sauce
2 teaspoons snipped fresh sage or ½ teaspoon dried sage, crushed
⅛ teaspoon ground black pepper
   Fresh sage leaves (optional)

1 Preheat oven to 375°F. In a covered medium saucepan cook sweet potatoes and garlic in enough boiling lightly salted water to cover for 15 to 20 minutes or until tender; drain well. Mash with a potato masher or beat with an electric mixer on low speed just until smooth. Gradually add milk and salt, mashing or beating to make potato mixture light and fluffy. Cover and keep warm.

2 Meanwhile, in a large skillet cook turkey and onion over medium heat until meat is brown, using a wooden spoon to break up meat as it cooks. Drain off fat. Stir zucchini, carrots, corn, and the water into meat mixture in skillet. Bring to boiling; reduce heat. Simmer, covered, for 5 to 10 minutes or until vegetables are tender.

3 Stir tomato sauce, Worcestershire sauce, snipped sage, and pepper into meat-vegetable mixture; heat through. Divide among four 10-ounce ramekins or individual casseroles, spreading evenly. Pipe or spoon mashed sweet potato mixture in mounds onto meat-vegetable mixture.

4 Bake for 20 to 25 minutes or until heated through. If desired, garnish with fresh sage leaves.

nutrition facts per serving: 278 cal., 1 g total fat (0 g sat. fat), 42 mg chol., 534 mg sodium, 43 g carb., 7 g dietary fiber, 24 g protein.

No-salt-added tomatoes reduce the sodium in this beefy polenta pie.
If you like, turn up the heat by opting for hot chili powder.

tamale pie

prep: 35 minutes **cook:** 10 minutes **bake:** 25 minutes **oven:** 350°F
makes: 6 servings

Nonstick cooking
    spray
1⅓ cups water
½ cup yellow cornmeal
½ cup cold water
½ teaspoon salt
8 ounces uncooked
    ground turkey
    breast or 90% or
    higher lean ground
    beef
½ cup chopped onion
    (1 medium)
½ cup chopped green
    and/or red sweet
    pepper (1 small)
1 clove garlic, minced
1 tablespoon chili
    powder
1 14.5-ounce can no-
    salt-added diced
    tomatoes, drained
1 11-ounce can whole
    kernel corn, drained
2 tablespoons tomato
    paste
2 tablespoons snipped
    fresh cilantro or
    parsley
½ cup shredded
    reduced-fat cheddar
    or Monterey Jack
    cheese (2 ounces)
Snipped fresh cilantro
    or parsley (optional)

1 Preheat oven to 350°F. Lightly coat a 2-quart square baking dish with cooking spray; set aside. In a small saucepan bring the 1⅓ cups water to boiling. In a small bowl stir together cornmeal, the ½ cup cold water, and ¼ teaspoon of the salt. Slowly add the cornmeal mixture to the boiling water, stirring constantly; cook and stir until mixture returns to boiling. Reduce heat to low. Cook about 10 minutes or until mixture is very thick, stirring occasionally.

2 Pour the hot mixture into the prepared baking dish. Cover and chill while preparing filling.

3 For filling, in a large skillet cook turkey, onion, sweet pepper, and garlic until meat is brown, using a wooden spoon to break up meat as it cooks. Drain off fat. Stir chili powder and the remaining ¼ teaspoon salt into meat mixture in skillet. Cook for 1 minute. Stir in tomatoes, corn, tomato paste, and 2 tablespoons cilantro.

4 Spoon the meat mixture on top of the chilled cornmeal mixture in baking dish.

5 Bake about 25 minutes or until heated through. Sprinkle with cheese. If desired, sprinkle with additional snipped cilantro.

nutrition facts per serving: 182 cal., 3 g total fat (1 g sat. fat), 22 mg chol., 546 mg sodium, 25 g carb., 4 g dietary fiber, 14 g protein.

Instead of using loads of calorie-laden regular sour cream, we lightened these enchiladas with a creamy filling that includes only a wisp of light sour cream.

chicken enchilada casserole

prep: 30 minutes bake: 25 minutes stand: 5 minutes oven: 350°F
makes: 6 servings

¾ cup water
½ cup chopped onion (1 medium)
½ teaspoon instant chicken bouillon granules
2 cloves garlic, minced
⅛ teaspoon ground black pepper
½ cup light sour cream
2 tablespoons nonfat dry milk powder
1 tablespoon all-purpose flour
1½ cups shredded cooked chicken breast or turkey breast (about 8 ounces)
1 8-ounce can no-salt-added tomato sauce
1 4-ounce can diced green chile peppers, drained, or 1 or 2 canned jalapeno chile peppers, rinsed, seeded, and finely chopped*
2 tablespoons snipped fresh cilantro or ½ teaspoon ground coriander
Nonstick cooking spray
4 6-inch corn tortillas, cut into 1-inch-wide strips
1 cup canned black beans or kidney beans, rinsed and drained
½ cup shredded reduced-fat Monterey Jack cheese (2 ounces)
Fresh cilantro leaves (optional)

1 Preheat oven to 350°F. For chicken filling, in a medium saucepan combine the water, onion, bouillon granules, garlic, and black pepper. Bring to boiling; reduce heat. Simmer, covered, about 3 minutes or until onion is tender. Do not drain. In a small bowl stir together sour cream, dry milk powder, and flour. Add to onion mixture; cook and stir until thickened and bubbly. Remove from heat; stir in chicken. Set filling aside.

2 In another small bowl combine tomato sauce, green chile peppers, and snipped cilantro; set aside.

3 Coat a 2-quart casserole with cooking spray. Arrange tortilla strips in the casserole. Top with chicken filling. Top with beans. Top with tomato sauce mixture.

4 Bake for 25 to 30 minutes or until heated through. Sprinkle with cheese. If desired, garnish with cilantro leaves. Let stand for 5 minutes before serving.

nutrition facts per serving: 219 cal., 6 g total fat (3 g sat. fat), 43 mg chol., 420 mg sodium, 23 g carb., 3 g dietary fiber, 19 g protein

*tip: Because chile peppers contain volatile oils that can burn your skin and eyes, avoid direct contact with them as much as possible. When working with chile peppers, wear plastic or rubber gloves. If your bare hands do touch the peppers, wash your hands and nails well with soap and warm water.

One time try broccoli and thyme. Another time use basil or tarragon and asparagus. Whatever you choose, this hearty casserole is sure to please.

potato, broccoli, and ham bake

prep: 30 minutes   bake: 30 minutes   stand: 5 minutes   oven: 400°F
makes: 6 servings

1   pound Yukon gold potatoes, sliced
1   8-ounce package light cream cheese (Neufchâtel), cubed
¾   cup fat-free milk
⅓   cup thinly sliced green onions
¼   teaspoon ground black pepper
1   tablespoon snipped fresh thyme, basil, or tarragon; or ½ teaspoon dried thyme, basil, or tarragon, crushed
4   ounces cooked ham, cut into bite-size pieces (about ¾ cup)
1   pound broccoli, trimmed and cut into small florets (about 4 cups), or 1 pound fresh asparagus, trimmed and cut into 2- to 3-inch pieces
2   tablespoons finely shredded Parmesan cheese

1 Preheat oven to 400°F. In a covered medium saucepan cook potatoes in enough boiling lightly salted water to cover for 5 to 7 minutes or just until tender; drain. Transfer to a 1½-quart baking dish; set aside.

2 For sauce, in the same saucepan combine cream cheese, milk, green onions, and pepper. Heat and whisk until smooth and cheese is melted. Remove from heat; stir in thyme.

3 Top potatoes with ham and broccoli. Evenly spoon sauce over. Bake, covered, for 20 minutes. Sprinkle with Parmesan cheese. Bake, uncovered, for 10 to 12 minutes more or until heated through. Let stand for 5 minutes before serving.

nutrition facts per serving: 230 cal., 11 g total fat (6 g sat. fat), 40 mg chol., 439 mg sodium, 22 g carb., 4 g dietary fiber, 12 g protein.

baked stuffed shells

prep: 40 minutes   bake: 37 minutes
stand: 10 minutes   oven: 350°F
makes: 4 servings

391

½	cup chopped onion (1 medium)
2	cloves garlic, minced
1	teaspoon olive oil
1	14.5-ounce can no-salt-added diced tomatoes, undrained
1	8-ounce can no-salt-added tomato sauce
1	tablespoon snipped fresh basil or ½ teaspoon dried basil, crushed
2	teaspoons snipped fresh oregano or ½ teaspoon dried oregano, crushed
¼	teaspoon salt
12	dried jumbo shell macaroni
1	12.3-ounce package extra-firm, silken-style tofu (fresh bean curd)
½	cup finely shredded Parmesan or Romano cheese (2 ounces)
¼	cup refrigerated or frozen egg product, thawed, or 1 egg
¼	teaspoon ground black pepper
½	cup shredded reduced-fat mozzarella cheese (2 ounces)
2	tablespoons shredded fresh basil (optional)

1 Preheat oven to 350°F. For sauce, in a medium saucepan cook onion and garlic in hot oil over medium heat about 5 minutes or until onion is tender, stirring occasionally. Add tomatoes, tomato sauce, dried basil and oregano (if using), and salt. Bring to boiling; reduce heat. Simmer, uncovered, about 15 minutes or until desired consistency. Remove from heat; stir in snipped fresh basil and oregano (if using). Reserve ¾ cup of the sauce; spread the remaining sauce in the bottom of a 2-quart rectangular baking dish. Set aside.

2 Meanwhile, cook pasta shells according to package directions; drain. Rinse with cold water; drain again.

3 For filling, place tofu in a blender or food processor. Cover and blend or process until smooth. Add Parmesan cheese, egg, and pepper. Cover and blend or process just until combined. Spoon about 3 tablespoons of the filling into each pasta shell. Arrange filled shells, filling sides up, on sauce in baking dish. Spoon the reserved ¾ cup sauce over shells.

4 Bake, covered, about 35 minutes or until heated through. Sprinkle with mozzarella cheese. Bake, uncovered, about 2 minutes more or until cheese is melted. Let stand for 10 minutes before serving. If desired, top with shredded fresh basil.

nutrition facts per serving: 351 cal., 8 g total fat (3 g sat. fat), 15 mg chol., 536 mg sodium, 48 g carb., 5 g dietary fiber, 21 g protein.

turkey and black bean
chimichangas

prep: 30 minutes bake: 10 minutes oven: 425°F makes: 6 chimichangas

Nonstick cooking
spray

6   10-inch whole wheat
flour tortillas

8   ounces uncooked
ground turkey
breast

½   cup chopped onion
(1 medium)

1   15-ounce can no-salt-
added black beans,
rinsed and drained,
or 1¾ cups cooked
black beans

1   14.5-ounce can no-
salt-added diced
tomatoes, drained

¼   cup salsa

¼   cup snipped fresh
cilantro

1   tablespoon lime juice

½   teaspoon ground
cumin

½   cup shredded
reduced-fat
Monterey Jack
cheese (2 ounces)
Snipped fresh cilantro
(optional)

1 Preheat oven to 425°F. Coat a baking sheet with cooking spray; set aside. Stack tortillas and wrap tightly in foil. Bake about 5 minutes or until heated through.

2 Meanwhile, for filling, in a large nonstick skillet cook ground turkey and onion over medium heat until turkey is brown and onion is softened, using a wooden spoon to break up meat as it cooks. Add black beans. Using a fork or potato masher, mash beans slightly. Stir in tomatoes, salsa, the ¼ cup snipped cilantro, lime juice, and cumin; heat through.

3 Spoon about ½ cup of the filling onto each tortilla, spooning filling just below the center. Fold bottom edge of tortilla up and over filling. Fold in sides; roll up from bottom. If necessary, secure with wooden toothpicks.

4 Place tortilla bundles, seam sides down, on the prepared baking sheet. Lightly coat tops and sides of bundles with cooking spray. Bake for 10 to 12 minutes or until tortillas are golden. Sprinkle with cheese; let stand for 1 minute before serving. If desired, sprinkle with additional snipped cilantro.

nutrition facts per chimichanga: 351 cal., 6 g total fat (2 g sat. fat), 30 mg chol., 718 mg sodium, 51 g carb., 11 g dietary fiber, 22 g protein.

nutrition note

Chimichangas can command a prominent spot in your healthful recipe rotation when they include lean protein sources, nonstarchy veggies, and flavor-boosting sauces and spices.

tex-mex chicken tostadas

start to finish: 25 minutes   oven: 350°F   makes: 4 servings

4   8-inch flour tortillas
12 ounces uncooked
    ground chicken
1   teaspoon chili
    powder
1   8-ounce jar medium
    or hot salsa
1   15-ounce can no-salt-
    added black beans
    or pinto beans
¼   cup thinly sliced
    radishes
1   cup chopped lettuce
1   2.25-ounce can sliced
    pitted ripe olives
2   tablespoons diced
    pimiento
2   tablespoons thinly
    sliced green
    onion (1)
¼   cup reduced-fat
    shredded cheddar
    cheese (1 ounce)
    Light sour cream
    (optional)

1 Preheat oven to 350°F. For tostada shells, place tortillas in a single layer directly on the middle oven rack. Bake about 6 minutes or until golden and crisp, turning once halfway through baking. (If tortillas bubble during baking, puncture bubbles with a fork.) Cover to keep warm; set aside.

2 Meanwhile, in a 10 inch nonstick skillet cook and stir chicken and chili powder over medium heat for 5 to 7 minutes or until chicken is brown, using a wooden spoon to break up meat as it cooks. Stir in salsa; set aside. Keep warm.

3 Drain beans, reserving liquid. In a small saucepan stir beans over low heat until heated through. Using a potato masher or fork, mash beans, adding enough of the reserved bean liquid to make of spreadable consistency; heat through.

4 To assemble, spread a warm tortilla with a thin layer of the beans. Top beans with some of the chicken mixture, radishes, lettuce, olives, pimiento, green onion, cheese, and, if desired, sour cream. Repeat with remaining tostadas.

nutrition facts per tostada. 410 cal., 13 g total fat (3 g sat. fat), 77 mg chol., 854 mg sodium, 46 g carb., 7 g dietary fiber, 28 g protein.

chipotle chicken
quesadillas

prep: 30 minutes   cook: 2 minutes per batch   oven: 300°F   makes: 4 servings

8   7-inch whole wheat
     tortillas
     Nonstick cooking
     spray
12   ounces skinless,
     boneless chicken
     breast halves, cut
     into thin bite-size
     strips
2   small red and/or
     green sweet
     peppers, seeded
     and chopped
2   cloves garlic, minced
¼   cup thinly sliced
     green onions (2)
1   canned chipotle chile
     pepper in adobo
     sauce, drained and
     finely chopped*
2   tablespoons lime juice
3   ounces queso fresco,
     crumbled, or ¾ cup
     shredded reduced-
     fat Monterey Jack
     cheese (3 ounces)
¼   cup light sour cream
     (optional)
1   teaspoon finely
     chopped canned
     chipotle chile
     pepper in adobo
     sauce* (optional)
4   cups shredded lettuce
     Salsa and/or lime
     wedges (optional)

1 Preheat oven to 300°F. Lightly coat one side of each tortilla with cooking spray. Place tortillas, coated sides down, on a tray or clean work surface; set aside.

2 Coat a large nonstick skillet with cooking spray. Heat skillet over medium-high heat. Add chicken, sweet peppers, and garlic; cook for 4 to 6 minutes or until chicken is no longer pink, stirring occasionally. Remove from heat; stir in green onions, 1 chipotle pepper, and lime juice.

3 Divide chicken-pepper mixture among tortillas, placing the mixture on one half of each tortilla. Sprinkle chicken mixture with cheese. Fold tortillas over filling; press down lightly.

4 Heat a nonstick skillet or griddle over medium-high heat; reduce heat to medium. Cook quesadillas, two or three at a time, for 2 to 3 minutes or until tortillas are lightly browned, turning once halfway through cooking. Keep quesadillas warm in the oven while cooking the remaining quesadillas.

5 If desired, in a small bowl stir together sour cream and the 1 teaspoon chipotle pepper. Cut each quesadilla into three wedges. Serve with lettuce. If desired, serve with sour cream mixture, salsa, and/or lime wedges.

nutrition facts per serving: 262 cal., 7 g total fat (0 g sat. fat), 49 mg chol., 440 mg sodium, 30 g carb., 18 g dietary fiber, 36 g protein.

*tip: Because chile peppers contain volatile oils that can burn your skin and eyes, avoid direct contact with them as much as possible. When working with chile peppers, wear plastic or rubber gloves. If your bare hands do touch the peppers, wash your hands and nails well with soap and warm water.

sweet-and-sour chicken

start to finish: 30 minutes makes: 6 servings

¾ cup reduced-sodium chicken broth
3 tablespoons red wine vinegar
2 tablespoons reduced-sodium soy sauce
4 teaspoons sugar
1 tablespoon cornstarch
1 clove garlic, minced
4 teaspoons canola oil
1½ cups thinly sliced carrots (3 medium)
1 large red sweet pepper, seeded and cut into bite-size strips
2 cups fresh snow pea pods
12 ounces skinless, boneless chicken breast halves, cut into 1-inch pieces
1 8-ounce can pineapple chunks (juice-pack), drained
3 cups hot cooked brown rice

1 For sauce, in a small bowl stir together broth, vinegar, soy sauce, sugar, cornstarch, and garlic; set aside.

2 In a large nonstick skillet heat 3 teaspoons of the oil over medium-high heat. Add carrots and sweet pepper; cook for 3 minutes. Add pea pods; cook and stir about 1 minute more or until vegetables are crisp-tender. Remove vegetable mixture from skillet; set aside.

3 Add the remaining 1 teaspoon oil to skillet. Add chicken to skillet; cook and stir for 3 to 4 minutes or until chicken is no longer pink. Push chicken from center of skillet. Stir sauce; add to center of skillet. Cook and stir until thickened and bubbly. Add vegetable mixture and pineapple chunks to skillet; heat through. Serve with hot cooked brown rice.

nutrition facts per serving: 270 cal., 5 g total fat (1 g sat. fat), 33 mg chol., 321 mg sodium, 39 g carb., 4 g dietary fiber, 18 g protein.

Chopped water chestnuts add extra crunch to the savory filling in these delightful morsels.

light 'n' crisp egg rolls

prep: 30 minutes   bake: 15 minutes   oven: 450°F   makes: 8 egg rolls

Nonstick cooking
  spray
2   teaspoons toasted
  sesame oil or canola
  oil
8   ounces lean boneless
  pork loin, cut into
  ½-inch pieces, or
  ground pork
½   cup chopped red
  sweet pepper
1   teaspoon grated
  fresh ginger or
  ¼ teaspoon ground
  ginger
1   clove garlic, minced
¾   cup finely chopped
  bok choy or napa
  cabbage
½   cup chopped canned
  water chestnuts
½   cup coarsely
  shredded carrot
  (1 medium)
¼   cup sliced green
  onions (2)
¼   cup bottled light
  Asian sesame
  ginger vinaigrette
  salad dressing
8   egg roll wrappers

1 Preheat oven to 450°F. Lightly coat a large baking sheet with cooking spray; set aside. For filling, in a medium nonstick skillet heat oil over medium-high heat. Add pork, sweet pepper, ginger, and garlic; cook for 3 to 4 minutes or until pork is no longer pink, stirring occasionally. If using ground pork, drain off fat. Add bok choy, water chestnuts, carrot, and green onions to pork mixture; cook and stir about 1 minute more or until any liquid evaporates. Stir in vinaigrette. Cool filling slightly.

2 For each egg roll, place an egg roll wrapper on a flat surface with a corner pointing toward you. Spoon about ⅓ cup of the filling across and just below center of each egg roll wrapper. Fold bottom corner over filling, tucking it under on the other side. Fold side corners over filling, forming an envelope shape. Roll egg roll toward remaining corner. Moisten top corner with water; press firmly to seal.

3 Place egg rolls, seam sides down, on the prepared baking sheet. Coat the tops and sides of the egg rolls with cooking spray. Bake for 15 to 18 minutes or until egg rolls are golden and crisp. Cool slightly before serving.

nutrition facts per egg roll: 167 cal., 4 g total fat (1 g sat. fat), 22 mg chol., 282 mg sodium, 23 g carb., 1 g dietary fiber, 10 g protein.

nutrition note

Yes, you can have crisp eggrolls, without frying with a lot of fat. Spray the egg roll wrappers with nonstick cooking spray, then bake at high-temperatures for a restaurant-style treat.

Using packaged cooked brown rice is the secret to keeping this recipe's prep time short.

coconut shrimp with mango rice pilaf

prep: 25 minutes bake: 8 minutes oven: 450°F makes: 4 servings

1   pound fresh or frozen extra-large shrimp in shells
    Nonstick cooking spray
¼   cup refrigerated or frozen egg product, thawed, or 2 egg whites, lightly beaten
¾   cup finely crushed reduced-fat or reduced-sodium shredded wheat crackers
⅓   cup shredded coconut
¼   teaspoon ground ginger
¼   teaspoon ground black pepper
1   8.8-ounce pouch cooked brown rice
½   cup chopped fresh mango or chopped jarred mango, rinsed and drained
⅓   cup sliced green onions
2   tablespoons snipped fresh cilantro

1 Thaw shrimp, if frozen. Preheat oven to 450°F. Lightly coat a large baking sheet with cooking spray; set aside. Peel and devein shrimp, leaving tails intact if desired. Rinse shrimp; pat dry with paper towels.

2 Place egg in a shallow dish. In another shallow dish combine crushed crackers, coconut, ginger, and pepper. Dip shrimp into egg, turning to coat. Dip in coconut mixture, pressing to coat except leaving tail uncoated. Arrange shrimp in a single layer on the prepared baking sheet.

3 Bake for 8 to 10 minutes or until shrimp are opaque and coating is lightly browned. Meanwhile, heat rice according to package directions. Transfer rice to a serving bowl; stir in mango and green onions. Serve rice with shrimp; sprinkle with cilantro.

nutrition facts per serving: 303 cal., 7 g total fat (2 g sat. fat), 129 mg chol., 249 mg sodium, 36 g carb., 3 g dietary fiber, 23 g protein.

sizzling catfish with cajun chips

start to finish: 30 minutes oven: 425°F makes: 2 servings

1 Thaw fish, if frozen. Rinse fish; pat dry with paper towels. If necessary, cut fish into two serving-size pieces; set aside. Prepare Cajun Tortilla Chips.

8 ounces fresh or frozen catfish fillets, ½ to ¾ inch thick
1 recipe Cajun Tortilla Chips
1 egg white, lightly beaten
1 tablespoon water
2 tablespoons yellow cornmeal
2 tablespoons finely chopped fresh poblano chile pepper*
1 tablespoon fine dry bread crumbs
1 tablespoon grated Parmesan cheese
⅛ teaspoon salt
2 tablespoons all-purpose flour
1 tablespoon canola oil
Lime wedges (optional)

2 In a shallow dish combine egg white and the water. In another shallow dish combine cornmeal, poblano chile pepper, bread crumbs, cheese, and salt. Place flour in a third shallow dish. Dip each piece of fish in flour, turning to coat. Dip in egg mixture, turning to coat. Dip in cornmeal mixture, turning to coat evenly.

3 In a large skillet heat the oil over medium heat. Add fish; cook for 8 to 10 minutes or until golden and fish flakes easily when tested with a fork, turning once halfway through cooking. If desired, garnish with lime wedges. Serve with Cajun Tortilla Chips.

nutrition facts per serving: 368 cal., 17 g total fat (3 g sat. fat), 55 mg chol., 331 mg sodium, 31 g carb., 3 g dietary fiber, 24 g protein.

cajun tortilla chips: Preheat oven to 425°F. Lightly coat two 6-inch corn tortillas on both sides with nonstick cooking spray. Sprinkle tortillas on both sides with ¼ teaspoon Cajun seasoning. Cut each tortilla into six pieces. Arranged tortilla pieces in a single layer on a baking sheet. Bake about 8 minutes or until lightly browned and crisp. Cool on a wire rack. Makes 12 chips.

*tip: Because chile peppers contain volatile oils that can burn your skin and eyes, avoid direct contact with them as much as possible. When working with chile peppers, wear plastic or rubber gloves. If your bare hands do touch the peppers, wash your hands and nails well with soap and warm water.

The addition of halibut, scallops, and clams turns ordinary corn chowder into an extraordinary meal-in-a-bowl.

seafood-corn chowder

prep: 25 minutes   cook: 12 minutes   makes: 6 servings

8	ounces fresh or frozen skinless halibut fillets
4	fresh or frozen sea scallops (about 8 ounces total)
¾	cup chopped green sweet pepper (1 medium)
½	cup chopped onion (1 medium)
2	cloves garlic, minced
1	tablespoon canola oil
4	medium tomatoes, cored and coarsely chopped
2	cups low-sodium vegetable broth
1	cup water
1	cup fresh or frozen whole kernel corn
1	teaspoon ground cumin
¼	teaspoon ground black pepper
1	10-ounce can or two 3.53-ounce packages whole baby clams, drained
¼	cup snipped fresh cilantro
	Cracked black pepper (optional)

1 Thaw halibut and scallops, if frozen. Cut halibut into 1-inch pieces and cut large scallops in halves or quarters; set aside. In a large saucepan cook sweet pepper, onion, and garlic in hot oil over medium heat about 5 minutes or until tender, stirring occasionally. Stir in tomatoes, broth, the water, corn, cumin, and ground black pepper. Bring to boiling; reduce heat. Simmer, covered, for 10 minutes.

2 Add halibut and scallops to tomato mixture. Return to boiling; reduce heat. Simmer, uncovered, for 2 to 3 minutes more or until halibut flakes easily when tested with a fork and scallops are opaque.

3 Stir in clams and cilantro. Serve immediately. If desired, sprinkle with cracked black pepper.

nutrition facts per serving: 205 cal., 5 g total fat (0 g sat. fat), 50 mg chol., 319 mg sodium, 15 g carb., 2 g dietary fiber, 26 g protein.

mexican chicken-tortilla soup

prep: 30 minutes   cook: 35 minutes   bake: 10 minutes   oven: 375°F
makes: 4 servings

2   medium bone-in chicken breast halves (about 1¼ pounds total)
1   14-ounce can reduced-sodium chicken broth
1¾ cups water
½   cup chopped onion (1 medium)
1   clove garlic, minced
½   teaspoon ground cumin
1   tablespoon vegetable oil
1   14.5-ounce can no-salt-added diced tomatoes, undrained
1   8-ounce can no-salt-added tomato sauce
1   4-ounce can whole green chile peppers, rinsed, seeded, and cut into thin bite-size strips
¼   cup snipped fresh cilantro or parsley
1   tablespoon snipped fresh oregano or 1 teaspoon dried oregano, crushed
4   6-inch corn tortillas
½   cup reduced-fat shredded cheddar or Monterey Jack cheese (2 ounces)

1 In a large saucepan combine chicken, broth, and the water. Bring to boiling; reduce heat. Simmer, covered, about 15 minutes or until chicken is tender and no longer pink. Remove chicken; set aside to cool, reserving cooking broth. Remove and discard chicken skin and bones. When cool enough to handle, use two forks to pull chicken apart into fine shreds. Set chicken aside. Strain cooking broth through a fine-mesh sieve. Skim fat from broth; set aside.

2 In the same saucepan cook onion, garlic, and cumin in hot oil until onion is tender. Stir in strained broth, tomatoes, tomato sauce, green chile peppers, cilantro, and oregano. Bring to boiling; reduce heat. Simmer, covered, for 20 minutes. Stir in chicken; heat through.

3 Meanwhile, preheat oven to 375°F. Cut tortillas in half. Cut each half crosswise into ¼- to ½-inch-wide strips. Place tortilla strips on a baking sheet. Bake for 7 to 10 minutes or until crisp.

4 Ladle soup into four soup bowls. Sprinkle each serving with shredded cheese and top with tortilla strips. Serve immediately.

nutrition facts per serving: 319 cal., 8 g total fat (2 g sat. fat), 61 mg chol., 594 mg sodium, 32 g carb., 7 g dietary fiber, 32 g protein.

special

occa

14

Company is coming! With
dishes like these—both
heavenly and healthful—
you can be good to yourself
as well as your guests.

sions

traditional roast turkey

prep: 20 minutes   roast: 3 hours   stand: 15 minutes   oven: 425°F/325°F
makes: 24 servings

1   12- to 14-pound
     turkey
1   tablespoon snipped
     fresh rosemary or
     1 teaspoon dried
     rosemary, crushed
1   tablespoon snipped
     fresh thyme or
     1 teaspoon dried
     thyme, crushed
1   tablespoon snipped
     fresh sage or
     1 teaspoon dried
     sage, crushed
½   teaspoon salt
½   teaspoon ground
     black pepper
1   tablespoon olive oil
     Fresh rosemary
     sprigs, fresh thyme
     sprigs, fresh sage
     leaves, and/or
     pomegranate pieces
     (optional)

1 Preheat oven to 425°F. Remove neck and giblets from turkey. Rinse inside of turkey; pat dry with paper towels. In a small bowl stir together snipped or dried rosemary, thyme, sage, salt, and pepper. Season inside of body cavity with half of the herb mixture. Pull neck skin to back; fasten with a skewer. Tuck ends of drumsticks under band of skin across tail, if available. If there is no band of skin, tie drumsticks securely to tail with 100-percent-cotton kitchen string. Twist wing tips under back.

2 Place turkey, breast side up, on a rack in a shallow roasting pan. Brush turkey with oil; sprinkle with the remaining herb mixture. If desired, insert an ovenproof meat thermometer into center of an inside thigh muscle. The thermometer should not touch bone. Cover turkey loosely with foil.

3 Roast for 30 minutes. Reduce oven temperature to 325°F. Roast for 2½ to 3 hours more or until thermometer registers 180°F. About 45 minutes before end of roasting, remove foil and cut band of skin or string between drumsticks so thighs will cook evenly. When turkey is done, the juices should run clear and the drumsticks should move easily in their sockets.

4 Remove turkey from oven. Transfer turkey to a serving platter; cover with foil. Let stand for 15 to 20 minutes before carving. If desired, garnish platter with rosemary sprigs, thyme sprigs, sage leaves, and/or pomegranate pieces.

nutrition facts per serving: 229 cal., 7 g total fat (2 g sat. fat), 137 mg chol., 123 mg sodium, 0 g carb., 0 g dietary fiber, 38 g protein.

glazed ham

prep: 15 minutes bake: 1 hour 30 minutes oven: 325°F
makes: 16 to 20 servings

1 5- to 6-pound cooked
   ham (rump half or
   shank portion)
24 whole cloves
   (optional)
1 recipe Orange Glaze
   Orange slices,
   cranberries, fresh
   sage leaves, and/
   or fresh rosemary
   sprigs (optional)
1 recipe Mint and
   Lemon Sprinkle
   (optional)

1 Preheat oven to 325°F. Score ham in a diamond pattern by making diagonal cuts at 1-inch intervals. If desired, stud ham with cloves. Place ham on a rack in a shallow roasting pan. If desired, insert an ovenproof meat thermometer into center of ham. The thermometer should not touch bone.

2 Bake for 1½ to 2¼ hours or until thermometer registers 140°F. Brush ham with some of the Orange Glaze during the last 20 minutes of baking.

3 Transfer ham to a serving platter. If desired, garnish platter with orange slices, cranberries, sage leaves, and/or rosemary sprigs. Serve with the remaining glaze and, if desired, Mint and Lemon Sprinkle.

nutrition facts per serving. 156 cal., 7 g total fat (1 g sat fat), 62 mg chol., 984 mg sodium, 7 g carb., 0 g dietary fiber, 16 g protein.

orange glaze: In a medium saucepan combine 2 teaspoons finely shredded orange peel, 1 cup orange juice, ½ cup packed brown sugar, 4 teaspoons cornstarch, and 1½ teaspoons dry mustard. Cook and stir over medium heat until thickened and bubbly. Cook and stir for 2 minutes more. Makes 1¼ cups glaze.

mint and lemon sprinkle: In a small bowl combine ½ cup snipped fresh mint, 1 tablespoon finely shredded lemon peel, and 2 cloves garlic, minced.

wild rice stuffing

prep: 15 minutes cook: 45 minutes makes: 6 servings (2½ cups total)

1¾ cups water
¼   cup uncooked wild
     rice, rinsed and
     drained
¼   cup uncooked regular
     brown rice
1   teaspoon instant
     chicken bouillon
     granules
⅛   to ¼ teaspoon ground
     sage or nutmeg
2   cups sliced fresh
     mushrooms
½   cup chopped celery
     (1 stalk)
⅓   cup sliced green
     onions
¼   cup sliced almonds or
     pine nuts, toasted
     (optional)

1 In a medium saucepan bring the water
to boiling. Stir in wild rice, brown rice,
bouillon granules, and sage. Return to boiling;
reduce heat. Simmer, covered, for 20 minutes.

2 Stir in mushrooms, celery, and green
onions. Simmer, covered, about 25 minutes
more or just until vegetables are tender,
stirring frequently. If desired, stir in almonds.
Serve immediately or use to stuff a 3½ - to
4-pound whole chicken.

nutrition facts per serving: 66 cal., 1 g total fat
(0 g sat. fat), 0 mg chol., 155 mg sodium, 13 g carb.,
1 g dietary fiber, 3 g protein.

make-ahead directions: Prepare as
directed. Transfer to a 1-quart casserole.
Cover and chill for 2 to 24 hours. To serve,
preheat oven to 375°F. Stir ¼ cup water
into stuffing. Bake, covered, about
30 minutes or until heated through.

nutrition note
*How many servings of grains you
should eat per day varies by your age
and activity level, but one guideline
is clear: According to the USDA, half
the grains you eat should be whole
grains. Here, the ½ cup brown and
wild rices equals 1 serving of
whole grain.*

Make holiday meals more healthful by serving this updated version of the traditional family favorite. The reduced-fat soup and cheddar cheese as well as fat-free milk and light sour cream help keep the fat in check.

heart-healthy
cheesy potatoes

prep: 15 minutes bake: 1 hour 5 minutes stand: 10 minutes
oven: 350°F makes: 12 servings

1 10.75-ounce can reduced-fat and reduced-sodium condensed cream of chicken soup

1 cup shredded reduced-fat sharp cheddar cheese (4 ounces)

½ cup fat-free milk

½ cup light sour cream

⅓ cup finely chopped onion (1 small) or 2 tablespoons dried minced onion

½ teaspoon ground black pepper

1 30- or 32-ounce package frozen shredded or diced hash brown potatoes, thawed

½ cup crushed cornflakes or crushed wheat cereal flakes

1 Preheat oven to 350°F. Lightly grease a 2-quart rectangular baking dish; set aside. In an extra-large bowl combine soup, cheese, milk, sour cream, onion, and pepper. Stir in potatoes. Transfer mixture to the prepared baking dish.

2 Bake, covered, for 45 minutes. Stir potatoes; sprinkle with cornflakes. Bake, uncovered, for 20 to 25 minutes more or until heated through and bubbly. Let stand for 10 minutes before serving.

nutrition facts per serving: 129 cal., 3 g total fat (2 g sat. fat), 11 mg chol., 236 mg sodium, 20 g carb., 1 g dietary fiber, 5 g protein.

If pumpkin pie is a must for the holidays, this version is a healthy way to fulfill the tradition.

light and luscious
pumpkin pie

prep: 30 minutes bake: 40 minutes oven: 450°F/375°F makes: 10 servings

1   recipe Oil Pastry
    Sugar (optional)
1   15-ounce can
      pumpkin
⅓   cup sugar
2   tablespoons honey
1   teaspoon ground
      cinnamon
¼   teaspoon ground
      ginger
¼   teaspoon ground
      nutmeg
½   cup refrigerated or
      frozen egg product,
      thawed, or 2 eggs,
      lightly beaten
1   teaspoon vanilla
¾   cup evaporated fat-
      free milk

1 Preheat oven to 450°F. Prepare Oil Pastry. On a well-floured surface, slightly flatten pastry. Roll pastry from center to edges into a 12-inch circle. Wrap pastry circle around rolling pin; unroll into a 9-inch pie plate. Ease pastry into pie plate without stretching it. Trim pastry to ½ inch beyond edge of pie plate, reserving scraps if desired. Fold under extra pastry even with edge of pie plate. Crimp edge as desired. Do not prick pastry. Line pastry with a double thickness of foil. Bake for 8 minutes. Remove foil. Bake for 5 minutes more. Cool on a wire rack. Reduce oven temperature to 375°F.

2 If desired, combine the reserved pastry scraps; flatten to ¼-inch thickness. Using desired cookie cutters, cut out shapes for top of pie. Place on an ungreased baking sheet. If desired, sprinkle with sugar. Bake for 7 to 10 minutes or until golden brown. Transfer to a wire rack; cool.

3 For filling, in a medium bowl combine pumpkin, ⅓ cup sugar, honey, cinnamon, ginger, and nutmeg. Add egg product and vanilla. Beat lightly with a fork just until combined. Gradually stir in evaporated milk. Pour filling into baked pastry shell.

4 To prevent overbrowning, cover edge of pie with foil. Bake for 40 to 45 minutes or until filling appears set (edge of filling may crack slightly).

5 Cool on a wire rack. If desired, top with baked pastry cutouts. Cover and chill within 2 hours.

nutrition facts per serving: 196 cal., 8 g total fat (1 g sat. fat), 1 mg chol., 108 mg sodium, 28 g carb., 2 g dietary fiber, 5 g protein.

oil pastry: In a medium bowl stir together 1⅓ cups all-purpose flour and ¼ teaspoon salt. Add ⅓ cup vegetable oil and 3 tablespoons fat-free milk all at once to flour mixture. Stir lightly with a fork until combined. Shape into a ball. Makes 1 pastry.

lattice-topped
apple pie

prep: 30 minutes bake: 40 minutes oven: 375°F makes: 8 servings

6   cups sliced cooking
    apples, such as
    Jonathan or Rome
    Beauty (about
    2 pounds)
3   tablespoons sugar
1   teaspoon ground
    cinnamon
1   tablespoon
    cornstarch
1   recipe Whole Wheat
    Pastry
    Fat-free milk

whole wheat pastry: In a medium bowl stir together ½ cup all-purpose flour, ¼ cup whole wheat pastry flour or whole wheat flour, 2 tablespoons toasted wheat germ, and ⅛ teaspoon ground nutmeg. Using a pastry blender, cut in 3 tablespoons butter until mixture resembles coarse crumbs. Sprinkle 1 tablespoon cold water over part of the flour mixture; toss gently with a fork. Push moistened dough to side of bowl. Repeat with additional cold water, 1 tablespoon at a time (2 to 3 tablespoons total), until all of the flour mixture is moistened. Shape into a ball. Makes 1 pastry.

1 Place apples in a 2-quart rectangular baking dish. In a small bowl combine sugar and cinnamon; reserve 1 teaspoon of the mixture. Stir cornstarch into the remaining sugar mixture. Sprinkle sugar-cornstarch mixture over apples; toss gently to combine.

2 Preheat oven to 375°F. Prepare Whole Wheat Pastry. On a lightly floured surface, slightly flatten pastry. Roll pastry from center to edges into a 10x5-inch rectangle. Cut pastry lengthwise into eight about ½-inch-wide strips.

3 Place five of the pastry strips crosswise on filling. Fold alternate strips back halfway. Place one of the remaining pastry strips in the center across the strips already in place. Unfold the folded strips; fold back the remaining crosswise strips. Place another of the remaining pastry strips across the first set of strips parallel to the strip in the center. Repeat the weaving steps with the remaining pastry strip. Trim pastry strips; tuck ends into dish. Brush pastry with milk; sprinkle with the reserved 1 teaspoon sugar mixture.

4 Bake for 40 to 45 minutes or until apples are tender. Serve warm or cool.

nutrition facts per serving: 152 cal., 5 g total fat (2 g sat. fat), 12 mg chol., 48 mg sodium, 26 g carb., 3 g dietary fiber, 2 g protein.

olive
deviled eggs

prep: 30 minutes stand: 15 minutes chill: 1 hour makes: 24 appetizers

12 eggs
¼ cup chopped
   pimiento-stuffed
   green olives
¼ cup light mayonnaise
   or salad dressing
1 tablespoon Dijon-
   style mustard
⅛ to ¼ teaspoon ground
   black pepper
   Snipped fresh chives
   and/or cracked
   black pepper
   (optional)

1 Place eggs in a single layer in a Dutch oven (do not stack eggs). Add enough cold water to cover the eggs by 1 inch. Bring to a rapid boil over high heat (water will have large rapidly breaking bubbles). Remove from heat. Let stand, covered, for 15 minutes; drain. Run cold water over the eggs or place them in ice water until cool enough to handle; drain.

2 Peel eggs. Cut eggs in half lengthwise and remove yolks; set whites aside. Place yolks in a medium bowl; mash with a fork. Stir in olives, mayonnaise, mustard, and ⅛ teaspoon pepper.

3 Stuff egg white halves with yolk mixture. Cover and chill for 1 hour before serving. If desired, garnish with chives and/or cracked pepper.

nutrition facts per appetizer: 49 cal., 4 g total fat (1 g sat. fat), 107 mg chol., 83 mg sodium, 1 g carb., 0 g dietary fiber, 3 g protein.

make-ahead directions: Prepare as directed, except cover and chill for up to 24 hours before serving.

The green bean casserole gets a new slim profile with the help of reduced-fat and reduced-sodium cream of mushroom soup. Almonds replace the standard fried onion rings on top.

light green bean casserole

prep: 15 minutes **bake:** 30 minutes **oven:** 350°F **makes:** 6 servings

1 10.75-ounce can reduced-fat and reduced-sodium cream of mushroom soup
¼ cup chopped roasted red sweet pepper or one 2-ounce jar diced pimiento, drained
¼ teaspoon salt
¼ teaspoon ground black pepper
3 9-ounce packages frozen French-cut green beans, thawed and drained
½ cup sliced almonds, toasted

1 Preheat oven to 350°F. In a large bowl combine soup, roasted sweet pepper, salt, and black pepper. Stir in green beans. Transfer mixture to an ungreased 2-quart rectangular baking dish. Sprinkle with toasted almonds.

2 Bake, uncovered, for 30 to 35 minutes or until heated through.

nutrition facts per serving: 128 cal., 5 g total fat, 1 mg chol., 286 mg sodium, 14 g carb., 5 g dietary fiber, 4 g protein.

zucchini crab cakes

start to finish: 30 minutes makes: 8 servings

2 teaspoons vegetable oil
1 cup coarsely shredded zucchini
¼ cup thinly sliced green onions (2)
1 egg, lightly beaten
⅓ cup seasoned fine dry bread crumbs
1 tablespoon Dijon-style mustard
1 teaspoon snipped fresh lemon thyme or thyme
⅛ to ¼ teaspoon cayenne pepper
1 cup cooked crabmeat, flaked, or one 6-ounce can crabmeat, drained, flaked, and cartilage removed
   Vegetable oil
8 ¼-inch slices red and/or yellow tomatoes
1 recipe Tomato-Sour Cream Sauce
   Thinly sliced green onions (optional)

1 In a medium skillet heat 2 teaspoons oil over medium-high heat. Add zucchini and ¼ cup green onions; cook for 3 to 5 minutes or just until vegetables are tender and liquid is evaporated, stirring occasionally. Cool slightly.

2 In a medium bowl combine egg, bread crumbs, mustard, thyme, and cayenne pepper. Add zucchini mixture and crabmeat; mix well. Using moistened hands, shape crab mixture into eight ½-inch-thick patties.

3 Lightly brush a grill pan or large skillet with additional oil; heat pan over medium heat. Add crab cakes; cook about 6 minutes or until heated through and golden brown, turning once. If cakes brown too quickly, reduce heat to medium low.

4 To serve, arrange crab cakes on top of tomato slices. Top with Tomato-Sour Cream Sauce and, if desired, sprinkle with additional green onions.

nutrition facts per serving: 98 cal., 5 g total fat (2 g sat. fat), 44 mg chol., 371 mg sodium, 6 g carb., 1 g dietary fiber, 7 g protein.

tomato-sour cream sauce: In a small bowl stir together ½ cup sour cream, 3 tablespoons finely chopped yellow tomato, 1 to 2 tablespoons lemon juice or lime juice, and ⅛ teaspoon seasoned salt. Makes ¾ cup.

chipotle-and-ranch-stuffed mushrooms

prep: 30 minutes **bake:** 10 minutes **oven:** 425°F **makes:** 24 appetizers

24 large fresh mushrooms (1½ to 2 inches in diameter)
⅓ cup finely chopped onion (1 small)
1 tablespoon olive oil
¾ cup frozen whole kernel corn, thawed and drained
1 8-ounce package reduced-fat cream cheese (Neufchâtel), softened
¼ cup light sour cream
1 1.0-ounce envelope ranch dry salad dressing mix
1 to 2 teaspoons finely chopped canned chipotle peppers in adobo sauce*
Snipped fresh cilantro (optional)

1 Preheat oven to 425°F. Remove stems from mushrooms. Finely chop stems; set aside. Place mushroom caps, stemmed sides down, in a 3-quart rectangular baking dish. Bake, uncovered, for 5 minutes; drain. Turn mushroom caps stemmed sides up.

2 Meanwhile, for filling, in a large skillet cook chopped mushroom stems and onion in hot oil over medium heat about 5 minutes or until tender, stirring occasionally. Add ½ cup of the corn; cook and stir for 1 minute. Stir in cream cheese, sour cream, salad dressing mix, and chipotle peppers. Cook and stir just until cream cheese is melted and smooth.

3 Spoon filling into mushroom caps, mounding slightly. Sprinkle with the remaining ¼ cup corn.

4 Bake for 10 to 15 minutes or until heated through. If desired, sprinkle with cilantro.

nutrition facts per appetizer: 46 cal., 3 g total fat (1 g sat. fat), 8 mg chol., 124 mg sodium, 3 g carb., 0 g dietary fiber, 2 g protein.

*tip: Because chile peppers contain volatile oils that can burn your skin and eyes, avoid direct contact with them as much as possible. When working with chile peppers, wear plastic or rubber gloves. If your bare hands do touch the peppers, wash your hands and nails well with soap and warm water.

tomato
crostini

prop: 20 minutes   stand: 20 minutes   broil: 4 minutes
makes: about 20 appetizers

1   cup seeded and
    chopped tomatoes
    (2 medium)
¼   cup finely chopped
    red onion
6   kalamata olives,
    pitted and finely
    chopped, or pitted
    ripe olives, finely
    chopped
1   tablespoon finely
    chopped poblano
    chile pepper*
1   tablespoon balsamic
    vinegar or red wine
    vinegar
1   clove garlic, minced
1   10-ounce loaf
    baguette-style
    French bread
5   ounces part-skim
    mozzarella cheese,
    thinly sliced

1 In a medium bowl stir together tomatoes, onion, olives, poblano chile pepper, vinegar, and garlic. Let stand at room temperature for 20 to 30 minutes to blend flavors, tossing occasionally.

2 Meanwhile, preheat broiler. Diagonally cut bread into ½-inch slices, discarding ends of loaf. Place bread slices on an extra-large baking sheet (use two large baking sheets if necessary). Broil, one sheet at a time if necessary, 3 to 4 inches from the heat for 2 to 3 minutes or until light brown, turning once halfway through broiling.

3 Divide cheese slices among toasted bread slices, cutting cheese to fit as necessary. Drain tomato mixture well. Spoon tomato mixture onto cheese-topped bread. Broil for 2 to 3 minutes more or until cheese is melted.

nutrition facts per appetizer: 64 cal., 2 g total fat (1 g sat. fat), 5 mg chol., 146 mg sodium, 9 g carb., 1 g dietary fiber, 3 g protein.

tip: Be sure to drain the tomato and olive mixture well to prevent the bread from becoming soggy.

*tip: Because chile peppers contain volatile oils that can burn your skin and eyes, avoid direct contact with them as much as possible. When working with chile peppers, wear plastic or rubber gloves. If your bare hands do touch the peppers, wash your hands and nails well with soap and warm water.

mushroom and goat cheese
phyllo triangles

prep: 1 hour stand: 30 minutes bake: 25 minutes oven: 350°F
makes: 36 appetizers

10 dried shiitake
    mushrooms
    Boiling water
 2 tablespoons butter
 1 clove garlic, minced
 3 cups finely chopped
    fresh button or
    cremini mushrooms
    (8 ounces)
 8 ounces soft goat
    cheese (chèvre)
 2 tablespoons snipped
    fresh parsley
 ½ teaspoon freshly
    ground black
    pepper
 ⅛ teaspoon salt
18 sheets frozen phyllo
    dough (14x9-inch
    rectangles), thawed
 ½ cup butter, melted

1 In a small bowl combine dried mushrooms and enough boiling water to cover. Let stand at room temperature about 30 minutes or until softened; drain. Rinse mushrooms; drain again. Remove and discard stems; finely chop mushroom caps.

2 For filling, in a large skillet heat 2 tablespoons butter over medium heat until melted. Add garlic; cook and stir for 15 seconds. Add chopped shiitake mushrooms and button mushrooms; cook about 10 minutes or until mushrooms are tender and liquid is evaporated, stirring occasionally. Remove from heat. Stir in cheese, parsley, pepper, and salt. Remove from heat; cool slightly.

3 Preheat oven to 350°F. Line a large baking sheet with parchment paper or foil; set aside. Unfold phyllo dough; place one sheet on a cutting board or other flat surface. Lightly brush with some of the melted butter. Place another sheet of phyllo on top; brush with butter. (Keep the remaining phyllo covered with plastic wrap until needed.)

4 Using a pizza cutter, cut the two layered sheets lengthwise into four 2¼-inch strips. Spoon a scant 1 tablespoon of the filling about 1 inch from an end of each dough strip. To fold into a triangle, bring a corner over filling so the short edge lines up with the side edge. Continue folding the triangular shape along the strip until the end is reached. Repeat with the remaining phyllo, butter, and filling.

5 Place triangles on the prepared baking sheet. Bake about 25 minutes or until light brown. Serve warm.

nutrition facts per appetizer: 72 cal., 5 g total fat (3 g sat. fat), 14 mg chol., 100 mg sodium, 4 g carb., 0 g dietary fiber, 2 g protein.

edamame **wontons**
prep: 50 minutes bake: 12 minutes oven: 400°F makes: 28 appetizers

1 teaspoon toasted
sesame oil
1 teaspoon canola oil or
olive oil
1 clove garlic, minced
1 12-ounce package
frozen shelled
sweet soybeans
(edamame)
Nonstick cooking
spray
⅓ cup thinly sliced
green onions
1 tablespoon hoisin
sauce
1 tablespoon reduced-
sodium soy sauce
28 wonton wrappers
Light teriyaki sauce
or Chinese-style hot
mustard (optional)

1 In a large skillet heat sesame oil and canola oil over medium-high heat. Add garlic; cook and stir for 15 seconds. Add frozen edamame; cook and stir for 5 to 7 minutes or until tender and starting to brown. Remove from heat; cool slightly.

2 Preheat oven to 400°F. Lightly coat a large baking sheet with cooking spray; set aside. For filling, in a food processor combine edamame mixture, green onions, hoisin sauce, and soy sauce. Cover and process until nearly smooth and mixture clings together, stopping to scrape down side as necessary.

3 Spoon about 1 tablespoon of the filling into the center of each wonton wrapper. Brush edges of wrapper with a little water. Fold one corner of wrapper to opposite corner to form a triangle; press edges to seal.

4 Arrange wonton triangles on the prepared baking sheet. Lightly coat triangles with cooking spray. Bake for 12 to 14 minutes or until triangles are crisp and golden brown. Serve warm. If desired, serve with teriyaki sauce.

nutrition facts per appetizer: 42 cal., 1 g total fat (0 g sat. fat), 1 mg chol., 77 mg sodium, 6 g carb., 1 g dietary fiber, 2 g protein.

oven method: Preheat oven to 450°F. Prepare Roasted Cherry Tomatoes as directed, except use a 13x9x2-inch baking pan. Bake for 10 to 12 minutes or until tomatoes are wilted, stirring occasionally. Prepare dough circles as directed, brush with oil mixture, and place on lightly greased baking sheets. Bake for 7 minutes; turn and top with cheese. Bake about 2 minutes more or until dough is cooked through and cheese is melted. Serve as directed.

These tasty little pizzas have a crisp texture when grilled and are chewy-crisp when baked. Look for frozen pizza dough among frozen breakfast pastries and baked goods.

roasted cherry tomato pizza poppers

prep: 1 hour grill: 4 minutes per batch makes: 56 to 60 appetizers

1   recipe Roasted
    Cherry Tomatoes
2   1-pound loaves
    frozen pizza dough,
    thawed
¼   cup olive oil
1   teaspoon dried basil,
    crushed
1   teaspoon dried
    oregano, crushed
12 to 14 ounces sliced
    mozzarella or
    provolone cheese,
    cut into 2-inch
    pieces
    Small fresh basil
    leaves (optional)

1 Prepare Roasted Cherry Tomatoes.

2 Meanwhile, on a lightly floured surface, roll pizza dough, one loaf at a time, into a 15x12-inch rectangle (if dough becomes difficult to roll, cover and let rest occasionally). Cover and let rest for 10 minutes. Using a 2- to 2½-inch round cutter, cut out circles; discard trimmings. Place dough circles on lightly greased baking sheets. In a small bowl combine oil, dried basil, and oregano; brush over both sides of dough circles. Prick circles all over with a fork.

3 For a charcoal grill with a cover, place dough circles, about 12 at a time,* on the well-greased grill rack directly over medium coals. Cover and grill for 2 minutes. Carefully turn circles and press down lightly to flatten. Top each with a piece of cheese. Cover and grill about 2 minutes more or until dough is cooked through and cheese is melted. Remove from grill; keep warm. Repeat with the remaining dough circles and cheese. (For a gas grill, preheat grill. Reduce heat to medium. Place dough circles on well-greased grill rack over heat. Cover and grill as above.)

4 Top dough circles with tomatoes and, if desired, basil leaves. Serve warm or at room temperature.

nutrition facts per appetizer: 64 cal., 2 g total fat (1 g sat. fat), 3 mg chol., 104 mg sodium, 8 g carb., 0 g dietary fiber, 2 g protein.

*tip: So dough circles do not overcook on the grill, it's best to grill a dozen or so at a time.

roasted cherry tomatoes: In a 13½x9½x3-inch disposable foil pan combine 4 cups red and/or yellow cherry or grape tomatoes, halved and/or quartered; 1 tablespoon olive oil; 2 teaspoons balsamic vinegar; 2 to 4 cloves garlic, minced; and ½ teaspoon dried oregano, crushed, or 1 teaspoon snipped fresh oregano. For a charcoal grill with or without a cover, place tomatoes in pan on the grill rack directly over medium coals. Grill, uncovered, for 8 to 9 minutes or until tomatoes are wilted, stirring occasionally. (For a gas grill, preheat grill. Reduce heat to medium. Place tomatoes in pan on grill rack over heat. Cover and grill as above.)

avocado pesto– stuffed tomatoes

prep: 40 minutes   stand: 30 minutes   makes: 30 appetizers

30	cherry tomatoes (about 2½ cups)
½	of a medium avocado, seeded, peeled, and cut up
2	ounces cream cheese, softened
2	tablespoons basil pesto
1	teaspoon lemon juice
	Snipped fresh basil (optional)
	Coarse ground black pepper (optional)

1 Cut a thin slice from the top of each tomato. If desired, cut a thin slice from the bottom of each tomato so it stands upright. Using a small spoon or melon baller, carefully hollow out tomatoes; invert onto paper towels. Let stand for 30 minutes to drain.

2 Meanwhile, for filling, in a food processor combine avocado, cream cheese, pesto, and lemon juice. Cover and process until smooth. If desired, spoon filling into a decorating bag fitted with a large plain round or open star tip.

3 Pipe or spoon filling into tomato cups and arrange on a serving platter. Serve immediately or cover loosely and chill for up to 4 hours. If desired, sprinkle with basil and pepper before serving.

nutrition facts per appetizer: 18 cal., 1 g total fat (1 g sat. fat), 2 mg chol., 16 mg sodium, 1 g carb., 0 g dietary fiber, 0 g protein.

Any cooking apple will work here, but Pink Lady, also known as the Crisp Pink variety of apple, adds a pink blush to this sauce. This sauce also pairs well with pork, turkey, or chicken.

chunky apple-sage appetizer

prep: 15 minutes cook: 10 minutes makes: 12 appetizers

¼ cup finely chopped
    red onion
1 tablespoon olive oil
2 cups chopped
    cooking apples,
    such as Pink Lady
    (3 medium)
2 tablespoons snipped
    fresh sage or
    2 teaspoons dried
    sage, crushed, or
    1 tablespoon
    snipped fresh
    thyme or 1 teaspoon
    dried thyme,
    crushed
2 tablespoons dried
    cranberries
1 tablespoon apple
    brandy (optional)
12 crisp flatbreads,
    large whole wheat
    crackers, or toasted
    pita wedges
6 tablespoons shredded
    reduced-fat sharp
    white cheddar
    cheese or Parmesan
    cheese

1 In a medium saucepan cook onion in hot oil over medium heat for 2 to 3 minutes or until softened, stirring occasionally. Stir in apples, sage, and dried cranberries.

2 Cook, covered, over medium heat for 10 to 12 minutes or until apples are softened, stirring occasionally. Remove from heat. If desired, stir in apple brandy. Cool slightly.

3 Spoon warm apple mixture onto flatbreads. Sprinkle with cheese.

nutrition facts per appetizer: 87 cal, 4 g total fat (1 g sat. fat), 1 mg chol., 66 mg sodium, 9 g carb., 2 g dietary fiber, 4 g protein.

make-ahead directions: Prepare as directed through Step 2. Cover and chill for up to 6 hours. Let stand at room temperature for 20 minutes before serving. Serve as directed.

sugar 'n' spice fruit dip

start to finish: 15 minutes makes: 1¼ cups

½   cup light cream
     cheese spread,
     softened*

½   cup light sour cream*

¼   cup low-sugar
     raspberry preserves
     or orange marmalade

1   teaspoon finely
     shredded lemon
     peel or orange peel
     (optional)

¼   teaspoon ground
     cinnamon, nutmeg,
     or allspice
     Ground cinnamon,
     nutmeg, or allspice
     (optional)
     Desired dippers,
     such as raspberries,
     clementine
     orange segments,
     individually
     wrapped 60-calorie
     dark chocolate
     sticks, cut-up
     peeled kiwifruit,
     apple slices, pear
     slices, and/or
     banana slices

1 In a medium bowl combine cream cheese and sour cream. Beat with an electric mixer on medium speed until smooth. Stir in preserves, lemon peel (if using), and ¼ teaspoon cinnamon.

2 Transfer dip to a serving bowl. If desired, sprinkle with additional cinnamon. Serve dip with desired dippers.

nutrition facts per 2 tablespoons dip: 47 cal., 3 g total fat (2 g sat. fat), 9 mg chol., 67 mg sodium, 4 g carb., 0 g dietary fiber, 2 g protein.

*tip: If desired, substitute Yogurt Cheese for the cream cheese and sour cream.

**tip: Use a brand of yogurt that contains no gums, gelatin, or fillers. These ingredients may prevent the whey from separating from the curd to make cheese.

yogurt cheese: Line a yogurt strainer, sieve, or a small colander with three layers of 100-percent-cotton cheesecloth or a clean paper coffee filter. Suspend lined strainer, sieve, or colander over a bowl. Spoon in one 16-ounce carton plain yogurt.** Cover with plastic wrap and chill for at least 24 hours. Discard liquid. Store cheese, covered, in the refrigerator for up to 1 week. Makes about 1 cup.

As you are grocery shopping, keep an eye out for salt-free seasoning blends in the herb and spice aisle. They're terrific for adding lots of flavor but very little sodium to a variety of foods.

pine nut–white
bean dip

prep: 15 minutes chill: 2 hours makes: 1½ cups

¼ cup soft bread crumbs

2 tablespoons fat-free milk

1 15-ounce can cannellini beans (white kidney beans) or Great Northern beans, rinsed and drained

¼ cup fat-free or light sour cream

3 tablespoons pine nuts, toasted

¼ teaspoon salt-free garlic and herb seasoning blend or other salt-free seasoning blend

⅛ teaspoon cayenne pepper

2 teaspoons snipped fresh oregano or basil or ½ teaspoon dried oregano or basil, crushed
Pine nuts, toasted (optional)
Fresh oregano or basil leaves (optional)
Assorted vegetable dippers

1 In a small bowl combine bread crumbs and milk. Let stand, covered, for 5 minutes.

2 Meanwhile, in a blender or food processor combine beans, sour cream, 3 tablespoons pine nuts, seasoning blend, and cayenne pepper. Cover and blend or process until nearly smooth. Add bread crumb mixture. Cover and blend or process until smooth. Stir in 2 teaspoons oregano. Transfer to a serving bowl. Cover and chill for 2 hours to blend flavors.

3 If desired, sprinkle with additional pine nuts and garnish with oregano leaves. Serve dip with vegetable dippers.

nutrition facts per 2 tablespoons dip: 40 cal., 1 g total fat (0 g sat. fat), 1 mg chol., 70 mg sodium, 7 g carb., 2 g dietary fiber, 3 g protein.

make-ahead directions: Prepare as directed, except cover and chill for up to 24 hours before serving.

quick

lower sodium

424

special occasions

quick

lower sodium

herbed cheese mini peppers

start to finish: 25 minutes makes: 20 appetizers

10 red, yellow, and/or orange miniature sweet peppers (6 to 8 ounces total)
1 8-ounce package reduced-fat cream cheese (Neufchâtel), softened
1 to 2 tablespoons snipped fresh oregano, rosemary, tarragon, or thyme, or ½ to 1 teaspoon dried oregano, rosemary, tarragon, or thyme, crushed
1 tablespoon lemon juice
1 tablespoon milk
Finely shredded lemon peel
Fresh oregano leaves (optional)

1 Cut each sweet pepper in half lengthwise; remove seeds. Set peppers aside.

2 In a small bowl stir together cream cheese, desired herb, lemon juice, and 1 tablespoon milk. If necessary, stir in enough additional milk to reach piping consistency.

3 Pipe or spoon cream cheese mixture into pepper halves. Sprinkle with lemon peel and, if desired, oregano leaves.

nutrition facts per appetizer: 32 cal., 3 g total fat (2 g sat. fat), 9 mg chol., 46 mg sodium, 1 g carb., 0 g dietary fiber, 1 g protein.

make-ahead directions: Prepare as directed, except cover and chill for up to 4 hours before serving.

edamame-avocado dip

start to finish: 20 minutes makes: 2½ cups

1 12-ounce package frozen shelled sweet soybeans (edamame), thawed
1 medium avocado, seeded, peeled, and cut up
¼ cup chopped onion
3 tablespoons lemon juice
2 tablespoons basil pesto
¾ teaspoon sea salt or kosher salt
¼ teaspoon freshly ground black pepper
Chopped tomato (optional)
Sea salt (optional)
Freshly ground black pepper (optional)
Pita chips or tortilla chips

1 In a food processor combine edamame, avocado, onion, lemon juice, pesto, ¾ teaspoon salt, and ¼ teaspoon pepper. Cover and process until nearly smooth. Transfer dip to a serving bowl.

2 If desired, top with tomato and additional salt and pepper. Serve dip with pita chips.

nutrition facts per 2 tablespoons dip: 48 cal., 3 g total fat (0 g sat. fat), 0 mg chol., 74 mg sodium, 3 g carb., 1 g dietary fiber, 2 g protein.

nutrition note

Bringing this dip to a gathering? Instead of a serving spoon, tuck in a 1-tablespoon measuring spoon to help you keep an eye on portion size.

original lime margarita
start to finish: 10 minutes makes: 2 servings

1 In a pitcher combine carbonated beverage, limeade, tequila, and triple sec. Divide ice between two margarita glasses. Pour tequila mixture over ice. Garnish with lime wedges.

⅔ cup diet lemon-lime carbonated beverage
⅔ cup light limeade
¼ cup (2 ounces) tequila
2 tablespoons (1 ounce) triple sec or desired orange liqueur
1½ cups ice cubes or crushed ice
2 lime wedges

nutrition facts per serving: 110 cal., 0 g total fat (0 g sat. fat), 0 mg chol., 25 mg sodium, 7 g carb., 0 g dietary fiber, 0 g protein.

nutrition note
Alcohol contains 7 calories per gram, almost as much as the 9 calories per gram that fat carries. So if you're watching your waistline, it's also important to watch your bar tab.

frosty mint cocktail

prep: 20 minutes   freeze: 12 hours   stand: 30 minutes
makes: 10 to 12 (12-ounce) servings

1   cup water
⅔   cup sugar
½   cup loosely packed
     fresh mint leaves
3   cups orange juice
1   6-ounce can
     unsweetened
     pineapple juice
⅓   cup lemon juice
     Small fresh mint
     leaves (optional)
1   1-liter bottle lemon-
     lime carbonated
     beverage or five to
     six 6-ounce bottles
     sparkling water
     with lemon flavor,
     chilled

1 In a small saucepan combine the water, sugar, and ½ cup mint leaves. Bring to boiling, reduce heat. Simmer, uncovered, for 2 minutes. Remove from heat. Strain through a fine-mesh sieve; discard mint leaves.

2 Pour sugar mixture into a 2-quart square baking dish. Stir in orange juice, pineapple juice, and lemon juice. Cover and freeze for at least 12 hours or until completely frozen.

3 To serve, let frozen mixture stand at room temperature for 30 minutes. Using a large metal spoon, scrape the top of the mixture to form a slush. Spoon slush into ten to twelve 12-ounce glasses, filling each glass half full. If desired, add additional mint leaves. Slowly pour carbonated beverage over slush. Serve immediately.

nutrition facts per serving: 134 cal., 0 g total fat (0 g sat. fat), 0 mg chol., 23 mg sodium, 34 g carb., 0 g dietary fiber, 1 g protein.

Orange and lime juices are included in this version of the Spanish red wine beverage.

sangria

prep: 10 minutes chill: 3 to 24 hours makes: 10 (about 4-ounce) servings

1 cup orange juice
¼ cup lime juice
1 750-milliliter bottle
  dry red wine
¼ to ⅓ cup sugar
  Ice cubes
  Small orange or lime
  wedges (optional)

1 In a large pitcher stir together orange juice and lime juice. Add wine and sugar, stirring until sugar is dissolved. Cover and chill for 3 to 24 hours.

2 Serve juice mixture over ice cubes. If desired, garnish each serving with an orange wedge.

nutrition facts per serving: 85 cal., 0 g total fat (0 g sat. fat), 0 mg chol., 4 mg sodium, 9 g carb., 0 g dietary fiber, 0 g protein.

white peach sangria

prep: 10 minutes chill: 4 to 24 hours makes: 10 (about 4-ounce) servings

1 cup peach juice blend
2 tablespoons orange
  juice
2 tablespoons lime
  juice
1 750-milliliter bottle
  dry white wine
2 medium white and/
  or yellow peaches,
  pitted and sliced
  Ice cubes
  Halved lime slices
  (optional)

1 In a large pitcher stir together peach juice, orange juice, and lime juice. Stir in wine and peach slices. Cover and chill for 4 to 24 hours.

2 Serve juice mixture over ice cubes. If desired, garnish each serving with a lime slice.

nutrition facts per serving: 91 cal., 0 g total fat (0 g sat. fat), 0 mg chol., 5 mg sodium, 9 g carb., 0 g dietary fiber, 0 g protein.

White Peach Sangria

sour apple martini
start to finish: 5 minutes makes: 2 servings

2 maraschino cherries
 with stems
⅓ cup (about 3 ounces)
 sour apple schnapps
2 tablespoons (1 ounce)
 vodka or gin
 Ice cubes
 Diet lemon-lime
 carbonated
 beverage, chilled

1 Divide cherries between two 4-ounce
martini glasses; set aside.

2 In a cocktail shaker combine schnapps and
vodka. Add ice cubes to fill shaker half full;
cover and shake until very cold.

3 Strain vodka mixture into the prepared
martini glasses. Slowly pour carbonated
beverage into glasses.

nutrition facts per serving: 147 cal., 0 g total fat
(0 g sat. fat), 0 mg chol., 12 mg sodium, 14 g carb.,
0 g dietary fiber, 0 g protein.

chocolate milkshake cocktail

start to finish: 20 minutes makes: 4 servings

Coarse sugar
Unsweetened cocoa
   powder
Orange wedges or
   lime wedges
1   cup light chocolate or
    chocolate chip ice
    cream
1⅓ cups fat-free
    chocolate milk
1   teaspoon vanilla
¼   teaspoon peppermint
    extract or 2 drops
    almond extract
    (optional)
½   ounce chocolate curls
4   maraschino cherries

1 Place sugar in a shallow dish; place cocoa powder in another shallow dish. Rub orange wedges around rims of four chilled martini glasses. Dip rims in sugar, then in cocoa powder. Divide ice cream among the prepared martini glasses.

2 In a small pitcher combine chocolate milk, vanilla, and peppermint extract (if using). Pour milk mixture over ice cream. Garnish with chocolate curls and cherries.

nutrition facts per serving: 151 cal., 4 g total fat (2 g sat. fat), 15 mg chol., 93 mg sodium, 25 g carb., 1 g dietary fiber, 5 g protein.

chocolate coffee milkshake cocktail: Prepare as directed, except reduce chocolate milk to ⅔ cup and add ½ cup cold, strong brewed coffee to milk mixture. Omit peppermint or almond extract. If desired, substitute coffee ice cream for the chocolate or chocolate chip ice cream.

per serving: 128 cal., 4 g total fat (2 g sat. fat), 14 mg chol., 68 mg sodium, 21 g carb., 1 g dietary fiber, 3 g protein.

no-guilt

des

Get out your magic wand. This selection of sweets—each weighing in at 200 calories or less per serving—is positively enchanting.

triple **chocolate** cookies

prep: 40 minutes stand: 20 minutes bake: 9 minutes per batch
freeze: 4 minutes oven: 350°F makes: 60 cookies

7	ounces bittersweet chocolate, chopped
5	ounces unsweetened chocolate, chopped
½	cup butter
⅓	cup all-purpose flour
¼	teaspoon baking powder
¼	teaspoon salt
1	cup granulated sugar
¾	cup packed brown sugar
4	eggs
¼	cup finely chopped pecans, toasted
1	recipe Chocolate Drizzle

1 In a 2-quart saucepan combine chocolates and butter. Heat and stir over low heat until melted and mixture is smooth. Remove from heat; let cool for 10 minutes. In a small bowl stir together flour, baking powder, and salt; set aside.

2 In a large bowl combine granulated sugar, brown sugar, and eggs. Beat with an electric mixer on medium to high speed for 2 to 3 minutes or until color lightens slightly. Beat in melted chocolate until combined. Add flour mixture to chocolate mixture. Beat until combined. Stir in pecans. Cover surface of cookie dough with plastic wrap. Let stand for 20 minutes (dough thickens as it stands).

3 Preheat oven to 350°F. Line cookie sheets with parchment paper or foil. Drop dough by rounded teaspoons 2 inches apart on prepared cookie sheets.

4 Bake about 9 minutes or just until tops are set. Let stand for 1 minute on cookie sheet. Transfer to a wire rack; cool completely.

5 Place cooled cookies on a cookie sheet lined with parchment or waxed paper. Spoon Chocolate Drizzle over cookies. Place the entire cookie sheet in the freezer for 4 to 5 minutes or until chocolate is firm.

nutrition facts per cookie: 92 cal., 6 g total fat (3 g sat. fat), 18 mg chol., 19 mg sodium, 11 g carb., 1 g dietary fiber, 1 g protein.

chocolate drizzle: In a small saucepan combine 1 cup semisweet chocolate pieces with 4 teaspoons shortening. Heat and stir over low heat until the chocolate melts and mixture is smooth. Remove from heat. Drizzle while still warm. Makes about 1 cup.

Bright red maraschino cherries, buried in a chocolaty dough, provide a tasty surprise.

chocolate-cherry
cookies

prep: 30 minutes   bake: 10 minutes per batch   oven: 350°F
makes: 42 to 48 cookies

1   10-ounce jar
    maraschino cherries
    (42 to 48)
½   cup butter, softened
1   cup sugar
¼   teaspoon baking
    powder
¼   teaspoon baking soda
¼   teaspoon salt
1   egg
1½ teaspoons vanilla
½   cup unsweetened
    cocoa powder
1½ cups all-purpose flour
1   cup semisweet
    chocolate pieces
½   cup sweetened
    condensed milk

1 Preheat oven to 350°F. Drain cherries, reserving juice. Halve any large cherries. In a medium bowl beat butter with an electric mixer on medium to high speed for 30 seconds. Add sugar, baking powder, baking soda, and salt. Beat until combined, scraping sides of bowl occasionally. Beat in egg and vanilla until combined. Beat in cocoa powder until combined. Beat in as much of the flour as you can with the mixer. Stir in any remaining flour.

2 Shape dough into 1-inch balls. Place about 2 inches apart on an ungreased cookie sheet. Using your thumb, make an indentation in the center of each ball. Place a cherry in each center.

3 For frosting, in a small saucepan heat and stir chocolate pieces and sweetened condensed milk over low heat until mixture is smooth. Stir in 4 teaspoons of the reserved cherry juice. (Thin frosting with additional cherry juice, if necessary.) Spoon about 1 teaspoon of the frosting over each cherry, spreading to cover.

4 Bake about 10 minutes or until edges are firm. Let stand for 1 minute on cookie sheet. Transfer to a wire rack; cool completely.

nutrition facts per cookie: 97 cal., 4 g total fat (2 g sat. fat), 13 mg chol., 56 mg sodium, 14 g carb., 0 g dietary fiber, 1 g protein.

chipotle-chocolate
brownies

prep: 25 minutes bake: 35 minutes oven: 325°F makes: 32 brownies

8	ounces semisweet chocolate, chopped
1	cup butter
2	cups all-purpose flour
¼	cup unsweetened Dutch-process cocoa powder
2½	cups sugar
1	tablespoon instant espresso coffee powder or instant coffee crystals
1½	teaspoons ground cinnamon
1	to 2 teaspoons ground chipotle chile pepper
2	teaspoons vanilla
6	eggs
	Unsweetened Dutch-process cocoa powder

1 Preheat oven to 325°F. Line a 13x9x2-inch baking pan with foil, extending the foil over the edges of the pan. Grease foil; set pan aside. In a small saucepan combine semisweet chocolate and butter; cook and stir over low heat until melted and mixture is smooth. Cool slightly. In a small bowl combine flour and ¼ cup cocoa powder; set aside.

2 In a large bowl combine sugar, coffee powder, cinnamon, and ground chipotle pepper. Add cooled chocolate mixture and vanilla. Beat with an electric mixer on medium speed for 1 minute, scraping sides of bowl occasionally. Add eggs, one at a time, beating on low speed just until combined. Add flour mixture, ½ cup at a time, beating after each addition just until combined. Beat on medium speed for 1 minute more. Spread batter evenly into prepared baking pan.

3 Bake for 35 to 40 minutes or until edges start to pull away from sides of pan. Cool in pan on a wire rack. Using the foil, lift uncut brownies from pan. Cut into bars. Sift additional cocoa powder over tops of brownies.

nutrition facts per brownie: 194 cal., 9 g total fat (5 g sat. fat), 55 mg chol., 55 mg sodium, 26 g carb., 1 g dietary fiber, 3 g protein.

chocolate–peanut
butter bars

prep: 25 minutes   bake: 20 minutes   oven: 350°F   makes: 36 bars

⅔ cup butter, softened
1 cup packed
   brown sugar
1 egg
2 teaspoons vanilla
½ teaspoon salt
2 cups all-purpose flour
1 12-ounce package
   semisweet
   chocolate pieces
3 tablespoons butter
¼ cup hot strong coffee
¼ cup reduced-fat
   peanut butter
1 cup powdered sugar

1 Preheat oven to 350°F. Lightly grease a 15x10x1-inch baking pan or line the pan with foil or parchment; set aside.

2 For cookie base, in a large bowl beat ⅔ cup butter with an electric mixer on medium to high for 30 seconds. Beat in brown sugar until combined, scraping sides of bowl occasionally. Beat in egg, vanilla, and salt until combined. Beat in as much flour as you can with the mixer. Stir in any remaining flour. Spread dough evenly in prepared pan.

3 Bake for 20 to 22 minutes or until edges are golden brown. Cool in pan completely on a wire rack.

4 For frosting, in a small saucepan combine chocolate and 3 tablespoons butter; cook and stir over low heat until melted and mixture is smooth. Remove from heat. Transfer chocolate mixture to a medium bowl. Whisk in coffee and peanut butter until combined. Whisk in powdered sugar until smooth. Spread frosting on cookie base. Let stand until frosting is set. Cut into bars.

nutrition facts per bar: 159 cal., 8 g total fat (5 g sat. fat), 17 mg chol., 79 mg sodium, 21 g carb., 1 g dietary fiber, 2 g protein.

peanut butter–
banana drops

prep: 20 minutes   bake: 8 minutes per batch   oven: 375°F
makes: about 40 cookies

1   16.5-ounce roll
    refrigerated peanut
    butter cookie dough
1   cup dried banana
    chips, coarsely
    crushed
1   cup semisweet
    chocolate pieces
¼   cup turbinado sugar,
    Demorara sugar,
    or colored coarse
    sugar

1 Preheat oven to 375°F. In a large bowl combine cookie dough, banana chips, and chocolate pieces. If necessary, knead dough until well mixed.

2 Place sugar in a small bowl. Shape dough into 1-inch balls. Roll balls in sugar to coat. Place 2 inches apart on an ungreased cookie sheet. Flatten balls slightly.

3 Bake for 8 to 10 minutes or until edges are golden brown. Transfer cookies to a wire rack; cool completely.

nutrition facts per cookie: 87 cal., 5 g total fat (2 g sat. fat), 3 mg chol., 47 mg sodium, 11 g carb., 0 g dietary fiber, 1 g protein.

to store: Layer cookies between waxed paper in an airtight container; cover. Store at room temperature for up to 3 days or freeze for up to 3 months.

raspberry and white chocolate brownies

prep: 30 minutes   bake: 35 minutes   oven: 350°F   makes: 20 brownies

½   cup butter
2   ounces white baking
     chocolate, chopped
⅔   cup sugar
2   eggs
1   teaspoon vanilla
1   cup all-purpose flour
½   cup chopped
     almonds, toasted
½   teaspoon baking
     powder
     Dash salt
1   cup fresh raspberries
2   ounces white baking
     chocolate, melted
     Fresh raspberries
     (optional)

1 In a medium saucepan heat and stir butter and the 2 ounces chopped white chocolate over low heat until melted and mixture is smooth; set aside to cool.

2 Preheat oven to 350°F. Line an 8x8x2-inch baking pan with foil, extending the foil over edges of pan. Grease foil; set pan aside.

3 Stir sugar into the cooled chocolate mixture. Add eggs, one at a time, beating with a wooden spoon just until combined. Stir in vanilla. In a small bowl stir together flour, almonds, baking powder, and salt. Add flour mixture to chocolate mixture; stir just until combined. Spread batter evenly in prepared pan. Sprinkle with the 1 cup raspberries.

4 Bake for 35 minutes. Cool in pan on a wire rack. Drizzle with the 2 ounces melted white chocolate.

5 Using the edges of the foil, lift uncut brownies out of pan. Cut into bars. Serve brownies the same day prepared with, if desired, additional raspberries.

nutrition facts per brownie: 146 cal., 8 g total fat (4 g sat. fat), 34 mg chol., 62 mg sodium, 16 g carb., 1 g dietary fiber, 2 g protein.

coconut macaroons

prep: 30 minutes bake: 20 minutes oven: 325°F makes: about 60 cookies

4 egg whites
1 teaspoon vanilla
¼ teaspoon cream of tartar
⅛ teaspoon salt
1⅓ cups sugar
1 14-ounce package flaked coconut (5⅓ cups)

1 Preheat oven to 325°F. Line cookie sheets with parchment paper; set aside. In a very large bowl beat egg whites, vanilla, cream of tartar, and salt with an electric mixer on high speed until soft peaks form (tips curl). Gradually add sugar, about 1 tablespoon at a time, beating until stiff peaks form (tips stand straight). Fold in coconut, half at a time.

2 Drop mixture from a teaspoon 1 inch apart into small mounds on prepared cookie sheets.*

3 Bake for 20 to 25 minutes or until bottoms are light brown. Transfer cookies to a wire rack and let cool.

nutrition facts per cookie: 49 cal., 2 g total fat (2 g sat. fat), 0 mg chol., 29 mg sodium, 7 g carb., 0 g dietary fiber, 1 g protein.

*tip: If you cannot use all the cookie mixture at once, cover and chill while first batch of cookies are baking.

snickerdoodles

prep: 25 minutes   chill: 1 to 2 hours   bake: 10 minutes per batch   oven: 375°F
makes: about 48 cookies

⅓ cup butter, softened
1 cup sugar
1 teaspoon baking
   powder
½ teaspoon ground
   nutmeg
¼ teaspoon baking soda
⅓ cup fat-free sour
   cream
1 egg, lightly beaten
1 teaspoon vanilla
2 cups all-purpose flour
   Nonstick cooking
   spray
2 tablespoons sugar
2 teaspoons
   unsweetened cocoa
   powder (optional)

1 In a large bowl beat butter with an electric mixer on medium to high speed for 30 seconds. Add the 1 cup sugar, baking powder, nutmeg, and baking soda. Beat until combined, scraping sides of bowl occasionally. Beat in sour cream, egg, and vanilla until combined. Beat in as much of the flour as you can with the mixer. Stir in any remaining flour. Cover and chill dough for 1 to 2 hours or until dough is easy to handle.

2 Preheat oven to 375°F. Lightly coat cookie sheets with cooking spray; set aside. In a small bowl combine the 2 tablespoons sugar and cocoa powder (if using). Shape dough into 1-inch balls. Roll balls in sugar or sugar-cocoa mixture to coat. Place balls about 2 inches apart on prepared cookie sheets.

3 Bake for 10 to 11 minutes or until edges are light brown. Transfer cookies to a wire rack; cool completely.

nutrition facts per cookie: 53 cal., 1 g total fat (1 g sat. fat), 8 mg chol., 25 mg sodium, 9 g carb., 0 g dietary fiber, 0 g protein.

toffee–pumpkin
pie bars

prep: 30 minutes bake: 40 minutes oven: 375°F makes: 32 bars

1 recipe Ginger Crumb
    Crust
1 15-ounce can pumpkin
¾ cup packed brown
    sugar
1 teaspoon ground
    cinnamon
¾ teaspoon ground
    ginger
½ teaspoon salt
¼ teaspoon ground
    cloves
4 eggs, lightly beaten
1½ cups half-and-half or
    light cream
½ cup toffee pieces
½ cup chopped pecans,
    toasted
    Caramel-flavor ice
    cream topping
    (optional)

1 Preheat oven to 375°F. Line a 13x9x2-inch baking pan with foil, extending the foil over the edges of the pan. Lightly grease foil. Press the Ginger Crumb Crust evenly and firmly onto bottom of prepared pan; set aside.

2 For filling, in a large bowl combine pumpkin, brown sugar, cinnamon, ginger, salt, and cloves. Add eggs; beat lightly with a fork until combined. Gradually add half-and-half; stir just until combined. Pour filling into crust-lined pan.

3 Bake for 40 to 45 minutes or until a knife inserted near the center comes out clean. Sprinkle top with toffee pieces and pecans. Cool in pan on a wire rack.

4 Using the foil, lift uncut bars out of pan. Cut into bars. Cover and chill within 2 hours. If desired, drizzle with caramel topping just before serving.

nutrition facts per bar: 145 cal., 8 g total fat (4 g sat. fat), 41 mg chol., 139 mg sodium, 17 g carb., 1 g dietary fiber, 2 g protein.

ginger crumb crust: In a medium bowl combine 2 cups crushed gingersnaps (about 35 cookies), ¼ cup sugar, and ¼ cup all-purpose flour. Add ½ cup melted butter and stir until well combined.

to store: Place bars in a single layer in an airtight container; cover. Store in the refrigerator for up to 2 days. Do not freeze.

Espresso coffee powder and bittersweet chocolate make this dense cake extra rich.

bittersweet chocolate cake with berries

prep: 25 minutes bake: 30 minutes oven: 350°F makes: 12 servings

Nonstick cooking
   spray
¾ cup sugar
½ cup water
1 tablespoon instant
   espresso coffee
   powder or
   2 tablespoons
   instant coffee
   powder
3 ounces bittersweet
   or semisweet
   chocolate, chopped
2 egg yolks
1 teaspoon vanilla
½ cup unsweetened
   cocoa powder
⅓ cup all-purpose flour
¼ teaspoon baking
   powder
5 egg whites
   Unsweetened cocoa
   powder (optional)
½ of an 8-ounce
   container frozen
   light whipped
   dessert topping,
   thawed
1½ cups fresh
   raspberries,
   blackberries, and/or
   blueberries

1 Preheat oven to 350°F. Lightly coat a 9-inch springform pan with cooking spray; set aside. In a medium saucepan stir together sugar, the water, and espresso coffee powder. Cook and stir over medium-low heat until the sugar dissolves and mixture almost boils. Stir in the chocolate until melted. Remove from heat.

2 Place eggs yolks in a small bowl; gradually stir chocolate mixture into egg yolks. Stir in vanilla (mixture may appear slightly grainy); set aside.

3 In a medium bowl stir together ½ cup cocoa powder, flour, and baking powder. Stir in chocolate-egg yolk mixture until smooth.

4 In a large bowl beat egg whites with an electric mixer on medium speed until stiff peaks form (tips stand straight). Stir a small amount of the beaten egg whites into the chocolate mixture to lighten. Gently fold chocolate mixture into remaining egg whites. Spread batter into the prepared pan.

5 Bake about 30 minutes or until the top springs back when lightly touched. Cool in pan on a wire rack for 10 minutes. Loosen and remove sides of pan. Cool completely. (Cake may fall slightly but evenly during cooling.)

6 To serve, cut cake into 12 wedges. If desired, sprinkle dessert plates with a little additional cocoa powder. Transfer wedges to dessert plates. Top each serving with whipped topping and berries.

nutrition facts per serving: 152 cal., 5 g total fat (3 g sat. fat), 34 mg chol., 31 mg sodium, 24 g carb., 2 g dietary fiber, 4 g protein.

tiny chocolate-cherry bombs

prep: 30 minutes   bake: 18 minutes   stand: 10 minutes   oven: 350°F
makes: about 55 tiny cupcakes

2	10-ounce jars maraschino cherries with stems
1¼	cups all-purpose flour
1	cup granulated sugar
½	cup unsweetened cocoa powder
½	teaspoon baking soda
½	teaspoon baking powder
¼	teaspoon salt
⅔	cup milk
⅓	cup butter, melted and cooled, or canola oil
2	tablespoons kirsch, cherry-flavored brandy, brandy, cherry juice or milk
1½	teaspoons vanilla
1	egg
1	cup powdered sugar

1 Preheat oven to 350°F. Line 1¾-inch muffin cups with silver and/or red foil bake cups. Drain cherries, reserving 2 tablespoons juice; set aside.

2 In a large bowl combine flour, granulated sugar, cocoa powder, baking soda, baking powder, and salt. Add milk, butter, kirsch, and vanilla. Beat with an electric mixer on low speed just until combined. Beat on medium speed for 2 minutes. Add egg; beat for 2 minutes more.

3 Spoon 1 tablespoon batter into each muffin cup. (If necessary, chill batter while first batch bakes.) Push a cherry into batter of each cup, keeping stem end up. (If you run out of cherries, just add an extra tablespoon of batter to the muffin cups for plain chocolate bombs.)

4 Bake for 18 to 20 minutes or until cake springs back when lightly touched. Cool cupcakes in muffin cups on wire racks for 10 minutes. Remove cupcakes from muffin cups. Cool completely on wire racks.

5 For icing, in a medium bowl combine powdered sugar and 1 tablespoon reserved cherry juice. Add additional juice, 1 teaspoon at a time, to make an icing of drizzling consistency. Drizzle over cupcakes and allow to set before serving.

nutrition facts per tiny cupcake: 66 cal., 1 g total fat (1 g sat. fat), 7 mg chol., 36 mg sodium, 13 g carb., 1 g dietary fiber, 1 g protein.

carrot cake cupcakes

prep: 25 minutes   bake: 20 minutes   oven: 350°F   cool: 5 minutes
makes: 12 cupcakes

Nonstick cooking
   spray
1   cup all-purpose flour
1   cup white whole
   wheat flour
1   cup sugar
2   tablespoons
   flaxseed meal
2   teaspoons ground
   cinnamon
1   teaspoon baking
   powder
1   teaspoon baking soda
⅛   teaspoon salt
2   cups shredded
   carrots (4 medium)
1   cup unsweetened
   applesauce
1   egg, lightly beaten
1   teaspoon vanilla
1   recipe Cream Cheese
   Frosting or ½ cup
   purchased cream
   cheese frosting

1 Preheat oven to 350°F. Coat twelve 2½-inch muffin cups with cooking spray or line with paper bake cups. In a large bowl combine all purpose flour, white whole wheat flour, sugar, flaxseed meal, cinnamon, baking powder, baking soda, and salt; set aside.

2 In a medium bowl combine carrots, applesauce, egg, and vanilla. Add carrot mixture to flour mixture; mix just until combined. Fill prepared muffin cups three-fourths full with batter.

3 Bake for 20 to 24 minutes or until toothpick inserted in center comes out clean. Cool in muffin cups on a wire rack for 5 minutes. Remove from muffin cups. Cool completely on a wire rack.

4 Top each cupcake with Cream Cheese Frosting.

nutrition facts per cupcake: 196 cal., 1 g total fat (0 g sat. fat), 19 mg chol., 245 mg sodium, 43 g carb., 2 g dietary fiber, 5 g protein.

cream cheese frosting: In a small bowl beat ⅓ cup fat-free cream cheese and ⅓ cup powdered sugar with an electric mixer on medium speed until smooth. If necessary, add 1 teaspoon fat-free milk to make a frosting of spreading consistency. Makes about ½ cup.

lemon-spice cupcakes

prep: 25 minutes bake: per package directions oven: 350°F
makes: 24 cupcakes

1   package 2-layer-size
      lemon cake mix
1   16-ounce can cream
      cheese frosting
1   teaspoon apple
      pie spice
12 purchased
      gingersnap cookies

1 Preheat oven to 350°F. Line twenty-four 2½-inch muffin cups with foil or paper bake cups; set aside. Prepare cake mix according to package directions for cupcakes. Fill prepared muffin cups two-thirds full with batter.

2 Bake according to package directions. Cool in muffin cups on a wire rack for 5 minutes. Remove from muffin cups. Cool completely on a wire rack.

3 In a small bowl stir together the cream cheese frosting and apple pie spice. Spread or pipe frosting on cupcakes. To serve, use a serrated knife to cut each cookie in half. Insert the cut side of each cookie half into a cupcake.

nutrition facts per cupcake: 183 cal., 5 g total fat (2 g sat. fat), 0 mg chol., 198 mg sodium, 33 g carb., 0 g dietary fiber, 1 g protein.

Swap the blackberries for your favorite summer fruits, such as strawberries, blueberries, or plum slices.

coconut fruit s'mores

start to finish: 25 minutes makes: 12 servings

4 ounces dark or semisweet chocolate, chopped
Nonstick cooking spray
3 tablespoons butter, melted and cooled
⅓ cup flaked coconut
12 marshmallows
1⅓ cups fresh blackberries
24 graham cracker squares

1 Preheat broiler. Place chocolate in a small microwave-safe bowl. Microwave, uncovered, on 50 percent power (medium) for 1½ minutes. Let stand for 5 minutes. Stir until melted and smooth. Let cool for 10 minutes.

2 Line a baking sheet with foil; lightly coat foil with cooking spray. Set aside. Place melted butter in a shallow dish. Place coconut in the another shallow dish. Roll marshmallows in melted butter; coat evenly with coconut.

3 Thread berries and marshmallows on twelve 6-inch skewers. Place skewers on prepared baking sheet. Sprinkle any remaining coconut over marshmallows. Spoon chocolate onto half of the graham crackers and arrange on a large serving platter.

4 Broil skewers 3 to 4 inches from heat for 1 to 1½ minutes or until coconut is light brown and marshmallows are puffed, turning once halfway through broiling.

5 To serve, immediately top each chocolate-coated graham cracker with a skewer. Use remaining graham crackers to push marshmallows and berries off skewers and form sandwiches.

nutrition facts per serving: 150 cal., 9 g total fat (5 g sat. fat), 8 mg chol., 120 mg sodium, 25 g carb., 2 g dietary fiber, 2 g protein.

wonton dessert stacks

prep: 20 minutes bake: 6 minutes oven: 350°F makes: 4 servings

Nonstick cooking
   spray
8 wonton wrappers
   Sugar
½ cup sliced
   strawberries
2 kiwi fruit, peeled
   and sliced
1 6-ounce carton low-
   fat lemon yogurt
2 fresh strawberries,
   cut in half

1 Preheat oven to 350°F. Line a large baking sheet with foil; lightly coat with cooking spray. Arrange wontons flat on the baking sheet; lightly coat each with additional cooking spray. Sprinkle lightly with sugar.

2 Bake for 6 to 8 minutes or until golden brown and crisp. Remove from oven. Cool slightly.

3 Meanwhile, in a medium bowl combine ½ cup sliced strawberries and kiwi fruit.

4 To serve, place 1 baked wonton wrapper on each of four dessert plates. Top each with some of the yogurt. Divide the fruit mixture evenly among the stacks. Top each with another baked wonton and the remaining yogurt. Garnish each with a strawberry half.

nutrition facts per serving: 127 cal., 1 g total fat (0 g sat. fat), 4 mg chol., 118 mg sodium, 26 g carb., 2 g dietary fiber, 4 g protein.

nutrition note
Good news for fans of Greek yogurt: You can use fat-free or low-fat Greek yogurt in this recipe, and in doing so, you'll step up the protein quotient.

banana cream pie squares

prep: 15 minutes bake: 5 minutes chill. 4 to 24 hours oven: 375°F
makes: 9 servings

24 reduced-fat vanilla
     wafers
 3 tablespoons tub-style
     vegetable oil spread
     with 40% to 50% fat
1½ cups fat-free milk
 1 4-serving size
     package vanilla
     or banana cream
     fat-free sugar-free
     instant pudding mix
 ½ of an 8-ounce
     container frozen
     light whipped
     dessert topping,
     thawed
 4 large bananas, sliced
 2 teaspoons
     lemon juice
     Frozen light whipped
     dessert topping,
     thawed
     Sliced almonds,
     toasted (optional)

1 Preheat oven to 375°F. For crust, place vanilla wafers in a food processor. Cover and process until finely crushed. Add vegetable oil spread. Cover and process until mixture begins to cling together. Transfer to a 2-quart square baking dish; press crumb mixture evenly into bottom of dish. Bake about 5 minutes or until light brown. Cool completely on a wire rack.

2 For filling, in a medium bowl combine milk and pudding mix. Whisk for 1 to 2 minutes or until pudding is thickened. Gently fold in ½ container whipped topping until combined.

3 In another medium bowl toss banana slices with lemon juice to coat. Layer half of the banana slices over cooled crust. Top with half of the filling. Repeat with remaining bananas and filling. Cover and chill for 4 to 24 hours.

4 To serve, cut into nine 2-inch square pieces. garnish each serving with additional whipped topping and/or, if desired, toasted almonds.

nutrition facts per serving: 179 cal., 5 g total fat (2 g sat. fat), 6 mg chol., 231 mg sodium, 31 g carb., 2 g dietary fiber, 3 g protein.

stovetop peach-raspberry cobbler

prep: 20 minutes bake: 15 minutes oven: 375°F makes: 4 servings

1 teaspoon sugar
Dash ground cinnamon
½ of a sheet frozen puff pastry, thawed according to package directions
1 egg, lightly beaten
3 tablespoons sugar
1 tablespoon cornstarch
¼ teaspoon ground cinnamon
1 16-ounce package frozen unsweetened peach slices
1 cup fresh raspberries
½ cup water
Vanilla ice cream (optional)

1 Preheat oven to 375°F. Grease a baking sheet. For puff pastry twists, in a small bowl combine the 1 teaspoon sugar and the dash cinnamon. Place puff pastry on a work surface. Brush pastry with beaten egg. Sprinkle with cinnamon-sugar mixture. Cut pastry lengthwise into 4 strips; cut each strip in half crosswise. Twist strips; place on prepared baking sheet.

2 Bake about 15 minutes or until brown and puffed; set aside.

3 Meanwhile, in a large saucepan combine the 3 tablespoons sugar, cornstarch, and the ¼ teaspoon cinnamon. Add frozen peaches, half of the raspberries, and the water; cook over medium heat until mixture is thickened and bubbly, stirring occasionally. Cook and stir for 2 minutes more. Remove from heat. Stir in the remaining raspberries.

4 Top fruit mixture with puff pastry twists. If desired, serve with ice cream.

nutrition facts per serving: 159 cal., 4 g total fat (1 g sat. fat), 53 mg chol., 34 mg sodium, 30 g carb., 4 g dietary fiber, 3 g protein.

apples and
peanut
butter crisp

prep: 20 minutes bake: 30 minutes oven: 375°F makes: 8 servings

6 medium red and/
   or green cooking
   apples, cored,
   peeled, if desired,
   and thinly sliced
2 tablespoons all-
   purpose flour
1 tablespoon packed
   brown sugar
⅔ cup quick-cooking
   rolled oats
2 tablespoons all-
   purpose flour
2 tablespoons packed
   brown sugar
¼ cup peanut butter
2 tablespoons chopped
   peanuts

1 Preheat oven to 375°F. Place apple slices in
a 2-quart square baking dish; set aside. In
a small bowl stir together the 2 tablespoons
flour and the 1 tablespoon brown sugar until
well combined. Sprinkle flour mixture over
apple slices in dish; toss to coat.

2 Bake, covered, for 15 minutes. Meanwhile,
in a medium bowl combine rolled oats,
the 2 tablespoons flour, and the 2 tablespoons
brown sugar. Using a fork, stir in peanut butter
until mixture resembles coarse crumbs. Stir in
peanuts. Uncover apple mixture; sprinkle with
oat mixture.

3 Bake, uncovered, for 15 to 20 minutes
more or until apples are tender and
topping is golden. Serve warm.

nutrition facts per serving: 174 cal., 6 g total fat
(1 g sat. fat), 0 mg chol., 51 mg sodium, 28 g carb.,
4 g dietary fiber, 4 g protein.

chocolate-almond torte

prep: 25 minutes stand: 30 minutes bake: 25 minutes cool: 15 minutes
oven: 350°F makes: 12 servings

¾ cup fat-free milk
⅓ cup unsweetened
 cocoa powder
2 ounces unsweetened
 chocolate, chopped
1 tablespoon balsamic
 vinegar
3 egg whites
 Nonstick cooking
 spray
¾ cup all-purpose flour
⅔ cup granulated sugar
½ teaspoon baking
 powder
¼ teaspoon baking soda
⅛ teaspoon salt
¼ cup granulated sugar
¼ cup sliced almonds
1 to 2 teaspoons
 powdered sugar
 (optional)

1 In a small saucepan combine milk and cocoa powder. Heat over medium heat, whisking constantly, until mixture just comes to a boil. Remove from heat. Whisk in unsweetened chocolate and vinegar until smooth. Cool to room temperature. Meanwhile, in a medium bowl, allow egg whites to stand at room temperature for 30 minutes.

2 Preheat oven to 350°F. Lightly coat an 8x2-inch round tart pan with removable bottom or 8-inch springform pan with cooking spray; set aside. In a large bowl stir together flour, the ⅔ cup granulated sugar, the baking powder, baking soda, and salt. Stir cooled chocolate mixture into flour mixture until well combined (batter will be thick); set aside.

3 Beat egg whites with an electric mixer on medium speed until soft peaks form (tips curl). Gradually add ¼ cup granulated sugar, about 1 tablespoon at a time, beating on high speed until stiff peaks form (tips stand straight). Gently fold one third of beaten egg whites into chocolate mixture. Fold in the remaining beaten egg whites just until combined. Spread batter into the prepared baking pan. Sprinkle almonds over batter.

4 Bake for 25 to 28 minutes or until a wooden toothpick inserted near the center comes out clean. Cool in pan on a wire rack for 15 minutes. Run sharp thin-blade knife around edges; remove sides of pan. Cool completely on a wire rack.

5 If desired, sprinkle lightly with powdered sugar just before serving.

nutrition facts per serving: 144 cal., 4 g total fat (2 g sat. fat), 0 mg chol., 81 mg sodium, 25 g carb., 1 g dietary fiber, 4 g protein.

The secret of Italy's smooth, rich frozen dessert is a custard prepared with lots of egg yolks.

triple chocolate gelato

prep: 20 minutes   cool: 20 minutes   chill: 6 to 24 hours   freeze: per manufacturer's directions   ripen: 4 hours (optional)   makes: 24 (½-cup) servings

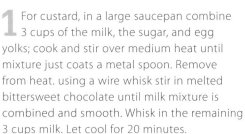

6   cups milk
1⅓   cups sugar
12   egg yolks, beaten
6   ounces bittersweet
     chocolate, chopped
     and melted
6   ounces dark
     chocolate, chopped
3   ounces white baking
     chocolate, chopped
     (optional)

1 For custard, in a large saucepan combine 3 cups of the milk, the sugar, and egg yolks; cook and stir over medium heat until mixture just coats a metal spoon. Remove from heat. using a wire whisk stir in melted bittersweet chocolate until milk mixture is combined and smooth. Whisk in the remaining 3 cups milk. Let cool for 20 minutes.

2 Cover surface of custard with plastic wrap. Chill for 6 to 24 hours. (Or place the saucepan in a sink of ice water. Let stand for 30 to 45 minutes or until cool, stirring occasionally.)

3 Stir in chopped dark chocolate and white chocolate (if using) into chilled custard just before freezing. Freeze custard in a 4- or 5-quart ice cream freezer according to the manufacturer's directions. If desired, ripen for 4 hours.

nutrition facts per ½ cup: 176 cal., 9 g total fat (3 g sat. fat), 110 mg chol., 30 mg sodium, 22 g carb., 1 g dietary fiber, 4 g protein.

triple chocolate truffles

prep: 45 minutes chill: 3½ hours stand: 30 minutes makes: 30 truffles

12 ounces semisweet chocolate, coarsely chopped

½ of an 8-ounce package cream cheese, softened and cut up

4 teaspoons instant coffee crystals

1 teaspoon water

1⅓ cups milk chocolate or semisweet chocolate pieces

2 tablespoons shortening

2 ounces milk chocolate, semisweet chocolate, and/or white baking chocolate, coarsely chopped

1 In a heavy medium saucepan cook and stir semisweet chocolate over very low heat until melted and smooth. Remove from heat. Stir in cream cheese until combined. Stir together coffee crystals and the water; add to the chocolate mixture and stir until mixture is smooth. Cover and chill about 2 hours or until firm.

2 Line a baking sheet or tray with waxed paper. Use a small cookie scoop to drop mounds of mixture on prepared baking sheet. Roll each mound in your hands to shape into 1-inch balls. Cover and chill for 1 to 2 hours or until firm.

3 In a heavy medium saucepan cook and stir 1⅓ cups milk chocolate and shortening over low heat until melted and mixture is smooth. Remove from heat, cool to room temperature.

4 Use a fork to dip truffles into chocolate mixture, allowing excess chocolate to drip back into saucepan. Return truffles to baking sheet; chill about 30 minutes or until firm.

5 In a heavy small saucepan cook and stir 2 ounces desired chocolate over low heat until melted and smooth. Drizzle over the tops of truffles. Chill for a few minutes or until set.

6 To store, place truffles in a tightly covered container in the refrigerator. Let stand at room temperature about 30 minutes before serving.

nutrition facts per truffle: 126 cal., 8 g total fat (5 g sat. fat), 6 mg chol., 21 mg sodium, 13 g carb., 1 g dietary fiber, 1 g protein.

The rich, gooey filling in these tarts has a hit of raspberry liqueur. Substitute your favorite liqueur or flavored syrup, or leave it out altogether.

chocolate-raspberry
tassies

prep: 40 minutes bake: 12 minutes cool: 10 minutes oven: 375°F
makes: 24 tassies

1 recipe Chocolate
   Pastry
6 ounces semisweet
   or bittersweet
   chocolate, chopped
   (1 cup)
2 tablespoons butter
1 large egg,
   lightly beaten
⅓ cup sugar
1 tablespoon raspberry
   liqueur or
   raspberry-flavored
   syrup
2 teaspoons vanilla
1 recipe Chocolate
   Buttercream
   (optional)

1 Preheat oven to 375°F. For pastry shells, divide the Chocolate Pastry into 24 balls. Using floured fingers, press each ball evenly onto bottom and up sides of 24 ungreased 1¾-inch muffin cups; set aside.

2 For filling, in small saucepan cook and stir chocolate and butter over medium-low heat until melted and mixture is smooth. Remove from heat. Stir in egg, sugar, liqueur, and vanilla. Spoon 1 scant tablespoon filling in each pastry shell.

3 Bake for 12 to 15 minutes or until pastry is firm and filling is puffed. Cool in pans for 10 minutes. Run sharp thin-blade knife around tassie edges; carefully remove from pans. Cool on a wire rack.

4 To serve, pipe or top with a small amount of Chocolate Buttercream.

nutrition facts per tassie: 138 cal., 7 g total fat (5 g sat. fat), 30 mg chol., 52 mg sodium, 16 g carb., 1 g dietary fiber, 2 g protein.

chocolate pastry: In a food processor combine 1¼ cups all-purpose flour, ⅓ cup sugar, ¼ cup unsweetened cocoa powder, and dash of salt. Pulse with on/off turns until combined. Cut ½ cup cold butter into small pieces. Add butter to flour mixture. Cover and process with on/off turns until mixture is crumbly. In a small bowl whisk together 1 egg yolk and 2 tablespoons cold water. Add egg mixture to flour mixture. Cover and process with on/off turns until dough forms a ball, adding additional cold water if necessary. Cover and chill about 1 hour or until dough is easy to handle, if necessary.

chocolate buttercream: In a medium bowl beat ¼ cup softened butter with an electric mixer on medium-high speed for 30 seconds. Gradually beat in 1 cup powdered sugar and 3 tablespoons unsweetened cocoa powder. Beat in 2 tablespoons milk. Gradually beat in 1 cup additional powdered sugar to make a frosting of spreading consistency. Makes about 1 cup.

to store: Place tassies in a single layer in an airtight container; cover. Store in the refrigerator for up to 3 days or freeze for up to 3 months.

Like cheesecake? Crave chocolate? Put them together to form a luscious union.

chocolate–
cream cheese pie
prep: 20 minutes   chill: 4 to 24 hours   makes: 10 servings

1 4-serving-size
   package fat-free
   sugar-free reduced-
   calorie chocolate
   instant pudding mix
1¾ cups fat-free milk
1 teaspoon vanilla
½ of an 8-ounce
   package reduced-
   fat cream cheese
   (Neufchâtel),
   softened
½ of an 8-ounce
   container frozen
   light whipped
   dessert topping,
   thawed
1 6-ounce chocolate-
   flavor crumb
   pie shell
1 tablespoon grated
   semisweet
   chocolate
1 cup fresh raspberries

1 In a medium bowl prepare pudding mix according to package directions, except use the 1¾ cups milk. Stir in vanilla; set aside.

2 Place cream cheese in a large microwave-safe bowl. Microwave, uncovered, on 100 percent power (high) for 15 seconds; stir. Microwave on 100 percent power (high) for 15 seconds more. Beat cream cheese with an electric mixer on medium speed for 15 seconds. Add half of the pudding mixture. Beat until smooth. Add the remaining pudding mixture. Beat until smooth. Fold in half of the whipped topping. Spread pudding mixture in pie shell. Cover and chill for 4 to 24 hours.

3 To serve, cut into wedges. Top individual servings with the remaining whipped topping and grated chocolate. Serve with raspberries.

nutrition facts per serving: 180 cal., 8 g total fat (4 g sat. fat), 9 mg chol., 285 mg sodium, 22 g carb., 1 g dietary fiber, 4 g protein.

strawberry
cream pie

prep: 30 minutes chill: 4 hours makes: 8 servings

2½ cups fresh
    strawberries
¼ cup sugar
1 envelope unflavored
    gelatin
2 tablespoons
    frozen limeade
    or lemonade
    concentrate,
    thawed
3 egg whites,
    lightly beaten
1 tablespoon tequila or
    orange juice
1 3-ounce package
    ladyfingers, split
2 tablespoons
    orange juice
½ of an 8-ounce
    container frozen
    light whipped
    dessert topping,
    thawed
    Sliced fresh
    strawberries
    (optional)
    Fresh mint sprigs
    (optional)

1 Place the 2½ cups strawberries in a blender or food processor. Cover and blend or process until nearly smooth. Measure pureed strawberries (should have about 1½ cups).

2 In a medium saucepan stir together sugar and gelatin. Stir in pureed strawberries and limeade concentrate. Cook and stir over medium heat until mixture is bubbly and gelatin is dissolved. Gradually stir about half of the hot gelatin mixture into egg whites. Return egg white mixture to saucepan. Cook and stir over low heat about 3 minutes or until mixture is slightly thickened (do not boil). Pour into a medium bowl; stir in tequila. Cover and chill about 2 hours or until mixture mounds when spooned, stirring occasionally.

3 Meanwhile, cut half of the split ladyfingers in half crosswise; stand on end around the outside edge of a 9-inch tart pan or springform pan that has a removable bottom. Arrange the remaining split ladyfingers in the bottom of the pan. Drizzle orange juice over ladyfingers.

4 Fold whipped topping into strawberry mixture. Pour mixture into the prepared pan, spreading evenly. Cover and chill about 2 hours or until set. If desired, garnish with additional strawberries and mint.

nutrition facts per serving: 130 cal., 3 g total fat (2 g sat. fat), 39 mg chol., 48 mg sodium, 22 g carb., 1 g dietary fiber, 4 g protein.

key lime pie

prep: 30 minutes bake: 8 minutes chill: 4½ hours oven: 350°F
makes: 8 servings

1½ cups small pretzel twists (2 ounces; about 34)
2 tablespoons sliced almonds, toasted
3 tablespoons butter, melted
1 3-ounce package (4 serving) sugar-free low-calorie lime-flavored gelatin or regular lime-flavored gelatin
1 cup boiling water
2 6-ounce cartons key lime pie lowfat yogurt
½ of an 8-ounce container frozen light whipped dessert topping, thawed
1 teaspoon finely shredded lime peel
Thin lime slices (optional)
Finely shredded lime peel (optional)

1 Preheat oven to 350°F. For crust, in a food processor combine pretzels and almonds. Cover and process until finely crushed. Add butter to pretzel mixture. Cover and process until combined. Press pretzel mixture on bottom and up sides of a 9-inch pie plate. Bake for 8 to 10 minutes or until light brown. Cool on a wire rack.

2 For filling, place gelatin in a medium bowl. Add the boiling water. Stir about 2 minutes or until gelatin dissolves. Cover and chill about 30 minutes or until mixture is partially set (the consistency of unbeaten egg whites). Fold in yogurt, whipped topping, and the 1 teaspoon lime peel. Pour filling into cooled crust. Chill for at least 4 hours.

3 If desired, garnish with lime slices and additional finely shredded lime peel.

nutrition facts per serving: 153 cal., 7 g total fat (5 g sat. fat), 13 mg chol., 180 mg sodium, 17 g carb., 0 g dietary fiber, 3 g protein.

464

This recipe can also be made with fresh pitted cherries, cranberries, or blueberries.

lemon-blackberry pie

prep: 40 minutes   bake: 43 minutes   oven: 400°F/350°F   makes: 12 servings

1   recipe Sweet Butter
    Pastry
3   eggs
2   egg whites
¾   cup sugar
¾   cup lemon juice
¼   cup butter, melted
¼   cup finely shredded
    lemon peel
1   cup fresh
    blackberries

1 Preheat oven to 400°F. On a lightly floured surface use your hands to slightly flatten the Sweet Butter Pastry. Roll pastry from center to edges into a 12-inch circle. Wrap pastry circle around rolling pin; unroll into a 9-inch pie plate. Trim pastry to ½ inch beyond edge of pie plate. Fold under extra pastry even with edge of pie plate. Crimp edge as desired. Prick bottom and sides of pastry with a fork. Line pastry with a double thickness of foil.

2 Bake for 8 minutes. Remove foil. Bake for 5 to 6 minutes more or until pastry is golden. Cool on a wire rack. Reduce oven temperature to 350°F.

3 For filling, in a large bowl combine eggs, egg whites, sugar, and lemon juice. Beat with an electric mixer on medium to high speed until thick and lemon colored. Stir in melted butter and lemon peel.

4 Place blackberries in bottom of the cooled pastry shell. Pour filling over blackberries.

5 Bake in the 350°F oven about 30 minutes or until filling is set. Cool on a wire rack.

nutrition facts per serving: 197 cal., 9 g total fat (5 g sat. fat), 73 mg chol., 131 mg sodium, 27 g carb., 1 g dietary fiber, 4 g protein.

sweet butter pastry: In a medium bowl stir together 1 cup all-purpose flour, 3 tablespoons sugar, and ¼ teaspoon salt. Using a pastry blender, cut in ¼ cup cold butter until pieces are pea size. Sprinkle 1 tablespoon cold water over part of the flour mixture; toss gently with a fork. Push moistened dough to side of bowl. Repeat with additional cold water, 1 tablespoon at a time (4 to 5 tablespoons total), until all of the mixture is moistened. Gather mixture into a ball, kneading gently until it holds together. Cover with plastic wrap and chill for 30 to 60 minutes or until dough is easy to handle, if necessary. Makes 1 pastry.

Lightly wetting your hands helps make the yummy cereal, apple, and peanut mixture easier to shape into balls.

peanut-apple crunch balls

prep: 20 minutes   stand: 30 minutes   makes: 18 balls

⅓ cup chunky
    peanut butter
¼ cup 68% vegetable oil
    spread
2 tablespoons honey
1 cup rice and wheat
    cereal flakes,
    crushed slightly
1 cup bran flakes,
    crushed slightly
⅓ cup finely snipped
    dried apples
2 tablespoons finely
    chopped peanuts
⅛ teaspoon apple
    pie spice
2 ounces white baking
    chocolate (with
    cocoa butter),
    chopped
¼ teaspoon shortening

1 In a medium saucepan combine peanut butter, vegetable oil spread, and honey. Cook over low heat just until melted and mixture is nearly smooth, whisking constantly. Stir in cereals, apples, peanuts, and apple pie spice until well mixed. Divide mixture into 18 portions. Using slightly wet hands, shape mixture into balls. Let stand on a baking sheet lined with waxed paper about 15 minutes or until firm.

2 In a small saucepan combine white baking chocolate and shortening. Cook and stir over low heat until melted. Drizzle balls with melted baking chocolate. Let stand about 15 minutes or until baking chocolate is set (if necessary, chill balls until baking chocolate is firm).

nutrition facts per ball: 94 cal., 6 g total fat (2 g sat. fat), 1 mg chol., 76 mg sodium, 9 g carb., 1 g dietary fiber, 2 g protein.

nutrition note

Nutritionally, there's no difference between smooth and chunky peanut butter, but the chunky variety adds a welcome crunch to this recipe. However, reduced-fat, reduced-sugar, and flavored peanut butters do vary nutritionally—so it pays to compare the labels.

index

index

metric information

The charts on this page provide a guide for converting measurements from the U.S. customary system, which is used throughout this book, to the metric system.

Product Differences

Most of the ingredients called for in the recipes in this book are available in most countries. However, some are known by different names. Here are some common American ingredients and their possible counterparts:

- Sugar (white) is granulated, fine granulated, or castor sugar.
- Powdered sugar is icing sugar.
- All-purpose flour is enriched, bleached, or unbleached white household flour. When self-rising flour is used in place of all-purpose flour in a recipe that calls for leavening, omit the leavening agent (baking soda or baking powder) and salt.
- Light-colored corn syrup is golden syrup.
- Cornstarch is cornflour.
- Baking soda is bicarbonate of soda.
- Vanilla or vanilla extract is vanilla essence.
- Green, red, or yellow sweet peppers are capsicums or bell peppers.
- Golden raisins are sultanas.

Volume and Weight

The United States traditionally uses cup measures for liquid and solid ingredients. The chart below shows the approximate imperial and metric equivalents. If you are accustomed to weighing solid ingredients, the following approximate equivalents will be helpful.

- 1 cup butter, castor sugar, or rice = 8 ounces = ½ pound = 250 grams
- 1 cup flour = 4 ounces = ¼ pound = 125 grams
- 1 cup icing sugar = 5 ounces = 150 grams

Canadian and U.S. volume for a cup measure is 8 fluid ounces (237 ml), but the standard metric equivalent is 250 ml.

1 British imperial cup is 10 fluid ounces.

In Australia, 1 tablespoon equals 20 ml, and there are 4 teaspoons in the Australian tablespoon.

Spoon measures are used for smaller amounts of ingredients. Although the size of the tablespoon varies slightly in different countries, for practical purposes and for recipes in this book, a straight substitution is all that's necessary. Measurements made using cups or spoons always should be level unless stated otherwise.

Common Weight Range Replacements

Imperial / U.S.	Metric
½ ounce	15 g
1 ounce	25 g or 30 g
4 ounces (¼ pound)	115 g or 125 g
8 ounces (½ pound)	225 g or 250 g
16 ounces (1 pound)	450 g or 500 g
1¼ pounds	625 g
1½ pounds	750 g
2 pounds or 2¼ pounds	1,000 g or 1 Kg

Oven Temperature Equivalents

Fahrenheit Setting	Celsius Setting*	Gas Setting
300°F	150°C	Gas Mark 2 (very low)
325°F	160°C	Gas Mark 3 (low)
350°F	180°C	Gas Mark 4 (moderate)
375°F	190°C	Gas Mark 5 (moderate)
400°F	200°C	Gas Mark 6 (hot)
425°F	220°C	Gas Mark 7 (hot)
450°F	230°C	Gas Mark 8 (very hot)
475°F	240°C	Gas Mark 9 (very hot)
500°F	260°C	Gas Mark 10 (extremely hot)
Broil	Broil	Grill

Electric and gas ovens may be calibrated using Celsius. However, for an electric oven, increase Celsius setting 10 to 20 degrees when cooking above 160°C. For convection or forced air ovens (gas or electric) lower the temperature setting 25°F/10°C when cooking at all heat levels.

Baking Pan Sizes

Imperial / U.S.	Metric
9×1½-inch round cake pan	22- or 23×4-cm (1.5 L)
9×1½-inch pie plate	22- or 23×4-cm (1 L)
8×8×2-inch square cake pan	20×5-cm (2 L)
9×9×2-inch square cake pan	22- or 23×4.5-cm (2.5 L)
11×7×1½-inch baking pan	28×17×4-cm (2 L)
2-quart rectangular baking pan	30×19×4.5-cm (3 L)
13×9×2-inch baking pan	34×22×4.5-cm (3.5 L)
15×10×1-inch jelly roll pan	40×25×2-cm
9×5×3-inch loaf pan	23×13×8-cm (2 L)
2-quart casserole	2 L

U.S. / Standard Metric Equivalents

⅛ teaspoon = 0.5 ml	
¼ teaspoon = 1 ml	
½ teaspoon = 2 ml	
1 teaspoon = 5 ml	
1 tablespoon = 15 ml	
2 tablespoons = 25 ml	
¼ cup = 2 fluid ounces = 50 ml	
⅓ cup = 3 fluid ounces = 75 ml	
½ cup = 4 fluid ounces = 125 ml	
⅔ cup = 5 fluid ounces = 150 ml	
¾ cup = 6 fluid ounces = 175 ml	
1 cup = 8 fluid ounces = 250 ml	
2 cups = 1 pint = 500 ml	
1 quart = 1 liter	